.NET Test Automation Recipes

Recipes

A Problem-Solution Approach

■ ■ ■

James D. McCaffrey

Apress®

.NET Test Automation Recipes: A Problem-Solution Approach

Copyright © 2006 by James D. McCaffrey

ISBN-13: 978-1-59059-663-0

ISBN-10: 1-59059-663-3

Printed and bound in the United States of America 9 8 7 6 5 4 3 2 1

Lead Editor: Jonathan Hassell
Technical Reviewer: Josh Kelling
Editorial Board: Steve Anglin, Ewan Buckingham, Gary Cornell, Jason Gilmore, Jonathan Gennick,
    Jonathan Hassell, James Huddleston, Chris Mills, Matthew Moodie, Dominic Shakeshaft, Jim Sumser,
    Keir Thomas, Matt Wade
Project Manager: Elizabeth Seymour
Copy Edit Manager: Nicole LeClerc
Copy Editor: Julie McNamee
Assistant Production Director: Kari Brooks-Copony
Production Editor: Katie Stence
Compositor: Lynn L'Heureux
Proofreader: Elizabeth Berry
Indexer: Becky Hornak
Cover Designer: Kurt Krames
Manufacturing Director: Tom Debolski

Distributed to the book trade worldwide by Springer-Verlag New York, Inc., 233 Spring Street, 6th Floor, New York, NY 10013. Phone 1-800-SPRINGER, fax 201-348-4505, e-mail orders-ny@springer-sbm.com, or visit http://www.springeronline.com.

For information on translations, please contact Apress directly at 2560 Ninth Street, Suite 219, Berkeley, CA 94710. Phone 510-549-5930, fax 510-549-5939, e-mail info@apress.com, or visit http://www.apress.com.

The source code for this book is available to readers at http://www.apress.com in the Source Code section.

Contents at a Glance

Contents

PART 1 ■■■ Windows Application Testing

PART 2 ■ ■ ■ Web Application Testing

PART 3 ■ ■ ■ **Data Testing**

About the Author

DR. JAMES MCCAFFREY works for Volt Information Sciences, Inc. He holds a doctorate from the University of Southern California, a master's in information systems from Hawaii Pacific University, a bachelor's in mathematics from California State University at Fullerton, and a bachelor's in psychology from the University of California at Irvine. He was a professor at Hawaii Pacific University, and worked as a lead software engineer at Microsoft on key products such as Internet Explorer and MSN Search.

About the Technical Reviewer

JOSH KELLING is a private consultant working in the business software industry. He is formally educated in physics and self-taught as a software developer with nearly 10 years of experience developing business and commercial software using Microsoft technologies. His focus has been primarily on .NET development since it was a beta product. He also enjoys teaching, skiing, hiking, hunting for wild mushrooms, and pool.

Acknowledgments

Many people made this book possible. First and foremost, Jonathan Hassell and Elizabeth Seymour of Apress, Inc. drove the concept, writing, editing, and publication of the entire project. My corporate vice presidents at Volt Information Sciences, Inc., Patrick Walker and Christina Harris, suggested the idea of this book in the first place and supported its development. The lead technical reviewer, Josh Kelling (Kelling Consulting) did a terrific job at finding and correcting my coding mistakes. I'm also grateful to Doug Walter (Microsoft), who contributed significantly to the technical accuracy of this book. Many of the sections of this book are based on a monthly column I write for Microsoft's MSDN Magazine. My editors at MSDN, Joshua Trupin and Stephen Toub, provided me with a lot of advice about writing, without which this book would never have gotten off the ground. And finally, my staff at Volt—Shirley Lin, Lisa Vo Carlson, and Grace Son—supplied indispensable administrative help.

Many Volt software engineers working at Microsoft acted as auxiliary technical and editorial reviewers for this book. Primary technical reviewers include: Evan Kaplan, Steven Fusco, Bruce Ritter, Peter Yan, Ron Starr, Gordon Lippa, Kirk Slota, Joanna Tao, Walter Wittel, Jay Gray, Robert Hopkins, Sam Abolrous, Rich Bixby, Max Guernsey, Larry Briones, Kristin Jaeger, Joe Davis, Andrew Lee, Clint Kreider, Craig Green, Daniel Bedassa, Paul Kwiatkowski, Mark Wilcox, David Blais, Mustafa Al-Hasnawi, David Grossberg, Vladimir Abashyn, Mitchell Harter, Michael Svob, Brandon Lake, David Reynolds, Rob Gilmore, Cyrus Jamula, Ravichandhiran Kolandaiswamy, and Rajkumar Ramasamy.

Secondary technical reviewers include Jerry Frost, Michael Wansley, Vanarasi Antony Swamy, Ted Keith, Chad Fairbanks, Chris Trevino, David Moy, Fuhan Tian, C.J. Eichholz, Stuart Martin, Justice Chang, Funmi Bolonduro, Alemeshet Alemu, Lori Shih, Eric Mattoon, Luke Burtis, Aaron Rodriguez, Ajay Bhat, Carol Snyder, Qiusheng Gao, Haik Babaian, Jonathan Collins, Dinesh Ravva, Josh Silveria, Brian Miller, Gary Roehl, Kender Talylor, Ahlee Ly, Conan Callen, Kathy Davis, and Florentin Ionescu.

Editorial reviewers include Christina Zubelli, Joey Gonzales, Tony Chu, Alan Vandarwarka, Matt Carson, Tim Garner, Michael Klevitsky, Mark Soth, Michael Roshak, Robert Hawkins, Mark McGee, Grace Lou, Reza Sorasi, Abhijeet Shah, April McCready, Creede Lambard, Sean McCallum, Dawn Zhao, Mike Agranov, Victor Araya Cantuarias, Jason Olsan, Igor Bodi, Aldon Schwimmer, Andrea Borning, Norm Warren, Dale Dey, Chad Long, Thom Hokama, Ying Guo, Yong Wang, David Shockley, Allan Lockridge, Prashant Patil, Sunitha Mutnuri, Ping Du, Mark Camp, Abdul Khan, Moss Willow, Madhavi Kandibanda, John Mooney, Filiz Kurban, Jesse Larsen, Jeni Jordan, Chris Rosson, Dean Thomas, Brandon Barela, and Scott Lanphear.

Introduction

What This Book Is About

This book presents practical techniques for writing lightweight software test automation in a .NET environment. If you develop, test, or manage .NET software, you should find this book useful. Before .NET, writing test automation was often as difficult as writing the code for the application under test itself. With .NET, you can write lightweight, custom test automation in a fraction of the time it used to take. By *lightweight automation*, I mean small, dedicated test harness programs that are typically two pages of source code or less in length and take less than two hours to write. The emphasis of this book is on practical techniques that you can use immediately.

Who This Book Is For

This book is intended for software developers, testers, and managers who work with .NET technology. This book assumes you have a basic familiarity with .NET programming but does not make any particular assumptions about your skill level. The examples in this book have been successfully used in seminars where the audience background has ranged from beginning application programmers to advanced systems programmers. The content in this book has also been used in teaching environments where it has proven highly effective as a platform for students who are learning intermediate level .NET programming.

Advantages of Lightweight Test Automation

The automation techniques in this book are intended to complement, not replace, other testing paradigms, such as manual testing, test-driven development, model-based testing, open source test frameworks, commercial test frameworks, and so on. Software test automation, including the techniques in this book, has five advantages over manual testing. We sometimes refer to these automation advantages with the acronym SAPES: test automation has better Speed, Accuracy, Precision, Efficiency, and Skill-Building than manual testing. Additionally, when compared with both open source test frameworks and commercial frameworks, lightweight test automation has the advantage of not requiring you to travel up a rather steep learning curve and perhaps even learning a proprietary scripting language. Compared with commercial test automation frameworks, lightweight test automation is much less expensive and is fully customizable. And compared with open source test frameworks, lightweight automation is more stable in the sense that you have fewer recurring version updates and bug fixes to deal with. But the single most important advantage of lightweight, custom test automation harnesses over commercial and open source test frameworks is subjective—lightweight automation actively encourages and promotes creative testing, whereas commercial and open source frameworks often tend to direct the types of automation you create to the types of tests that are best supported by the framework. The single biggest disadvantage of lightweight test automation is manageability. Because lightweight test harnesses are so easy to write, if you aren't careful, your testing effort can become overwhelmed by the sheer number of test harnesses, test case data, and test case result files you create. Test process management is outside the scope of this book, but it is a challenging topic you should not underestimate when writing lightweight test automation.

Coding Issues

All the code in this book is written in the C# language. Because of the unifying influence of the underlying .NET Framework, you can refactor the code in this book to Visual Basic .NET without too much trouble if necessary. All the code in this book was tested and ran successfully on both Windows XP Professional (SP2) and Windows Server 2003, and with Visual Studio .NET 2003 (with Framework 1.1) and SQL Server 2000. The code was also tested on Visual Studio 2005 (with Framework 2.0) and SQL Server 2005; however, if you are developing in that environment, you'll have to make a few minor changes. I've coded the examples so that any changes you have to make for VS 2005 and SQL Server 2005 are flagged quickly. I decided that presenting just code for VS 2003 and SQL Server 2000 was a better approach than to sprinkle the book text with many short notes describing the minor development platform differences for VS 2005 and SQL Server 2005. The code in this book is intended strictly for 32-bit systems and has not been tested against 64-bit systems.

If you are new to software test automation, you'll quickly find that coding as a tester is significantly different from coding as a developer. Most of the techniques in this book are coded using a traditional, scripting style, rather than in an object-oriented style. I've found that automation code is easier to understand when written in a scripting style but this is a matter of opinion. Also, most of the code examples are not parameterized or packaged as methods. Again, this is for clarity. Most of the normal error-checking code, such as checking the values of input parameters to methods, is omitted. Error-traps are absolutely essential in production test automation code (after all, you are expecting to find errors) but error-checking code is often three or four times the size of the core code being checked. The code in this book is specifically designed for you to modify, which includes wrapping into methods, adding error-checks, incorporating into other test frameworks, and encapsulating into utility classes and libraries.

Most of the chapters in this book present dummy applications to test against. By design, these dummy applications are not examples of good coding style, and these applications under test often contain deliberate errors. This keeps the size of the dummy applications small and also simulates the unrefined nature of an application's state during the development process. For example, I generally use default control names such as textBox1 rather than use descriptive names, I keep local variable names short (such as s for a string variable), I sometimes place multiple statements on the same line, and so forth. I've actually left a few minor "severity 4" bugs (typographical errors) in the screenshots in this book; you might enjoy looking for them.

In most cases, I've tried to be as accurate as possible with my terminology. For example, I use the term *method* when dealing with a subroutine that is a field/member in a C# class, and I use the term *function* when referring to a C++ subroutine in a Win32 API library. However, I make exceptions when I feel that a slightly incorrect term is more understandable or readable. For example, I sometimes use the term *string variable* instead of the more accurate *string object* when referring to a C# string type item.

This book uses a problem-solution structure. This approach has the advantage of organizing various test automation tasks in a convenient way. But to keep the size of the book reasonable, most of the solutions are not complete, standalone blocks of code. This means that I often do not declare variables, explicitly discuss the namespaces and project references used in the solution, and so on. Many of the solutions in a chapter refer to other solutions within the same chapter, so you'll have to make reasonable assumptions about dependencies and how to turn the solution code into complete test harnesses. To assist you in understanding how the sections of a chapter work together, the last section of every chapter presents a complete, standalone program.

Contents of This Book

In most computer science books, the contents of the book are summarized in the introduction. I will forego that practice and say instead that the best way to get a feel for what is contained in this book is to scan the table of contents; I know that's what I always do. That said however, let me mention four specific topics in this book that have generated particular interest among my colleagues. Chapter 1, "API Testing," is in many ways the most fundamental type of all software testing. If you are new to software testing, you will not only learn useful testing techniques, but you'll also learn many of the basic principles of software testing. Chapter 3, "Windows-Based UI Testing," presents powerful techniques to manipulate an application through its user interface. Even software testers with many years of experience are surprised at how easy UI test automation is using .NET and the techniques in that chapter. Chapter 5, "Request-Response Testing," demonstrates the basic techniques to test any Web-based application. Web developers and testers are frequently surprised at how powerful these techniques are in a .NET environment. Chapter 10, "Combinations and Permutations," gives you the tools you need to programmatically generate test cases that take into account all combinations and rearrangements of input values. Both new and experienced testers have commented that combinatorics with .NET makes test case generation significantly more efficient than previously.

Using the Code in This Book

This book is intended to provide practical help for you in developing and testing software. This means that, within reason, you may use the code in this book in your systems and documentation. Obvious exceptions include situations where you are reproducing a significant portion of the code in this book on a Web site or magazine article, or using examples in a conference talk, and so on. Most authors, including me, appreciate citations if you use examples from their book in a paper or article. All code is provided without warranty of any kind.

PART 1

■ ■ ■

Windows Application Testing

CHAPTER 1

■■■

API Testing

1.0 Introduction

The most fundamental type of software test automation is automated API (Application Programming Interface) testing. API testing is essentially verifying the correctness of the individual methods that make up your software system rather than testing the overall system itself. API testing is also called unit testing, module testing, component testing, and element testing. Technically, the terms are very different, but in casual usage, you can think of them as having roughly the same meaning. The idea is that you must make sure the individual building blocks of your system work correctly; otherwise, your system as a whole cannot be correct. API testing is absolutely essential for any significant software system. Consider the Windows-based application in Figure 1-1. This StatCalc application calculates the mean of a set of integers. Behind the scenes, StatCalc references a MathLib.dll library, which contains methods named ArithmeticMean(), GeometricMean(), and HarmonicMean().

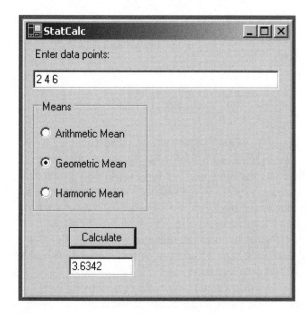

Figure 1-1. *The system under test (SUT)*

The goal is to test these three methods, not the whole StatCalc application that uses them. The program being tested is often called the SUT (system under test), AUT (application under test), or IUT (implementation under test) to distinguish it from the test harness system. The techniques in this book use the term AUT.

The methods under test are housed in a namespace MathLib with a single class named Methods and have the following signatures:

```
namespace MathLib
{
  public class Methods
  {
    public static double ArithmeticMean(params int[] vals)
    {
      // calculate and return arithmetic mean
    }

    private static double NthRoot(double x, int n)
    {
      // calculate and return the nth root;
    }

    public double GeometricMean(params int[] vals)
    {
      //use NthRoot to calculate and return geometric mean
    }

    public static double HarmonicMean(params int[] vals)
    {
      // this method not yet implemented
    }

  } // class Methods
} // ns MathLib
```

Notice that the ArithmeticMean() method is a static method, GeometricMean() is an instance method, and HarmonicMean() is not yet ready for testing. Handling static methods, instance methods, and incomplete methods are the three most common situations you'll deal with when writing lightweight API test automation. Each of the methods under test accepts a variable number of integer arguments (as indicated by the params keyword) and returns a type double value. In most situations, you do not test private helper methods such as NthRoot(). Any errors in a helper will be exposed when testing the method that uses the helper. But if you have a helper method that has significant complexity, you'll want to write dedicated test cases for it as well by using the techniques described in this chapter.

Manually testing this API would involve creating a small tester program, copying the Methods class into the program, hard-coding some input values to one of the methods under test, running the stub program to get an actual result, visually comparing that actual result with an expected result to determine a pass/fail result, and then recording the result in an Excel spreadsheet or similar data store. You would have to repeat this process hundreds of times to even begin to have confidence that the methods under test work correctly. A much better approach is to write test automation. Figure 1-2 shows a sample run of test automation that uses some of the techniques in this chapter. The complete program that generated the program shown in Figure 1-2 is presented in Section 1.15.

```
 C:\Book\Code\Ch1Code\ApiTest\bin\Debug\ApiTest.exe              _ □ X

CaseID Result Method          Details
=============================================

0001    Pass   ArithmeticMean  actual = 4.6667
0002    Pass   ArithmeticMean  actual = 3.0000
0003    Pass   ArithmeticMean  actual = 10.5000
0004    *FAIL* GeometricMean   actual = 5.6569 expected = 6.6569
0005    Pass   GeometricMean   actual = 0.0000
0006    Pass   GeometricMean   actual = 4.0000
0007           HarmonicMean    Not yet implemented
0008           HarmonicMean    Not yet implemented

=============== end test run ================

Pass = 5 Fail = 1
```

Figure 1-2. *Sample API test automation run*

Test automation has five advantages over manual testing:

- Speed: You can run thousands of test cases very quickly.

- Accuracy: Not as susceptible to human error, such as recording an incorrect result.

- Precision: Runs the same way every time it is executed, whereas manual testing often runs slightly differently depending on who performs the tests.

- Efficiency: Can run overnight or during the day, which frees you to do other tasks.

- Skill-building: Interesting and builds your technical skill set, whereas manual testing is often mind-numbingly boring and provides little skill enhancement.

The following sections present techniques for preparing API test automation, running API test automation, and saving the results of API test automation runs. Additionally, you'll learn techniques to deal with tricky situations, such as methods that can throw exceptions or that can accept empty string arguments. The following sections also show you techniques to manage API test automation, such as programmatically sending test results via e-mail.

1.1 Storing Test Case Data

Problem

You want to create and store API test case data in a simple text file.

Design

Use a colon-delimited text file that includes a unique test case ID, one or more input values, and one or more expected results.

Solution

```
0001:ArithmeticMean:2 4 8:4.6667
0002:ArithmeticMean:1 5:3.0000
0003:ArithmeticMean:1 2 4 8 16 32:10.5000
```

Comments

When writing automated tests, you can store test case data externally to the test harness or you can embed the data inside the harness. In general, external test case data is preferable because multiple harnesses can share the data more easily, and the data can be more easily modified. Each line of the file represents a single test case. Each case has four fields separated by the ':' character—test case ID, method to test, test case inputs separated by a single blank space, and expected result. You will often include additional test case data, such as a test case title, description, and category. The choice of delimiting character is arbitrary for the most part. Just make sure that you don't use a character that is part of the inputs or expected values. For instance, the colon character works nicely for numeric methods but would not work well when testing methods with URLs as inputs because of the colon that follows "http". In many lightweight test-automation situations, a text file is the best approach for storage because of simplicity. Alternative approaches include storing test case data in an XML file or SQL table. Weaknesses of using text files include their difficulty at handling inherently hierarchical data and the difficulty of seeing spurious control characters such as extra <CR><LF>s.

The preceding solution has only three test cases, but in practice you'll often have thousands. You should take into account boundary values (using input values exactly at, just below, and just above the defined limits of an input domain), null values, and garbage (invalid) values. You'll also create cases with permuted (rearranged) input values like

```
0002:ArithmeticMean:1 5:3.0000
0003:ArithmeticMean:5 1:3.0000
```

Determining the expected result for a test case can be difficult. In theory, you'll have a specification document that precisely describes the behavior of the method under test. Of course, the reality is that specs are often incomplete or nonexistent. One common mistake when determining expected results, and something you should definitely not do, is to feed inputs to the method under test, grab the output, and then use that as the expected value. This approach does not test the method; it just verifies that you get the same (possibly incorrect) output. This is an example of an invalid test system.

During the development of your test harness, you should create some test cases that deliberately generate a fail result. This will help you detect logic errors in your harness. For example:

```
0004:ArithmeticMean:1 5:6.0000:deliberate failure
```

In general, the term *API testing* is used when the functions or methods you are testing are stored in a DLL. The term *unit testing* is most often used when the methods you are testing are in a class (which of course may be realized as a DLL). The terms *module testing, component testing,* and *element testing* are more general terms that tend to be used when testing functions and methods not realized as a DLL.

1.2 Reading Test Case Data

Problem

You want to read each test case in a test case file stored as a simple text file.

Design

Iterate through each line of the test case file using a while loop with a System.IO.StreamReader object.

Solution

```
FileStream fs = new FileStream("..\\..\\TestCases.txt", FileMode.Open);
StreamReader sr = new StreamReader(fs);

string line;

while ((line = sr.ReadLine()) != null)
{
  // parse each test case line
  // call method under test
  // determine pass or fail
  // log test case result
}

sr.Close();
fs.Close();
```

Comments

In general, console applications, rather than Windows-based applications, are best suited for lightweight test automation harnesses. Console applications easily integrate into legacy test systems and can be easily manipulated in a Windows environment. If you do design a harness as a Windows application, make sure that it can be fully manipulated from the command line.

This solution assumes you have placed a `using System.IO;` statement in your harness so you can access the `FileStream` and `StreamReader` classes without having to fully qualify them. We also assume that the test case data file is named `TestCases.txt` and is located two directories above the test harness executable. Relative paths to test case data files are generally better than absolute paths like `C:\\Here\\There\\TestCases.txt` because relative paths allow you to move the test harness root directory and subdirectories as a whole without breaking the harness paths. However, relative paths may break your harness if the directory structure of your test system changes. A good alternative is to parameterize the path and name of the test case data file:

```
static void Main(string[] args)
{
  string testCaseFile = args[0];
  FileStream fs = new FileStream(testCaseFile, FileMode.Open);
  // etc.
}
```

Then you can call the harness along the lines of

```
C:\Harness\bin\Debug>Run.exe   ..\..\TestCases.txt
```

In this solution, `FileStream` and `StreamReader` objects are used. Alternatively, you can use static methods in the `System.IO.File` class such as `File.Open()`. If you expect that two or more test harnesses may be accessing the test case data file simultaneously, you can use the overloaded `FileStream` constructor that includes a `FileShare` parameter to specify how the file will be shared.

1.3 Parsing a Test Case

Problem

You want to parse the individual fields of a character-delimited test case.

Design

Use the `String.Split()` method, passing as the input argument the delimiting character and storing the return value into a string array.

Solution

```
string line, caseID, method;
string[] tokens, tempInput;
string expected;

while ((line = sr.ReadLine()) != null)
```

```
{
  tokens = line.Split(':');
  caseID = tokens[0];
  method = tokens[1];
  tempInput = tokens[2].Split(' ');
  expected = tokens[3];
  // etc.
}
```

Comments

After reading a line of test case data into a string variable line, calling the Split() method with the colon character passed in as an argument will break the line into the parts between the colons. These substrings are assigned to the string array tokens. So, tokens[0] will hold the first field, which is the test case ID (for example "001"), tokens[1] will hold the string identifying the method under test (for example "ArithmeticMean"), tokens[2] will hold the input vector as a string (for example "2 4 8"), and tokens[3] will hold the expected value (for example "4.667"). Next, you call the Split() method using a blank space argument on tokens[2] and assign the result to the string array tempInput. If tokens[2] has "2 4 8", then tempInput[0] will hold "2", tempInput[1] will hold "4", and tempInput[2] will hold "8".

If you need to use more than one separator character, you can create a character array containing the separators and then pass that array to Split(). For example,

```
char[] separators = new char[]{'#',':','!'};
string[] parts = line.Split(separators);
```

will break the string variable line into pieces wherever there is a pound sign, colon, or exclamation point character and assign those substrings to the string array parts.

The Split() method will satisfy most of your simple text-parsing needs for lightweight test-automation situations. A significant alternative to using Split() is to use regular expressions. One advantage of using regular expressions is that they are more powerful, in the sense that you can get a lot of parsing done in very few lines of code. One disadvantage of regular expressions is that they are harder to understand by those who do not use them often because the syntax is relatively unusual compared with most C# programming constructs.

1.4 Converting Data to an Appropriate Data Type

Problem

You want to convert your test case input data or expected result from type string into some other data type, so you can pass the data to the method under test or compare the expected result with an actual result.

Design

Perform an explicit type conversion with the appropriate static Parse() method.

Solution

```
int[] input = new int[tempInput.Length];
for (int i = 0; i < input.Length; ++i)
  input[i] = int.Parse(tempInput[i]);
```

Comments

If you store your test case data in a text file and then parse the test case inputs, you will end up with type string. If the method under test accepts any data type other than string you need to convert the inputs. In the preceding solution, if the string array tempInput holds {"2","4","8"} then you first create an integer array named input with the same size as tempInput. After the loop executes, input[0] will hold 2 (as an integer), input[1] will hold 4, and input[2] will hold 8. Including type string, the C# language has 14 data types that you'll deal with most often as listed in Table 1-1.

Table 1-1. *Common C# Data Types and Corresponding .NET Types*

C# Type	Corresponding .NET Type
int	Int32
short	Int16
long	Int64
uint	Uint32
ushort	Uint16
ulong	Uint64
byte	Byte
sbyte	Sbyte
char	Char
bool	Boolean
float	Single
double	Double
decimal	Decimal

Each of these C# data types supports a static Parse() method that accepts a string argument and returns the calling data type. For example,

```
string s1 = "345.67";
double d = double.Parse(s1);
string s2 = "true";
bool b = bool.Parse(s2);
```

will assign numeric 345.67 to variable d and logical true to b. An alternative to using Parse() is to use static methods in the System.Convert class. For instance,

```
string s1 = "345.67";
double d = Convert.ToDouble(s1);
string s2 = "true";
bool b = Convert.ToBoolean(s2);
```

is equivalent to the preceding `Parse()` examples. The `Convert` methods transform to and from .NET data types (such as `Int32`) rather than directly to their C# counterparts (such as `int`). One advantage of using `Convert` is that it is not syntactically C#-centric like `Parse()` is, so if you ever recast your automation from C# to VB.NET you'll have less work to do. Advantages of using the `Parse()` method include the fact that it maps directly to C# data types, which makes your code somewhat easier to read if you are in a 100% C# environment. In addition, `Parse()` is more specific than the `Convert` methods, because it accepts only type `string` as a parameter (which is exactly what you need when dealing with test case data stored in a text file).

1.5 Determining a Test Case Result

Problem

You want to determine whether an API test case passes or fails.

Design

Call the method under test with the test case input, fetch the return value, and compare the actual result with the expected result read from the test case.

Solution

```
string method, expected;
double actual = 0.0;

if (method == "ArithmeticMean")
{
  actual = MathLib.Methods.ArithmeticMean(input);
  if (actual.ToString("F4") == expected)
    Console.WriteLine("Pass");
  else
    Console.WriteLine("*FAIL*");
}
else
{
  Console.WriteLine("Method not recognized");
}
```

Comments

After reading data for a test case, parsing that data, and converting the test case input to an appropriate data type if necessary, you can call the method under test. For your harness to be able to call the method under test, you must add a project reference to the DLL (in this example, `MathLib`) to the harness. The preceding code first checks to see which method the data will be applied to. In a .NET environment, methods are either static or instance. `ArithmeticMean()` is a static method, so it is called directly using its class context, passing in the integer array input as the argument, and storing the return result in the `double` variable actual. Next, the return value obtained from the method call is compared with the expected return value (supplied by the test case data). Because the expected result is type `string`, but the actual result is type `double`, you must convert one or the other. Here the actual result is converted to a string with four decimal places to match the format of the expected result. If we had chosen to convert the expected result to type `double`

```
if (actual == double.Parse(expected))
  Console.WriteLine("Pass");
else
  Console.WriteLine("*FAIL*");
```

we would have ended up comparing two `double` values for exact equality, which is problematic as types `double` and `float` are only approximations. As a general rule of thumb, you should convert the expected result from type `string` except when dealing with type `double` or `float` as in this example.

GeometricMean()is an instance method, so before calling it, you must instantiate a `MathLib.Methods` object. Then you call `GeometricMean()` using its object context. If the actual result equals the expected result, the test case passes, and you print a pass message to console:

```
if (method == "GeometricMean")
{
  MathLib.Methods m = new MathLib.Methods();
  actual = m.GeometricMean(input);
  if (actual.ToString("F4") == expected)
    Console.WriteLine("Pass");
  else
    Console.WriteLine("*FAIL*");
}
```

You'll usually want to add additional information such as the test case ID to your output statements, for example:

```
Console.WriteLine(caseID + " Pass");
```

For test cases that fail, you'll often want to print the actual and expected values to help diagnose the failure, for example:

```
Console.WriteLine(caseID + "  *FAIL*  " + method + " actual = " +
                  actual.ToString("F4") + " expected = " + expected);
```

A design question you must answer when writing API tests is how many methods will each lightweight harness test? In many situations, you'll write a different test harness for every method under test; however, you can also combine testing multiple methods in a single harness. For example, to test both the `ArithmeticMean()` and `GeometricMean()` methods, you could combine test case data into a single file:

```
0001:ArithmeticMean:2 4 8:4.6667
0002:ArithmeticMean:1 5:3.0000
0004:GeometricMean :1 2 4 8 16 32:6.6569
0006:GeometricMean :2 4 8:4.0000
```

(The trailing blank space in "GeometricMean " is for readability only.) Then you can modify the test harness logic to branch on the value for the method under test:

```
if (method == "ArithmeticMean")
{
  // code to test ArithmeticMean here
}
else if (method == "GeometricMean ")
{
  // code to test GeometricMean here
}
else
{
  Console.WriteLine("Unknown method"");
}
```

The decision to combine testing multiple methods in one harness usually depends on how close the methods' signatures are to each other. If the signatures are close as in this example (both methods accept a variable number of integer arguments and return a double), then combining their tests may save you time. If your methods' signatures are very different, then you'll usually be better off writing separate harnesses.

When testing an API method, you must take into account whether the method is *stateless* or *stateful*. Most API methods are stateless, which means that each call is independent. Or put another way, each call to a stateless method with a given input set will produce the same result. Sometimes we say that a stateless method has no memory. On the other hand, some methods are stateful, which means that the return result can vary. For example, suppose you have a Fibonacci generator method that returns the sum of its two previous integer results. So the first and second calls return 1, the third call returns 2, the fourth call returns 3, the fifth call returns 5, and so on. When testing a stateful method, you must make sure your test harness logic prepares the method's state correctly.

Your test harness must be able to access the API methods under test. In most cases, you should add a project reference to the DLL that is housing the API methods. However, in some situations, you may want to physically copy the code for the methods under test into your test harness. This approach is necessary when testing a private helper method (assuming you do not want to change the method's access modifier from public to private).

1.6 Logging Test Case Results

Problem

You want to save test case results to external storage as a simple text file.

Design

Inside the main test case processing loop, use a `System.IO.StreamWriter` object to write a test case ID and a pass or fail result.

Solution

```
// open StreamReader sr here

FileStream ofs = new FileStream("..\\..\\TestResults.txt",
                                FileMode.CreateNew);
StreamWriter sw = new StreamWriter(ofs);

string line, caseID, method, expected;
double actual = 0.0;

while ((line = sr.ReadLine()) != null)
{
  // parse "line" here
  if (method == "ArithmeticMean")
  {
    actual = MathLib.Methods.ArithmeticMean(input);
    if (actual.ToString("F4") == expected)
      sw.WriteLine(caseID + " Pass");
    else
      sw.WriteLine(caseID + " *FAIL*");
  }
  else
  {
    sw.WriteLine(caseID + " Unknown method");
  }
} // while

sw.Close();
ofs.Close();
```

Comments

In many situations, you'll want to write your test case results to external storage instead of, or in addition to, displaying them in the command shell. The simplest form of external storage is a text file. Alternatives include writing to a SQL table or an XML file. You create a `FileStream` object and a `StreamWriter` object to write test case results to external storage. In this solution, the `FileMode.CreateNew` argument creates a new text file named `TestResults.txt` two directories above the test harness executable. Using a relative file path allows you to move your entire test harness directory structure if necessary. Then you can use the `StreamWriter` object to write test results to external storage just as you would to the console.

When passing in a FileMode.CreateNew "TestResults.txt" argument, if a file with the name TestResults.txt already exists, an exception will be thrown. You can avoid this by using a FileMode.Create argument, but then any existing TestResults.txt file will be overwritten, and you could lose test results. One strategy is to parameterize the test results file name

```
static void Main(string[] args)
{
  string testResultsFile = args[0];
  FileStream ofs = new FileStream(testResultsFile,
                                  FileMode.CreateNew);
  StreamWriter sw = new StreamWriter(ofs);
  // etc.
}
```

and pass in a new manually generated test results file name for each run:

```
C:\Harness\bin\Debug>Run.exe  Results-12-25-06.txt
```

Alternatives include writing results to a programmatically time-stamped file.

Our examples so far have either written test results to the command shell or to a .txt file, but you can write results to both console and external storage:

```
if (actual.ToString("F4") == expected)
{
  Console.WriteLine(caseID + " Pass");
  sw.WriteLine(caseID + " Pass");
}
else
{
  Console.WriteLine(caseID + " *FAIL*");
  sw.WriteLine(caseID + " *FAIL*");
}
```

When the StreamWriter.WriteLine() statement executes, it does not actually write results to your output file. Results are buffered and then flushed out only when the StreamWriter.Close() statement executes. You can force results to be written by explicitly issuing a StreamWriter.Flush() statement. This is usually most important when you have a lot of test cases or when you catch an exception—be sure to close any open streams in either the catch block or the finally block so that buffered results will be written to file and not lost:

```
catch(Exception ex)
{
  Console.WriteLine("Unexpected fatal error: " + ex.Message);
  sw.Close();
  // close other open streams
}
```

1.7 Time-Stamping Test Case Results

Problem

You want to time-stamp your test case results so you can distinguish the results of different test runs.

Design

Use the `DateTime.Now` property passed as an argument to the static `CreateDirectory()` method to create a time-stamped folder. Alternatively, you can pass `DateTime.Now` to the `FileStream()` constructor to create a time-stamped file name.

Solution

```
string folder = "Results" + DateTime.Now.ToString("s");
folder = folder.Replace(":","-");
Directory.CreateDirectory("..\\..\\" + folder);
string path = "..\\..\\" + folder + "\\TestResults.txt";
FileStream ofs = new FileStream(path, FileMode.Create);
StreamWriter sw = new StreamWriter(ofs);
```

Comments

You create a folder name using the `DateTime.Now` property, which grabs the current system date and time. Passing an "s" argument to the `ToString()` method returns a date-time string in a sortable pattern like "2006-07-30T13:57:00". You can use many other formatting arguments with `ToString()`, but a sortable pattern will help you manage test results better than a non-sortable pattern. You must replace the colon character with some other character (here we use a hyphen) because colons are not valid in a path or file name.

Next, you create the time-stamped folder using the static `CreateDirectory()` method, and then you can pass the entire path and file name to the `FileStream` constructor. After instantiating a `StreamWriter` object using the `FileStream` object, you can use the `StreamWriter` object to write into a file named `TestResults.txt`, which is located inside the time-stamped folder.

A slight variation on this idea is to write all results to the same folder but time-stamp their file names:

```
string stamp = DateTime.Now.ToString("s");
stamp = stamp.Replace(":","-");
string path = "..\\..\\TestResults-" + stamp + ".txt";
FileStream ofs = new FileStream(path, FileMode.Create);
StreamWriter sw = new StreamWriter(ofs);
```

This variation assumes that an arbitrary result directory is located two directories above the test harness executable directory. If the directory does not exist, an exception is thrown. The test case result file name becomes the time-stamp value appended to the string `TestResults-` with a `.txt` extension added, for example, `TestResults-2006-12-25T23-59-59.txt`.

1.8 Calculating Summary Results

Problem

You want to tally your test case results to track the number of test cases that pass and the number of cases that fail.

Design

Use simple integer counters initialized to 0 at the beginning of each test run.

Solution

```
int numPass = 0, numFail = 0;

while ((line = sr.ReadLine()) != null)
{
  // parse "line" here
  if (method == "ArithmeticMean")
  {
    actual = MathLib.Methods.ArithmeticMean(input);
    if (actual.ToString("F4") == expected)
    {
      Console.WriteLine("Pass");
      ++numPass;
    }
    else
    {
      Console.WriteLine("*FAIL*");
      ++numFail;
    }
  }
  else
  {
    Console.WriteLine("Unknown method");
    // no effect on numPass or numFail
  }
} // loop

Console.WriteLine("Number cases passed = " + numPass);
Console.WriteLine("Number cases failed = " + numFail);
Console.WriteLine("Total cases         = " + (numPass + numFail));
double percent = ((double)numPass)  / (numPass + numFail);
Console.WriteLine("Percent passed      = " + percent.ToString("P"));
```

Comments

It is often useful to calculate and record summary metrics such as the total number of test cases that pass and the number that fail. If you track these numbers daily, you can gauge the progress of the quality of your software system. You might also want to record and track the percentage of test cases that pass because most product specifications have exit criteria such as, "for milestone MM3, a full API test pass will achieve a 99.95% test case pass rate." You can declare integer variables and initialize them to 0 outside the main test loop. If a test case passes, you increment the pass counter; if the test case fails, you increment the fail counter. After all tests have been run, you can display your summary metrics and/or write them to external storage.

In the preceding solution we track the number of test cases that pass and the number that fail and then add them to determine the total number of cases run. You may also want to initialize and insert a counter numCases that increments after every test case so you can verify your test harness logic:

```
if (actual.ToString("F4") == expected)
{
  Console.WriteLine("Pass");
  ++numPass;
  ++numCases;
}
else
{
  Console.WriteLine("*FAIL*");
  ++numFail;
  ++numCases;
}
// etc.
if ((numPass + numFail) != numCases)
  Console.WriteLine("Warning: Counter logic failure");
```

When calculating a percent pass rate, be careful to cast either the numerator or denominator to type double so that the result of the division operation is implicitly converted to type double:

```
double percent = ((double)numPass)  / (numPass + numFail);
```

If you don't cast, you will be performing integer division and always get either 1.0 (100%) or 0.0 (0%) for the result. Instead of using an explicit C# cast to type double, you can perform an implicit cast by multiplying by 1.0:

```
double percent = (numPass * 1.0)  / (numPass + numFail);
```

This old technique has the advantage of being language-independent but the disadvantage of doing more work than is necessary.

1.9 Determining a Test Run Total Elapsed Time

Problem

You want to determine the total elapsed run time for a test run.

Design

Use the DateTime.Now property to record the time when the test run started and when the test run ended. Then use a TimeSpan object to calculate the elapsed time for the test run.

Solution

```
DateTime startTime = DateTime.Now;

while ((line = sr.ReadLine()) != null)
{
  // run tests
}

DateTime endTime = DateTime.Now;
TimeSpan elapsedTime = endTime - startTime;
Console.WriteLine("Elapsed time = " + elapsedTime.ToString());
```

Comments

Calling the DateTime.Now property retrieves the current system time on the test harness machine. You fetch a start time before your tests execute and an end time after the test run concludes. To determine the elapsed time, you find the difference between the start and end times. DateTime objects support an overloaded subtraction operator ("–") that returns a TimeSpan object. You can think of a DateTime value as being an instant in time and a TimeSpan value as being a time-duration.

You have to be somewhat careful about exactly where you place the statements that find the test run start and end times. The guiding principle is to place them as much as possible so that you capture time spent executing your tests, but not so much that you are capturing test harness overhead activities that can vary.

The purpose of recording and storing/displaying the total elapsed time of your daily test run is so that you can detect any significant change in the performance characteristics of your API methods. If the total elapsed time of a test run increases greatly one day, then you need to investigate. If you discover that a code change in one of the methods under test produced the performance degradation, you'll find out immediately and can decide to recast the code or accept the performance penalty. If a code change was not the cause of the performance hit, then you may have a problem with your test harness system (for example some rogue process running and using up CPU time.) Another cause of a change in test run elapsed time would be increasing (or decreasing) the number of tests in the test case data file.

One of the advantages of test automation is that you can execute many thousands of test cases quickly. When you are dealing with a huge number of test case results, you may want to log only summary metrics (the number of cases that passed and the number that failed) and details only about failed test cases. In a situation like this, determining and logging the test run elapsed time is important because it can uncover test harness problems that can be hidden when you don't have detailed test results to examine.

1.10 Dealing with null Input/null Expected Results

Problem
You want to verify the correct handling of null arguments passed to API methods under test.

Design
Use a special string token to represent null in your test case data file. Add logic to your test harness that converts the null-token to a null input value.

Solution
Suppose the original ArithmeticMean() method under test is modified to handle null input:

```
public static double ArithmeticMean(params int[] vals)
{
  if (vals == null) return 0.0; // modification

  double sum = 0.0;
  foreach (int v in vals)
    sum += v;
  return (double)(sum / vals.Length);
} // ArithmeticMean
```

You can add a null-token to your test case data like this:

```
0001:ArithmeticMean:2 4 8:4.6667
0002:ArithmeticMean:NULL:0.0000
```

Then process the token like this:

```
string line, caseID, method;
string[] tokens, tempInput;
int[] input = null;
double expected, actual;
```

```
while ((line = sr.ReadLine()) != null)
{
  tokens = line.Split(':');
  caseID = tokens[0];
  method = tokens[1];

  if (tokens[2] == "NULL") // null input
    input = null;
  else
  {
    tempInput = tokens[2].Split(' ');
    input = new int[tempInput.Length];
    for (int i = 0; i < input.Length; ++i)
      input[i] = int.Parse(tempInput[i]);
  }

  expected = double.Parse(tokens[3]);

  actual = MathLib.Methods.ArithmeticMean(input);

  if (actual == expected)
    Console.WriteLine(caseID + " Pass");
  else
    Console.WriteLine(caseID + " *FAIL*");
} // while
```

Comments

Testing API methods for null input arguments is essential. Because we can't store a null value directly in the test case data, we use the string token "NULL". Using "NULL" is arbitrary but makes the test case data and code more readable than alternatives like "nil" or "invalid". When we read and parse a test case, we check for the string "NULL" and then branch to special logic in the test harness. The exact logic you use will depend on the behavior of the method under test. Notice that we assigned null to our input variable at declaration time:

```
int[] input = null;
```

and then reassign a null value if we read "NULL" from the test case file:

```
if (tokens[2] == "NULL")
  input = null;
```

This is technically unnecessary but makes our code more readable and easier to modify. Dealing with a null expected result uses the same idea as dealing with a null input argument. Suppose a new method named Hypergeometric() is added to the MathLib library under test, and that the Hypergeometric() method returns null if all input arguments are 0. To test, we store a string token such as "NULL" in the test case file:

```
0001:Hypergeometric:0 0 0 0:NULL:
0002:Hypergeometric:1 3 5 7:2 4:
```

and then add logic to the test harness:

```
object expected = null;

while ((line = sr.ReadLine()) != null)
{
  if (tokens[3] == "NULL")
    expected = null;
  else
    // parse tokens[3] into object expected here

  // etc.
}
```

1.11 Dealing with Methods that Throw Exceptions

Problem

You want to test a method that throws an exception.

Design

Embed a special string token in your test case data file to signal that an exception should be thrown, and place the call to the method under test in a `try` block so you can catch the exception if it is thrown.

Solution

Add a token "`Exception`" as the expected value field in your test case data:

```
0004:GeometricMean :1 2 4 8 16 32:6.6569
0005:GeometricMean :0 0 0 0:Exception
0006:GeometricMean :2 4 8:4.0000
```

and then process inside the main test loop like this:

```
MathLib.Methods m = new MathLib.Methods();
if (tokens[3] == "Exception")
{
  try
  {
    actual = m.GeometricMean(input);
  }
  catch(Exception ex)
```

```
  {
    Console.WriteLine(caseID + " Pass");
    continue;
  }
  Console.WriteLine(caseID + " *FAIL* no exception thrown");
}
else
{
  // use regular test logic
}
```

Comments

A common situation is that methods will throw an exception for certain input. For example, a method that performs a division operation with one of its input arguments may throw an exception if the value of the argument is 0. In this example, we assume the original GeometricMean() method has been modified so that passing all zero values to the method throws an exception by design. We check for this special input by examining the test case data for an "Exception" string. If we find it, we branch to code that wraps the call to GeometricMean() in a try block. If an exception is thrown as expected, control is transferred to the catch block, and we print a pass result. Then we move to the next test case when the continue statement is executed. If calling GeometricMean() does not throw an exception, control will reach the

```
Console.WriteLine(caseID + " *FAIL* no exception thrown");
```

statement. Notice you do not want to wrap calls to the method under test that do not throw an exception in a try block because if the method does throw an exception, you'll get a pass result. Dealing with methods that throw an exception can be messy in terms of integrating that special logic into the "regular" logic of your test harness. Because of this, a good strategy is to create two different lightweight test harnesses—one harness for test cases that do not throw exceptions and one harness just for cases that do.

The preceding solution is designed so that we test only that an exception is thrown, not necessarily a particular exception. In some situations, you may want to check for a specific exception. One way to do this is to embed the exception message in your test case file and check for it in your harness logic. For example, suppose the GeometricMean() method contains this code:

```
if (denominator == 0)
  throw new Exception("Invalid division");
```

You could create this test case:

```
0005:GeometricMean :0 0 0 0:Invalid division
```

and then test inside the main test loop like this:

```
expected = tokens[3]; // "Invalid division"
try
{
  actual = m.GeometricMean(input);
}
catch(Exception ex)
{
  if (ex.Message == expected)
  {
    Console.WriteLine(caseID + " Pass; correct exception");
    continue;
  }
  else
  {
    Console.WriteLine(caseID + " *FAIL*; wrong exception");
  }
}
Console.WriteLine(caseID + " *FAIL*; no exception thrown");
```

1.12 Dealing with Empty String Input Arguments

Problem

You want to test empty string arguments passed to API methods under test.

Design

Use a special string token to represent an empty string in your test case file and then add branching logic to your test harness that passes a true empty string argument to the API method under test.

Solution

Create test case data like this:

```
0001:SubString:put:computer:true
0002:SubString:xyz:computer:false
0003:SubString:emptystring:computer:true
```

and add special logic to the test harness to handle the "emptystring" token like this:

```
tokens = line.Split(':');

if (tokens[2] == "emptystring") // special input
  arg1 = "";
else
  arg1 = tokens[2];

bool actual = StringLib.Methods.SubString(arg1, tokens[3]);

if (actual == bool.Parse(tokens[4]))
  Console.WriteLine("Pass");
else
  Console.WriteLine("*FAIL*");
```

Comments

When testing API methods that accept string arguments, you should always test for empty strings. One way to deal with this is to store a special string token such as "emptystring" in your test case data file and then branch your test case logic when that token is read. Suppose, for example, you are testing a custom StringLib library containing a custom SubString() method that accepts two string arguments and returns true if the first argument is contained within the second argument. By design, the custom SubString() method returns true if an empty string is passed to its first parameter.

Unlike null input, it is possible to indirectly store empty string input in a test case data file. For example, the test case data string

```
0003:SubString::computer:true
```

when parsed by String.Split() into a string array named tokens will store an empty string into tokens[2] because of the two consecutive colon characters. However, in general, it's much better to store a special string token because it makes your test case data easier to read and validate programmatically.

The technique of embedding special string tokens in your test case data file to deal with empty string input can be used to test for other unusual input too. For example, suppose you are testing a method that accepts a character input argument. You will want to test for control characters such as <CR> and <LF>, and ASCII vs. Unicode characters. You can store strings like "<cr>", "<lf>", and "\u0041" in your test case data and then add special logic to your harness to deal with them:

```
char input;

if (tokens[2] == "<CR>") // special input
  input = '\x000d';
else
  input = char.Parse(tokens[2]);
```

If you have a lot of special tokens in your test case data file as is often the case, you can keep your harness code cleaner and more scalable by writing a helper method Map(), which converts the input value read from the test case data file into the appropriate value. For example, you could write:

```
private static char Map(string token)
{
  if (token == "<CR>")
    return '\x000d';
  else if (token == "<LF>")
    return '\x000a';
  // etc.
  else
    return char.Parse(token);
}
```

and then use it in your harness like this:

```
char input = Map(tokens[2]);
```

1.13 Programmatically Sending E-mail Alerts on Test Case Failures

Problem

You want your test harness to programmatically send an e-mail message when a test case fails.

Design

Use the System.Web.Mail class to create a MailMessage object. Supply properties such as To and Subject, and add details of the test case failure to the Body property.

Solution

```
if (method == "ArithmeticMean")
{
  actual = MathLib.Methods.ArithmeticMean(input);
  if (actual.ToString("F4") == expected)
  {
    Console.WriteLine("Pass");
  }
  else
```

```
  {
    Console.WriteLine("*FAIL*. Sending e-mail");
    try
    {
      MailMessage m = new MailMessage();
      m.From = "Test Automation Harness";
      m.To = "you@somewhere.com";
      m.Subject = "Test Case Failure";

      m.BodyEncoding = System.Text.Encoding.ASCII;
      m.BodyFormat = MailFormat.Html;
      m.Priority = MailPriority.High;

      m.Body = "Test case " + caseID + " failed";
      SmtpMail.SmtpServer = "127.0.0.1";
      SmtpMail.Send(m);
    }
    catch(Exception ex)
    {
      Console.WriteLine("Fatal error sending mail: " + ex.Message);
    }

  } // test case failed
}
```

Comments

Because test automation often runs unattended, you may want to send an e-mail message to yourself or one of your team members when a test case fails, so that the test case failure does not lie unnoticed in a log file somewhere. You may also want to send an e-mail message summarizing the test run results. There are several ways to programmatically send e-mail in a .NET environment, but using the MailMessage class in the System.Web.Mail namespace is usually the easiest. The code in this solution assumes you have first added a project reference to the System.Web namespace (it's not accessible by a console application by default) and placed a

```
using System.Web.Mail;
```

statement in your harness code.

After instantiating a MailMessage object, you supply values for properties From, To, Subject, BodyEncoding, BodyFormat, and Body. You can also set the optional Priority property to MailPriority.High. You set the BodyEncoding value to one of the encoding representations from System.Text.Encoding. You will usually use Encoding.ASCII, but you can use Encoding.Unicode or Encoding.UTF8 if you want to. The BodyFormat property can be set to MailFormat.Html or MailFormat.Text. Either will work fine as long as there are no quirks in your e-mail system. The Body property is a string that holds the text of the message. At a minimum, you'll want to include the test case ID that failed and the actual and expected return values.

In theory, programmatically sending e-mail is easy, but in practical terms, a lot of things can go wrong. You have to deal with relay servers, proxy servers, network security policies, and firewalls, just to name a few. Because of this, your best strategy is to make sure that whenever feasible, your test harness machine is running as isolated as possible from other machines. This will help prevent unintended side effects as well as make sending e-mail from your test harness much more reliable.

1.14 Launching a Test Harness Automatically

Problem

You want your test harness program to launch automatically.

Design

Use the Windows Task Scheduler.

Solution

You will often want to launch your test automation automatically. For example you might schedule a test automation harness to start at 2:00 A.M. so that it runs overnight, and the test results are ready to review when you come to work. The Windows Task Scheduler makes it easy to schedule tasks in a Windows environment. You specify the test harness executable, the schedule of when you want the harness to run, and the security context under which you want the harness to run.

If you have several lightweight test-automation harnesses that you want to run, you can create a .BAT file with commands to launch them. For example,

```
@echo off
echo Starting test automation sequence
echo.
C:\TestHarness1\bin\Debug\Run.exe
C:\TestHarness2\bin\Debug\Run.exe
C:\TestHarness3\bin\Debug\Run.exe
echo.
echo Test automation sequence complete
```

If your harnesses explicitly log test case results to external files, then this is all you need. If your harnesses log test case results to the command shell, then you can easily save them to external storage using system redirection such as:

```
C:\TestHarness1\bin\Debug\Run.exe  >  C:\Results\Harness1Results.txt
C:\TestHarness2\bin\Debug\Run.exe  >  C:\Results\Harness2Results.txt
```

Comments

For most lightweight test-automation situations, using .BAT files to manage multiple test harnesses is simple and effective. An alternative is to write a C# master harness that coordinates and calls the worker automation harnesses. You can write statements that call the worker harnesses by using the static Start() method in the System.Diagnostics.Process namespace:

```
Console.WriteLine("Starting test automation sequence\n");
Process.Start("C:\\TestHarness1\\bin\\Debug\\Run.exe");
Process.Start("C:\\TestHarness2\\bin\\Debug\\Run.exe");
Process.Start("C:\\TestHarness3\\bin\\Debug\\Run.exe");
Console.WriteLine("\n Test automation sequence complete\n");
```

and then schedule this one master program using the Task Scheduler. An advantage of using a .BAT file master solution is simplicity. An advantage of using a C# master solution is that you have increased power to do things like catch exceptions and add branching logic to execute a worker harness only if a preceding harness test results meet some condition.

Instead of using the Windows Task Scheduler to automatically launch a test harness, you can use the old at command. Scheduling a test harness or master harness program to run using the at command is more difficult than using the Windows Task Scheduler. You should only use at if your test system does not support the Task Scheduler or if you are integrating a new test harness system into an existing system that uses the at command.

1.15 Example Program: ApiTest

This program combines many of the techniques we've seen in this chapter into a complete lightweight API test harness. The methods under test are ArithmeticMean(), GeometricMean(), and HarmonicMean() as described at the beginning of this chapter. The complete lightweight test harness listing is shown in Listing 1-1. The program reads test case data a line at a time from the file TestCases.txt. Then the harness parses the test case ID, which includes the method to test, input values, and an expected result. Input values are sent to the method under test, and an actual result value is obtained and compared with the test case expected result value. A pass or fail result is sent to the command shell and logged to the file TestResults.txt.

Listing 1-1. *Program ApiTest*

```
using System;
using System.IO;
using MathLib; // houses methods under test

namespace TestAutomation
{
  class Class1
  {
    [STAThread]
    static void Main(string[] args)
```

```
      {
        try
        {
          FileStream ifs = new FileStream("..\\..\\TestCases.txt",
                                          FileMode.Open);
          StreamReader sr = new StreamReader(ifs);
          string stamp = DateTime.Now.ToString("s");
          stamp = stamp.Replace(":", "-");
          FileStream ofs = new FileStream("..\\..\\TestResults" +
                          stamp + ".txt", FileMode.CreateNew);
          StreamWriter sw = new StreamWriter(ofs);

          string line, caseID, method;
          string[] tokens, tempInput;
          string expected;
          double actual = 0.0;
          int numPass = 0, numFail = 0;

          Console.WriteLine("\nCaseID Result Method   Details");
          Console.WriteLine("==================================\n");

          while ((line = sr.ReadLine()) != null)
          {
            tokens = line.Split(':');
            caseID = tokens[0];
            method = tokens[1];
            tempInput = tokens[2].Split(' ');
            expected = tokens[3];

            int[] input = new int[tempInput.Length];
            for (int i = 0; i < input.Length; ++i)
              input[i] = int.Parse(tempInput[i]);

            if (method == "ArithmeticMean")
            {
              actual = MathLib.Methods.ArithmeticMean(input);
              if (actual.ToString("F4") == expected)
              {
                Console.WriteLine(caseID + "   Pass   " + method +
                        " actual = " + actual.ToString("F4"));
                sw.WriteLine(caseID + "   Pass   " + method +
                        " actual = " + actual.ToString("F4"));
                ++numPass;
              }
              else
```

```
        {
          Console.WriteLine(caseID + "  *FAIL*  " + method +
                  " actual = " + actual.ToString("F4") +
                  " expected = " + expected);
          sw.WriteLine(caseID + "  *FAIL*  " + method +
                  " actual = " + actual.ToString("F4") +
                  " expected = " + expected);
          ++numFail;
        }
      }
      else if (method == "GeometricMean ")
      {
        MathLib.Methods m = new MathLib.Methods();
        actual = m.GeometricMean(input);
        if (actual.ToString("F4") == expected)
        {
          Console.WriteLine(caseID + "   Pass   " + method +
                  " actual = " + actual.ToString("F4"));
          sw.WriteLine(caseID + "   Pass   " + method +
                  " actual = " + actual.ToString("F4"));
          ++numPass;
        }
        else
        {
          Console.WriteLine(caseID + "  *FAIL*  " + method +
                  " actual = " + actual.ToString("F4") +
                  " expected = " + expected);
          sw.WriteLine(caseID + "  *FAIL*  " + method +
                  " actual = " + actual.ToString("F4") +
                  " expected = " + expected);
          ++numFail;
        }
      }
      else
      {
        Console.WriteLine(caseID + "            " + method +
                " Not yet implemented");
        sw.WriteLine(caseID + "            " + method +
                " Not yet implemented");
      }
    } // test case loop
```

```
        Console.WriteLine("\n========= end test run ==========");
        Console.WriteLine("\nPass = " + numPass +
                        " Fail = " + numFail);
        sw.WriteLine(Environment.NewLine + "Pass = " + numPass +
                        " Fail = " + numFail);
        sr.Close();
        ifs.Close();
        sw.Close();
        ofs.Close();
      }
      catch(Exception ex)
      {
        Console.WriteLine("Fatal error: " + ex.Message);
      }
      Console.ReadLine();
    } // Main()
  } // class Class1
} // ns TestAutomation
```

When run with this test case data file:

```
0001:ArithmeticMean:2 4 8:4.6667
0002:ArithmeticMean:1 5:3.0000
0003:ArithmeticMean:1 2 4 8 16 32:10.5000
0004:GeometricMean :1 2 4 8 16 32:6.6569
0005:GeometricMean :0:0.0000
0006:GeometricMean :2 4 8:4.0000
0007:HarmonicMean  :2 4 8:3.4286
0008:HarmonicMean  :2 3 6:3.0000
```

the output is

```
0001   Pass   ArithmeticMean actual = 4.6667
0002   Pass   ArithmeticMean actual = 3.0000
0003   Pass   ArithmeticMean actual = 10.5000
0004   *FAIL* GeometricMean  actual = 5.6569 expected = 6.6569
0005   Pass   GeometricMean  actual = 0.0000
0006   Pass   GeometricMean  actual = 4.0000
0007          HarmonicMean   Not yet implemented
0008          HarmonicMean   Not yet implemented

Pass = 5 Fail = 1
```

Test case 0004 has a deliberately incorrect expected value to check the validity of the test harness logic.

CHAPTER 2

■ ■ ■

Reflection-Based UI Testing

2.0 Introduction

The most fundamental and simplest form of application testing is manual testing through the application's user interface (UI). Paradoxically, automated testing through a user interface (automated UI testing for short) is challenging. The .NET environment provides you with many classes in the System.Reflection namespace that can access and manipulate an application at run time. Using reflection, you can write lightweight automated UI tests. For example, suppose you had a simple form-based Windows application, as shown in the foreground of Figure 2-1.

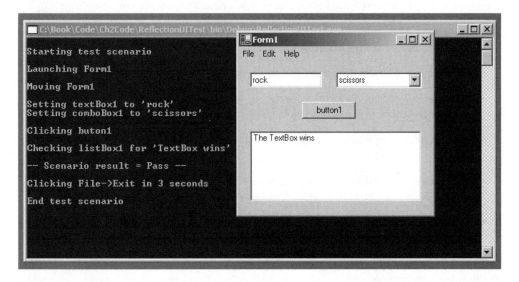

Figure 2-1. *Reflection-based UI testing*

A user types *paper*, *rock*, or *scissors* into the TextBox control, and a second user selects one of those strings from the ComboBox control. When either user clicks on the Button control, a message with the winner is displayed in the ListBox control. The key code for this dummy application is

```
private void button1_Click(object sender, System.EventArgs e)
{
  string tb = textBox1.Text;
  string cb = comboBox1.Text;

  if (tb == cb)
    listBox1.Items.Add("Result is a tie");
  else if (tb == "paper" && cb == "rock" ||
          tb == "rock" && cb == "scissors" ||
          tb == "scissors" && cb == "paper")
    listBox1.Items.Add("The TextBox wins");
  else
    listBox1.Items.Add("The ComboBox wins");
}
```

Note that this is not an example of good coding, and many deliberate errors are included. For example, the ComboBox player can win by leaving the ComboBox control empty. This simulates the unrefined character of an application while still under development. Using the techniques in this chapter, you can write automated UI tests as shown in the background of Figure 2-1. To write reflection-based lightweight UI test automation, you must be able to perform six tasks programmatically (each test automation task corresponds to a section in this chapter):

- Launch the application under test (AUT) from your test-harness program in a way that allows the two programs to communicate.

- Manipulate the application form to simulate a user moving and resizing the form.

- Examine the application form properties to verify that the resulting state of the application is correct so you can determine a test scenario pass or fail result.

- Manipulate the application control properties to simulate actions such as a user typing into a TextBox control.

- Examine the application control properties to verify that the resulting state of the application is correct so you can determine a test scenario pass or fail result.

- Invoke the application methods to simulate actions such as a user clicking on a Button control.

The techniques in this chapter are very lightweight. The main advantage of using these reflection-based test techniques is that they are very quick and easy to implement. The main disadvantages are that they apply only to pure .NET applications and that they cannot deal with complex test scenarios. The techniques in Chapter 3 provide you with lower-level, more powerful UI test-automation techniques at the expense of increased complexity.

2.1 Launching an Application Under Test

Problem

You want to launch the AUT so that you can manipulate it.

Design

Spin off a separate thread of execution from the test harness by creating a `Thread` object and then associate that thread with an application state wrapper class.

Solution

```
using System;
using System.Reflection;
using System.Windows.Forms;
using System.Threading;

class Class1
{
    [STAThread]
    static void Main(string[] args)
    {
      try
      {
        Console.WriteLine("Launching Form");
        Form theForm = null;
        string formName = "AUT.Form1";
        string path = "..\\..\\..\\AUT\\bin\\Debug\\AUT.exe";

        Assembly a = Assembly.LoadFrom(path);
        Type t1 = a.GetType(formName);
        theForm = (Form)a.CreateInstance(t1.FullName);

        AppState aps = new AppState(theForm);
        ThreadStart ts = new ThreadStart(aps.RunApp);
        Thread thread = new Thread(ts);
        thread.ApartmentState = ApartmentState.STA;
        thread.IsBackground = true;
        thread.Start();
```

```
      Console.WriteLine("\nForm launched");
    }
    catch(Exception ex)
    {
      Console.WriteLine("Fatal error: " + ex.Message);
    }
  } // Main()
  private class AppState
  {
    public readonly Form formToRun;

    public AppState(Form f)
    {
      this.formToRun = f;
    }

    public void RunApp()
    {
      Application.Run(formToRun);
    }
  } // class AppState

} // class Class1
```

To test a Windows-based form application through its UI using reflection techniques, you must launch the application on a separate thread of execution within the test-harness process. If, instead, you launch an AUT using the `Process.State()` method like this:

```
string exePath = "..\\..\\..\\AUT\\bin\\Debug\\AUT.exe";
System.Diagnostics.Process.Start(exePath);
```

the application will launch, but your test harness will not be able to directly communicate with the application because the harness and the application will be running in separate processes. The trick to enable harness-application communication is to spin off a separate thread from the harness. This way, the harness and the application will be running in the same process context and can communicate with each other.

Comments

If your test harness is a console application, you can add the following `using` statements so you won't have to fully qualify classes and objects:

```
using System.Reflection;
using System.Windows.Forms;
using System.Threading;
```

The `System.Reflection` namespace houses the primary classes you'll be using to access the AUT. The `System.Windows.Forms` namespace is not accessible to a console application by default, so you must add a project reference to the `System.Windows.Forms.dll` file. The `System.Threading` namespace allows you to create a separate thread of execution for the AUT.

Start by getting a reference to the application `Form` object:

```
Form theForm = null;
string formName = "AUT.Form1";
string path = "..\\..\\..\\AUT\\bin\\Debug\\AUT.exe";

Assembly a = Assembly.LoadFrom(path);
Type t1 = a.GetType(formName);
theForm = (Form)a.CreateInstance(t1.FullName);
```

The heart of obtaining a reference to the `Form` object under test is to use the `Assembly.CreateInstance()` method. This is slightly tricky because `CreateInstance()` is called from the context of an `Assembly` object and accepts an argument for the full name of the instance being created. Furthermore, an `Assembly` object is created using a factory mechanism instead of the more usual constructor instantiation with the new keyword. Additionally, the full name argument is called from a `Type` context. In short, you must first create an `Assembly` object using `Assembly.Load()`, passing in the path to the assembly. Then you create a `Type` object using `Assembly.GetType()`, passing in the full `Form` class name. And, finally, you create a reference to the `Form` object under test using `Assembly.CreateInstance()`, passing in the `Type.FullName` property. Notice that you must use the full form name (e.g., `"AUT.Form1"`) rather than the shortened form name (e.g., `"Form1"`).

The code to launch the `Form` under test is best understood by working backwards. The goal is to create a new `Thread` object and then call its `Start()` method; however, to create a `Thread` object, you need to pass a `ThreadStart` object to the `Thread` constructor. To create a `ThreadStart` object, you need to pass a target method to the `ThreadStart` constructor. This target method must return `void`, and it is the method to invoke when the thread begins execution. Now in the case of a `Form` object, you want to call the `Application.Run()` method. Although it seems a bit awkward, the easiest way to pass `Application.Run()` to `ThreadStart` is to create a separate wrapper class:

```
private class AppState
{
  public readonly Form formToRun;

  public AppState(Form f)
  {
    this.formToRun = f;
  }

  public void RunApp()
  {
    Application.Run(formToRun);
  }
}
```

This `AppState` class is just a wrapper around a `Form` object and a call to the `Application.Run()` method. We do this to pass `Application.Run()` to `ThreadStart` in a convenient way. With this class in place, you can instantiate an `AppState` object and pass `Application.Run()` indirectly to the `ThreadStart` constructor:

```
AppState aps = new AppState(theForm);
ThreadStart ts = new ThreadStart(aps.RunApp);
```

With the ThreadStart object created, you can create a new Thread, set its properties if necessary, and start the thread up:

```
Thread thread = new Thread(ts);
thread.ApartmentState = ApartmentState.STA;
thread.IsBackground = true;
thread.Start();
```

An alternative to creating a Thread object directly is to call the ThreadPool.QueueUserWorkItem() method. That method creates a thread indirectly and requires a starting method to be passed to a WaitCallBack object. This approach would look like

```
Form theForm = null;
string formName = "AUT.Form1";
string path = "..\\..\\..\\AUT\\bin\\Debug\\AUT.exe";

Assembly a = Assembly.LoadFrom(path);
Type t1 = a.GetType(formName);
theForm = (Form)a.CreateInstance(t1.FullName);

ThreadPool.QueueUserWorkItem(new WaitCallback(RunApp), theForm);
```

where

```
static void RunApp(object o)
{
  Application.Run(o as Form);
}
```

This ThreadPool technique is somewhat simpler than the ThreadStart solution but does not give you as much control over the thread of execution.

You can increase the modularity of this technique by refactoring your code as a method:

```
static Form LaunchApp(string path, string formName)
{
  Form result = null;
  Assembly a = Assembly.LoadFrom(path);
  Type t = a.GetType(formName);
  result = (Form)a.CreateInstance(t.FullName);
  AppState aps = new AppState(result);
  ThreadStart ts = new ThreadStart(aps.RunApp);
  Thread thread = new Thread(ts);
  thread.Start();
  return result;
}
```

which you can call like this:

```
Form theForm = null;
string path = "..\\..\\..\\AUT\\bin\\Debug\\AUT.exe";
string formName = "AUT.Form1";
theForm = LaunchApp(path, formName);
```

2.2 Manipulating Form Properties

Problem

You want to set the properties of a Windows form-based application.

Design

Get a reference to the property you want to set using the Type.GetProperty() method. Then use the PropertyInfo.SetValue() method in conjunction with the Form.Invoke() method and a method delegate.

Solution

```
string formName = "AUT.Form1";
string path = "..\\..\\..\\AUT\\bin\\Debug\\AUT.exe";
Form theForm = LaunchApp(path, formName); // see Section 2.1

Thread.Sleep(1500);
Console.WriteLine("\nSetting Form1 Location to x=10, y=20");
System.Drawing.Point pt = new System.Drawing.Point(10,20);
object[] o = new object[] { theForm, "Location", pt };
Delegate d = new SetFormPropertyValueHandler(SetFormPropertyValue);
if (theForm.InvokeRequired)
{
    theForm.Invoke(d, o);
}
else
{
  Console.WriteLine("Unexpected logic flow");
}
```

where

```
delegate void SetFormPropertyValueHandler(Form f,
                                          string propertyName,
                                          object newValue);

static void SetFormPropertyValue(Form f, string propertyName,
                                 object newValue)
```

```
{
  Type t = f.GetType();
  PropertyInfo pi = t.GetProperty(propertyName);
  pi.SetValue(f, newValue, null);
}
```

Comments

To simulate user interaction with a Windows-based form application, you may want to move the form or resize the form. One way to do this using a reflection-based technique is to use the `PropertyInfo.SetValue()` method. Although the idea is simple in principle, the details are tricky. You can best understand the technique by working backwards. The .NET Framework has a `PropertyInfo.SetValue()` method that can set the value of a property of an object. But the `SetValue()` method requires a `PropertyInfo` object context. However, a `PropertyInfo` object requires a `Type` object context. So you start by creating a `Type` object from the `Form` object you want to manipulate. Then you get a `PropertyInfo` object from the `Type` object, and then you call the `SetValue()` method. So, if there were no hidden issues you could simply write code like this:

```
theForm = LaunchApp(path, formName); // see Section 2.1
Console.WriteLine("\nSetting Form location to x=10, y=20");
Type t = theForm.GetType();
PropertyInfo pi = t.GetProperty("Location");
Point pt = new Point(10,20);
pi.SetValue(theForm, pt, null);
```

Unfortunately, there is a serious hidden issue that you must deal with. Before explaining that hidden issue, let's examine the `SetValue()` method. `SetValue()` accepts three arguments. The `PropertyInfo` object, whose `SetValue()` method you call, represents a property, such as a `Form` object's `Location` property. The first argument to `SetValue()` is the object to manipulate, which in this case is the `Form` object. The second argument is the new value of the property, which in this example is a new `Point` object. The third argument is necessary because some properties are indexed. When a property is not indexed, as is usually the case with form controls, you can just pass a `null` value as the argument.

The hidden issue with calling the `PropertyInfo.SetValue()` method is that you are not calling `SetValue()` from the main `Form` thread; you are calling `SetValue()` from a thread created by the test-automation harness. In situations like this, you should not call `SetValue()` directly. A full explanation of this issue is outside the scope of this book, but the conclusion is that you should call `SetValue()` indirectly by calling the `Form.Invoke()` method. This is a bit tricky because `Form.Invoke()` requires a delegate object that calls `SetValue()` and an object that represents the arguments for `SetValue()`. So in pseudo-code, you need to do this:

```
if (theForm.InvokeRequired)
  theForm.Invoke(a method delegate, an object array);
else
  Console.WriteLine("Unexpected logic flow");
```

The `InvokeRequired` property in this situation should always be true because the `Form` object was launched by a different thread (the automation harness). If `InvokeRequired` is not true, there is a logic error and you may want to print a warning message.

So, now you need a method delegate. Before you create the delegate, which you can think of as an alias for a real method, you create the real method that will actually do the work:

```
static void SetFormPropertyValue(Form f, string propertyName,
                                 object newValue)
{
  Type t = f.GetType();
  PropertyInfo pi = t.GetProperty(propertyName);
  pi.SetValue(f, newValue, null);
}
```

Notice that this method is almost exactly like the naive code if the whole InvokeRequired hidden issue did not exist. After creating the real method, you create a delegate that matches the real method:

```
delegate void SetFormPropertyValueHandler(Form f, string propertyName,
                                          object newValue);
```

In short, if you pass a reference to delegate SetFormPropertyValueHandler(), control is transferred to the associated SetFormPropertyValue() method (assuming you associate the two in the delegate constructor).

Now that we've dealt with the delegate parameter to the Form.Invoke() method, we have to deal with the object array parameter. This parameter represents arguments that are passed to the delegate and then, in turn, are passed to the associated real method. In this case, the delegate requires a Form object, a property name as a string, and a location as a Point object:

```
System.Drawing.Point pt = new System.Drawing.Point(10,20);
object[] o = new object[] { theForm, "Location", pt };
```

Putting these ideas and code together, you can write

```
delegate void SetFormPropertyValueHandler(Form f,
                                          string propertyName,
                                          object newValue);

static void SetFormPropertyValue(Form f, string propertyName,
                                 object newValue)
{
  Type t = f.GetType();
  PropertyInfo pi = t.GetProperty(propertyName);
  pi.SetValue(f, newValue, null);
}

static void Main(string[] args)
{
  Form theForm = null;

  string formName = "AUT.Form1";
  string path = "..\\..\\..\\AUT\\bin\\Debug\\AUT.exe";
  theForm = LaunchApp(path, formName); // see Section 2.1
  Console.WriteLine("\nSetting Form1 Location to 10,20");
```

```
  System.Drawing.Point pt = new System.Drawing.Point(10,20);
  object[] o = new object[] { theForm, "Location", pt };
  Delegate d = new SetFormPropertyValueHandler(SetFormPropertyValue);
  if (theForm.InvokeRequired)
    theForm.Invoke(d, o);
  else
    Console.WriteLine("Unexpected logic flow");
  //etc.
}
```

And now manipulating the properties of the application form is very easy. For example, suppose you want to change the size of the form. Here's how:

```
Console.WriteLine("\nSetting Form1 Size to 300x400");

System.Drawing.Size size = new System.Drawing.Size(300,400);
object[] o = new object[] { theForm, "Size", size };
Delegate d = new SetFormPropertyValueHandler(SetFormPropertyValue);
if (theForm.InvokeRequired)
{
  theForm.Invoke(d, o);
}
else
  Console.WriteLine("Unexpected logic flow");

Console.WriteLine("\n And now setting Form1 Size to 200x500");

Thread.Sleep(1500);

size = new System.Drawing.Size(200,500);
o = new object[] { theForm, "Size", size };
d = new SetFormPropertyValueHandler(SetFormPropertyValue);
if (theForm.InvokeRequired)
{
  theForm.Invoke(d, o);
}
else
  Console.WriteLine("Unexpected logic flow");
```

You can significantly increase the modularity of this technique by wrapping up the code into a single method combined with a delegate:

```
delegate void SetFormPropertyValueHandler(Form f,
  string propertyName, object newValue);

static void SetFormPropertyValue(Form f, string propertyName,
                                 object newValue)
```

```
{
  if (f.InvokeRequired)
  {
    // Console.WriteLine("in invoke required");
    Delegate d =
      new SetFormPropertyValueHandler(SetFormPropertyValue);
    object[] o = new object[] { f, propertyName, newValue };
    f.Invoke(d, o);
    return;
  }
  else
  {
    // Console.WriteLine("in the else part");
    Type t = f.GetType();
    PropertyInfo pi = t.GetProperty(propertyName);
    pi.SetValue(f, newValue, null);
  }
}
```

With this helper method, you can make clean calls in your test harness such as

```
Form theForm = null;
string formName = "AUT.Form1";
string path = "..\\..\\..\\AUT\\bin\\Debug\\AUT.exe";
theForm = LaunchApp(path, formName); // see Section 2.1

System.Drawing.Point pt = new System.Drawing.Point(10,10);
SetFormPropertyValue(theForm, "Location", pt);
Thread.Sleep(1500);

pt = new System.Drawing.Point(200,300);
SetFormPropertyValue(theForm, "Location", pt);
Thread.Sleep(1500);
```

This SetFormPropertyValue() wrapper is slightly tricky because it is self-referential. (A recursive method calls itself directly; a self-referential method calls itself indirectly.) When called in the Main() method of your harness, InvokeRequired is initially true because the calling automation thread does not own the form. Execution branches to the Form.Invoke() statement, which, in turn, calls the SetFormPropertyValueHandler() delegate that calls back into the associated SetFormPropertyValue() method. But the second time through the wrapper, InvokeRequired will be false, because the call comes from the originating thread. Control transfers to the else part of the logic, where the PropertyInfo.SetValue() changes the Form property. If you remove the commented lines of code and run, you'll see how the path of execution works.

Because placing Thread.Sleep() delays is so common in UI test automation, you may want to add a delay parameter to all the wrapper methods in this chapter:

```
static void SetFormPropertyValue(Form f, string propertyName,
                                 object newValue, int delay)
{
  Thread.Sleep(delay);
  // other code as before
}
```

So, if you wanted to delay 1,500 milliseconds (1.5 seconds), you can call SetFormPropertyValue() like this:

```
Point point = new Point(50,75);
SetFormPropertyValue (theForm, "Location", point, 1500);
```

In a lightweight test-automation situation, the most common form properties you will manipulate are Size and Location. However, the techniques in the section allow you to set any form property. For example, suppose you want to manipulate the form title bar. You can do this by passing "Text" as the property name argument and a string for the new title:

```
Form theForm = null;
string formName = "AUT.Form1";
string path = "..\\..\\..\\AUT\\bin\\Debug\\AUT.exe";
theForm = LaunchApp(path, formName); // see Section 2.1

SetFormPropertyValue(theForm, "Text", "SomeNewTitle");
Thread.Sleep(1500);
```

2.3 Accessing Form Properties

Problem

You want to retrieve the properties of an application form object.

Design

Use the Type.GetProperty() method to get a reference to the property you want to examine. Then use the PropertyInfo.GetValue() method in conjunction with a method delegate to get the value of the property.

Solution

```
if (theForm.InvokeRequired)
{
  Delegate d = new GetFormPropertyValueHandler(GetFormPropertyValue);
  object[] o = new object[] { theForm, "Location" };
  Point p = (Point)theForm.Invoke(d, o);
  Console.WriteLine("Form1 location = " + p.X + " " + p.Y);
}
```

```
else
{
  Console.WriteLine("Unexpected logic flow");
}
```

where

```
delegate object GetFormPropertyValueHandler(Form f,
                                            string propertyName);

static object GetFormPropertyValue(Form f, string propertyName)
{
  Type t = f.GetType();
  PropertyInfo pi = t.GetProperty(propertyName);
  object result = pi.GetValue(f, null);
  return result;
}
```

Comments

When performing lightweight reflection-based UI test automation, you may want to retrieve properties of the application form such as the Location and Size properties. This allows you to verify the state of the Form object under test and determine a test scenario pass/fail result. The key to obtaining the value of a form property is to use the PropertyInfo.GetValue() method. Unfortunately, there is a hidden issue—you should not call GetValue() directly from a thread that is not the main form thread. This issue is discussed in detail in "Section 2.2 Manipulating Form Properties." If the hidden issue did not exist, you could get a form property like this:

```
string formName = "AUT.Form1";
string path = "..\\..\\..\\AUT\\bin\\Debug\\AUT.exe";
theForm = LaunchApp(path, formName); // see Section 2.1

Type t = theForm.GetType();
PropertyInfo pi = t.GetProperty("Location");
Point p = (Point)pi.GetValue(theForm, null);

Console.WriteLine("Form1 location = " + p.X + " " + p.Y);
```

But because you are calling GetValue() from the test-harness thread instead of the main Form object thread, you should call Form.Invoke() with a delegate like this:

```
if (theForm.InvokeRequired)
{
  Delegate d = new GetFormPropertyValueHandler(GetFormPropertyValue);
  object[] o = new object[] { theForm, "Location" };
  Point p = (Point)theForm.Invoke(d, o);
  Console.WriteLine("Form1 location = " + p.X + " " + p.Y);
}
```

```
else
{
  Console.WriteLine("Unexpected logic flow");
}
```

where

```
delegate object GetFormPropertyValueHandler(Form f,
                                            string propertyName);

static object GetFormPropertyValue(Form f, string propertyName)
{
  Type t = f.GetType();
  PropertyInfo pi = t.GetProperty(propertyName);
  return pi.GetValue(f, null);
}
```

In short, you call Form.Invoke() with a delegate argument. Control of execution is transferred to the delegate, which is in turn mapped to a helper method that calls the PropertyInfo.GetValue() method. This strategy solves the Invoke() issue. You can significantly increase the modularity of your test automation by wrapping up the code in this solution like this:

```
delegate object GetFormPropertyValueHandler(Form f,
                                            string propertyName);

static object GetFormPropertyValue(Form f, string propertyName)
{
  if (f.InvokeRequired)
  {
    Delegate d =
      new GetFormPropertyValueHandler(GetFormPropertyValue);
    object[] o = new object[] { f, propertyName };
    object iResult = f.Invoke(d, o);
    return iResult;
  }
  else
  {
    Type t = f.GetType();
    PropertyInfo pi = t.GetProperty(propertyName);
    object gResult = pi.GetValue(f, null);
    return gResult;
  }
}
```

This can be called in the following way:

```
Point p = (Point)GetFormPropertyValue(theForm, "Location");
Console.WriteLine("Form location = " + p.X + " " + p.Y);
```

This GetFormPropertyValue() wrapper is a bit tricky because it is self-referential. When called in the Main() method of your harness, InvokeRequired is initially true, because the calling thread does not own the form. Execution branches to the Form.Invoke() statement, which, in turn, calls the GetFormPropertyValueHandler() delegate that calls back into the associated GetFormPropertyValue() method. But on the second pass through the wrapper, InvokeRequired will be false because the call comes from the originating thread. Control transfers to the else part of the logic, where the PropertyInfo.GetValue() retrieves the form property. With this technique, you can retrieve the value of any form property. For example:

```
string title = (string)GetFormPropertyValue(theForm, "Text");
Console.WriteLine("Form title = " + title);
Size size = (Size)GetFormPropertyValue(theForm, "Size");
Console.WriteLine("Form size = " + size.Height + " x " + size.Width);
```

2.4 Manipulating Control Properties

Problem

You want to set the value of a control property.

Design

Obtain a reference to the control you want to manipulate using the Form.GetType(), Type.GetField(), and FieldInfo.GetValue() methods. Then use the PropertyInfo.SetValue() method in conjunction with a method delegate to set the value of the target control.

Solution

```
if (theForm.InvokeRequired)
{
  Delegate d =
    new SetControlPropertyValueHandler(SetControlPropertyValue);
  object[] o = new object[] { theForm, "textBox1", "Text", "foo" };
  Console.WriteLine("Setting textBox1 to 'foo'");
  theForm.Invoke(d, o);
}
else
{
  Console.WriteLine("Unexpected logic flow");
}
```

where

```
static BindingFlags flags = BindingFlags.Public |
                            BindingFlags.NonPublic |
                            BindingFlags.Static |
                            BindingFlags.Instance;
```

```
delegate void SetControlPropertyValueHandler(Form f,
        string controlName, string propertyName, object newValue);

static void SetControlPropertyValue(Form f, string controlName,
        string propertyName, object newValue)
{
  Type t1 = f.GetType();
  FieldInfo fi = t1.GetField(controlName, flags);
  object ctrl = fi.GetValue(f);
  Type t2 = ctrl.GetType();
  PropertyInfo pi = t2.GetProperty(propertyName); //?
  pi.SetValue(ctrl, newValue, null);
}
```

Comments

When writing lightweight reflection-based UI test automation, you may need to simulate user actions by manipulating properties of controls on the application form. Examples include setting the Text property value of a TextBox control to simulate a user typing and setting the Checked property value of a RadioButtonList item to true to simulate a user clicking on the item. The key to setting the value of a control's property is to use the PropertyInfo.SetValue() method. Unfortunately, as described in Sections 2.2 "Manipulating Form Properties" and 2.3 "Accessing Form Properties," there is a hidden issue—you should not call SetValue() directly from a thread that is not the main Form thread. If the hidden issue did not exist, you could set the value of a control like this:

```
BindingFlags flags = BindingFlags.Public | BindingFlags.NonPublic |
                     BindingFlags.Static | BindingFlags.Instance;

Console.WriteLine("Setting textBox1 to 'foo'");
Type t1 = theForm.GetType();
FieldInfo fi = t1.GetField("textBox1", flags);
object ctrl = fi.GetValue(theForm);
Type t2 = ctrl.GetType();
PropertyInfo pi = t2.GetProperty("Text");
pi.SetValue(ctrl, "foo", null);
```

    The BindingFlags object is a filter for many of the methods in the System.Reflection namespace. In lightweight test-automation situations, you almost always filter for Public, NonPublic, Instance, and Static methods, as we've done in this example. Because this is such a common pattern, you'll often find it convenient to declare a single class-scope BindingFlags object, rather than recode a new object for each call that requires a BindingFlags argument.

    To manipulate a control, you begin by getting a Type object from the parent Form object. This is the first of two Type objects you'll need. Then you use the Type object to obtain a reference to a FieldInfo object by using the GetField() method. With this intermediate FieldInfo object, you can now get a reference to the actual control object by calling FieldInfo.GetValue(). This is not entirely intuitive but the pattern is always the same. Next, you use the control object and get its Type by calling GetType(). Then you can use this second Type object to get a PropertyInfo object using the GetProperty() method. At this point, you have references to the control object and one of its properties. Finally, you can manipulate the value of the control's property by using the SetValue() method.

The first two arguments passed to SetValue() are the control object to manipulate and the new value for the control's property. The third argument represents optional index values. You only need this when you are dealing with indexed properties. This value should be a null reference for nonindexed properties, as is almost always the case for controls. Although some controls, such as the ListBox control, have components that are indexed (the Items property, for example), the control itself is not indexed.

As described earlier, the hidden issue is that you should not directly call SetValue() on a control object from a thread that does not own the control's parent Form object. Doing so can lead to complex thread synchronization problems. Because you are working from the test-harness thread instead of the Form thread, the Form.InvokeRequired property is always true. The recommended technique in situations like this is to call Form.Invoke(), passing a delegate object that is associated with a method that actually calls SetValue(). Implementing this idea gives you the code in this solution.

You can significantly increase the modularity of this technique by wrapping the code up into a single method combined with a delegate object:

```
static BindingFlags flags = BindingFlags.Public |
                            BindingFlags.NonPublic |
                            BindingFlags.Static |
                            BindingFlags.Instance;

delegate void SetControlPropertyValueHandler(Form f,
  string controlName, string propertyName, object newValue);

static void SetControlPropertyValue(Form f, string controlName,
  string propertyName, object newValue)
{
  if (f.InvokeRequired)
  {
    //Console.WriteLine("in invoke req.");
    Delegate d =
      new SetControlPropertyValueHandler(SetControlPropertyValue);
    object[] o = new object[]{f, controlName, propertyName, newValue};
    f.Invoke(d, o);
  }
  else
  {
    //Console.WriteLine("in else part");
    Type t1 = f.GetType();
    FieldInfo fi = t1.GetField(controlName, flags);
    object ctrl = fi.GetValue(f);
    Type t2 = ctrl.GetType();
    PropertyInfo pi = t2.GetProperty(propertyName);
    pi.SetValue(ctrl, newValue, null);
  }
}
```

The method can be called like this:

```
SetControlPropertyValue(theForm, "textBox1", "Text", "paper");
SetControlPropertyValue(theForm, "comboBox1", "Text", "rock");
```

This SetControlPropertyValue() wrapper improves the modularity of your automation code, but is somewhat tricky because it references itself. When SetControlPropertyValue() is called in the Main() method of your harness, InvokeRequired is initially true because the calling thread does not own the form. Execution branches to the Form.Invoke() statement, which, in turn, calls the SetControlPropertyValueHandler() delegate that calls back into the associated SetControlPropertyValue() method. But the second time through the wrapper, InvokeRequired will be false because the call now comes from the originating thread. Execution transfers to the else part of the logic, where the PropertyInfo.SetValue() changes the control's property. If you remove the commented lines of code and run, you'll see how the path of execution works.

2.5 Accessing Control Properties

Problem

You want to retrieve the properties of a control on a Windows form-based application.

Design

Obtain a reference to the control you want to manipulate using the Form.GetType(), Type.GetField(), and FieldInfo.GetValue() methods. Then use the PropertyInfo.GetValue() method in conjunction with a method delegate to retrieve the value of the target control.

Solution

```
if (theForm.InvokeRequired)
{
  Delegate d =
    new GetControlPropertyValueHandler(GetControlPropertyValue);
  object[] o = new object[] { theForm, "textBox1", "Text" };
  string txt = (string)theForm.Invoke(d, o);
  Console.WriteLine("textBox1 has " + txt);
}
else
{
  Console.WriteLine("Unexpected logic flow");
}
```

where

```
static BindingFlags flags = BindingFlags.Public |
                            BindingFlags.NonPublic |
                            BindingFlags.Static |
                            BindingFlags.Instance;
```

```
delegate object GetControlPropertyValueHandler(Form f,
  string controlName, string propertyName);

static object GetControlPropertyValue(Form f, string controlName,
  string propertyName)
{
  Type t1 = f.GetType();
  FieldInfo fi = t1.GetField(controlName, flags);
  object ctrl = fi.GetValue(f);
  Type t2 = ctrl.GetType();
  PropertyInfo pi = t2.GetProperty(propertyName);
  object result = pi.GetValue(ctrl, null);
  return result;
}
```

Comments

When writing lightweight reflection-based UI test automation, you may want to retrieve properties of controls on the application form. Examples include the Text property value of a TextBox control and the ObjectCollection property of a ListBox control. You must do this to verify the state of the AUT and determine a pass/fail test result. The key to obtaining the value of a control's property is to use the PropertyInfo.GetValue() method. But there is a hidden issue—you should not call GetValue() directly from a thread that is not the main Form thread. This issue is discussed in detail in Sections 2.2, 2.3, and 2.4. If the hidden issue did not exist, you could easily get a control property like this:

```
// launch object theForm

Type t1 = theForm.GetType();
FieldInfo fi = t1.GetField("textBox1", flags);
object ctrl = fi.GetValue(theForm);
Type t2 = ctrl.GetType();
PropertyInfo pi = t2.GetProperty("Text");
string txt = (string)pi.GetValue(ctrl, null);
Console.WriteLine("TextBox1 Text is " + txt);
```

To access the property of a control object, you start by getting a Type object from the parent Form object. This is the first of two Type objects you'll need. Then you use that Type object to obtain a reference to a FieldInfo object by using the GetField() method. The flags argument in this example is a BindingFlags object, as described in Section 2.4, and it acts as a filter. With the FieldInfo object, you can now get a reference to the actual control object by calling FieldInfo.GetValue(). Next, you use the control object and get its Type by calling GetType(). Then you can use this second Type object to get a PropertyInfo object using the GetProperty() method. At this point, you have references to the control object and one of its properties. Finally, you can manipulate the value of the control's property by using the GetValue() method.

The GetValue() method accepts two arguments. The first argument to GetValue() is the parent control object. The second argument is an optional array of index values. You only need this when you are dealing with indexed properties. This value should be null for nonindexed properties, as is almost always the case for controls. Although some controls, such as the ListBox control, have components that are indexed (the Items property for example), the control property itself is not indexed.

The hidden issue is that you should not directly call GetValue() on a Form object from a thread that does not own the form. Doing so can lead to thread problems. Because you are working from the test-harness thread instead of the Form thread, the Form.InvokeRequired property is always true. The recommended technique in situations like this is to call Form.Invoke(), passing a delegate object that is associated with a method that actually calls PropertyInfo.GetValue().

You can significantly increase the modularity of this technique by wrapping the code into a single method in conjunction with a delegate:

```
delegate object GetControlPropertyValueHandler(Form f,
  string controlName, string propertyName);

static object GetControlPropertyValue(Form f, string controlName,
  string propertyName)
{
  if (f.InvokeRequired)
  {
    Delegate d =
      new GetControlPropertyValueHandler(GetControlPropertyValue);
    object[] o = new object[] { f, controlName, propertyName };
    object iResult = f.Invoke(d, o);
    return iResult;
  }
  else
  {

    Type t1 = f.GetType();
    FieldInfo fi = t1.GetField(controlName, flags);
    object ctrl = fi.GetValue(f);
    Type t2 = ctrl.GetType();
    PropertyInfo pi = t2.GetProperty(propertyName);
    object gResult = pi.GetValue(ctrl, null);
    return gResult;
  }
}
```

with class-scope object

```
static BindingFlags flags = BindingFlags.Public |
                            BindingFlags.NonPublic |
                            BindingFlags.Static |
                            BindingFlags.Instance;
```

The logic behind this self-referential wrapping technique is explained in detail in the "Comments" part of Sections 2.2, 2.3, and 2.4. With this wrapper method, you can make clean calls in your test harness like this:

```
string txt =
  (string)GetControlPropertyValue(theForm, "textBox1", "Text");
Console.WriteLine("TextBox1 holds " + txt);

ListBox.ObjectCollection oc =
(ListBox.ObjectCollection)GetControlPropertyValue(theForm,
                              "listBox1", "Items");
if (oc.Count > 0)
{
  string s = oc[0].ToString();
  Console.WriteLine("The first line in listBox1 is " + s);
}

if (oc.Contains("The TextBox wins"))
  Console.WriteLine("Found 'The TextBox wins' in listBox1");
else
  Console.WriteLine("Did not find 'The TextBox wins' in listBox1");
```

Notice that for a ListBox control, you retrieve the Items property, which is a collection of type ListBox.ObjectCollection. This component is indexed so you can access each string in the collection or iterate through all the strings using square bracket syntax.

2.6 Invoking Methods

Problem

You want to invoke a method of a form-based application.

Design

Get a reference to the method you want to invoke using the Form.GetType() and Type.GetMethod() methods. Then use the MethodInfo.Invoke() method in conjunction with an AutoResetEvent object and a method delegate to call the target method.

Solution

```
if (theForm.InvokeRequired)
{
  Delegate d = new InvokeMethodHandler(InvokeMethod);
  object[] parms = new object[] { null, EventArgs.Empty };
  object[] o = new object[] { theForm, "button1_Click", parms };
  theForm.Invoke(d, o);
  are.WaitOne();
}
```

```
else
{
  Console.WriteLine("Unexpected logic flow");
}
```

where

```
static BindingFlags flags = BindingFlags.Public |
                            BindingFlags.NonPublic |
                            BindingFlags.Static |
                            BindingFlags.Instance;

static AutoResetEvent are = new AutoResetEvent(false);

delegate void InvokeMethodHandler(Form f, string methodName,
                                  params object[] parms);
static void InvokeMethod(Form f, string methodName,
                         params object[] parms)
{
  Type t = f.GetType();
  MethodInfo mi = t.GetMethod(methodName, flags);
  mi.Invoke(f, parms);
  are.Set();
}
```

Comments

When writing lightweight reflection-based UI test automation, you usually need to invoke methods that are part of the application form to simulate user actions. Examples include invoking a button1_Click() method, which handles actions when a user clicks on a button1 control, and invoking a menuItem2_Click() method, which handles actions when a user clicks on a menuItem2 menu item. Notice that reflection-based UI automation simulates a button click by directly invoking the button control's associated method rather than by firing an event. When a real user clicks on a button, it generates a Windows message that is processed by the control and turned into a managed event. This causes a particular method to be invoked. So, reflection-based UI automation will not catch the logic error if the AUT has the wrong method wired to a button click event.

The key to invoking methods is to use the MethodInfo.Invoke() method. If there were no hidden issues, you could invoke a method like this:

```
Type t = theForm.GetType();
MethodInfo mi = t.GetMethod("button1_Click", flags);
mi.Invoke(theForm, new object[] { null, EventArgs.Empty });
```

where

```
static BindingFlags flags = BindingFlags.Public |
                            BindingFlags.NonPublic |
                            BindingFlags.Static |
                            BindingFlags.Instance;
```

The `BindingFlags` object is a filter for many of the methods in the `System.Reflection` namespace and is discussed in Section 2.4. The `MethodInfo.Invoke()` method accepts two arguments. The first argument is the parent `Form` object that owns the method being invoked. The second argument is an object array containing the arguments that must be passed to the method being invoked. In this example, the `button1_Click()` method has a signature of

```
private void button1_Click(object sender, System.EventArgs e)
```

So you need to pass values for parameters `sender` and `e`, representing the object associated with the `button1_Click()` method and optional event data the method might need. For lightweight UI test automation, you can ignore these parameters and simply pass `null` and `EventArgs.Empty`.

As described in Sections 2.3, 2.3, and 2.4, there is a hidden issue—you should not call `MethodInfo.Invoke()` directly from a thread that is not the main `Form` thread. The solution to this hidden invoke issue is to call `MethodInfo.Invoke()` indirectly through a `Delegate` object:

```
if (theForm.InvokeRequired)
{
  Delegate d = new InvokeMethodHandler(InvokeMethod);
  object[] parms = new object[] { null, EventArgs.Empty };
  object[] o = new object[] { theForm, "button1_Click", parms };
  theForm.Invoke(d, o);
}
else
{
  Console.WriteLine("Unexpected logic flow");
}
```

where

```
static BindingFlags flags = BindingFlags.Public |
                            BindingFlags.NonPublic |
                            BindingFlags.Static |
                            BindingFlags.Instance;
delegate void InvokeMethodHandler(Form f, string methodName,
                                  params object[] parms);
static void InvokeMethod(Form f, string methodName,
                         params object[] parms)
{
  Type t = f.GetType();
  MethodInfo mi = t.GetMethod(methodName, flags);
  mi.Invoke(f, parms);
}
```

This code will work *most* of the time; however, programmatically invoking a method has a second, very subtle, hidden issue involving synchronization. Suppose your test harness invokes a method on the AUT, and that method directly or indirectly spins off a new thread of execution. Before your test harness takes any further action, you must wait until control is returned to the test harness. There are two solutions to this timing problem. The first is a crude but effective approach: place Thread.Sleep() statements in your test harness to slow the automation down. For example:

```
if (theForm.InvokeRequired)
{
  Delegate d = new InvokeMethodHandler(InvokeMethod);
  object[] parms = new object[] { null, EventArgs.Empty };
  object[] o = new object[] { theForm, "button1_Click", parms };
  theForm.Invoke(d, o);
  Thread.Sleep(2000);
}
else
{
  Console.WriteLine("Unexpected logic flow");
}
```

where

```
static BindingFlags flags = BindingFlags.Public |
                            BindingFlags.NonPublic |
                            BindingFlags.Static |
                            BindingFlags.Instance;
delegate void InvokeMethodHandler(Form f, string methodName,
                                  params object[] parms);
static void InvokeMethod(Form f, string methodName,
                         params object[] parms)
{
  Type t = f.GetType();
  MethodInfo mi = t.GetMethod(methodName, flags);
  mi.Invoke(f, parms);
  Thread.Sleep(2000);
}
```

However, this crude approach has a big problem: there's no way to determine how long to pause so you must make your delay times long. This leads to a test harness with multiple lengthy delays. A better solution to the timing problem is to use an AutoResetEvent object for synchronization. You declare a class scope object like

```
static AutoResetEvent are = new AutoResetEvent(false);
```

which creates an object that can have a value of signaled or not-signaled. The false argument means initialize the object to not-signaled. Then, whenever you want to pause your automation, you insert the statement are.WaitOne(). This sets the value of the AutoResetEvent object to not-signaled. The current thread of execution halts until the AutoResetEvent object is set to signaled from an are.Set() statement. Putting these ideas together led to this code:

```
if (theForm.InvokeRequired)
{
  Delegate d = new InvokeMethodHandler(InvokeMethod);
  object[] parms = new object[] { null, EventArgs.Empty };
  object[] o = new object[] { theForm, "button1_Click", parms };
  theForm.Invoke(d, o);
  are.WaitOne();
}
else
{
  Console.WriteLine("Unexpected logic flow");
}
```

where

```
static BindingFlags flags = BindingFlags.Public |
                            BindingFlags.NonPublic |
                            BindingFlags.Static |
                            BindingFlags.Instance;

static AutoResetEvent are = new AutoResetEvent(false);

delegate void InvokeMethodHandler(Form f, string methodName,
                                  params object[] parms);
static void InvokeMethod(Form f, string methodName,
                         params object[] parms)
{
  Type t = f.GetType();
  MethodInfo mi = t.GetMethod(methodName, flags);
  mi.Invoke(f, parms);
  are.Set();
}
```

So, at the beginning of the code, the test-automation thread does not own the main test Form object thread, and the InvokeRequired property is true. Execution control is transferred to the InvokeMethodHandler() delegate, which in turn is associated with an InvokeMethod() helper method. InvokeMethod() actually performs the work by calling MethodInfo.Invoke(). For synchronization, calling AutoResetEvent.WaitOne() blocks the thread of execution, allowing the MethodInfo.Invoke() method to complete execution. Calling AutoResetEvent.Set() signals that the thread of execution can resume.

You can greatly modularize this technique by wrapping the code in a single self-referential method in conjunction with a delegate and an AutoResetEvent object:

```
delegate void InvokeMethodHandler(Form f, string methodName,
                                  params object[] parms);
```

```
static void InvokeMethod(Form f, string methodName,
                          params object[] parms)
{
  if (f.InvokeRequired)
  {
    Delegate d = new InvokeMethodHandler(InvokeMethod);
    f.Invoke(d, new object[] {f, methodName, parms});
    are.WaitOne();
  }
  else
  {
    Type t = f.GetType();
    MethodInfo mi = t.GetMethod(methodName, flags);
    mi.Invoke(f, parms);
    are.Set();
  }
}
```

where

```
static BindingFlags flags = BindingFlags.Public |
                            BindingFlags.NonPublic |
                            BindingFlags.Static |
                            BindingFlags.Instance;
```

```
static AutoResetEvent are = new AutoResetEvent(false);
```

With this convenient wrapper method you can make clean calls:

```
object[] parms = new object[] { null, EventArgs.Empty };
InvokeMethod(theForm, "button1_Click", parms );
```

The InvokeMethod() wrapper is self-referencing. On the initial call to InvokeMethod() from your test harness, InvokeRequired is true because the call is coming from your test harness. Control of execution transfers to the Form.Invoke() method, which passes control to the InvokeMethodHandler() delegate. The delegate is associated with the original InvokeMethod() method, so execution control reenters InvokeMethod(). The second time through the helper method, InvokeRequired will be false, so control is transferred to the else block where MethodInfo.Invoke() actually invokes the method passed in as an argument to the helper.

2.7 Example Program: ReflectionUITest

This program (see Listing 2-1) combines several of the techniques in the chapter to demonstrate a lightweight reflection-based UI test-automation scenario. The scenario tests the "paper-rock-scissors" form application described in the introduction to this chapter. The test scenario launches the application, moves the form, and then simulates typing *rock* into the TextBox control and a user selecting *scissors* from the ComboBox control. Then the scenario simulates a button click. The automation checks to see if the expected TextBox1 wins string is in the ListBox control, and determines a scenario pass or fail result. The scenario finishes by simulating a user selecting File ➤ Exit to close the application. Figure 2-1 in the introduction to this chapter shows the result of running this test scenario.

This program assumes you have added project references to the System.Windows.Forms and System.Drawing namespaces. You can extend this automation scenario by using some of the techniques described in Chapter 1 and Chapter 4. For example, you can log test results to external storage, or parameterize the scenario to accept multiple input states.

Listing 2-1. *Program ReflectionUITest*

```
using System;
using System.Reflection;
using System.Windows.Forms;
using System.Threading;
using System.Drawing;

namespace ReflectionUITest
{
  class Class1
  {
    static BindingFlags flags = BindingFlags.Public |
                                BindingFlags.NonPublic |
                                BindingFlags.Static |
                                BindingFlags.Instance;
    static AutoResetEvent are = new AutoResetEvent(false);

    [STAThread]
    static void Main(string[] args)
    {
      try
      {
        Console.WriteLine("\nStarting test scenario");
        Console.WriteLine("\nLaunching Form1");
        Form theForm = null;
        string formName = "AUT.Form1";
        string path = "..\\..\\..\\AUT\\bin\\Debug\\AUT.exe";
        theForm = LaunchApp(path, formName);

        Console.WriteLine("\nMoving Form1");
        Point pt = new Point(320, 100);
        SetFormPropertyValue(theForm, "Location", pt);

        Console.WriteLine("\nSetting textBox1 to 'rock'");
        SetControlPropertyValue(theForm, "textBox1", "Text", "rock");
        Console.WriteLine("Setting comboBox1 to 'scissors'");
        SetControlPropertyValue(theForm, "comboBox1", "Text",
                                "scissors");
```

```
        Console.WriteLine("\nClicking button1");
        object[] parms = new object[]{ null, EventArgs.Empty };
        InvokeMethod(theForm, "button1_Click", parms);

        bool pass = true;

        Console.WriteLine("\nChecking listBox1 for 'TextBox wins'");
        ListBox.ObjectCollection oc =
            (ListBox.ObjectCollection)
                GetControlPropertyValue(theForm, "listBox1",
                                              "Items");
        string s = oc[0].ToString();
        if (s.IndexOf("TextBox wins") == -1)
          pass = false;

        if (pass)
          Console.WriteLine("\n-- Scenario result = Pass --");
        else
          Console.WriteLine("\n-- Scenario result = *FAIL* --");

        Console.WriteLine("\nClicking File->Exit in 3 seconds");
        Thread.Sleep(3000);
        InvokeMethod(theForm, "menuItem2_Click", parms);

        Console.WriteLine("\nEnd test scenario");
      }
      catch(Exception ex)
      {
        Console.WriteLine("Fatal error: " + ex.Message);
      }
    } // Main()

    static Form LaunchApp(string path, string formName)
    {
      Form result = null;
      Assembly a = Assembly.LoadFrom(path);
      Type t = a.GetType(formName);
      result = (Form)a.CreateInstance(t.FullName);
      AppState aps = new AppState(result);
      ThreadStart ts = new ThreadStart(aps.RunApp);
      Thread thread = new Thread(ts);
      thread.Start();
      return result;
    }
    private class AppState
    {
      public readonly Form formToRun;
      public AppState(Form f)
```

```
  {
    this.formToRun = f;
  }
  public void RunApp()
  {
    Application.Run(formToRun);
  }
} // class AppState

delegate void SetFormPropertyValueHandler(Form f,
  string propertyName, object newValue);
static void SetFormPropertyValue(Form f, string propertyName,
  object newValue)
{
  if (f.InvokeRequired)
  {
    Delegate d =
      new SetFormPropertyValueHandler(SetFormPropertyValue);
    object[] o = new object[] { f, propertyName, newValue };
    f.Invoke(d, o);
    are.WaitOne();
  }
  else
  {
    Type t = f.GetType();
    PropertyInfo pi = t.GetProperty(propertyName);
    pi.SetValue(f, newValue, null);
    are.Set();
  }
}

delegate void SetControlPropertyValueHandler(Form f,
  string controlName, string propertyName, object newValue);
static void SetControlPropertyValue(Form f, string controlName,
  string propertyName, object newValue)
{
  if (f.InvokeRequired)
  {
    Delegate d =
      new SetControlPropertyValueHandler(SetControlPropertyValue);
    object[] o = new object[] { f, controlName, propertyName,
      newValue };
    f.Invoke(d, o);
    are.WaitOne();
  }
```

```
      else
      {
        Type t1 = f.GetType();
        FieldInfo fi = t1.GetField(controlName, flags);
        object ctrl = fi.GetValue(f);
        Type t2 = ctrl.GetType();
        PropertyInfo pi = t2.GetProperty(propertyName);
        pi.SetValue(ctrl, newValue, null);
        are.Set();
      }
    }


    delegate void InvokeMethodHandler(Form f, string methodName,
      params object[] parms);
    static void InvokeMethod(Form f, string methodName,
      params object[] parms)
    {
      if (f.InvokeRequired)
      {
        Delegate d = new InvokeMethodHandler(InvokeMethod);
        f.Invoke(d, new object[] {f, methodName, parms});
        are.WaitOne();
      }
      else
      {
        Type t = f.GetType();
        MethodInfo mi = t.GetMethod(methodName, flags);
        mi.Invoke(f, parms);
        are.Set();
      }
    }


    delegate object GetControlPropertyValueHandler(Form f,
      string controlName, string propertyName);
    static object GetControlPropertyValue(Form f, string controlName,
      string propertyName)
    {
      if (f.InvokeRequired)
      {
        Delegate d =
          new GetControlPropertyValueHandler(GetControlPropertyValue);
        object[] o = new object[] { f, controlName, propertyName };
        object iResult = f.Invoke(d, o);
        are.WaitOne();
        return iResult;
      }
```

```
      else
      {
        Type t1 = f.GetType();
        FieldInfo fi = t1.GetField(controlName, flags);
        object ctrl = fi.GetValue(f);
        Type t2 = ctrl.GetType();
        PropertyInfo pi = t2.GetProperty(propertyName);
        object gResult = pi.GetValue(ctrl, null);
        are.Set();
        return gResult;
      }
    }
  } // Class1
} // ns
```

■ ■ ■

CHAPTER 3

Windows-Based UI Testing

3.0 Introduction

This chapter describes how to test an application through its user interface (UI) using low-level Windows-based automation. These techniques involve calling Win32 API functions such as FindWindow() and sending Windows messages such as WM_LBUTTONUP to the application under test (AUT). Although these techniques have been available to developers and testers for many years, the .NET programming environment dramatically simplifies the process. Figure 3-1 demonstrates the kind of lightweight test automation you can quickly create.

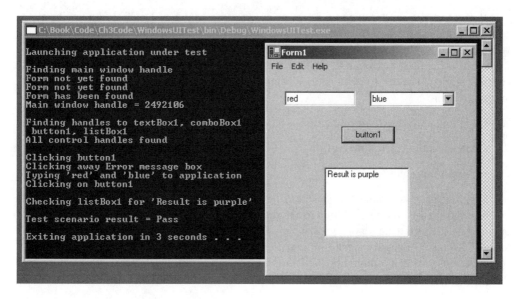

Figure 3-1. *Windows-based UI test run*

The dummy AUT is a color-mixer application. The key code for the application is

```
void button1_Click(object sender, System.EventArgs e)
{
  string tb = textBox1.Text;
  string cb = comboBox1.Text;

  if (tb == "<enter color>" || cb == "<pick>")
    MessageBox.Show("You need 2 colors", "Error");
  else
  {
    if (tb == cb)
      listBox1.Items.Add("Result is " + tb);
    else if (tb == "red" && cb == "blue" ||
             tb == "blue" && cb =="red")
      listBox1.Items.Add("Result is purple");
    else
      listBox1.Items.Add("Result is black");
  }
}
```

Notice that the application may generate an error message box. Dealing with low-level constructs such as message boxes and the main menu are tasks that can be handled well by Win32 functions. The fundamental idea is that every Windows-based control is a window. Each control/window has a handle that can be used to access, manipulate, and examine the control/window. The three key categories of tasks in lightweight, low-level Windows-based UI automation are

- Finding a window/control handle

- Manipulating a window/control

- Examining a window/control

Keeping this task-organization structure in mind will help you arrange your test automation.
The code in this chapter is written in a traditional procedural style rather than in an object-oriented style. This is a matter of personal preference, and you may want to recast the techniques to an OOP (object-oriented programming) style. Additionally, you may want to modularize the code solutions further by combining them into a .NET class library. The test automation harness that produced the test run shown in Figure 3-1 is presented in Section 3.10.

3.1 Launching the AUT

Problem

You want to launch a Windows form-based application so you can test it through its UI.

Design

Use the System.Diagnostics.Process.Start() method.

Solution

```
static void Main(string[] args)
{
  try
  {
    Console.WriteLine("\nLaunching application under test");

    string path = "..\\..\\..\\WinApp\\bin\\Debug\\WinApp.exe";
    Process p = Process.Start(path);
    if (p == null)
      Console.WriteLine("Warning: process may already exist");

    // run UI test scenario here

    Console.WriteLine("\nDone");
  }
  catch(Exception ex)
  {
    Console.WriteLine("Fatal error: " + ex.Message);
  }
}
```

There are several ways to launch a Windows form application so that you can test it through its UI using Windows-based techniques. The simplest way is to use the Process.Start() static method located in the System.Diagnostics namespace.

Comments

The Process.Start() method has four overloads. The overload used in this solution accepts a path to the AUT and returns a Process object that represents the resources associated with the application. You need to be a bit careful with the Process.Start() return value. A return of null does not necessarily indicate failure; null is also returned if an existing process is reused. Regardless, a return of null is not good because your UI test automation will often become confused if more than one target application is running. This idea is explained more fully in Section 3.2.

If you need to pass arguments to the AUT, you can use the Process.Start() overload that accepts a second argument, which represents command-line arguments to the application. For example:

```
Process p = null;
p = Process.Start("SomeApp.exe", "C:\\Somewhere\\Somefile.txt");
if (p == null)
  Console.WriteLine("Warning: process may already exist");
```

The Process.Start() method also supports an overload that accepts a ProcessStartInfo object as an argument. A ProcessStartInfo object can direct the AUT to launch and run in a variety of ways; however, this technique is rarely needed in a lightweight test automation scenario. The Process.Start() method is asynchronous, so when you use it to launch the AUT, be careful about attempting to access the application through your test harness until after you are sure the application has launched. This problem is discussed and solved in Section 3.2.

3.2 Obtaining a Handle to the Main Window of the AUT

Problem

You want to obtain a handle to the application main window.

Design

Use the FindWindow() Win32 API function with the .NET platform invoke (P/Invoke) mechanism.

Solution

```
class Class1
{
  [DllImport("user32.dll", EntryPoint="FindWindow",
    CharSet=CharSet.Auto)]
  static extern IntPtr FindWindow(string lpClassName,
    string lpWindowName);

  [STAThread]
  static void Main(string[] args)
  {
    try
    {
      // launch AUT; see Section 3.1

      IntPtr mwh = IntPtr.Zero; // main window handle
      bool formFound = false;
      int attempts = 0;

      while (!formFound && attempts < 25)
      {
        if (mwh == IntPtr.Zero)
        {
          Console.WriteLine("Form not yet found");
          Thread.Sleep(100);
          ++attempts;
          mwh = FindWindow(null, "Form1");
        }
        else
        {
          Console.WriteLine("Form has been found");
          formFound = true;
        }
      }

      if (mwh == IntPtr.Zero)
        throw new Exception("Could not find main window");
```

```
      Console.WriteLine("\nDone");
    }
    catch(Exception ex)
    {
      Console.WriteLine("Fatal error: " + ex.Message);
    }
  }
} // Class1
```

To manipulate and examine the state of a Windows application, you must obtain a handle to the application's main window. A window handle is a system-generated value that you can think of as being both an ID for the associated window and a way to access the window.

Comments

In a .NET environment, a window handle is type System.IntPtr, which is a platform-specific type used to represent either a pointer (memory address) or a handle. To obtain a handle to the main window of an AUT, you can call the Win32 API FindWindow() function. The FindWindow() function is essentially a part of the Windows operating system, which is available to you. Because FindWindow() is part of Windows, it is written in traditional C++ and not managed code. The C++ signature for FindWindow() is

```
HWND FindWindow(LPCTSTR lpClassName, LPCTSTR lpWindowName);
```

This function accepts a window class name and a window name as arguments, and it returns a handle to the window. To call into unmanaged code like the FindWindow() function from C#, you can use a .NET mechanism called *platform invoke* (P/Invoke). P/Invoke functionality is contained in the System.Runtime.InteropServices namespace. The mechanism is very elegant. In essence, you create a C# wrapper, or alias for the Win32 function you want to use, and then call that alias. You start by placing a

```
using System.Runtime.InteropServices;
```

statement in your test harness so you can easily access P/Invoke functionality. Next you determine a C# signature for the unmanaged function you want to call. This really involves deter- mining C# data types that map to the return type and parameter types of the unmanaged function. In the case of FindWindow(), the unmanaged return type is HWND, which is a Win32 data type representing a handle to a window. As explained earlier, the corresponding C# data type is System.IntPtr. The Win32 FindWindow() function accepts two parameters of type LPCTSTR. Although the details are fairly deep, this is basically a Win32 data type that can be represented by a C# type string.

■**Note** One of the greatest productivity-enhancing improvements that .NET introduced to application development is a vastly simplified data type model. To use the P/Invoke mechanism, you must determine the C# equivalents to Win32 data types. A detailed discussion of the mappings between Win32 data types and .NET data types is outside the scope of this book, but fortunately most mappings are fairly obvious. For example, the Win32 data types LPCSTR, LPCTSTR, LPCWSTR, LPSTR, LPTSTR, and LPWSTR usually map to the C# string data type.

After determining the C# alias method signature, you can place a class-scope `DllImport` attribute with the C# method signature that corresponds to the Win32 function signature into your test harness:

```
[DllImport("user32.dll", EntryPoint="FindWindow",
          CharSet=CharSet.Auto)]
static extern IntPtr FindWindow(string lpClassName,
                                string lpWindowName);
```

The "user32.dll" argument specifies the DLL file where the unmanaged function you want to use is located. Because the `DllImport` attribute is expecting a DLL, the `.dll` extension is optional; however, including it makes your code more readable. The `EntryPoint` attribute specifies the name of the Win32 API function that you will be calling through the C# alias. If the C# method name is exactly the same as the Win32 function name, you may omit the `EntryPoint` argument. But again, putting the argument in the attribute makes your code easier to read and maintain. The `CharSet` argument is optional but should be used whenever the C# method alias has a return type or one or more parameters that are type `char` or `string`. Specifying `CharSet.Auto` essentially means to let the .NET Framework take care of all character type conversions, for example, ASCII to Unicode. The `CharSet.Auto` argument dramatically simplifies working with type `char` and type `string`.

When you code the C# method alias for a Win32 function, you almost always use the `static` and `extern` modifiers because most Win32 functions are static functions rather than instance functions in C# terminology, and Win32 functions are external to your test harness. You may name the C# method anything you like but keeping the C# method name the same as the Win32 function name is the most readable approach. Similarly, you can name the C# parameters anything you like, but again, a good strategy is to make C# parameter names the same as their Win32 counterparts.

With the P/Invoke plumbing in place, if a subtle timing issue did not exist, you could now get the handle to the main window of the AUT like this:

```
IntPtr mwh = FindWindow(null, "Form1");
```

Before explaining the timing issue, let's look at the method call. The second argument to `FindWindow()` is the window name. In help documentation, this value is sometimes called the window title or the window caption. In the case of a Windows form application, this will usually be the form name. The first argument to `FindWindow()` is the window class name. A window class name is a system-generated string that is used to register the window with the operating system. Note that the term "class name" in this context is an old pre-OOP term and is not at all related to the idea of a C# language class container structure. Window/control class names are not unique, so they have little value when trying to find a window/control.

In this example, if you pass `null` as the window class name when calling `FindWindow()`, `FindWindow()` will return the handle of the first instance of a window with name `"Form1"`. This means you should be very careful about having multiple AUTs active, because you may get the wrong window handle.

If you attempt to obtain the application main window handle in the simple way just described, you are likely to run into a timing issue. The problem is that your AUT may not be fully launched and registered. A poor way to deal with this problem is to place `Thread.Sleep()` calls with large delays into your test harness to give the application time to launch. A better

way to deal with this issue is to wrap the call to FindWindow() in a while loop with a small
delay, checking to see if you get a valid window handle:

```
IntPtr mwh = IntPtr.Zero; // main window handle
bool formFound = false;

while (!formFound)
{
  if (mwh == IntPtr.Zero)
  {
    Console.WriteLine("Form not yet found");
    Thread.Sleep(100);
    mwh = FindWindow(null, "Form1");
  }
  else
  {
    Console.WriteLine("Form has been found");
    formFound = true;
  }
}
```

You use a Boolean flag to control the while loop. If the value of the main window handle is
IntPtr.Zero, then you delay the test automation by 100 milliseconds (one-tenth of a second)
using the Thread.Sleep() method from the System.Threading namespace. This approach could
lead to an infinite loop if the main window handle is never found, so in practice you will often
want to add a counter to limit the maximum number of times you iterate through the loop:

```
IntPtr mwh = IntPtr.Zero; // main window handle
bool formFound = false;
int attempts = 0;

while (!formFound && attempts < 25)
{
  if (mwh == IntPtr.Zero)
  {
    Console.WriteLine("Form not yet found");
    Thread.Sleep(100);
    ++attempts;
    mwh = FindWindow(null, "Form1");
  }
  else
  {
    Console.WriteLine("Form has been found");
    formFound = true;
  }
}

if (mwh == IntPtr.Zero)
  throw new Exception("Could not find Main Window");
```

If the value of the main window handle variable is still `IntPtr.Zero` after the while loop terminates, you know that the handle was never found, and you should abort the test run by throwing an exception.

You can increase the modularity of your lightweight test harness by wrapping the code in this solution in a helper method. For example, if you write

```
static IntPtr FindMainWindowHandle(string caption)
{
  IntPtr mwh = IntPtr.Zero;
  bool formFound = false;
  int attempts = 0;

  do
  {
    mwh = FindWindow(null, caption);
    if (mwh == IntPtr.Zero)
    {
      Console.WriteLine("Form not yet found");
      Thread.Sleep(100);
      ++attempts;
    }
    else
    {
      Console.WriteLine("Form has been found");
      formFound = true;
    }
  } while (!formFound && attempts < 25);

  if (mwh != IntPtr.Zero)
    return mwh;
  else
    throw new Exception("Could not find Main Window");
} // FindMainWindowHandle()
```

then you can make a clean call in your harness `Main()` method like this:

```
Console.WriteLine("Finding main window handle");
IntPtr mwh = FindMainWindowHandle("Form1");
Console.WriteLine("Handle to main window is " + mwh);
```

Depending on the complexity of your AUT, you may want to parameterize the delay time and the maximum number of attempts, leading to a helper signature such as

```
static IntPtr FindMainWindowHandle(string caption, int delay,
                                   int maxTries)
```

which can be called like this:

```
Console.WriteLine("Finding main window handle");
int delay = 100;
int maxTries = 25;
IntPtr mwh = FindMainWindowHandle("Form1", delay, maxTries);
Console.WriteLine("Handle to main window is " + mwh);
```

3.3 Obtaining a Handle to a Named Control

Problem

You want to obtain a handle to a control/window that has a window name.

Design

Use the `FindWindowEx()` Win32 API function with the .NET P/Invoke mechanism.

Solution

```
IntPtr mwh = IntPtr.Zero; // main window handle
// obtain main window handle here; see Section 3.2

Console.WriteLine("Finding handle to textBox1");
IntPtr tb = FindWindowEx(mwh, IntPtr.Zero, null, "<enter color>");
if (tb == IntPtr.Zero)
  throw new Exception("Unable to find textBox1");
else
  Console.WriteLine("Handle to textBox1 is " + tb);

Console.WriteLine("Finding handle to button1");
IntPtr butt = FindWindowEx(mwh, IntPtr.Zero, null, "button1");
if (butt == IntPtr.Zero)
  throw new Exception("Unable to find button1");
else
  Console.WriteLine("Handle to button1 is " + butt);
```

where a class-scope `DllImport` attribute is

```
[DllImport("user32.dll", EntryPoint="FindWindowEx",
  CharSet=CharSet.Auto)]
static extern IntPtr FindWindowEx(IntPtr hwndParent,
  IntPtr hwndChildAfter, string lpszClass, string lpszWindow);
```

To access and manipulate a control on a form-based application, you must obtain a handle to the control. In a Windows environment, all GUI controls are themselves windows. So, a button control is a window, a textbox control is a window, and so forth. To get a handle to a control/window, you can use the `FindWindowEx()` Win32 API function.

Comments

To call a Win32 function such as FindWindowEx() from a C# test harness, you can use the P/Invoke mechanism as described in Section 3.2. The Win32 FindWindowEx() function has this C++ signature:

```
HWND FindWindowEx(HWND hwndParent, HWND hwndChildAfter,
                  LPCTSTR lpszClass, LPCTSTR lpszWindow);
```

The FindWindowEx() function accepts four arguments. The first argument is a handle to the parent window of the control you are seeking. The second argument is a handle to a control and directs FindWindowEx() where to begin searching; the search begins with the next child control. The third argument is the class name of the target control, and the fourth argument is the window name/title/caption of the target control.

As discussed in Section 3.2, the C# equivalent to the Win32 type HWND is IntPtr and the C# equivalent to type LPCTSTR is string. Because the Win32 FindWindowEx() function is located in file user32.dll, you can insert this class-scope attribute and C# alias into the test harness:

```
[DllImport("user32.dll", EntryPoint="FindWindowEx",
  CharSet=CharSet.Auto)]
static extern IntPtr FindWindowEx(IntPtr hwndParent,
  IntPtr hwndChildAfter, string lpszClass, string lpszWindow);
```

Notice that the C# alias method signature uses the same function name and same parameter names as the Win32 function for code readability. With this P/Invoke plumbing in place, you can obtain a handle to a named control:

```
// get main window handle in variable mwh; see Section 3.2

Console.WriteLine("Finding handle to textBox1");
IntPtr tb = FindWindowEx(mwh, IntPtr.Zero, null, "<enter color>");

Console.WriteLine("Finding handle to button1");
IntPtr butt = FindWindowEx(mwh, IntPtr.Zero, null, "button1");
```

The first argument is the handle to the main window form that contains the target control. By specifying IntPtr.Zero as the second argument, you instruct FindWindowEx() to search all controls on the main form window. You ignore the target control class name by passing in null as the third argument. The fourth argument is the target control's name/title/caption.

You should not assume that a call to FindWindowEx() has succeeded. To check, you can test if the return handle has value IntPtr.Zero along the lines of

```
if (tb == IntPtr.Zero)
  throw new Exception("Unable to find textBox1");

if (butt == IntPtr.Zero)
  throw new Exception("Unable to find button1");
```

So, just how do you determine a control name/title/caption? The simplest way is to use the Spy++ tool included with Visual Studio .NET. The Spy++ tool is indispensable for lightweight UI test automation. Figure 3-2 shows Spy++ after its window finder has been placed on the button1 control of the AUT shown in the foreground of Figure 3-1.

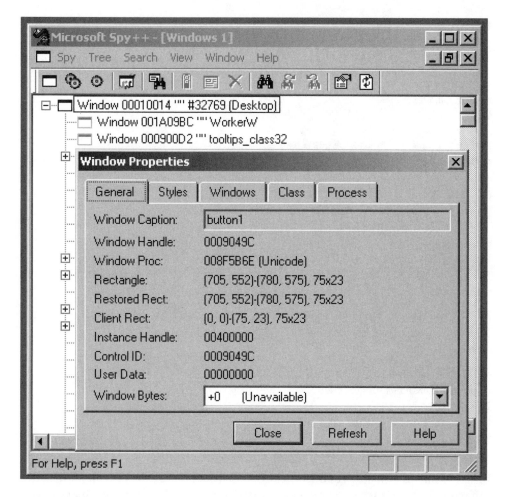

Figure 3-2. *The Spy++ tool*

In addition to a control's caption, Spy++ provides other useful information such as the control's class name, Windows events related to the control, and the control's parent, child, and sibling controls.

3.4 Obtaining a Handle to a Non-Named Control

Problem

You want to obtain a handle to a control that does not have a window name.

Design

Write a FindWindowByIndex() helper method that finds the control by using its implied index value.

Solution

```
static IntPtr FindWindowByIndex(IntPtr hwndParent, int index)
{
  if (index == 0)
    return hwndParent;
  else
  {
    int ct = 0;
    IntPtr result = IntPtr.Zero;
    do
    {
      result = FindWindowEx(hwndParent, result, null, null);
      if (result != IntPtr.Zero)
        ++ct;
    } while (ct < index && result != IntPtr.Zero);

    return result;
  }
}
```

and then call like this:

```
Console.WriteLine("Finding handle to listBox1");
IntPtr lb = FindWindowByIndex(mwh, 3);
if (lb == IntPtr.Zero)
  throw new Exception("Unable to find listBox1");
else
  Console.WriteLine("Handle to listBox1 is " + lb);
```

   To access and manipulate a control on a form-based application, you must obtain a handle to the control. If the target control has a unique window name, then you can obtain its handle using the techniques in Section 3.3. But a control may not have a name/caption/title. Examples include empty textbox controls and empty listbox controls. Furthermore, controls may have nonunique names. To deal with these situations, you can write a helper method that uses the Win32 FindWindowEx() function to return a control handle based on the control's order index value.

Comments

The index value of a control is implied rather than explicit. The idea is that each control on a form has a predecessor and a successor control (except for the first control, which has no predecessor, and the last control, which has no successor). This predecessor-successor relationship can be used to find window handles.

   Before examining this control index order concept further, let's imagine that we know the index value of a control and see how the FindWindowByIndex() helper method works to return the control handle. Suppose, for example, that an application has a listbox control, and the index of the control is 3. This means that index 0 represents the main form window, and indexes 1 and 2 represent predecessor controls to the listbox control. The FindWindowByIndex() helper method accepts two arguments. The first argument is a handle to the parent control, and the second is a control index. If the index argument is 0, the FindWindowByIndex() method immediately returns the handle to the parent control. This design choice is arbitrary. The heart of the helper method is a call to FindWindwEx() inside a loop:

```
int ct = 0;
do
{
  result = FindWindowEx(hwndParent, result, null, null);
  if (result != IntPtr.Zero)
    ++ct;
} while (ct < index && result != IntPtr.Zero);
```

Each call to FindWindowEx() returns a handle to the next available control because you pass in as arguments the current window handle, the result returned in the preceding iteration of the loop, null, and null again, as the first, second, third, and fourth arguments, respectively. As explained in Section 3.3, the second argument to FindWindowEx() directs the method where to begin searching, and passing null as the third and fourth arguments means to find the first available window/control regardless of class name or window name. If this loop executes n times, variable result will hold the handle of the nth window/control, or IntPtr.Zero if the control could not be found.

So, if you know the index value of a control, you can get the control handle using the FindWindowByIndex() helper method. But just how do you determine a control's implied index value? There are two simple ways to get this index value. First, if you have access to the AUT source code, you can get a control index value because the value is the order in which the control is added to the main form control. For example, suppose the AUT code contains

```
this.Controls.Add(this.comboBox1);
this.Controls.Add(this.button1);
this.Controls.Add(this.listBox1);
this.Controls.Add(this.textBox1);
```

The implied index of the comboBox1 control is 1, the index of button1 is 2, the index of listBox1 is 3, and the index of textBox1 is 4. Note that the implied index value of a control is not the same as the control tab order. Now if you do not have access to the source code of the AUT, you can still determine the index value of each control by examining the predecessors and successors of the controls with the Spy++ tool as described in Section 3.3.

The FindWindowByIndex() helper method gives you a way to deal with controls with nonunique names. Suppose your AUT has two buttons with the same label:

```
this.Controls.Add(this.button1); // window name is "Click me"
this.Controls.Add(this.button2); // window name also "Click me"
```

You can still obtain handles to each button control:

```
IntPtr butt1 = FindWindowByIndex(mwh, 1);
IntPtr butt2 = FindWindowByIndex(mwh, 2);
```

3.5 Sending Characters to a Control

Problem

You want to send characters to a text-based control.

Design

Use the Win32 SendMessage() function with a WM_CHAR notification message.

Solution

```
// launch app; see Section 3.1
// get main window handle; see Section 3.2
// get handle to textBox1 as tb; see Sections 3.3 and 3.4

Console.WriteLine("Sending 'x' to textBox1");
uint WM_CHAR = 0x0102;
SendMessage1(tb, WM_CHAR, 'x', 0);

Console.WriteLine("Now adding 'foo' to textBox1");
string s = "foo";
foreach (char c in s)
{
  SendMessage1(tb, WM_CHAR, c, 0);
}
```

where the class-scope DllImport attribute is

```
[DllImport("user32.dll", EntryPoint="SendMessage",
  CharSet=CharSet.Auto)]
static extern void SendMessage1(IntPtr hWnd, uint Msg,
  int wParam, int lParam);
```

A common lightweight UI test automation task is to simulate a user typing characters into a UI control. One way to do this is to use the Win32 SendMessage() function with the .NET P/Invoke mechanism.

Comments

The SendMessage() function has this C++ signature:

```
LRESULT SendMessage(HWND hWnd, UINT Msg,
                    WPARAM wParam, LPARAM lParam);
```

There are four parameters. The first parameter is a handle to the window/control that you are sending a Windows message to. The second parameter is the Windows message to send to the control. The third and fourth parameters are generic and their meaning and data type depend upon the Windows message. Similarly, the meaning and type of the return value for SendMessage() depend upon the message being sent. So, before you can create a C# signature alias for the C++ SendMessage() function, you need to examine the particular Windows message you will be sending. In this case, you want to send a WM_CHAR message. The WM_CHAR message is sent to the control that has keyboard focus when a key is pressed. WM_CHAR is actually a Windows symbolic constant defined as 0x0102. If you look up "WM_CHAR" in the integrated Visual Studio .NET Help, you will find that wParam parameter specifies the character code of the key pressed. The lParam parameter specifies various key-state masks such as the repeat count, scan code, extended-key flag, context code, previous key-state flag, and transition-state flag values. So, with this information in hand, you can create a C# signature like:

```
[DllImport("user32.dll", EntryPoint="SendMessage",
  CharSet=CharSet.Auto)]
static extern void SendMessage1(IntPtr hWnd, uint Msg,
  int wParam, int lParam);
```

You use a C# method alias name of SendMessage1() rather than SendMessage() because there will be several different C# signatures depending on the particular Windows message passed to the SendMessage() function. As explained in Section 3.2, a C# IntPtr type corresponds to a C++ HWND type. All Windows messages are type uint, and the WM_CHAR message requires two int parameters for the scan code of the key pressed and a value for the key-state mask.

With this code in place, you can send a character to a control like this:

```
Console.WriteLine("Finding handle to textBox1");
IntPtr tb = FindWindowEx(mwh, IntPtr.Zero, null, "<enter color>");

Console.WriteLine("Sending 'x' to textBox1");
uint WM_CHAR = 0x0102;
SendMessage1(tb, WM_CHAR, 'x', 0);
```

Notice that an implicit type conversion is occurring here. When you pass a character such as 'x' as the third argument to SendMessage(), the character will be implicitly converted to type int.

You can increase the modularity of your test automation by wrapping the essential code into two helper methods:

```
static void SendChar(IntPtr hControl, char c)
{
  uint WM_CHAR = 0x0102;
  SendMessage1(hControl, WM_CHAR, c, 0);
}

static void SendChars(IntPtr hControl, string s)
{
  foreach (char c in s)
  {
    SendChar(hControl, c);
  }
}
```

Then you can make clean calls such as

```
Console.WriteLine("Sending 'x' to textBox1");
SendChar(tb, 'x');

Console.WriteLine("Now adding 'foo' to textBox1");
SendChars(tb, "foo");
```

3.6 Clicking on a Control

Problem

You want to automate a mouse click on a control.

Design

Use the Win32 `PostMessage()` function with `WM_LBUTTONDOWN` and `WM_LBUTTONUP` notification messages.

Solution

```
Console.WriteLine("Clicking on button1");
uint WM_LBUTTONDOWN = 0x0201;
uint WM_LBUTTONUP   = 0x0202;
PostMessage1(butt, WM_LBUTTONDOWN, 0, 0);
PostMessage1(butt, WM_LBUTTONUP, 0, 0);
```

where a class-scope `DllImport` attribute is

```
[DllImport("user32.dll", EntryPoint="PostMessage",
  CharSet=CharSet.Auto)]
static extern bool PostMessage1(IntPtr hWnd, uint Msg,
  int wParam, int lParam);
```

Comments

A common lightweight UI test automation task is to simulate a user clicking on a UI control. One way to do this is to use the Win32 `PostMessage()` function with the .NET P/Invoke mechanism. The `PostMessage()` function has this C++ signature:

```
BOOL PostMessage(HWND hWnd, UINT Msg,
                 WPARAM wParam, LPARAM lParam);
```

The `PostMessage()` function is closely related to the `SendMessage()` function described in Section 3.5. In lightweight test automation scenarios, you will use `SendMessage()` most often. The primary difference between `SendMessage()` and `PostMessage()` is that `SendMessage()` calls the specified procedure and does not return until after the procedure has processed the Windows message; `PostMessage()` returns without waiting for the message to be processed. In the case of a mouse button click action, you want control to return to the test automation harness without waiting for the thread to process the message. In practical terms, deciding whether to use `SendMessage()` or `PostMessage()` is difficult. You should consider the actions associated with the message you want to send; if the actions are very closely related and must happen more or less together, try `PostMessage()`, otherwise try `SendMessage()`. Regardless, you may have to experiment to get the desired effect.

The `PostMessage()` function accepts four arguments: a handle to the window/control that you are posting a Windows message to, the Windows message to post to the control, and generic arguments whose data type and meaning depend upon the Windows message being posted. To create a C# signature alias for the C++ `PostMessage()` function, you need to examine the particular Windows message you will be posting. In this instance, you want to post a `WM_LBUTTONDOWN` (mouse left button down) message followed by a `WM_LBUTTONUP` message. As with all Windows messages, `WM_LBUTTONDOWN` and `WM_LBUTTONUP` are symbolic constants, in this case 0x0201 and 0x0202, respectively. The `wParam` parameter for both messages indicates whether various virtual keys are down while the mouse button is being clicked. A value of 0 means no keys are down when the mouse button is clicked. The `lParam` parameter specifies where in the target control the mouse clicks at; a value of 0 means the upper-left corner of the control (the low byte is the x coordinate, and the high byte is the y coordinate). With this information in hand, you can create a C# signature such as

```
[DllImport("user32.dll", EntryPoint="PostMessage",
  CharSet=CharSet.Auto)]
static extern bool PostMessage1(IntPtr hWnd, uint Msg,
  int wParam, int lParam);
```

Choose a C# method alias name of `PostMessage1()` rather than `PostMessage()` because there may be several different C# signatures depending on the particular Windows message passed to the `PostMessage()` function. As explained in Section 3.2, a C# `IntPtr` type corresponds to a C++ `HWND` type.

After you have placed the P/Invoke plumbing in your lightweight test automation harness, you can simulate a user clicking on a control:

```
// get button1 handle into variable 'butt'; see Section 3.3
Console.WriteLine("Clicking on button1");
uint WM_LBUTTONDOWN = 0x0201;
uint WM_LBUTTONUP   = 0x0202;
PostMessage1(butt, WM_LBUTTONDOWN, 0, 0);
PostMessage1(butt, WM_LBUTTONUP, 0, 0);
```

Notice that you are ignoring the `PostMessage1()` return value. Win32 function return values are often used for error-checking, and you should take advantage of them. Somewhat surprisingly, however, Windows message return values are often not very helpful in lightweight UI test automation. The main reason for this is that the return values are generally intended for use by the message receiver; however, in a test automation situation, you are effectively the message sender.

You can increase the modularity of your test automation by wrapping the essential control-click code into a helper method:

```
static void ClickOn(IntPtr hControl)
{
  uint WM_LBUTTONDOWN = 0x0201;
  uint WM_LBUTTONUP   = 0x0202;
  PostMessage1(hControl, WM_LBUTTONDOWN, 0, 0); // button down
  PostMessage1(hControl, WM_LBUTTONUP, 0, 0); // button up
}
```

Then you can make calls such as

```
// get button1 handle into variable 'butt'; see Section 3.3

Console.WriteLine("Clicking on button1");
ClickOn(butt);
```

In addition to using this solution to click on button controls, you can use the technique to give focus to a control in situations where a real user might do so, so that you can send characters to the control. For example:

```
// get comboBox1 handle into variable 'cb'; see Section 3.4

Console.WriteLine("Clicking on comboBox1 to set keyboard focus");
ClickOn(cb);
Thread.Sleep(500);
Console. WriteLine("Now sending 'foo' to comboBox1");
SendChars(cb, "foo");
```

3.7 Dealing with Message Boxes

Problem

You want to deal with a message box, such as clicking it away.

Design

Treat the message box as a top-level window/control rather than as a child control, and use the Win32 FindWindow() function with the P/Invoke mechanism.

Solution

```
Console.WriteLine("Clicking button1");
ClickOn(butt); // see Section 3.6
// generates a message box with title "Error" and button "OK"
```

```
Console.WriteLine("\nLooking for Message Box");
IntPtr mb = IntPtr.Zero;
bool mbFound = false;
int tries = 0;
while (!mbFound && tries < 25)
{
  mb = FindWindow(null, "Error");
  ++tries;

  if (mb == IntPtr.Zero)
  {
    Console.WriteLine("Message Box window not yet found");
    Thread.Sleep(100);
  }
  else
  {
    Console.WriteLine("Message Box found; handle = " + mb);
    mbFound = true;
  }
} // while

Console.WriteLine("Clicking away Message Box in 2.5 seconds");
Thread.Sleep(2500);

IntPtr okButt = FindWindowEx(mb, IntPtr.Zero, null, "OK");
ClickOn(okButt);
```

The key to dealing with message box windows is to realize that message box controls are not child controls of the application form. Message box controls are top-level windows, so you treat them just as you would the main application form. You can think of a message box as a tiny subprogram that runs independently from the AUT. So, first you get a handle to the message box, and then you get a handle to the "OK" button (or other control on the message box), which you can then manipulate.

Comments

The heart of the technique to obtain a handle to a message box is to call the Win32 API FindWindow() function using the .NET P/Invoke mechanism. This technique is described in detail in Section 3.2. To summarize, you create a C# alias for the Win32 FindWindow() function using a class-scope DllImport attribute. The C# FindWindow() method alias accepts the target message box class name (which is rarely useful), accepts the window name/title/caption, and returns a handle to the message box:

```
IntPtr mb = IntPtr.Zero;
mb = FindWindow(null, "Error");
```

After you obtain a handle to a message box, if you want to simulate a user clicking the box away as is usually the case, you obtain a handle to the OK button using the FindWindowEx() function as described in Section 3.3:

```
IntPtr okButt = FindWindowEx(mb, IntPtr.Zero, null, "OK");
```

The FindWindowEx() method accepts a handle to the parent control (the message box), a handle to the window/control to begin searching at (a value of IntPtr.Zero means search all child controls), the target control class name (rarely useful so we usually pass in null), and the target control name/title/caption. An alternative way to get the handle to the message box OK button is to use the FindWindowByIndex() helper method described in Section 3.4. For example, if the OK button is the only control on a message box, then you can get a handle to the button with

```
IntPtr okButt = FindWindowByIndex(mb, 1);
```

Because message box controls are top-level windows, a slight delay may occur before they are ready to be accessed. This is especially true if you are running your lightweight test automation under a stress condition (reduced system resources). So, you can use the same idea as presented in Section 3.2—place the call to FindWindow() in a while loop with a slight delay, checking each time through the loop until the message box handle variable does not have a IntPtr.Zero value:

```
Console.WriteLine("\nLooking for message box");
IntPtr mb = IntPtr.Zero;
bool mbFound = false;
int attempts = 0;
while (!mbFound && attempts < 25)
{
  mb = FindWindow(null, "Error");
  ++attempts;

  if (mb == IntPtr.Zero)
  {
    Console.WriteLine("Message Box window not found yet . . . ");
    Thread.Sleep(100);
  }
  else
  {
    Console.WriteLine("Message Box window found with ptr = " + mb);
    mbFound = true;
  }
}
```

You can increase the modularity of this solution by wrapping the code up into a helper method:

```
static IntPtr FindMessageBox(string caption)
{
  IntPtr result = IntPtr.Zero;
  bool mbFound = false;
  int attempts = 0;
```

```
  do
  {
    result = FindWindow(null, caption);
    if (result == IntPtr.Zero)
    {
      Console.WriteLine("Message Box not yet found");
      Thread.Sleep(100);
      ++attempts;
    }
    else
    {
      Console.WriteLine("Message Box has been found");
      mbFound = true;
    }
  } while (!mbFound && attempts < 25);

  if (result != IntPtr.Zero)
    return result;
  else
    throw new Exception("Could not find Message Box");
}
```

With this helper method, you can now make calls like this:

```
Console.WriteLine("\nLooking for message box");
IntPtr mb = FindMessageBox("Error");
Console.WriteLine("Message box handle = " + mb);
```

Except for some minor details such as the progress messages, this helper method is exactly the same as the helper method to find the main window handle presented in the discussion section of Section 3.2. Therefore, you could combine them both into a single helper:

```
static IntPtr FindTopLevelWindow(string caption)
{
  // code as shown previously
}
```

Then, make calls like this:

```
// launch AUT here; see Section 3.1

Console.WriteLine("\nLooking for main window handle");
IntPtr mwh = FindTopLevelWindow ("Form1");
Console.WriteLine("Main window handle = " + mwh);

ClickOn(butt); // see Section 3.6

Console.WriteLine("\nLooking for message box");
IntPtr mb = FindTopLevelWindow ("Error");
Console.WriteLine("Message box handle = " + mb);
```

This approach is more efficient than having two separate helper methods and makes technical sense, but the downside is that your code will be slightly harder to read and modify for specific message box or main window issues. A compromise approach is to write a single FindTopLevelWindow() method as shown previously and then write tiny wrapper methods such as

```
static IntPtr FindMainWindowHandle(string caption, int delay, int maxTries)
{
  return FindTopLevelWindow(caption, delay, maxTries);
}

static IntPtr FindMessageBox(string caption)
{
  int delay = 100;
  int maxTries = 25;
  return FindTopLevelWindow(caption, delay, maxTries);
}
```

3.8 Dealing with Menus

Problem

You want to simulate a user clicking on a main menu item such as Help ➤ About or File ➤ Exit.

Design

Use the Win32 API functions GetMenu(), GetSubMenu(), GetMenuItemID(), and SendMessage() with a WM_COMMAND Windows message.

Solution

```
// Launch AUT; See Section 3.1
// Get main window handle into mwh; See Section 3.2

IntPtr hMainMenu = GetMenu(mwh);
Console.WriteLine("Handle to main menu is " + hMainMenu);

IntPtr hHelp = GetSubMenu(hMainMenu, 2);
Console.WriteLine("\nHandle to Help is " + hHelp);

int iAbout = GetMenuItemID(hHelp, 0);
Console.WriteLine("\nIndex to About is " + iAbout);

uint WM_COMMAND = 0x0111;
SendMessage2(mwh, WM_COMMAND, iAbout, IntPtr.Zero);
```

where class-scope attributes are

```
// Menu routines
[DllImport("user32.dll")]
static extern IntPtr GetMenu(IntPtr hWnd);

[DllImport("user32.dll")]
static extern IntPtr GetSubMenu(IntPtr hMenu, int nPos);

[DllImport("user32.dll")]
static extern int GetMenuItemID(IntPtr hMenu, int nPos);

[DllImport("user32.dll", EntryPoint="SendMessage",
  CharSet=CharSet.Auto)]
static extern void SendMessage2(IntPtr hWnd, uint Msg,
  int wParam, IntPtr lParam);
```

Comments

Suppose your AUT has a main menu structured like this:

```
File    Edit    Help
  New     Cut     About
  Save    Copy    Update
  Print   Paste
  Exit
```

The preceding solution would simulate a user clicking on Help ➤ About. The GetMenu() function returns a handle to the main application menu. The GetSubMenu() function accepts a parent menu handle and a 0-based submenu index, and returns a handle to a submenu. In this example, if variable hMainMenu holds a handle to the main menu, then the call GetSubMenu(hMainMenu, 2) would return a handle to the Help part of the main menu, GetSubMenu(hMainMenu, 0) would return a handle to the File part of the main menu, and so on. After you have the submenu handle, the next step is to get an index value of the item you want to manipulate using the GetMenuItemID() function. If hHelp holds a handle to the Help part of the main menu, the call GetMenuItemID(hHelp, 0) returns the index of the About part of the submenu and GetMenuItemID(hHelp, 1) returns the index of the Update part of the submenu.

After obtaining an index to the menu item you want to manipulate, the last step to simulate clicking on the menu item is to call the SendMessage() Win32 API function using a WM_COMMAND message. If variable iAbout holds the index of the About item in the Help submenu, then the statements

```
uint WM_COMMAND = 0x0111;
SendMessage2(mwh, WM_COMMAND, iAbout, IntPtr.Zero);
```

will simulate a user clicking on Help ➤ About.

A common task in lightweight UI test automation scenarios is to simulate a user performing a File ➤ Exit. If File is the first menu item, and Exit is the first submenu item under File, then the pattern is

```
Console.WriteLine("\nDoing a File -> Exit in 2.5 seconds");
Thread.Sleep(2500);
IntPtr hMainMenu = GetMenu(mwh);
IntPtr hFile = GetSubMenu(hMainMenu, 0);
int iExit = GetMenuItemID(hFile, 0);
uint WM_COMMAND = 0x0111;
SendMessage2(mwh, WM_COMMAND, iExit, IntPtr.Zero);
```

The WM_COMMAND message is sent when the user selects a command item from a menu. Like all Windows messages, it is really just a constant; in this case, the value is 0x0111. Notice we are using a C# alias named SendMessage2(). As discussed in Section 3.2, the C# alias signatures for the Win32 SendMessage() and the PostMessage() functions depend on the message being sent/posted. In the case of WM_COMMAND, the wParam parameter represents two values. The high-order word of wParam specifies the notification code if the message comes from a control. If the message is from an accelerator, this value is 1; if the message is from a menu, this value is 0. The low-order word of wParam specifies the identifier of the menu item. In other words, the wParam parameter is type int. The lParam parameter specifies the handle to the control sending the message (if the message is from a control) or null if the message is not from a control (which is the case when notification comes from a user-initiated event). In other words, the lParam parameter is type IntPtr. Therefore, you create a DllImport attribute of

```
[DllImport("user32.dll", EntryPoint="SendMessage",
  CharSet=CharSet.Auto)]
static extern void SendMessage2(IntPtr hWnd, uint Msg,
  int wParam, IntPtr lParam);
```

You could rely on .NET overloading and just use one common SendMessage() alias signature, but creating separate SendMessageX()-style alias signatures tends to be a bit more readable in general. The .NET alias signatures for GetMenu(), GetSubMenu(), and GetMenuItemID() follow their Win32 counterparts. Because these functions are used in only one way, you do not give them a MethodNameX()-style alias, such as GetMenu1() for example.

The pattern to simulate more complex menu structures follows the same general pattern as the preceding solution. For example, suppose you have a menu structure like this:

```
File    Edit    Help
                    HelpItem0 [0]
                    HelpItem1 [1]
                    HelpItem2 [2]
                      HelpItem2SubItem0 [0]
                      HelpItem2SubItem1 [1]
                    HelpItem3 [3]
```

To simulate a user selecting Help ➤ HelpItem2 ➤ HelpItem2SubItem1, you could write this code:

```
IntPtr hMainMenu = GetMenu(mwh);
Console.WriteLine("Handle to main menu is " + hMainMenu);

IntPtr hHelp = GetSubMenu(hMainMenu, 2);
Console.WriteLine("\nHandle to Help is " + hHelp);

IntPtr hSub = GetSubMenu(hHelp, 2);
Console.WriteLine("\nHandle to HelpItem2 is  " + hSub);

int iSub = GetMenuItemID(hSub, 1);
Console.WriteLine("\nIndex to HelpItem2SubItem1 is " + iSub);

uint WM_COMMAND = 0x0111;
SendMessage2(mwh, WM_COMMAND, iSub, IntPtr.Zero);
```

3.9 Checking Application State

Problem

You want to check the contents of a control on the AUT.

Design

Use the WM_GETTEXT message with the SendMessage() Win32 API function.

Solution

```
// launch AUT; see Section 3.1
// get handle to textBox1 into variable tb; see Section 3.3
// manipulate app; see Sections 3.5 and 3.6

Console.WriteLine("\nChecking the contents of textBox1");
uint WM_GETTEXT = 0x000D;
byte[] buffer = new byte[256];
string text = null;
int numFetched = SendMessage3(tb, WM_GETTEXT, 256, buffer);
text = System.Text.Encoding.Unicode.GetString(buffer);
Console.WriteLine("Fetched " + numFetched + " chars");
Console.WriteLine("TextBox1 contains = " + text);
```

where

```
[DllImport("user32.dll", EntryPoint="SendMessage",
  CharSet=CharSet.Auto)]
static extern int SendMessage3(IntPtr hWndControl,
  uint Msg, int wParam, byte[] lParam);
```

Comments

To determine a pass or fail test result when performing lightweight UI test automation, you must be able to programmatically examine the AUT to determine if the result state is what is expected. For example, you may need to determine if an expected text string is in a textbox control. The WM_GETTEXT message used with the SendMessage() function is one of several ways to retrieve the text from a textbox control or a combobox control. As described in Section 3.2, the C# method signature for SendMessage() depends on the particular message being sent. In the case of WM_GETTEXT, the wParam parameter is the maximum number of characters to fetch from the control, so you can use the C# int data type. The lParam parameter is a pointer to a buffer array to receive the text fetched from the control, so you can use a C# byte array. This leads to the following class-scope DllImport attribute to create a C# alias for SendMessage() when used in conjunction with a WM_GETTEXT message:

```
[DllImport("user32.dll", EntryPoint="SendMessage",
  CharSet=CharSet.Auto)]
static extern int SendMessage3(IntPtr hWndControl, uint Msg,
  int wParam, byte[] lParam);
```

With this P/Invoke plumbing in place, you can prepare the call to retrieve the text in a textbox control like this:

```
uint WM_GETTEXT = 0x000D;
byte[] buffer = new byte[256];
string text = null;
```

The Windows message WM_GETTEXT is just a symbolic constant with value 0x000D. You declare a byte array to hold the text in the control we are examining. In this example, placing a hard-coded 256 value in the automation is a simple approach but assumes the text in the target control is no longer than 256 bytes (or 128 Unicode characters). If you need to determine the actual size of the text in the target control, you can use the WM_GETTEXTLENGTH message first, and then use that return value to allocate your buffer array.

Now, if variable tb holds the handle to textBox1, you can make the call to SendMessage() like this:

```
int numFetched = SendMessage3(tb, WM_GETTEXT, 256, buffer);
text = System.Text.Encoding.Unicode.GetString(buffer);
```

This technique works for simple text-based controls. For example, you can retrieve the text in a combobox control in the exact same way. More complex controls, such as listbox controls, require a different approach:

```
Console.WriteLine("\nChecking contents of listBox1 for 'foo'");
uint LB_FINDSTRING = 0x018F;
int result = SendMessage4(lb, LB_FINDSTRING, -1, "foo");
if (result >= 0)
  Console.WriteLine("Found 'foo'");
else
  Console.WriteLine("Did not find 'foo'");
```

where

```
[DllImport("user32.dll", EntryPoint="SendMessage",
  CharSet=CharSet.Auto)]
static extern int SendMessage4(IntPtr hWnd, uint Msg,
  int wParam, string lParam);
```

The LB_FINDSTRING message can be used to determine if a particular string is in a listbox control. The wParam parameter specifies which item in the listbox to begin searching at, with a value of -1 indicating to search the entire control. The lParam parameter is the target string to search for. The return value is a 0-based index of the location of the target string in the listbox, or -1 if the target is not found.

3.10 Example Program: WindowsUITest

This program combines several of the techniques from this chapter to create a lightweight test automation harness to test the Windows application shown in the foreground of Figure 3-1. The program is a test scenario with test inputs hard-coded into the harness, rather than using test case inputs read from an external file. The test automation first launches the color-mixer AUT. Then the test scenario clicks the button control to generate an error message box. Next the automation clicks the error message box away and then simulates a user typing "red" and "blue" to the application. The automation clicks the button control again and then examines the listbox control, looking for an expected "Result is purple" string. The complete light-weight test harness is listed in Listing 3-1. When run, the output will be as shown in Figure 3-1 in the introduction section of this chapter.

Listing 3-1. *Program WindowsUITest*

```
using System;
using System.Diagnostics;
using System.Runtime.InteropServices;
using System.Threading;

namespace WindowsUITest
{
  class Class1
  {
    [STAThread]
    static void Main(string[] args)
    {
      try
      {
        Console.WriteLine("\nLaunching application under test");

        string path = "..\\..\\..\\WinApp\\bin\\Debug\\WinApp.exe";
        Process p = Process.Start(path);
```

```
Console.WriteLine("\nFinding main window handle");
IntPtr mwh = FindMainWindowHandle("Form1", 100, 25);
Console.WriteLine("Main window handle = " + mwh);

Console.WriteLine("\nFinding handles to textBox1, comboBox1");
Console.WriteLine(" button1, listBox1");

// you may want to add delays here to make sure Form has rendered
IntPtr tb = FindWindowEx(mwh, IntPtr.Zero, null, "<enter color>");
IntPtr cb = FindWindowByIndex(mwh, 1);
IntPtr butt = FindWindowEx(mwh, IntPtr.Zero, null, "button1");
IntPtr lb = FindWindowByIndex(mwh, 3);

if (tb == IntPtr.Zero || cb == IntPtr.Zero ||
    butt == IntPtr.Zero || lb == IntPtr.Zero)
  throw new Exception("Unable to find all controls");
else
  Console.WriteLine("All control handles found");

Console.WriteLine("\nClicking button1");
ClickOn(butt);

Console.WriteLine("Clicking away Error message box");
Thread.Sleep(1000);
IntPtr mb = FindMessageBox("Error");
if (mb == IntPtr.Zero)
  throw new Exception("Unable to find message box");
IntPtr okButt = FindWindowEx(mb, IntPtr.Zero, null, "OK");
if (okButt == IntPtr.Zero)
  throw new Exception("Unable to find OK button");
ClickOn(okButt);

Console.WriteLine("Typing 'red' and 'blue' to application");
SendChars(tb, "red");
ClickOn(cb);
SendChars(cb, "blue");

Console.WriteLine("Clicking on button1");
ClickOn(butt);
Console.WriteLine("\nChecking listBox1 for 'purple'");

uint LB_FINDSTRING = 0x018F;
int result = SendMessage4(lb, LB_FINDSTRING, -1,
                          "Result is purple");
if (result >= 0)
  Console.WriteLine("\nTest scenario result = Pass");
else
  Console.WriteLine("\nTest scenario result = *FAIL*");
```

```
      Console.WriteLine("\nExiting app in 3 seconds . . . ");
      Thread.Sleep(3000);
      IntPtr hMainMenu = GetMenu(mwh);
      IntPtr hFile = GetSubMenu(hMainMenu, 0);
      int iExit = GetMenuItemID(hFile, 0);
      uint WM_COMMAND = 0x0111;
      SendMessage2(mwh, WM_COMMAND, iExit, IntPtr.Zero);

      Console.WriteLine("\nDone");
      Console.ReadLine();
    }
    catch(Exception ex)
    {
      Console.WriteLine("Fatal error: " + ex.Message);
    }
} // Main()

static IntPtr FindTopLevelWindow(string caption, int delay,
                                   int maxTries)
{
  IntPtr mwh = IntPtr.Zero;
  bool formFound = false;
  int attempts = 0;

  do
  {
    mwh = FindWindow(null, caption);
    if (mwh == IntPtr.Zero)
    {
      Console.WriteLine("Form not yet found");
      Thread.Sleep(delay);
      ++attempts;
    }
    else
    {
      Console.WriteLine("Form has been found");
      formFound = true;
    }
  } while (!formFound && attempts < maxTries);

  if (mwh != IntPtr.Zero)
    return mwh;
  else
    throw new Exception("Could not find Main Window");
} // FindTopLevelWindow()
```

```
static IntPtr FindMainWindowHandle(string caption, int delay, int maxTries)
{
  return FindTopLevelWindow(caption, delay, maxTries);
}

static IntPtr FindMessageBox(string caption)
{
  int delay = 100;
  int maxTries = 25;
  return FindTopLevelWindow(caption, delay, maxTries);
}

static IntPtr FindWindowByIndex(IntPtr hwndParent, int index)
{
  if (index == 0)
    return hwndParent;
  else
  {
    int ct = 0;
    IntPtr result = IntPtr.Zero;
    do
    {
      result = FindWindowEx(hwndParent, result, null, null);
      if (result != IntPtr.Zero)
        ++ct;
    } while (ct < index && result != IntPtr.Zero);

    return result;
  }
} // FindWindowByIndex()

static void ClickOn(IntPtr hControl)
{
  uint WM_LBUTTONDOWN = 0x0201;
  uint WM_LBUTTONUP   = 0x0202;
  PostMessage1(hControl, WM_LBUTTONDOWN, 0, 0);
  PostMessage1(hControl, WM_LBUTTONUP, 0, 0);
}

static void SendChar(IntPtr hControl, char c)
{
  uint WM_CHAR = 0x0102;
  SendMessage1(hControl, WM_CHAR, c, 0);
}
```

```csharp
static void SendChars(IntPtr hControl, string s)
{
  foreach (char c in s)
  {
    SendChar(hControl, c);
  }
}

// P/Invoke Aliases

[DllImport("user32.dll", EntryPoint="FindWindow",
  CharSet=CharSet.Auto)]
static extern IntPtr FindWindow(string lpClassName,
  string lpWindowName);

[DllImport("user32.dll", EntryPoint="FindWindowEx",
  CharSet=CharSet.Auto)]
static extern IntPtr FindWindowEx(IntPtr hwndParent,
  IntPtr hwndChildAfter, string lpszClass, string lpszWindow);

// for WM_CHAR message
[DllImport("user32.dll", EntryPoint="SendMessage",
  CharSet=CharSet.Auto)]
static extern void SendMessage1(IntPtr hWnd, uint Msg,
  int wParam, int lParam);

// for WM_COMMAND message
[DllImport("user32.dll", EntryPoint="SendMessage",
  CharSet=CharSet.Auto)]
static extern void SendMessage2(IntPtr hWnd, uint Msg,
  int wParam, IntPtr lParam);

// for WM_LBUTTONDOWN and WM_LBUTTONUP messages
[DllImport("user32.dll", EntryPoint="PostMessage",
  CharSet=CharSet.Auto)]
static extern bool PostMessage1(IntPtr hWnd, uint Msg,
  int wParam, int lParam);

// for WM_GETTEXT message
[DllImport("user32.dll", EntryPoint="SendMessage",
  CharSet=CharSet.Auto)]
static extern int SendMessage3(IntPtr hWndControl, uint Msg,
  int wParam, byte[] lParam);
```

```
    // for LB_FINDSTRING message
    [DllImport("user32.dll", EntryPoint="SendMessage",
      CharSet=CharSet.Auto)]
    static extern int SendMessage4(IntPtr hWnd, uint Msg,
      int wParam, string lParam);

    // Menu routines
    [DllImport("user32.dll")] //
    static extern IntPtr GetMenu(IntPtr hWnd);

    [DllImport("user32.dll")] //
    static extern IntPtr GetSubMenu(IntPtr hMenu, int nPos);

    [DllImport("user32.dll")] //
    static extern int GetMenuItemID(IntPtr hMenu, int nPos);

  } // class
} // ns
```

■■■

Test Harness Design Patterns

4.0 Introduction

One of the advantages of writing lightweight test automation instead of using a third-party testing framework is that you have great flexibility in how you can structure your test harnesses. A practical way to classify test harness design patterns is to consider the type of test case data storage and the type of test-run processing. The three fundamental types of test case data storage are flat, hierarchical, and relational. For example, a plain-text file is usually flat storage; an XML file is typically hierarchical; and SQL data is often relational. The two fundamental types of test-run processing are streaming and buffered. Streaming processing involves processing one test case at a time; buffered processing processes a collection of test cases at a time. This categorization leads to six fundamental test harness design patterns:

- Flat test case data, streaming processing model

- Flat test case data, buffered processing model

- Hierarchical test case data, streaming processing model

- Hierarchical test case data, buffered processing model

- Relational test case data, streaming processing model

- Relational test case data, buffered processing model

Of course, there are many other ways to categorize, but thinking about test harness design in this way has proven to be effective in practice. Now, suppose you are developing a poker game application as shown in Figure 4-1.

Figure 4-1. *Poker Game AUT*

Let's assume that the poker application references a PokerLib.dll library that houses classes to create and manipulate various poker objects. In particular, a Hand() constructor accepts a string argument such as "Ah Kh Qh Jh Th" (ace of hearts through ten of hearts), and a Hand.GetHandType() method returns an enumerated type with a string representation such as "RoyalFlush". As described in Chapter 1, you need to thoroughly test the methods in the PokerLib.dll library. This chapter demonstrates how to test the poker library using each of the six fundamental test harness design patterns and explains the advantages and disadvantages of each pattern. For example, Section 4.3 uses this hierarchical test case data:

```xml
<?xml version="1.0" ?>
<testcases>
  <case id="0001">
    <input>Ac Ad Ah As Tc</input>
    <expected>FourOfAKindAces</expected>
  </case>
  <case id="0002">
    <input>4s 5s 6s 7s 3s</input>
    <expected>StraightSevenHigh</expected>
  </case>
  <case id="0003">
    <input>5d 5c Qh 5s Qd</input>
    <expected>FullHouseFivesOverQueens</expected>
  </case>
</testcases>
```

and uses a streaming processing model to produce this result:

```xml
<?xml version="1.0" encoding="utf-8"?>
<TestResults>
  <case id="0001">
    <result>Pass</result>
  </case>
  <case id="0002">
    <input>4s 5s 6s 7s 3s</input>
    <expected>StraightSevenHigh</expected>
    <actual>StraightFlushSevenHigh</actual>
    <result>*FAIL*</result>
  </case>
  <case id="0003">
    <result>Pass</result>
  </case>
</TestResults>
```

Although the techniques in this chapter demonstrate the six fundamental design patterns by testing a .NET class library, the patterns are general and apply to testing any type of software component.

The streaming processing model, expressed in pseudo-code, is

```
loop
  read a single test case from external store
  parse test case data into input(s) and expected(s)
  call component under test
  determine test case result
  save test case result to external store
end loop
```

The buffered processing model, expressed in pseudo-code, is

```
loop // 1. read all test cases
  read a single test case from external store into memory
end loop

loop // 2. run all test cases
  read a single test case from in-memory store
  parse test case data into input(s) and expected(s)
  call component under test
  determine test case result
  store test case result to in-memory store
end loop

loop // 3. save all results
  save test case result from in-memory store to external store
end loop
```

The streaming processing model is simpler than the buffered model, so it is often your best choice. However, in two common scenarios, you should consider using the buffered processing model. First, if the aspect in the system under test (SUT) involves file input/output, you often want to minimize test harness file operations. This is especially true if you are monitoring performance. Second, if you need to perform any preprocessing of your test case input (for example, pulling in and filtering test case data from more than one data store) or postprocessing of your test case results (for example, aggregating various test case category results), it's almost always more convenient to have data in memory where you can process it.

4.1 Creating a Text File Data, Streaming Model Test Harness

Problem

You want to create a test harness that uses text file test case data and a streaming processing model.

Design

In one continuous processing loop, use a StreamReader object to read a test case data into memory, then parse the test case data into input and expected values using the String.Split() method, and call the component under test (CUT). Next, check the actual result with the expected result to determine a test case pass or fail. Then, write the results to external storage with a StreamWriter object. Do this for each test case.

Solution

Begin by creating a tagged and end-of-file delimited test case file:

```
[id]=0001
[input]=Ac Ad Ah As Tc
[expected]=FourOfAKindAces

[id]=0002
[input]=4s 5s 6s 7s 3s
[expected]=StraightSevenHigh

[id]=0003
[input]=5d 5c Qh 5s Qd
[expected]=FullHouseFivesOverQueens

*

```

Then process using `StreamReader` and `StreamWriter` objects:

```
Console.WriteLine("\nBegin Text File Streaming model test run\n");

FileStream ifs = new FileStream("..\\..\\..\\TestCases.txt",
                                FileMode.Open);
StreamReader sr = new StreamReader(ifs);
FileStream ofs = new FileStream("TextFileStreamingResults.txt",
                                FileMode.Create);
StreamWriter sw = new StreamWriter(ofs);

string id, input, expected, blank, actual;

while (sr.Peek() != '*')
{
  id = sr.ReadLine().Split('=')[1];
  input = sr.ReadLine().Split('=')[1];
  expected = sr.ReadLine().Split('=')[1];
  blank = sr.ReadLine();

  string[] cards = input.Split(' ');
  Hand h = new Hand(cards[0], cards[1], cards[2], cards[3], cards[4]);
  actual = h.GetHandType().ToString();

  sw.WriteLine("====================");
  sw.WriteLine("ID       = " + id);
  sw.WriteLine("Input    = " + input);
  sw.WriteLine("Expected = " + expected);
  sw.WriteLine("Actual   = " + actual);
```

```
  if (actual == expected)
    sw.WriteLine("Pass");
  else
    sw.WriteLine("*FAIL*");
}
sw.WriteLine("====================");

sr.Close(); ifs.Close();
sw.Close(); ofs.Close();

Console.WriteLine("\nDone");
```

Comments

You begin by creating a test case data file. As shown in the techniques in Chapter 1, you could structure the file with each test case on one line:

```
0001:Ac Ad Ah As Tc:FourOfAKindAces
0002:4s 5s 6s 7s 3s:StraightSevenHigh:deliberate error
0003:5d 5c Qh 5s Qd:FullHouseFivesOverQueens
```

When using this approach, notice that the meaning of each part of the test case data is implied (the first item is the case ID, the second is the input, and the third is the expected result). A more flexible solution is to provide some structure to your test case data by adding tags such as "[id]" and "[input]". This allows you to easily perform rudimentary validity checks. For example:

```
string temp = sr.ReadLine(); // should be the ID
if (temp.StartsWith("[id]"))
  id = temp.Split('=')[1];
else
  throw new Exception("Invalid test case line");
```

You can perform validity checks on your test case data via a separate program that you run before you run the test harness, or you can perform validity checks inside the test harness itself. In addition to validity checks, structure tags also allow you to deal with test case data that has a variable number of inputs.

This technique assumes that you have added a project reference to the PokerLib.dll library under test and that you have supplied appropriate using statements so you don't have to fully qualify classes and objects:

```
using System;
using PokerLib;
using System.IO;
```

You should also always wrap your test harness code in try-catch-finally blocks:

```
static void Main(string[] args)
{
  // Open any files here
  try
  {
    // main harness code here
  }
  catch(Exception ex)
  {
    Console.WriteLine("Fatal error: " + ex.Message);
  }
  finally
  {
    // Close any open streams here
  }

} // Main()
```

When the code in this section is run with the preceding test case input data, the output is

```
====================
ID        = 0001
Input     = Ac Ad Ah As Tc
Expected = FourOfAKindAces
Actual    = FourOfAKindAces
Pass
====================
ID        = 0002
Input     = 4s 5s 6s 7s 3s
Expected = StraightSevenHigh
Actual    = StraightFlushSevenHigh
*FAIL*
====================
ID        = 0003
Input     = 5d 5c Qh 5s Qd
Expected = FullHouseFivesOverQueens
Actual    = FullHouseFivesOverQueens
Pass
====================
```

Test case #0002 is an intentional failure. Using a special character token in the test case data file to signal end-of-file is an old but effective technique. With such a token in place, you can use the StreamReader.Peek() method to check the next input character without actually consuming it from the associated stream.

To create meaningful test cases, you must understand how the SUT works. This can be difficult. Techniques to discover information about the SUT are discussed in Section 4.8. This solution represents a minimal test harness. You can extend the harness, for example, by adding summary counters of the number of test cases that pass and the number that fail by using the techniques in Chapter 1.

4.2 Creating a Text File Data, Buffered Model Test Harness

Problem

You want to create a test harness that uses text file test case data and a buffered processing model.

Design

Read all test case data into an ArrayList collection that holds lightweight TestCase objects. Then iterate through the test cases ArrayList object, executing each test case and storing the results into a second ArrayList object that holds lightweight TestCaseResult objects. Finally, iterate through the results ArrayList object, saving the results to an external text file.

Solution

Begin by creating lightweight TestCase and TestCaseResult classes:

```
class TestCase
{
  public string id;
  public string input;
  public string expected;

  public TestCase(string id, string input, string expected)
  {
    this.id = id;
    this.input = input;
    this.expected = expected;
  }
} // class TestCase

class TestCaseResult
{
  public string id;
  public string input;
  public string expected;
  public string actual;
  public string result;
```

```
  public TestCaseResult(string id, string input, string expected,
                          string actual, string result)
  {
    this.id = id;
    this.input = input;
    this.expected = expected;
    this.actual = actual;
    this.result = result;
  }
} // class TestCaseResult
```

Notice these class definitions use `public` data fields for simplicity. A reasonable alternative is to use a C# struct type instead of a `class` type. The data fields for the `TestCase` class should match the test case input data. The data fields for the `TestCaseResult` class should generally contain most of the fields in the `TestCase` class, the fields for the actual result of calling the CUT, and the test case pass or fail result. Because of this, a design option for you to consider is placing a reference to a `TestCase` object in the definition of the `TestCaseResult` class. For example:

```
class TestCaseResult
{
  public TestCase tc;
  public string actual;
  public string result;

  public TestCaseResult(TestCase tc, string actual, string result)
  {
    this.tc = tc;
    this.actual = actual;
    this.result = result;
  }
} // class TestCaseResult
```

You may also want to include fields for the date and time when the test case was run. You process the test case data using three loop control structures and two `ArrayList` objects like this:

```
Console.WriteLine("\nBegin Text File Buffered model test run\n");

FileStream ifs = new FileStream("..\\..\\..\\TestCases.txt",
                               FileMode.Open);
StreamReader sr = new StreamReader(ifs);
FileStream ofs = new FileStream("TextFileBufferedResults.txt",
                               FileMode.Create);
StreamWriter sw = new StreamWriter(ofs);

string id, input, expected = "", blank, actual;
TestCase tc = null;
TestCaseResult r = null;
```

```
// 1. read all test case data into memory
ArrayList tcd = new ArrayList(); // test case data
while (sr.Peek() != '*')
{
  id = sr.ReadLine().Split('=')[1];
  input = sr.ReadLine().Split('=')[1];
  expected = sr.ReadLine().Split('=')[1];
  blank = sr.ReadLine();
  tc = new TestCase(id, input, expected);
  tcd.Add(tc);
}
sr.Close(); ifs.Close();

// 2. run all tests, store results to memory
ArrayList tcr = new ArrayList(); // test case result
for (int i = 0; i < tcd.Count; ++i)
{
  tc = (TestCase)tcd[i];
  string[] cards = tc.input.Split(' ');
  Hand h = new Hand(cards[0], cards[1], cards[2], cards[3], cards[4]);
  actual = h.GetHandType().ToString();

  if (actual == tc.expected)
    r = new TestCaseResult(tc.id, tc.input, tc.expected,
                           actual, "Pass");
  else
    r = new TestCaseResult(tc.id, tc.input, tc.expected,
                           actual, "*FAIL*");

  tcr.Add(r);
} // main processing loop

// 3. emit all results to external storage
for (int i = 0; i < tcr.Count; ++i)
{
  r = (TestCaseResult)tcr[i];
  sw.WriteLine("====================");
  sw.WriteLine("ID       = " + r.id);
  sw.WriteLine("Input    = " + r.input);
  sw.WriteLine("Expected = " + r.expected);
  sw.WriteLine("Actual   = " + r.actual);
  sw.WriteLine(r.result);
}
sw.WriteLine("====================");

sw.Close(); ofs.Close();

Console.WriteLine("\nDone");
```

Comments

The buffered processing model has three distinct phases. First, you read all test case data into memory. Although you can do this in many ways, experience has shown that your harness will be much easier to maintain if you create a very lightweight class for the test case data. Don't get carried away and try to make a universal test case class that can accommodate any kind of test case input, however, because you'll end up with a class that is so general it's too awkward to use effectively.

You have many choices of the kind of data structure to store your TestCase objects into. A System.Collections.ArrayList object is simple and effective. Because test case data is processed strictly sequentially in some situations, you may want to consider using a Stack or a Queue collection.

In the second phase of the buffered processing model, you iterate through each test case in the ArrayList object that holds TestCase objects. After retrieving the current TestCase object, you execute the test and determine a result. Then you instantiate a new TestCaseResult object and add it to the ArrayList that holds TestCaseResult objects. Although it's not a major issue, you do need to take some care to avoid confusing your objects. Notice that you'll have two ArrayList objects, a TestCase object and a TestCaseResult object, both of which contain a test case ID, test case input, and expected result.

In the third phase of the buffered processing model, you iterate through each test case result in the result ArrayList object and write information to an external text file. Of course, you can also easily emit results to an XML file, SQL database, or other external storage. If you run this code with the test case data file from Section 4.1

```
[id]=0001
[input]=Ac Ad Ah As Tc
[expected]=FourOfAKindAces
etc.
```

you will get the identical output as in Section 4.1:

```
====================
ID       = 0001
Input    = Ac Ad Ah As Tc
Expected = FourOfAKindAces
Actual   = FourOfAKindAces
Pass
====================
etc.
```

You can modularize this technique by writing three helper methods that wrap the code in the section. With these helper methods, your harness might look like:

```
class Class1
{
  static void Main(string[] args)
  {
    ArrayList tcd = null; // test case data
    ArrayList tcr = null; // test case results
    tcd = ReadData("..\\TestCases.txt");
    tcr = RunTests(tcd);
    SaveResults(tcr, "..\\TestResults.txt");
  }
  static ArrayList ReadData(string file)
  {
    // code here
  }
  static ArrayList RunTests(ArrayList testdata)
  {
    // code here
  }
  static void SaveResults(ArayList results, string file)
  {
    // code here
  }
}
class TestCase
{
  // code here
}
class TestCaseResult
{
  // code here
}
```

4.3 Creating an XML File Data, Streaming Model Test Harness

Problem

You want to create a test harness that uses XML file test case data and a streaming processing model.

Design

In one continuous processing loop, use an `XmlTextReader` object to read a test case into memory, then parse the test case data into input and expected values using the `GetAttribute()` and `ReadElementString()` methods, and call the CUT. Next, check the actual result with the expected result to determine a test case pass or fail. Then, write the results to external storage using an XmlTextWriter object. Do this for each test case.

Solution

Begin by creating an XML test case file:

```
<?xml version="1.0" ?>
<testcases>
  <case id="0001">
    <input>Ac Ad Ah As Tc</input>
    <expected>FourOfAKindAces</expected>
  </case>
  <case id="0002">
    <input>4s 5s 6s 7s 3s</input>
    <expected>StraightSevenHigh</expected>
  </case>
  <case id="0003">
    <input>5d 5c Qh 5s Qd</input>
    <expected>FullHouseFivesOverQueens</expected>
  </case>
</testcases>
```

Then process the test case data using XmlTextReader and XmlTextWriter objects:

```
Console.WriteLine("\nBegin XML File Streaming model test run\n");

XmlTextReader xtr = new XmlTextReader("..\\..\\..\\TestCases.xml");
xtr.WhitespaceHandling = WhitespaceHandling.None;
XmlTextWriter xtw = new XmlTextWriter("XMLFileStreamingResults.xml",
                                  System.Text.Encoding.UTF8);
xtw.Formatting = Formatting.Indented;
string id, input, expected, actual;

xtw.WriteStartDocument();
xtw.WriteStartElement("TestResults"); // root node

while (!xtr.EOF) // main loop
{
  if (xtr.Name == "testcases" && !xtr.IsStartElement())
    break;

  while (xtr.Name != "case" || !xtr.IsStartElement())
    xtr.Read(); // go to a <case> element if not there yet
```

```
  id = xtr.GetAttribute("id");
  xtr.Read(); // advance to <input>
  input = xtr.ReadElementString("input"); // go to <expected>
  expected = xtr.ReadElementString("expected"); // go to </case>
  xtr.Read(); // go to next <case> or </testcases>

  string[] cards = input.Split(' ');
  Hand h = new Hand(cards[0], cards[1], cards[2], cards[3], cards[4]);
  actual = h.GetHandType().ToString();

  xtw.WriteStartElement("case");

  xtw.WriteStartAttribute("id", null);
  xtw.WriteString(id); xtw.WriteEndAttribute();

  xtw.WriteStartElement("input");
  xtw.WriteString(input); xtw.WriteEndElement();

  xtw.WriteStartElement("expected");
  xtw.WriteString(expected); xtw.WriteEndElement();

  xtw.WriteStartElement("actual");
  xtw.WriteString(actual); xtw.WriteEndElement();

  xtw.WriteStartElement("result");
  if (actual == expected)
    xtw.WriteString("Pass");
  else
    xtw.WriteString("*FAIL*");
  xtw.WriteEndElement(); // </result>

  xtw.WriteEndElement(); // </case>
} // main loop

xtw.WriteEndElement(); // </TestResults>
xtr.Close();
xtw.Close();

Console.WriteLine("\nDone");
```

The XmlTextReader.Read() method advances one XML node at a time through the XML file. Because XML is hierarchical, keeping track of exactly where you are within the file is a bit tricky. To write results, you use an XmlTextWriter object with the WriteStartElement(), the WriteString(), and the WriteEndElement() methods, along with the WriteStartAttribute() and WriteEndAttribute() methods.

Comments

The use of XML for test case storage has become very common. The key to understanding this technique is to understand the `Read()` and `ReadElementString()` methods of the `System.Xml.XmlTextReader` class. To an `XmlTextReader` object, an XML file is a sequence of nodes. For example, if you do not count whitespace, the XML file

```
<?xml version="1.0" ?>
<foo att="x">
  <bar>99</bar>
</foo>
```

has six nodes: the XML declaration, `<foo>`, `<bar>`, 99, `</bar>`, and `</foo>`. This means that the statement

```
xtr.WhitespaceHandling = WhitespaceHandling.None;
```

in your harness is critical because without it you would have to keep track of blank lines, tab characters, end-of-line sequences, and so on. The `Read()` method advances one node at a time. Unlike many `Read()` methods in other classes, the `XmlTextReader.Read()` method does not return significant data. The `ReadElementString()` method, on the other hand, returns the data between begin and end tags of its argument and advances to the next node after the end tag. Because XML attributes are not nodes, you have to extract attribute data using the `GetAttribute()` method.

When run with the preceding test case data, this code produces the following as output:

```
<?xml version="1.0" encoding="utf-8"?>
<TestResults>
  <case id="0001">
    <input>Ac Ad Ah As Tc</input>
    <expected>FourOfAKindAces</expected>
    <actual>FourOfAKindAces</actual>
    <result>Pass</result>
  </case>
  <case id="0002">
    <input>4s 5s 6s 7s 3s</input>
    <expected>StraightSevenHigh</expected>
    <actual>StraightFlushSevenHigh</actual>
    <result>*FAIL*</result>
  </case>
  <case id="0003">
    <input>5d 5c Qh 5s Qd</input>
    <expected>FullHouseFivesOverQueens</expected>
    <actual>FullHouseFivesOverQueens</actual>
    <result>Pass</result>
  </case>
</TestResults>
```

Because XML is so flexible, you can use many alternative structures. For example, you can store all data as attributes:

```
<?xml version="1.0" ?>
<testcases>
 <case id="0001" input="Ac Ad Ah As Tc" expected="FourOfAKindAces"/>
 <case id="0002" input="4s 5s 6s 7s 3s" expected="StraightSevenHigh"/>
 etc.
</testcases>
```

This flexibility characteristic of XML is both a strength and a weakness. From a lightweight test automation point of view, the main disadvantage of XML is that you have to slightly modify your test harness code for every XML test case data structure.

Processing an XML test case file with this loop structure:

```
while (!xtr.EOF) // main loop
{
  if (xtr.Name == "testcases" && !xtr.IsStartElement()) break;

  // process file here
}
```

may look a bit odd at first glance. The loop exits on end-of-file or when at the </testcases> tag. But this structure is more readable than alternatives. When marching through the XML file, you can either Read() your way one node at a time or get a bit more sophisticated with code such as:

```
while (xtr.Name != "testcase" || !xtr.IsStartElement() )
  xtr.Read(); // advance to <testcase> tag
```

The choice of technique you use is purely a matter of style. Writing an XML element with XmlTextWriter tends to be a bit wordy but is straightforward. For example:

```
xtw.WriteStartElement("alpha");
xtw.WriteStartElement("beta");

xtw.WriteString("b");

xtw.WriteEndElement(); // writes </beta>
xtw.WriteEndElement(); // writes </alpha>
```

would create

```
<alpha>
  <beta>b</beta>
</alpha>
```

Notice that the WriteEndElement() method does not accept an argument; the end element written is kept on an internal stack structure and popped off the stack.

Writing an XML attribute follows a pattern similar to writing an element. For example:

```
xtw.WriteStartElement("alpha");
xtw.WriteStartAttribute("beta", null);
xtw.WriteString("b");
xtw.WriteEndAttribute();
xtw.WriteEndElement();
```

produces as output:

```
<alpha beta="b" />
```

4.4 Creating an XML File Data, Buffered Model Test Harness

Problem

You want to create a test harness that uses XML file test case data and a buffered processing model.

Design

To create a harness structure that uses a buffered processing model with XML test case data, you follow the same pattern as in Section 4.2 combined with the XML reading and writing techniques demonstrated in Section 4.3. You read all test case data into an ArrayList collection that holds lightweight TestCase objects, iterate through that ArrayList object, execute each test case, store the results into a second ArrayList object that holds lightweight TestCaseResult objects, and finally save the results to an external XML file.

Solution

With lightweight TestCase and TestCaseResult classes in place (see Section 4.2), you can write:

```
Console.WriteLine("\nBegin XML File Buffered model test run\n");

XmlTextReader xtr = new XmlTextReader("..\\..\\..\\TestCases.xml");
xtr.WhitespaceHandling = WhitespaceHandling.None;
XmlTextWriter xtw = new XmlTextWriter("XMLFileStreamingResults.xml",
                                 System.Text.Encoding.UTF8);
xtw.Formatting = Formatting.Indented;

string id, input, expected, actual;
TestCase tc = null;
TestCaseResult r = null;
```

```
// 1. read all test case data into memory
ArrayList tcd = new ArrayList();
while (!xtr.EOF) // main loop
{
  if (xtr.Name == "testcases" && !xtr.IsStartElement()) break;

  while (xtr.Name != "case" || !xtr.IsStartElement())
    xtr.Read(); // advance to a <case> element if not there yet

  id = xtr.GetAttribute("id");
  xtr.Read(); // advance to <input>
  input = xtr.ReadElementString("input"); // advance to <expected>
  expected = xtr.ReadElementString("expected"); // advance to </case>
  tc = new TestCase(id, input, expected);
  tcd.Add(tc);

  xtr.Read(); // advance to next <case> or </TestResults>
}
xtr.Close();

// 2. run all tests, store results to memory
ArrayList tcr = new ArrayList();
for (int i = 0; i < tcd.Count; ++i)
{
  tc = (TestCase)tcd[i];
  string[] cards = tc.input.Split(' ');
  Hand h = new Hand(cards[0], cards[1], cards[2], cards[3], cards[4]);
  actual = h.GetHandType().ToString();

  if (actual == tc.expected)
    r = new TestCaseResult(tc.id, tc.input, tc.expected, actual, "Pass");
  else
    r = new TestCaseResult(tc.id, tc.input, tc.expected, actual, "*FAIL*");

  tcr.Add(r);
} // main processing loop

// 3. emit all results to external storage
xtw.WriteStartDocument();
xtw.WriteStartElement("TestResults"); // root node

for (int i = 0; i < tcr.Count; ++i)
{
  r = (TestCaseResult)tcr[i];
  xtw.WriteStartElement("case");

  xtw.WriteStartAttribute("id", null);
  xtw.WriteString(r.id); xtw.WriteEndAttribute();
```

```
xtw.WriteStartElement("input");
xtw.WriteString(r.input); xtw.WriteEndElement();

xtw.WriteStartElement("expected");
xtw.WriteString(r.expected); xtw.WriteEndElement();

xtw.WriteStartElement("actual"); xtw.WriteString(r.actual);
xtw.WriteEndElement();

xtw.WriteStartElement("result");
xtw.WriteString(r.result); xtw.WriteEndElement();

xtw.WriteEndElement(); // </case>
}
xtw.WriteEndElement(); // </TestResults>

xtw.Close();

Console.WriteLine("\nEnd test run\n");
```

Comments

All the pertinent details to this technique are discussed in Sections 4.2 (buffered processing models) and 4.3 (reading and writing XML). If this code is run using the XML test case data file from Section 4.3:

```
<?xml version="1.0" ?>
<testcases>
  <case id="0001">
    <input>Ac Ad Ah As Tc</input>
    <expected>FourOfAKindAces</expected>
  </case>
  etc.
</testcases>
```

the output will be identical to that produced by the technique code in Section 4.3:

```
<?xml version="1.0" encoding="utf-8"?>
<TestResults>
  <case id="0001">
    <input>Ac Ad Ah As Tc</input>
    <expected>FourOfAKindAces</expected>
    <actual>FourOfAKindAces</actual>
    <result>Pass</result>
  </case>
  etc.
</TestResults>
```

Notice that this technique is starting to get a bit messy, mostly due to the large number of statements required to read and write XML. This makes it an excellent candidate for modularization by wrapping the code to read data, run tests, and save data into three helper methods. Furthermore, because the technique uses helper classes TestCase and TestCaseResult, recasting this solution to an OOP design is an attractive option. Such a design could take many forms, but here is one possibility:

```
class XMLBufferedHarness
{
    private ArrayList tcd = null; // test case data
    private ArrayList tcr = null; // test case results
    private XmlTextReader xtr = null;
    private XmlTextWriter xtw = null;

    public XMLBufferedHarness(string datafile, string resultfile)
    {
      // initialize tcd, tcr, xtr, xtw here
    }

    public void ReadData()
    {
      // use xtr to read datafile into tcd here
    }

    public void RunTests()
    {
      // run tests, store results to tcr here
    }

    public void SaveResults()
    {
      // save results to resultfile here
    }

    class TestCase
    {
      // see Section 4.2
    }

    class TestCaseResult
    {
      // see Section 4.2
    }

}
```

With this class in place, you can write very clean harness code like this:

```
static void Main(string[] args)
{
  string data = "TestCases.xml";
  string result = "TestResults.xml";
  XMLBufferedHarness h = new XMLBufferedHarness(data, result);
  h.ReadData();
  h.RunTests();
  h.SaveResults();
} // Main()
```

This approach has the advantage of being more modular than a non-OOP approach. However, the methods are very specific to a particular test scenario, meaning you'd have to significantly rewrite the methods for each CUT and associated XML test case file.

This technique uses an XmlTextReader object to iterate through the XML test case data file and store test case data into memory. You have two significant alternatives: the XmlSerializer class and the XmlDocument class. The techniques to use these classes to read and parse test case data into memory are explained in Chapter 12.

4.5 Creating a SQL Database for Lightweight Test Automation Storage

Problem

You want to create a SQL database for a lightweight test automation harness.

Design

Write a lightweight T-SQL script and run it using the Query Analyzer or the osql.exe programs.

Solution

```
-- makeDbTestPoker.sql
use master
go

if exists (select * from sysdatabases where name='dbTestPoker')
 drop database dbTestPoker
go

create database dbTestPoker
go

use dbTestPoker
go
```

```
create table tblTestCases
(
caseid char(4) primary key,
input char(14) not null,
expected varchar(35) not null,
)
go

insert into tblTestCases
 values('0001','Ac Ad Ah As Tc','FourOfAKindAces')
insert into tblTestCases
 values('0002','4s 5s 6s 7s 3s','StraightSevenHigh')
insert into tblTestCases
 values('0003','5d 5c Qh 5s Qd','FullHouseFivesOverQueens')
go

create table tblTestResults
(
resultid int identity(1,1) primary key,
caseid char(4) not null,
input char(14) not null,
expected varchar(35) not null,
actual varchar(35) not null,
result char(4) not null,
runat datetime not null
)
go
```

Comments

An alternative to using text files or XML files for your test case storage is to use a SQL database. SQL is particularly appropriate when you have many test cases (making the use of huge text files awkward) or when your SUT has a long development cycle (making management of many test case result files awkward).

To run a SQL script, you can paste the code into the Query Analyzer program that ships with Microsoft SQL Server, and execute it directly. An alternative is to run the script using the osql.exe command-line program, which also ships with SQL Server. If the preceding script is saved as makeDbTestPoker.sql, you can run it like this:

```
>osql -S(local) -E -i makeDbTestPoker.sql
```

The -S switch specifies the name of the SQL Server machine. The -E switch means to use a *trusted connection* (explained later in this section). The -i switch specifies the name of the SQL script to run.

The preceding script starts by setting the current database context to the "master" database, which is necessary to create or drop a database. Next, you check to see if the database dbTestPoker already exists by querying the sysdatabases system database. If dbTestPoker exists, then you drop it. Dropping a SQL database is surprisingly easy, so when using SQL for test automation, be sure to back up your databases often. After creating database `dbTestPoker`, you switch context to that database. A common mistake is to forget to switch context, when all subsequent SQL commands will be directed at the master database. Next, you create a SQL table to hold test case data. The `primary key` argument to the `caseid` column means that each `caseid` value must be unique. The `not null` arguments mean that each test case must have an input and expected value. After creating the test case data table, you use the T-SQL `insert` command to populate the table. The last step is to create a table to hold test case results. Because each test run adds additional test results to the table, you usually want to include a column that holds the date and time when the test case result was added to the SQL database:

```
runat datetime not null
```

This technique creates a single database with a single test results table. An alternative approach is to create a new table for each test harness run. As a general rule, however, placing all harness run results into a single table is better than creating multiple tables—one table with thousands of rows of data is easier to manage than thousands of tables with any number of rows of data. If you do plan to put all test results into a single table, then you should create a column that uniquely identifies the test case result. The simplest way to do this is by adding an identity column to your test case data table definition:

```
resultid int identity(1,1) primary key
```

The `identity(1,1)` modifier instructs SQL Server to automatically generate an integer value for the `resultid` column, starting with value 1, and increasing by 1 on each insert operation.

The technique in this section assumes that your test harness will be using a trusted connection. SQL Server requires a default Windows Authentication mode, which means in essence to integrate Windows security with SQL. This mode is the one used by a trusted connection. But SQL Server also supports an optional, additional SQL Authentication mode that can be used to gain access to SQL databases. The interaction between Windows Authentication and SQL Authentication modes can be tricky and is outside the scope of this book.

4.6 Creating a SQL Data, Streaming Model Test Harness

Problem

You want to create a test harness that uses SQL test case data and a streaming processing model.

Design

In one continuous processing loop, use a `SqlDataReader` object from the `System.Data.SqlClient` namespace to read a test case into memory from SQL, then parse the test case data into input and expected values using the `GetString()` method, and call the CUT. Next, check the actual result with the expected result to determine a test case pass or fail. Write the results to external storage using a `SqlCommand` object with a SQL `insert` statement as an argument. Do this for each test case. This technique assumes you have previously prepared a SQL database with test case data and a table to hold test results. See Section 4.5 for details.

Solution

```
using System.Data.SqlClient;
Console.WriteLine("\nBegin SQL Streaming model test run\n");

SqlConnection isc = new SqlConnection("Server=(local);
  Database=dbTestPoker;Trusted_Connection=yes");
SqlConnection osc = new SqlConnection("Server=(local);
  Database=dbTestPoker;Trusted_Connection=yes");

SqlCommand scSelect = new SqlCommand("SELECT * FROM tblTestCases", isc);
isc.Open();
osc.Open();
SqlDataReader sdr;
sdr = scSelect.ExecuteReader();
string caseid, input, expected, actual, result;

while (sdr.Read()) // main loop
{
  caseid = sdr.GetString(0); // parse input
  input = sdr.GetString(1);
  expected = sdr.GetString(2);
  string[] cards = input.Split(' ');

  Hand h = new Hand(cards[0], cards[1], cards[2], cards[3], cards[4]);
  actual = h.GetHandType().ToString();

  if (actual == expected) // emit results
    result = "Pass";
  else
    result = "FAIL";

  string runat = DateTime.Now.ToString("s");
  string insert = "INSERT INTO tblTestResults
    VALUES('" + caseid + "','" + input + "','" + expected +
            "','" + actual + "','" + result + "','" + runat + "')";
  SqlCommand scInsert = new SqlCommand(insert, osc);
  scInsert.ExecuteNonQuery();
} // while

sdr.Close();
isc.Close();
osc.Close();

Console.WriteLine("\nEnd test run\n");
```

Comments

Although there are several ways to iterate through a SQL table, the simplest is to use the SqlDataReader class. A SqlDataReader object gives you a way of reading a forward-only stream of rows from a SQL Server database. Notice that to create a SqlDataReader object, you use a factory mechanism by calling the ExecuteReader() method of the SqlCommand object, rather than directly by using a constructor and the new keyword. You also must prepare the SqlCommand object by passing in a T-SQL select statement to the SqlCommand constructor, so that the resulting SqlDataReader object knows how to traverse through the rows of its associated table.

If the code in this section is run with the input data from Section 4.5:

```
insert into tblTestCases
 values('0001','Ac Ad Ah As Tc','FourOfAKindAces')
insert into tblTestCases
 values('0002','4s 5s 6s 7s 3s','StraightSevenHigh')
insert into tblTestCases
 values('0003','5d 5c Qh 5s Qd','FullHouseFivesOverQueens')
```

then table tblTestResults in database dbTestPoker will hold this result data:

resultid	caseid	input	expected
1	0001	Ac Ad Ah As Tc	FourOfAKindAces
2	0002	4s 5s 6s 7s 3s	StraightSevenHigh
3	0003	5d 5c Qh 5s Qd	FullHouseFivesOverQueens

actual	result	runat
FourOfAKindAces	Pass	2006-06-15 07:50:20.000
StraightFlushSevenHigh	FAIL	2006-06-15 07:50:20.000
FullHouseFivesOverQueens	Pass	2006-06-15 07:50:20.000

The values in the runat column will be the date and time when the results were inserted into the SQL table.

You use the SqlDataReader.GetString() method to extract each column value as a string. The GetString() method accepts a zero-based column index rather than a column name as a string as you might expect. So you must write caseid = sdr.GetString(0); rather than caseid = sdr.GetString("caseid"); which would be more readable.

If you insert all test case results into one SQL table rather than creating a new table to hold the results of each test run, you usually should time-stamp the result. A simple way to do this is to fetch the current system date and time:

```
string runat = DateTime.Now.ToString("s");
```

The "s" argument will format the DateTime object into a sortable pattern such as:

```
'2006-09-20T11:46:41.000'
```

SQL Server understands this format, and a C# string variable in this format is converted into a SQL `datetime` data type automatically when you insert it into a `datetime` column.

The technique used in this solution to insert a row of data into the SQL test results table is rather ugly. If you were inserting literals into the results table, code might look like this:

```
string insert = "INSERT INTO tblTestResults
 VALUES('0001', 'Ac Ad Ah As Kc', 'FourOfAKindAces',
        'FourOfAKindAces', 'Pass', '2006-09-20 11:46:41.000')";
```

But because you are inserting values stored in variables, you have to build up a fairly complex insert string like this:

```
string insert = "INSERT INTO tblTestResults VALUES('" + caseid +
 "','" + input + "','" + expected + "','" + actual + "','" + result +
 "','" + runat + "')";
```

Creating such SQL strings can be an error-prone process, so you must be careful when coding them. An alternative to writing such long strings is to create a SQL stored procedure and then call it from your harness. For example, if your SQL database creation script contains this user stored procedure T-SQL code:

```
create procedure usp_insert
@caseid char(4),
@input char(14),
@expected varchar(35),
@actual varchar(35),
@result char(4),
@runat datetime

as

insert into tblTestResults
values(@caseid, @input, @expected, @actual, @result, @runat)

go
```

then you can prepare a `SqlCommand` object like this:

```
SqlConnection osc = new SqlConnection("Server=(local);
  Database=dbTestPoker; Trusted_Connection=yes");

SqlCommand sp = new SqlCommand("usp_insert", osc);
sp.CommandType = CommandType.StoredProcedure;

SqlParameter paramCaseID = sp.Parameters.Add("@caseid",
                                            SqlDbType.Char, 4);
SqlParameter paramInput = sp.Parameters.Add("@input",
                                            SqlDbType.Char, 14);
SqlParameter paramExpected = sp.Parameters.Add("@expected",
                                            SqlDbType.VarChar, 35);
```

```
SqlParameter paramActual = sp.Parameters.Add("@actual",
                                        SqlDbType.VarChar, 35);
SqlParameter paramResult = sp.Parameters.Add("@result",
                                        SqlDbType.Char, 4);
SqlParameter paramRunAt = sp.Parameters.Add("@runat",
                                        SqlDbType.DateTime);

osc.Open();
```

And then in the main processing loop, you can insert test case results in SQL like this:

```
// read caseid, input, expected from test case data here
// run test and get actual, result here
string runat = DateTime.Now.ToString("s");

paramCaseID.Value = caseid;
paramInput.Value = input;
paramExpected.Value = expected;
paramActual.Value = actual;
paramResult.Value = result;
paramRunAt.Value = runat;

sp.ExecuteNonQuery(); // insert using usp_insert
```

This technique has the advantage of reducing complexity by eliminating an ugly SQL insert command string, but has the disadvantage of increasing complexity by adding many more lines of code to your test harness.

4.7 Creating a SQL Data, Buffered Model Test Harness

Problem

You want to create a test harness that uses SQL test case data and a buffered processing model.

Design

To create a harness structure that uses a buffered processing model with SQL test case data, you follow the same pattern as in Section 4.2 combined with the SQL reading and writing techniques demonstrated in Section 4.6. You use a SqlDataReader object to read all test case data into an ArrayList collection that holds lightweight TestCase objects. Next, you iterate through that ArrayList object, execute each test case, and store the results into a second ArrayList object that holds lightweight TestCaseResult objects. Then you save the results to an external SQL database.

Solution

With lightweight TestCase and TestCaseResult classes in place (see Section 4.2), you can write:

```
Console.WriteLine("\nBegin SQL Buffered model test run\n");

SqlConnection isc = new SqlConnection("Server=(local);
  Database=dbTestPoker; Trusted_Connection=yes");
SqlConnection osc = new SqlConnection("Server=(local);
  Database=dbTestPoker;Trusted_Connection=yes");
isc.Open();
osc.Open();

SqlCommand scSelect = new SqlCommand("SELECT * FROM tblTestCases", isc);
SqlDataReader sdr = scSelect.ExecuteReader();

string caseid, input, expected = "", actual;
TestCase tc = null; // see Section 4.2
TestCaseResult r = null;

// 1. read all test case data into memory
ArrayList tcd = new ArrayList();
while (sdr.Read()) // main loop
{
  caseid = sdr.GetString(0);
  input = sdr.GetString(1);
  expected = sdr.GetString(2);
  tc = new TestCase(caseid, input, expected);
  tcd.Add(tc);
}
isc.Close();

// 2. run all tests, store results to memory
ArrayList tcr = new ArrayList();
for (int i = 0; i < tcd.Count; ++i)
{
  tc = (TestCase)tcd[i];
  string[] cards = tc.input.Split(' ');
  Hand h = new Hand(cards[0], cards[1], cards[2], cards[3], cards[4]);
  actual = h.GetHandType().ToString();

if (actual == tc.expected)
  r = new TestCaseResult(tc.id, tc.input, tc.expected, actual, "Pass");
else
  r = new TestCaseResult(tc.id, tc.input, tc.expected, actual, "FAIL");

tcr.Add(r);
} // main processing loop
```

```
// 3. emit all results to external SQL storage
for (int i = 0; i < tcr.Count; ++i)
{
  r = (TestCaseResult)tcr[i];
  string runat = DateTime.Now.ToString("s");
  string insert = "INSERT INTO tblTestResults
    VALUES('" + r.id + "','" + r.input + "','" + r.expected +
           "','" + r.actual + "','" + r.result + "','" + runat + "')";
SqlCommand scInsert = new SqlCommand(insert, osc);
scInsert.ExecuteNonQuery();
}
osc.Close();

Console.WriteLine("\nDone");
```

Comments

All the pertinent details to this technique are discussed in Sections 4.2 and 4.4 (buffered processing models), and Section 4.6 (reading and writing SQL). If the following code is run using the SQL test case data file from Section 4.5:

```
insert into tblTestCases
 values('0001','Ac Ad Ah As Tc','FourOfAKindAces')
insert into tblTestCases
 values('0002','4s 5s 6s 7s 3s','StraightSevenHigh')
insert into tblTestCases
 values('0003','5d 5c Qh 5s Qd','FullHouseFivesOverQueens')
```

then the output will be identical to that produced by the technique in Section 4.6:

```
resultid  caseid  input            expected
====================================================================
1         0001    Ac Ad Ah As Tc   FourOfAKindAces
2         0002    4s 5s 6s 7s 3s   StraightSevenHigh
3         0003    5d 5c Qh 5s Qd   FullHouseFivesOverQueens


          actual                 result  runat
====================================================================
          FourOfAKindAces        Pass    2006-06-15 07:50:20.000
          StraightFlushSevenHigh FAIL    2006-06-15 07:50:20.000
          FullHouseFivesOverQueens Pass  2006-06-15 07:50:20.000
```

Using a buffered test automation-processing model makes it easy for you to perform test case data filtering or test case results filtering. For example, suppose you want to filter your test cases so that only certain suites of tests are run rather than all your tests. *Test suite* means a collection of test cases, usually a subset of a larger set of tests. Following are examples of common test suite categorizations:

- Developer Regression Tests (DRTs): A set of tests run on some new code (typically a set of classes or methods) before a developer checks in the code to the main build system. Designed to verify that the new code has not broken existing functionality.

- Build Verification Tests (BVTs): A set of tests run on a new build of the SUT immediately after the build process. Designed to verify that the new build has minimal functionality and can be released to the test team for further testing.

- Daily Test Runs (DTRs): A set of tests run by the test team every day. Designed to verify that previous functionality is still correct, uncover new functionality and performance bugs, and so on.

- Weekly Test Runs (WTRs): A set of tests that is more extensive than Daily Test Run test cases but only run once a week due primarily to time constraints.

- Milestone Test Runs (MTRs): A comprehensive set of tests run before the release of a major or minor milestone. May require several days to run.

- Full Test Pass (FTP): Running every test case available. Typically requires several days to run.

Of course, there are many variations on these categories of test suites, but the general principle is that you'll have many test cases and you'll run various subsets of test cases at different times. This holds true whether you are working in a traditional spiral software development methodology environment or in any of a number of currently fashionable methodologies, such as test-driven development, extreme programming, agile development, and so on.

4.8 Discovering Information About the SUT

Problem

You want to discover information about the SUT so that you can create meaningful test cases.

Solution

One of the greatest challenges of software testing in almost any environment is discovering the essential information about the SUT (SUT) so that you can test it meaningfully. There are six primary ways to perform system discovery in a .NET environment:

- Read traditional specification documents.

- Examine SUT source code.

- Write experimental stub programs.

- Use XML auto-documentation.

- Examine .NET intermediate language code.

- Use reflection techniques.

Comments

In a very small production environment where developers test their own code, system discovery may not be an issue. As the size of a development effort increases, however, the discovery process becomes more difficult. The most common approach is for you to read traditional written specification documents that describe the SUT. In theory at least, every system has a set of documents, usually written by senior developers, managers, or architects, that completely and precisely describes the SUT. In reality, of course, such specification documents are often out-of-date, incomplete, or even nonexistent. Regardless, examining traditional specification documents is an important way to determine how to create meaningful test cases.

You can examine the source code of the SUT to gain insights on how to test your system, although in some cases, this may not be possible for security or legal reasons. Even when source code examination is possible, reviewing the source code for a complex SUT can be enormously time consuming. When you have access to system source code while developing test cases, the situation is sometimes called *white box* or *clear box* testing. When you do not have access to source code, the situation is sometimes called *black box* testing. When you have partial access to system source code, for example, the signatures of methods but not the body of the method, the situation is sometimes called *gray box* testing. These labels are some of the most overused but least-useful terms in software testing. However, the principles behind these labels are important. You cannot test every possible input to a system (see Chapter 10 for discussions of this idea), so the more you know about your SUT, the better your test cases will be. Although there has been much research in the area of automatic test case generation, currently test case development is still for the most part a human activity where experience and intuition play a big role.

A third discovery mechanism available to you is to experiment with the SUT by creating small stub programs. Again, this is not always possible for legal and security reasons and even when possible, it may not be a realistic technique: large software systems can be so complex that trying to understand them through experimentation just requires too much time. The development environment is often so dynamic that by the time you've figured a part of the system out, it has changed. This is not to say that experimentation is not important. On the contrary, initial experimentation with stub programs is usually the key first step when developing lightweight test automation.

The Visual Studio .NET IDE allows developers to add XML-based comments into their source code and have an XML-based document created automatically at project build time. In source code files, lines that begin with "///" and that precede user-defined items such as classes, delegates, interfaces, fields, events, properties, methods, or namespace declarations, can be processed as comments and placed in a file. There is a recommended set of tags. For example, the <param> tag is used to describe parameters. When used, the compiler verifies that the parameter exists and that all parameters are described in the documentation. This mechanism requires developers to expend extra effort, but the payoff is that system specs are always up to date.

Because .NET-compliant languages compile to an intermediate language, a terrific way to expose information about a SUT is to examine the SUT's intermediate language. The .NET environment provides developers and testers with a tool named ILDASM. The ILDASM tool parses .NET Framework .exe or .dll assemblies and shows the information in human-readable format. ILDASM also displays namespaces and types, including their interfaces. The use of ILDASM for system discovery is essential for any lightweight test automation situation.

The sixth primary way for you to discover information about the SUT is through the .NET reflection mechanism. Reflection means the process of programmatically obtaining information about .NET assemblies and the types defined within them. Using classes in the System.Reflection namespace, you can easily write short utility scripts that expose a wide range of data about the SUT. For example:

```
Console.WriteLine("\nBegin Reflection Discovery");
string assembly = "..\\..\\..\\LibUnderTest\\PokerLib.dll";
Assembly a = Assembly.LoadFrom(assembly);
Console.WriteLine("Assembly name = " + a.GetName());

Type[] tarr = a.GetTypes();
BindingFlags flags = BindingFlags.NonPublic | BindingFlags.Public |
                     BindingFlags.Static | BindingFlags.Instance;

foreach(Type t in tarr)
{
  Console.WriteLine(" Type name = " + t.Name);

  MemberInfo[] members = t.GetMembers(flags);
  foreach (MemberInfo mi in members) // fields, methods, ctors, etc.
  {
    if (mi.MemberType == MemberTypes.Field)
      Console.WriteLine("  (Field) member name = " + mi.Name);
  } // each member

  MethodInfo[] miarr = t.GetMethods(); // public only
  foreach (MethodInfo mi in miarr)
  {
    Console.WriteLine("  Method name = " + mi.Name);
    Console.WriteLine("   Return type = " + mi.ReturnType);
    ParameterInfo[] piarr = mi.GetParameters();
    foreach (ParameterInfo pi in piarr)
    {
      Console.WriteLine("   Parameter name = " + pi.Name);
      Console.WriteLine("   Parameter type = " + pi.ParameterType);
    }
  } // each method
} // each Type

Console.WriteLine("\nDone");
```

This example loads the PokerLib.dll assembly and then iterates through each type (classes, enumerations, interfaces, and so on) in the assembly. Then for each type, you iterate through each member (fields, methods, properties, constructors, and so on), printing some information if you hit a field. After iterating through the members, you iterate through each method, printing the method's name, return type, parameter names, and parameter types.

4.9 Example Program: PokerLibTest

This demonstration program combines several of the techniques in this chapter to create a lightweight test automation harness to test the PokerLib.dll library described in Section 4.1. The harness reads test case data from a SQL database, processes test cases using a buffered model, and emits test results to an XML file. If the test case input is

```
caseid  input           expected
======================================================
0001    Ac Ad Ah As Tc  FourOfAKindAces
0002    4s 5s 6s 7s 3s  StraightSevenHigh
0003    5d 5c Qh 5s Qd  FullHouseFivesOverQueens
```

then the resulting XML output (where the runat attribute will be the value of the date and time the harness executed) is

```xml
<?xml version="1.0" encoding="utf-8"?>
<TestResults>

  <case id="0001" runat="2006-10-28T12:41:36">
    <input>Ac Ad Ah As Tc</input>
    <expected>FourOfAKindAces</expected>
    <actual>FourOfAKindAces</actual>
    <result>Pass</result>
  </case>

  <case id="0002" runat="2006-10-28T12:41:36">
    <input>4s 5s 6s 7s 3s</input>
    <expected>StraightSevenHigh</expected>
    <actual>StraightFlushSevenHigh</actual>
    <result>FAIL</result>
  </case>

  <case id="0003" runat="2006-10-28T12:41:36">
    <input>5d 5c Qh 5s Qd</input>
    <expected>FullHouseFivesOverQueens</expected>
    <actual>FullHouseFivesOverQueens</actual>
    <result>Pass</result>
  </case>

</TestResults>
```

The complete lightweight test harness is presented in Listing 4-1.

Listing 4-1. *Program PokerLibTest*

```
using System;
using System.Collections;
using System.Data.SqlClient;
using System.Xml;
using PokerLib;

namespace PokerLibTest
{
  class Class1
  {
    [STAThread]
    static void Main(string[] args)
    {
      try
      {
        Console.WriteLine("\nBegin PokerLibTest run\n");

        SqlConnection isc = new SqlConnection("Server=(local);
          Database=dbTestPoker;Trusted_Connection=yes");
        isc.Open();
        SqlCommand scSelect = new SqlCommand("SELECT * FROM tblTestCases",
                                             isc);
        SqlDataReader sdr = scSelect.ExecuteReader();

        string caseid, input, expected = "", actual;
        TestCase tc = null;
        TestCaseResult r = null;

        // 1. read all test case data from SQL into memory
        ArrayList tcd = new ArrayList();
        while (sdr.Read())
        {
          caseid = sdr.GetString(0);
          input = sdr.GetString(1);
          expected = sdr.GetString(2);
          tc = new TestCase(caseid, input, expected);
          tcd.Add(tc);
        }
        isc.Close();

        // 2. run all tests, store results to memory
        ArrayList tcr = new ArrayList();
        for (int i = 0; i < tcd.Count; ++i)
        {
          tc = (TestCase)tcd[i];
          string[] cards = tc.input.Split(' ');
```

```
    Hand h = new Hand(cards[0], cards[1], cards[2],
                      cards[3], cards[4]);
    actual = h.GetHandType().ToString();
    string runat = DateTime.Now.ToString("s");

    if (actual == tc.expected)
      r = new TestCaseResult(tc.id, tc.input, tc.expected,
                             actual, "Pass", runat);
    else
      r = new TestCaseResult(tc.id, tc.input, tc.expected,
                             actual, "FAIL", runat);
    tcr.Add(r);
}

// 3. emit all results to external XML storage
XmlTextWriter xtw = new XmlTextWriter("PokerLibResults.xml",
  System.Text.Encoding.UTF8);
xtw.Formatting = Formatting.Indented;
xtw.WriteStartDocument();
xtw.WriteStartElement("TestResults"); // root node

for (int i = 0; i < tcr.Count; ++i)
{
  r = (TestCaseResult)tcr[i];
  xtw.WriteStartElement("case");

  xtw.WriteStartAttribute("id", null);
  xtw.WriteString(r.id); xtw.WriteEndAttribute();

  xtw.WriteStartAttribute("runat", null);
  xtw.WriteString(r.runat); xtw.WriteEndAttribute();

  xtw.WriteStartElement("input");
  xtw.WriteString(r.input); xtw.WriteEndElement();

  xtw.WriteStartElement("expected");
  xtw.WriteString(r.expected); xtw.WriteEndElement();

  xtw.WriteStartElement("actual");
  xtw.WriteString(r.actual); xtw.WriteEndElement();

  xtw.WriteStartElement("result");
  xtw.WriteString(r.result); xtw.WriteEndElement();

  xtw.WriteEndElement(); // </case>
}
xtw.WriteEndElement(); // </TestResults>
xtw.Close();
```

```csharp
        Console.WriteLine("\nDone");
        Console.ReadLine();
      }
      catch(Exception ex)
      {
        Console.WriteLine("Fatal error: " + ex.Message);
        Console.ReadLine();
      }
    } // Main()

    class TestCase
    {
      public string id;
      public string input;
      public string expected;

      public TestCase(string id, string input, string expected)
      {
        this.id = id;
        this.input = input;
        this.expected = expected;
      }
    } // class TestCase

    class TestCaseResult
    {
      public string id;
      public string input;
      public string expected;
      public string actual;
      public string result;
      public string runat;

      public TestCaseResult(string id, string input, string expected,
        string actual, string result, string runat)
      {
        this.id = id;
        this.input = input;
        this.expected = expected;
        this.actual = actual;
        this.result = result;
        this.runat = runat;
      }
    } // class TestCaseResult

  } // Class1
} // ns
```

PART 2

Web Application Testing

■ ■ ■

CHAPTER 5

Request-Response Testing

5.0 Introduction

The most fundamental type of Web application testing is request-response testing. You programmatically send an HTTP request to a Web server, and then after the Web server processes the request and sends an HTTP response (usually in the form of an HTML page), you capture the response and examine it for an expected value. The request-response actions normally occur together, meaning that in a lightweight test automation situation, it is unusual for you to send an HTTP request and not retrieve the response, or to retrieve an HTTP response from a request you did not create. Accordingly, most of the techniques in this chapter show you how to send an HTTP request and fetch the HTTP response, or how to examine an HTTP response for an expected value. Consider the simple ASP.NET Web application shown in Figure 5-1.

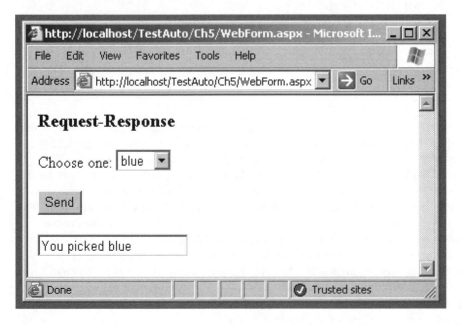

Figure 5-1. *Web AUT*

The code that produced the Web application shown in Figure 5-1 is

```html
<html>
  <head>
    <script language="c#" runat="server">
      void Button1_Click(object sender, System.EventArgs e)
      {
        TextBox1.Text = "You picked " + DropDownList1.SelectedValue;
      }
    </script>
  </head>
  <body>
    <h3>Request-Response</h3>
    <form id="Form1" method="post" runat="server">

      <p>Choose one:
      <asp:DropDownList id="DropDownList1" runat="server">
        <asp:ListItem Value="red">red</asp:ListItem>
        <asp:ListItem Value="blue">blue</asp:ListItem>
        <asp:ListItem Value="green">green</asp:ListItem>
      </asp:DropDownList>

      <p><asp:Button id="Button1" text="Send" onclick=
          "Button1_Click" runat="server" />

      <p><asp:TextBox id="TextBox1" runat="server" /></p>

    </form>
  </body>
</html>
```

Notice that for simplicity, the C# logic and HTML display code are combined in the same file rather than the more usual approach of storing them in separate files using the ASP.NET code-behind mechanism (as when you create a Web application using Visual Studio .NET). This ASP.NET Web application is coded in C#, but the request-response testing techniques in this chapter will work for ASP.NET applications written in any .NET-compliant language.

To test this application manually, you select a color from the Choose One drop-down list and click the Send button. The drop-down value is sent as part of an HTTP request to the ASP.NET Web server. The server processes the request and constructs an HTTP response. The response is returned to the Internet Explorer (IE) client where the HTML is rendered in friendly form as shown in Figure 5-1. You have to visually examine the result for some indication that the HTTP response was correct (the message in the text box control in this case). Manually testing a Web application in this way is slow, inefficient, error-prone, and tedious. A better approach is to write lightweight test automation.

An automated request-response test programmatically sends an HTTP request that contains the same information as the result of a user selecting a drop-down value, and the test programmatically examines the HTTP response for data that indicates a correct response as shown in Figure 5-2.

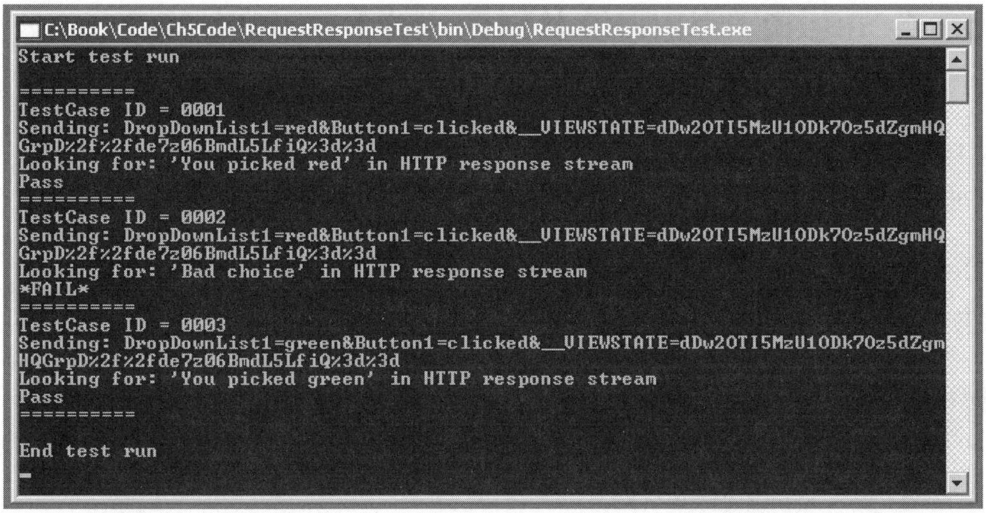

Figure 5-2. *Request-response test run*

The .NET Framework provides you with three fundamental ways and two low-level ways to send an HTTP request and retrieve the corresponding HTTP response. Listed from easiest-to-use but least-flexible to hardest-to-use but most-flexible, following are the five ways to send and retrieve HTTP data:

- WebClient: Particularly simple to use but does not allow you to send authentication credentials.

- WebRequest - WebResponse: Gives you more flexibility, including the ability to send authentication credentials.

- HttpWebRequest - HttpWebResponse: Gives you full control at the expense of a slight increase in complexity.

- TcpClient: A low-level class available to you, but except in unusual situations, it isn't needed for lightweight request-response test automation.

- Socket: A very low-level class not often used in lightweight test automation.

The .NET Framework also has an HttpRequest class, but it's a base class that is not intended to be used directly. The techniques in this chapter use the three higher-level classes (WebClient, WebRequest - WebResponse, and HttpWebRequest - HttpWebResponse). The TcpClient and Socket classes are explained in Chapter 8. The test harness that produced the test run shown in Figure 5-2 is presented in Section 5.12.

5.1 Sending a Simple HTTP GET Request and Retrieving the Response

Problem

You want to send a simple HTTP GET request and retrieve the HTTP response.

Design

Create an instance of the WebClient class and use its DownloadData() method.

Solution

```
string uri = "http://server/path/WebForm.aspx";

WebClient wc = new WebClient();
Console.WriteLine("Sending an HTTP GET request to " + uri);
byte[] bResponse = wc.DownloadData(uri);
string strResponse = Encoding.ASCII.GetString(bResponse);
Console.WriteLine("HTTP response is: ");
Console.WriteLine(strResponse);
```

Comments

The WebClient class is part of the System.Net namespace, which is accessible by default from the console application. Using the WebClient.DownloadData() method to fetch an HTTP response is particularly simple, but DownLoadData() only returns a byte array that must be converted into a string using the System.Text.Encoding.ASCII.GetString() method. An alternative is to use the WebClient.OpenRead() method and associate it with a stream:

```
string uri = " http://server/path/WebForm.aspx";

WebClient wc = new WebClient();
Console.WriteLine("Sending an HTTP GET request to " + uri);
Stream st = wc.OpenRead(uri);
StreamReader sr = new StreamReader(st);
string res = sr.ReadToEnd();
sr.Close();
st.Close();
Console.WriteLine("HTTP Response is ");
Console.WriteLine(res);
```

The WebClient class is most useful when you are testing static HTML pages rather than ASP.NET Web applications. This code may be used to examine an ASP.NET application response but to expand this code into an automated test, you need to examine the HTTP response for an expected value. The techniques in this section are used in Section 5.8 to programmatically determine an ASP.NET Web application ViewState value. The techniques in Section 5.11 show you how to examine an HTTP response for an expected value.

5.2 Sending an HTTP Request with Authentication and Retrieving the Response

Problem

You want to send an HTTP request with network authentication credentials and retrieve the HTTP response.

Design

Create a WebRequest object and create a NetworkCredential object. Assign the NetworkCredential object to the Credentials property of WebRequest object and fetch the HTTP response using the WebRequest.GetResponse() method.

Solution

```
string uri = " http://server/path/WebForm.aspx";
WebRequest wreq = WebRequest.Create(uri);

string uid = "someDomainUserID";
string pwd = "theDomainPassword";
string domain = "theDomainName";
NetworkCredential nc = new NetworkCredential(uid, pwd, domain);
wreq.Credentials = nc;
Console.WriteLine("Sending authenticated request to " + uri);
WebResponse wres = wreq.GetResponse();
Stream st = wres.GetResponseStream();
StreamReader sr = new StreamReader(st);
string res = sr.ReadToEnd();

sr.Close();
st.Close();
Console.WriteLine("HTTP Response is ");
Console.WriteLine(res);
```

Comments

If you need to send an HTTP request with network authentication credentials (user ID, domain, and password), you can use the WebRequest and WebResponse classes. These classes are located in the System.Web namespace, which is not accessible by default in a console application, so you have to add a project reference to file System.Web.dll. Notice that a WebRequest object is created using a factory mechanism with the Create() method rather than the more usual constructor approach using the new keyword. After creating a NetworkCredential object, you can attach that object to the WebRequest object. The WebResponse object is returned by a call to the WebRequest.GetResponse() method; there is no explicit "Send" method as you might have expected. The response stream can be associated, like any stream, to a StreamReader object so that you can fetch the entire HTTP response as a string using the ReadToEnd() method.

The WebRequest and WebResponse classes are actually abstract base classes. In practical terms, you'll use WebRequest - WebResponse for relatively simple HTTP requests that require authentication. If authentication isn't necessary, the WebClient class is often a better choice. If you need to send an HTTP POST request, the HttpWebRequest and HttpWebResponse classes are often a better choice. The WebRequest and WebResponse classes support asynchronous calls, but this is rarely needed in lightweight test automation situations. The code in this section may be used to examine an ASP.NET application response, but to expand this code into an automated test, you need to examine the HTTP response for an expected value as described in Section 5.11.

5.3 Sending a Complex HTTP GET Request and Retrieving the Response

Problem

You want to send an HTTP GET Request and have full control over the request properties.

Design

Create an instance of an HttpWebRequest class and fetch the HTTP response using the GetResponse() method.

Solution

```
string uri = " http://server/path/WebForm.aspx";

HttpWebRequest req = (HttpWebRequest)WebRequest.Create(uri);
req.Method = "GET";
req.MaximumAutomaticRedirections = 3;
req.Timeout = 5000;

Console.WriteLine("Sending HTTP request");
HttpWebResponse res = (HttpWebResponse)req.GetResponse();
Stream resst = res.GetResponseStream();
StreamReader sr = new StreamReader(resst);

Console.WriteLine("HTTP Response is: ");
Console.WriteLine(sr.ReadToEnd());
sr.Close();
resst.Close();
```

Comments

The HttpWebRequest and HttpWebResponse classes are your best all around choice for sending and receiving HTTP data in lightweight test automation scenarios. They support a wide range of useful properties. These classes are located in the System.Net namespace, which is accessible by default in a console application. Notice that an HttpWebRequest object is created using a factory mechanism with the Create() method rather than the more usual constructor approach using the new keyword. Also, there is no explicit "Send" method as you might have expected; an HttpWebResponse object is returned by a call to the HttPWebRequest.GetResponse() method. You can associate the response stream to a StreamReader object so that you can retrieve the entire HTTP response as a string using the ReadToEnd() method. You can also retrieve the HTTP response line-by-line using the StreamReader.ReadLine() method.

This technique shows how you can limit the number of request redirections and set a timeout value. Following are a few of the HttpWebRequest properties that are most useful for lightweight test automation:

- AllowAutoRedirect: Gets or sets a value that indicates whether the request should follow redirection responses.

- CookieContainer: Gets or sets the cookies associated with the request.

- Credentials: Provides authentication information for the request.

- KeepAlive: Gets or sets a value indicating whether to make a persistent connection to the Internet resource.

- MaximumAutomaticRedirections: Gets or sets the maximum number of redirects that the request will follow.

- Proxy: Gets or sets proxy information for the request.

- SendChunked: Gets or sets a value indicating whether to send data in segments to the Internet resource.

- Timeout: Gets or sets the timeout value for a request.

- UserAgent: Gets or sets the value of the User-Agent HTTP header.

The purpose of each of these properties is fairly obvious from their names, and they are fully documented in case you need to use them.

5.4 Retrieving an HTTP Response Line-by-Line

Problem

You want to retrieve an HTTP response line-by-line rather than as an entire string.

Design

Obtain the HTTP response stream using the HttpWebRequest.GetResponse() method and pass that stream to a StreamReader() constructor. Then use the StreamReader.ReadLine() method inside a while loop.

Solution

```
// send an HTTP request using the WebClient class,
// the WebRequest class, or the HttpWebRequest class
```

```
Stream st = null;

// attach Stream st to an HTTP response using the
// WebClient.OpenRead() method, the WebRequest.GetResponseStream()
// method, or the HttpWebRequest.GetResponse() method
StreamReader sr = new StreamReader(st);
string line = null;

Console.WriteLine("HTTP response line-by-line: ");
while ((line = sr.ReadLine()) != null)
{
  Console.WriteLine(line);
}

sr.Close();
st.Close();
```

Comments

Each of the three fundamental ways to send an HTTP request (WebClient, WebRequest, HttpWebRequest) supports a method that returns their associated HTTP response as a Stream object. The Stream object can be associated to a StreamReader object that has several ways to fetch stream data. Using the StreamReader.ReadToEnd() method, you can retrieve the HTTP response as one big string. This is fine for most test automation situations, but sometimes you want to retrieve the HTTP response a line at a time. For instance, if the response is very large, you may not want to store it into one huge string. Or if you are searching the response for a target string, searching line-by-line is sometimes more efficient. To search line-by-line, you can use the StreamReader.ReadLine() method in conjunction with a while loop. The ReadLine() method returns a string consisting of everything up to and including a newline character, or null if no characters are available.

In addition to fetching an HTTP response stream a line at a time, you can also retrieve the response a block of characters at a time:

```
// attach response stream to Stream st
// associate st to StreamReader sr

char[] block = new char[3];
int ct = 0;
while ((ct = sr.Read(block, 0, 3)) != 0)
{
  for (int i = 0; i < ct; i++)
    Console.Write(block[i] + " ");
}
```

Code like this is useful when you want to examine the HTTP response at the character level rather than at the line or string level. In this example, you prepare a character array block of size 3 to hold the response. The StreamReader.Read() method reads 3 characters (or as many characters as are available in the stream), stores the characters into an array block starting at position 0, and returns the actual number of characters read. If 0 characters are read, that means the stream has been exhausted and you can exit the while loop. Notice that a degenerative case is defined when you declare a character array of size 1; in this situation, you are reading a single character at a time.

5.5 Sending a Simple HTTP POST Request to a Classic ASP Web Page

Problem

You want to send a simple HTTP POST request to a classic ASP page/script and retrieve the resulting HTTP response.

Design

Create an instance of the HttpWebRequest class. Set the object's Method property to "POST" and the ContentType property to "application/x-www-form-urlencoded". Add the POST data to the request using the GetRequestStream() method and the Stream.Write() method. Fetch the HTTP response using the HttpWebRequest.GetResponse() method.

Solution

```
string url = "http://localhost/TestAuto/Ch5/classic.asp";
string data = "inputBox1=orange";
byte[] buffer = Encoding.ASCII.GetBytes(data);

HttpWebRequest req = (HttpWebRequest)WebRequest.Create(url);
req.Method = "POST";
req.ContentType = "application/x-www-form-urlencoded";
req.ContentLength = buffer.Length;

Stream reqst = req.GetRequestStream();
reqst.Write(buffer, 0, buffer.Length);
reqst.Flush();
reqst.Close();

Console.WriteLine("\nPosting 'orange'");
HttpWebResponse res = (HttpWebResponse)req.GetResponse();
Stream resst = res.GetResponseStream();
StreamReader sr = new StreamReader(resst);

Console.WriteLine("\nGrabbing HTTP response\n");
Console.WriteLine(sr.ReadToEnd());
sr.Close();
resst.Close();
Console.WriteLine("Done");
```

Comments

Suppose you have an HTML page form like this:

```
<html>
<!-- classic.html -->
  <body>
    <form name="theForm" method="post" action="classic.asp">
      <p>Enter color:
      <input type="text" name="inputBox1"/>
      </p>
      <input type="submit" value="Send It"/>
    </form>
  </body>
</html>
```

And you have a related classic ASP page/script like this:

```
<html>
<!-- classic.asp -->
  <body>
    <p>You submitted: </p>
    <%
      strColor = Request.Form("inputBox1")
      Response.Write(strColor)
    %>
    <p>Bye</p>
  </body>
</html>
```

If a user loads page classic.html into a Web client such as IE, an "Enter color:" prompt and a text field are displayed. After entering some text and clicking on the submit button, an HTTP request containing the HTML form data is sent to the Web server. The Web server accepts the POST request and runs the classic.asp script. The script grabs the value entered in the text field and inserts it into the HTML result stream, which is then sent as an HTTP response back to the client (where the HTML would be rendered in human-friendly form).

To send an HTTP request directly to page/script classic.asp and retrieve the HTTP response, the most flexible option is to use the HttpWebRequest class. The key is to first set up data to post as a string of name-value pairs connected with &:

```
string data = "inputBox1=orange&inputBox2=green";
```

Next, you must convert the post data from type string into a byte array using the System. Text.Encoding.ASCII.GetBytes() method because all HTTP data is transferred as bytes. After creating an HttpWebRequest object, you must set the request object's Method property to "POST" and the ContentType to "application/x-www-form-urlencoded". You can think of the ContentType value as a magic string that tells the Web server to interpret the HTTP request data as HTML form data. You must set the value of the ContentLength property to the length of the post data stored in the byte array. Notice that because the ContentLength property is required, you must prepare the post data before setting up the HttpWebRequest object. After setting up the request, you obtain the request stream using the `HttpWebRequest.GetRequestStream()` method so that you can add the post data into the stream. You do this by writing to the stream like this:

```
reqst.Write(buffer, 0, buffer.Length);
```

You specify what byte array to write into the request stream, the starting position within the byte array, and the number of bytes to write. If you use the `Length` property as the number of bytes to write, you will write the entire byte array to the request stream. Now you can send the HTTP request and retrieve the HTTP response as a string using a `StreamReader` object. If the preceding solution is run, the output is

```
Posting 'orange'

Grabbing HTTP response:

<html>
<!-- classic.asp -->
  <body>
    <p>You submitted: </p>
    orange
    <p>Bye</p>
  </body>
</html>
Done
```

This technique uses the `HttpWebRequest` and `HttpWebResponse` classes, but you can use the `WebClient` class or the `WebRequest` and `WebResponse` classes, too. The technique in this section is useful to examine an HTTP response from a classic ASP Web application, but to extend the solution into test automation, you must search the HTTP response for an expected value as discussed in Section 5.11.

This technique assumes that the `POST` data string does not contain any characters that may be misinterpreted by the Web server such as blank spaces and ampersands. To deal with such characters see Section 5.7. This solution also assumes that the HTTP request-response does not travel through a proxy server. To deal with proxy servers, see the "Comments" section in Section 5.6.

5.6 Sending an HTTP POST Request to an ASP.NET Web Application

Problem

You want to send an HTTP `POST` request to an ASP.NET Web application and retrieve the resulting HTTP response.

Design

Create an HttpWebRequest object. Set the object's Method property to "POST" and the ContentType property to "application/x-www-form-urlencoded". Concatenate the application's ViewState value to the POST data. If your Web application is running on ASP.NET 2.0, you must also concatenate the application's EventValidation value to the POST data. Add the POST data to the request using the GetRequestStream() method and the Stream.Write() method. Fetch the HTTP response using the HttpWebRequest.GetResponse() method.

Solution

```
string url = "http://localhost/TestAuto/Ch5/WebForm.aspx";
string data = "TextBox1=red&TextBox2=empty&Button1=clicked";
string vs = "dDwtMTQwNDA4NDA4ODs7PeWiylVlaimBKuqooykeHvDojL2i";
vs = HttpUtility.UrlEncode(vs);
data += "&__VIEWSTATE=" + vs;
byte[] buffer = Encoding.ASCII.GetBytes(data);

HttpWebRequest req = (HttpWebRequest)WebRequest.Create(url);
req.Method = "POST";
req.ContentType = "application/x-www-form-urlencoded";
req.ContentLength = buffer.Length;

Stream reqst = req.GetRequestStream();
reqst.Write(buffer, 0, buffer.Length);
reqst.Flush();
reqst.Close();

HttpWebResponse res = (HttpWebResponse)req.GetResponse();
Stream resst = res.GetResponseStream();
StreamReader sr = new StreamReader(resst);

Console.WriteLine("\nGrabbing HTTP response:\n");
Console.WriteLine(sr.ReadToEnd());
sr.Close();
resst.Close();

Console.WriteLine("Done");
```

Comments

Suppose you have this ASP.NET Web application named WebForm1.aspx:

```
<html>
  <head>
    <script language="c#" runat="server">
      void Button1_Click(object sender, System.EventArgs e)
```

```
      {
        if (TextBox1.Text == "red")
          TextBox2.Text = "Roses are red";
        else if (TextBox1.Text == "blue")
          TextBox2.Text = "The sky is blue";
        else
          TextBox2.Text = "unknown color";
      }
    </script>
  </head>
  <body>
    <h3>Color Commenter</h3>
    <form id="Form1" method="post" runat="server">
      <p>Enter color:
      <asp:TextBox id="TextBox1" runat="server"/></p>
      <p>My comment:
      <asp:TextBox id="TextBox2" runat="server" /></p>
      <p><asp:Button id="Button1" text="Send"
          onclick="Button1_Click" runat="server" />
    </form>
  </body>
</html>
```

This Web application was created manually rather than by using Visual Studio .NET, which would have resulted in the C# logic code and the HTML display code being in different files. This fact does not affect how you automate the application. The Web application has two text fields and a button control. The user enters a string such as "red" into the TextBox1 control. Clicking on the Button1 control sends an HTTP request to the Web server. The ASP.NET server logic checks the value in TextBox1 and creates an HTTP response page that displays a short message such as "Roses are red" in TextBox2. If the code in this solution executes, the output is

```
Sending TextBox1=red

Grabbing the HTTP response:

<html>
  <head>

  </head>
  <body>
    <h3>Color Commenter</h3>
    <form name="Form1" method="post" action="WebForm.aspx"
        id="Form1">
<input type="hidden" name="__VIEWSTATE"
 value="dDwtMTQwNDA4NDA
         4ODs7PuWdy3VjanmrKIqoo7kBHkDzjH2p" />
```

```
      <p>Enter color:
      <input name="TextBox1" type="text" value="red"
          id="TextBox1" /></p>
      <p>My comment:
      <input name="TextBox2" type="text" value="Roses are red"
          id="TextBox2" /></p>
      <p><input type="submit" name="Button1" value="Send"
          id="Button1" />
    </form>
  </body>
</html>
```

Done

Notice that the value attribute of the TextBox2 input tag is "Roses are red". To send an HTTP request directly to an ASP.NET Web application and retrieve the HTTP response, your most flexible option is to use the HttpWebRequest class. The first step is to set up data to post a string of name-value pairs:

```
string data = "TextBox1=red&TextBox2=empty&Button1=clicked";
```

The "TextBox1=red" is self-explanatory. The "TextBox2=empty" and the "Button1=clicked" part of the post data are there to keep the ViewState value synchronized between the client test automation program and the ASP.NET Web server. Every ASP.NET Web application has a ViewState value that represents the state of the application after each request-response round trip. The ViewState value is a Base64-encoded string. By creating and maintaining a ViewState value, the Web server can maintain application state between successive HTTP requests. You must determine the ViewState value and add it to the post data:

```
string vs = "dDwtMTQwNDA4NDA4ODs7PuWdy3VjanmrKIqoo7kBHkDzjH2p";
vs = HttpUtility.UrlEncode(vs);
data += "&__VIEWSTATE=" + vs;
```

Because the ViewState value can have characters that may confuse the ASP.NET Web server (&, for example), you should apply the HttpUtility.UrlEncode() method to the ViewState value. The HttpUtility class is contained in the System.Web namespace, which is not accessible by default to a console application, so you'll have to add a project reference to System.Web.dll (see Section 5.7 for details). Note that two underscore characters appear before the VIEWSTATE. You have two ways to determine an initial ViewState value. The first, as demonstrated here, is to manually find the value by simply launching IE (or another client), loading the WebForm.aspx application, and then choosing View ➤ Source. The second way to determine an initial ViewState value is to programmatically send an HTTP request to WebForm.aspx and then programmatically grab the ViewState value from the HTTP response. This technique is explained in Section 5.8.

Exactly which components of an ASP.NET application contribute to the ViewState value and how the ViewState value is calculated by the ASP.NET Web server is not fully documented, so it requires some trial and error to determine exactly what to place in the post data string. For instance, in this example, you can leave out the "TextBox2=empty" portion of the string, however the "Button1=clicked" is necessary. The "empty" and "clicked" string values are arbitrary. In other words, you can type "Button1=foo" or even "Button1=" and the ViewState value will remain synchronized, and your automation will succeed. Using string constants such as "empty" and "clicked" makes your code more readable at the expense of possibly misleading code reviewers into thinking there is something special about those values. When adding the ViewState value to a post data string, the position of the ViewState value does not matter. However, your code will be more readable if you place the ViewState value at the end of the string.

In ASP.NET 2.0, a new EventValidation feature was added for security against fraudulent postbacks. The framework posts encrypted data, which is part of the __EVENTVALIDATION hidden field. The hidden field is generated as the last element in the Web application form element. So in an ASP.NET 2.0 environment, you have to add the EventValidation value to the POST data like this:

```
string ev = "d+waMTswVDA4NDA4OQs7buWdy3VwbjkrKIqoo7kBHkDzjH2p";
ev = HttpUtility.UrlEncode(ev);
data += "&__EVENTVALIDATION=" + ev;
```

After building up the post data string, you must convert it into a byte array using the System.Text.Encoding.ASCII.GetBytes() method, because all HTTP traffic works at the byte level. Next, you must set the request object's Method property to "POST" and the ContentType to "application/x-www-form-urlencoded". The ContentType value is a string that tells the Web server that the HTTP request data should be interpreted as HTML form data. Then, you need to set the value of the ContentLength property to the length of the post data stored in the byte array. After setting up the request, you can obtain the request stream using the HttpWebRequest.GetRequestStream() method so that you can add the post data into the HTTP request stream:

```
reqst.Write(buffer, 0, buffer.Length);
```

You specify which byte array to write into the stream, the starting position within the byte array, and the total number of bytes to write. Finally, you are ready to send the HTTP request and retrieve the HTTP response:

```
HttpWebResponse res = (HttpWebResponse)req.GetResponse();
Stream resst = res.GetResponseStream();
```

You can then fetch the response as a string using a StreamReader object. The technique presented here is useful to examine an HTTP response from an ASP.NET Web application, but to extend the solution into true test automation, you must search the response for an expected value.

If you must deal with a proxy server, you can easily add the optional Proxy property to an HttpWebRequest object:

```
// instantiate HttpWebRequest req here
string proxy = "someProxyMachineNameOrIPAddress";
req.Proxy = new WebProxy(proxy, true);
```

You pass the name or IP address of the proxy server machine as a string to a WebProxy constructor and attach the resulting object to the HttpWebRequest object. The Boolean argument specifies whether or not to ignore the proxy server for local addresses; true means ignore the proxy server for local addresses.

You can significantly increase the modularity of and extend your test automation by factoring the code in this section into a helper method:

```
private static bool ResponseHasTarget(string uri,
                                      string postData,
                                      string target)
{
  // create HttpWebRequest
  // add postData to request stream
  // obtain HttpResponse stream
  // attach response to StreamReader object sr
  string result = sr.ReadToEnd();

  if (result.IndexOf(target) >= 0)
    return true;
   else
    return false;
}
```

The helper accepts the URI of the Web application (such as `"http://server/path/WebForm.aspx"`), the data that is to be posted to the application (such as `"TextBox1=red&TextBox2=blue"`), and a target string (such as `"The result is purple"`). The method returns true if the HTTP response associated with the HTTP request contains the target string and returns false if the target string is not in the HTTP response. The example program in Section 5.12 has a complete implementation of the helper method `ResponseHasTarget()`.

5.7 Dealing with Special Input Characters

Problem

You want to handle special characters such as "&" in your HTTP POST data.

Design

Use the `HttpUtility.UrlEncode()` method to convert potentially troublesome characters into their character-entity equivalents.

Solution

```
string badValueForTextBox1 = "this&that";
string goodValueForTextBox1 =
  HttpUtility.UrlEncode(badValueForTextBox1);
string data = "TextBox1=" + goodValueForTextBox1;
```

Comments

If you place characters (such as blank spaces) and/or punctuation (such as "&") into an HTTP request stream, the receiving ASP.NET Web server may misinterpret them. URL encoding converts characters that are not allowed in a URL into character-entity equivalents. For example, when embedded in a string to be transmitted in a URL, the characters "<" and ">" are encoded as %3c and %3d, respectively.

The `HttpUtility.UrlEncode()` method handles the mapping of potentially troublesome characters into a three-character sequence starting with "%". The `UrlEncode()` method is located inside the `System.Web` namespace. Suppose you have an ASP.NET Web application that contains this code:

```
if (TextBox1.Text == "this&that")
  TextBox2.Text = "Oh really";
else
  TextBox2.Text = "unknown input";
```

To test this logic, you need to post the string "this&that" to the Web application. If you try this directly as

```
string data = "TextBox1=this&that";
```

you will get an HTTP response with `"unknown input"` as the `TextBox2` attribute instead of `"Oh really"` because the Web server will get confused by the "&" character embedded in the `POST` data. To solve this issue, you can use the `HttpUtility.UrlEncode()` method that converts the "&" character to the sequence "%26". When the Web server receives the HTTP request, the %26 will be URL decoded into a "&" character and your automation logic will succeed.

One strategy you can employ is to always apply `HttpUtility.UrlEncode()` to your input `POST` data even when it does not contain troublesome characters:

```
string anyValue = "whatever";
anyValue = HttpUtility.UrlEncode(anyValue);
string data = "TextBox1=" + anyValue;
```

The downside to this strategy is that when testing, you sometimes want to actually send troublesome characters. One approach is to create two harnesses: one that always performs a `UrlEncode()` on the value part of name-value post pairs and one that never performs a `UrlEncode()`. Another approach is to parameterize your harness to read input `POST` data and expected values from an external test case data store and to include a value in the test case data to indicate whether the input data should be URL encoded or not:

```
001!TextBox1!red!noencode!Roses are red
002!TextBox1!this&that!encode!Oh really
003!TextBox1!this&that!noencode!unknown input
```

You then use branching logic to determine whether you should URL-encode or not:

```
while ((line = sr.ReadLine()) != null) // test loop
{
  tokens = line.Split('!');

  if (tokens[3] == "encode")
    input = HttpUtility.UrlEncode(tokens[2]);
  else
    input = tokens[2];

  data = tokens[1] + "=" + input;
  // etc.
}
```

5.8 Programmatically Determining a ViewState Value and an EventValidation Value

Problem

You want to programmatically determine an initial `ViewState` value (and an initial `EventValidation` value under ASP.NET 2.0) for an ASP.NET Web application.

Design

Use a `WebClient` object to send a simple, initial probing HTTP request to the application. Fetch the HTTP probe response and parse out the `ViewState` value (and the `EventValidation` value under ASP.NET 2.0) using the `String.IndexOf()` and `String.SubString()` methods.

Solution

If you are running under ASP.NET 1.1:

```
string uri = "http://server/path/WebForm.aspx";

WebClient wc = new WebClient();
Stream st = wc.OpenRead(uri);
StreamReader sr = new StreamReader(st);
string res = sr.ReadToEnd();
sr.Close();
st.Close();
int start = res.IndexOf("__VIEWSTATE", 0) + 20;
int end = res.IndexOf("\"", start);
string vs = res.Substring(start, (end-start));
Console.WriteLine("ViewState = " + vs);
```

If you are running under ASP.NET 2.0:

```
string uri = "http://server/path/WebForm.aspx";

WebClient wc = new WebClient();
Stream st = wc.OpenRead(uri);
StreamReader sr = new StreamReader(st);
string res = sr.ReadToEnd();
sr.Close();
st.Close();

int startVS = res.IndexOf("__VIEWSTATE", 0) + 37;
int endVS = res.IndexOf("\"", startVS);
string vs = res.Substring(startVS, (endVS-startVS));
Console.WriteLine("ViewState = " + vs);
```

```
int startEV = res.IndexOf("__EVENTVALIDATION", 0) + 49;
int endEV = res.IndexOf("\"", startEV);
string ev = res.Substring(startEV, (endEV-startEV));
Console.WriteLine("EventValidation = " + ev);
```

Comments

Before you can programmatically send an HTTP request to an ASP.NET Web application, you must determine the application's ViewState value (and the application's EventValidation value if you are running under ASP.NET 2.0). These are Base64-encoded values that represent the state of the Web application after each request-response round trip. This built-in mechanism is similar to how Web developers must maintain state in classic ASP Web pages by using HTML hidden input values. Although you can manually determine the ViewState value of an ASP.NET Web application by launching the application in a client such as IE and then choosing View ➤ Source, many times a better technique is to programmatically determine the ViewState value. The idea is to send an HTTP request for the Web application, retrieve the HTTP response into a string, and then parse the ViewState value out from the response string.

After instantiating a WebClient object and attaching a stream to the HTTP response with the OpenRead() method, you fetch the entire response string into variable res using the ReadToEnd() method. The ViewState value is embedded in an HTML input tag:

```
<input type="hidden" name="__VIEWSTATE" value="dDwtMTQwNDA4N==" />
```

To extract the ViewState value in ASP.NET 1.1, you first get the location within the entire response string where the identifying "__VIEWSTATE" string occurs:

```
int start = res.IndexOf("__VIEWSTATE", 0) + 20;
```

If you add 20 to that index value, the index will point to the double-quote character just before the ViewState value. (Note: two underscores appear before VIEWSTATE). Next, you get an index pointing to the double-quote character that is just after the ViewState value:

```
int end = res.IndexOf("\"", start);
```

Notice you need to escape the double-quote character. After you have the indexes of the two double-quote characters that delimit the ViewState value, you can extract and save the ViewState value using the SubString() method:

```
string vs = res.Substring(start, (end-start));
```

You can increase the modularity of your lightweight test automation code by recasting this solution into a method that accepts a URI string and returns a ViewState string:

```
private static string ViewState(string uri)
{
  try
  {
    WebClient wc = new WebClient();
    Stream st = wc.OpenRead(uri);
    StreamReader sr = new StreamReader(st);
    string res = sr.ReadToEnd();
    sr.Close();
    st.Close();
    int start = res.IndexOf("__VIEWSTATE", 0) + 20;
    int end = res.IndexOf("\"", start);
    string vs = res.Substring(start, (end-start));
    return vs;
  }
  catch
  {
    throw new Exception("Fatal error finding ViewState");
  }
}
```

With this helper method, you can append a `ViewState` value to a `POST` data string:

```
string uri = "http://server/path/WebForm.aspx";
string postData = "TextBox1=red&";

string vs = ViewState(uri);
vs = HttpUtility.UrlEncode(vs);

postData += "__VIEWSTATE=" + vs;
```

Because a `ViewState` value may contain characters such as "&" that need to be URL encoded, you must apply the `HttpUtility.UrlEncode()` method to the `ViewState` value at some point. A design decision you'll have to make is whether to apply `UrlEncode()` inside your helper method or outside the helper as you've done here. You must also be careful where you place the connecting "&" characters.

The code in this solution is referred to as "brittle." Brittle code makes assumptions about external dependencies and will break if those dependencies change. Notice the hard-coded 20 value in the code. The external dependency here is the way in which an ASP.NET 1.1 Web server returns the `ViewState` value to the calling client. The 20 assumes that exactly 20 characters appear between the start of "__VIEWSTATE" and the double-quote character that appears before the `ViewState` value. If, for example, a future modification to ASP.NET results in characters other than the two underscore characters in front of `VIEWSTATE`, then your test automation will break. Writing brittle code is almost always unacceptable in a development environment, but you can often get away with it in lightweight test automation. The idea is that lightweight automation is supposed to be quick and easy, which means you are willing to accept the consequences of brittle code—if the automation breaks, then you'll just have to fix it.

In ASP.NET 2.0, the ViewState value occurs 37 characters after the start of the "__VIEWSTATE" string because the 17-character string id="__VIEWSTATE" (with a preceding blank space) is added to the HTML hidden input element. Additionally, the new EventValidation value occurs 49 characters after the start of the "__EVENTVALIDATION" string. So, in an ASP.NET 2.0 environment, you can either write separate ViewState() and EventValidation() methods that programmatically fetch their values, or you can combine the logic into a single ViewStateEventValidation() method that returns a URL-encoded string containing both values like this:

```
private static string ViewStateAndEventValidation(string uri)
{
  try
  {
    WebClient wc = new WebClient();
    Stream st = wc.OpenRead(uri);
    StreamReader sr = new StreamReader(st);
    string res = sr.ReadToEnd();
    sr.Close();
    st.Close();

    int startVS = res.IndexOf("__VIEWSTATE", 0) + 37;
    int endVS = res.IndexOf("\"", startVS);
    string vs = res.Substring(startVS, (endVS-startVS));
    vs = HttpUtility.UrlEncode(vs);

    int startEV = res.IndexOf("__EVENTVALIDATION", 0) + 49;
    int endEV = res.IndexOf("\"", startEV);
    string ev = res.Substring(startEV, (endEV-startEV));
    ev = HttpUtility.UrlEncode(ev);

    return "&__VIEWSTATE=" + vs + "&__EVENTVALIDATION=" + ev;

  }
  catch
  {
    throw new Exception("Fatal error finding ViewState or EventValidation");
  }
}
```

With this method, setting up POST data to an ASP.NET 2.0 Web application looks like this:

```
string uri = "http://server/path/WebForm.aspx";
string postData = "TextBox1=red";
postData += ViewStateAndEventValidation(uri);
```

Executing this code results in the variable postData having a value resembling

```
"TextBox1=red&__VIEWSTATE=%2fQazwJ&__EVENTVALIDATION=%2fMaR4d8j="
```

where the actual values for ViewState and EventValidation depend on the particular Web AUT.

5.9 Dealing with CheckBox and RadioButtonList Controls

Problem

You want to send an HTTP request indicating a CheckBox or RadioButtonList control is checked.

Design

Modify the POST data string to include a name-value pair with the ID of the control you want to manipulate and the new value of the control.

Solution

```
string url = "http://server/path/WebForm.aspx";
string data = "CheckBox1=checked&RadioButtonList1=Alpha";
string viewstate = HttpUtility.UrlEncode("dDwtMTQ2MzgwNTQ2MD==");

data += "&__VIEWSTATE=" + viewstate;
// send data to Web application here
```

Comments

Two of the most common ASP.NET Web application controls are CheckBox and RadioButtonList. Suppose you have this Web application:

```
<html>
  <head>
    <script language="c#" runat="server">
      void Button1_Click(object sender, System.EventArgs e)
      {
        if (CheckBox1.Checked == true)
          TextBox1.Text = "CheckBox is checked";
        else
          TextBox1.Text = "CheckBox NOT checked";

        if (RadioButtonList1.Items[0].Selected == true)
          TextBox2.Text = "Alpha selected";
        else if (RadioButtonList1.Items[1].Selected == true)
          TextBox2.Text = "Beta selected";
      }
    </script>
  </head>
  <body>
    <h3>CheckBox and RadioButtonList</h3>
    <form id="Form1" method="post" runat="server">
```

```
      <p>Check or not:
      <asp:CheckBox id="CheckBox1" runat="server" />

      <p>Select one:
      <asp:RadioButtonList id="RadioButtonList1" runat="server">
        <asp:ListItem Value="Alpha">Alpha</asp:ListItem>
        <asp:ListItem Value="Beta">Beta</asp:ListItem>
      </asp:RadioButtonList>

      <p><asp:Button id="Button1" text="Send" onclick="Button1_Click"
 runat="server" />

      <p>My obervations:
      <p><asp:TextBox id="TextBox1" runat="server" /></p>
      <p><asp:TextBox id="TextBox2" runat="server" /></p>

    </form>
  </body>
</html>
```

This Web application checks to determine whether the CheckBox1 control is checked and whether the radio button with value Alpha or with Beta is selected, and prints a brief diagnostic message in a TextBox control. To programmatically send an HTTP request that corresponds to CheckBox1 being checked and Alpha being selected in RadioButtonList1, you can set up a POST data string like this:

```
string data = "CheckBox1=checked&RadioButtonList1=Alpha";
data += "&TextBox1=empty&TextBox2=empty&Button1=clicked";
```

If you submit this data to the Web application, the HTTP response includes the following:

```
<p>My obervations:
<p><input name="TextBox1" type="text" value="CheckBox is checked"
    id="TextBox1" /></p>
<p><input name="TextBox2" type="text" value="Alpha selected"
    id="TextBox2"
/></p>
```

To indicate that CheckBox1 is unchecked, you send an HTTP request with a name-value pair that has no value component: "CheckBox1=". Similarly, to indicate that none of the RadioButtonList1 options are selected, you send "RadioButtonList1=".

5.10 Dealing with DropDownList Controls

Problem

You want to send an HTTP request indicating the selected value of a DropDownList control.

Design

Modify the POST data string to include the ID of the DropDownList control and the selected value you want to indicate has been chosen in name-value form.

Solution

```
string url = "http://server/path/WebForm.aspx";
string data = "DropDownList1=SomeOption";
string viewstate = HttpUtility.UrlEncode("dDwtMTQ2MzgwNTQ2MD==");

data += "&__VIEWSTATE=" + viewstate;
// send data to Web application here
```

Comments

A common Web control used in ASP.NET Web applications is the DropDownList control. For example, suppose you have this application:

```
<html>
  <head>
    <script language="c#" runat="server">
      void Button1_Click(object sender, System.EventArgs e)
      {
        TextBox1.Text = DropDownList1.SelectedValue;
      }
    </script>
  </head>
  <body>
    <h3>DropDownList</h3>
    <form id="Form1" method="post" runat="server">

      <p>Choose one:
      <asp:DropDownList id="DropDownList1" runat="server">
        <asp:ListItem Value="ant">ant</asp:ListItem>
        <asp:ListItem Value="bug">bug</asp:ListItem>
        <asp:ListItem Value="cat">cat</asp:ListItem>
      </asp:DropDownList>

      <p><asp:Button id="Button1" text="Send" onclick="Button1_Click"
runat="server" />

      <p>You chose:
      <p><asp:TextBox id="TextBox1" runat="server" /></p>

    </form>
  </body>
</html>
```

This application grabs the selected value on control DropDownList1 and displays that value in TextBox1. To programmatically send an HTTP request that corresponds to "bug" selected in DropDownList1, you can set up a POST data string like this:

```
string data = "DropDownList1=bug&TextBox1=empty";
data += "&Button1=clicked";
```

If you submit this data to the Web application, the HTTP response includes the following:

```
<p>You chose:
<p><input name="TextBox1" type="text" value="bug"
    id="TextBox1" /></p>
```

5.11 Determining a Request-Response Test Result

Problem

You want to determine whether a request-response test case passes or fails.

Design

Read the HTTP response a line at a time using the StreamReader.ReadLine() method. Parse each line of the HTTP response using the String.IndexOf() method for an identifying target string that unambiguously determines a pass or fail test result.

Solution

```
// set up url here
// set up post data in byte array buffer here

HttpWebRequest req = (HttpWebRequest)WebRequest.Create(url);
req.Method = "POST";
req.ContentType = "application/x-www-form-urlencoded";
req.ContentLength = buffer.Length;
// write buffer into request stream here

HttpWebResponse res = (HttpWebResponse)req.GetResponse();
// get response stream and associate to StreamReader sr here

string expected = "someTargetString";
bool expectedFound = false;
string line = null;
while ((line = sr.ReadLine()) != null && !expectedFound)
{
  if (line.IndexOf(expected) >= 0)
  {
    Console.WriteLine("expected value found");
    expectedFound = true;
  }
}
```

```
if (expectedFound)
  Console.WriteLine("Pass");
else
  Console.WriteLine("Fail");
```

Comments

The essence of performing a request-response test of an ASP.NET Web application is to send an HTTP request to the application, retrieve the HTTP response, and examine the response for an identifying expected value. The following sets up the request, sends the request, and associates the response with a Stream object:

```
HttpWebResponse res = (HttpWebResponse)req.GetResponse();
Stream resst = res.GetResponseStream(); // fetch HTTP response
```

You then create a StreamReader object from the stream so that you access the response stream:

```
StreamReader sr = new StreamReader(resst);
```

You need to assign a target string to search for in the HTTP response:

```
string expected = "someTargetString";
```

The expected string is some string that, if found in the HTTP response, will uniquely identify a correct response. This is not always easy to specify. For example, suppose you have a Web application with a DropDownList control that has options "red", "blue", and "green". If the user selects "red" from the control, a message such as "apples are red" is displayed in a TextBox control. If you naively use the string "red" as an expected target, you will always get a pass result because "red" will be in the HTML <option> tag:

```
<select name="DropDownList1" id="DropDownList1">
  <option value="red">red</option>
  <option value="blue">blue</option>
  <option value="green">green</option>
</select>
```

Red will also be in the HTML <input> result tag:

```
<input name="TextBox1" type="text" value="apples are red"
    id="TextBox1" />
```

You can avoid this pitfall by making the expected target more specific:

```
string expected = "value=\"apples are red\"";
```

You search the HTTP response line-by-line. You declare a Boolean variable expectedFound and set it to false and declare a string variable line to hold one line of the HTTP response. Next, you examine each line of the HTTP response:

```
while ((line = sr.ReadLine()) != null && !expectedFound)
{
  if (line.IndexOf(expected) >= 0)
  {
    Console.WriteLine("Found expected target");
    expectedFound = true;
  }
}
```

The loop will exit if it reaches the end of the HTTP response stream or if the target expected value is found. After the loop terminates, if expectedFound is still set to false, the loop exited because it reached the end of the stream and did not find the expected target, and the test case fails. If expectedValue has been set to true, that means the loop exited because it found the expected target, and the test case passes.

As an alternative, you can retrieve the HTTP response as one big string using the StreamReader.ReadToEnd() method and then search it using String.IndexOf():

```
string entireResponse = sr.ReadToEnd();
if (entireResponse.IndexOf(expected) >= 0)
  Console.WriteLine("Pass");
else
  Console.WriteLine("*FAIL*");
```

This approach is simpler but may not be feasible if the HTTP response is very large.

In lightweight test automation, you often can create test bed scenarios where a unique identifying string or other characteristic is used. In some situations, however, you may need to search for a nonunique target string in the HTTP response. One solution to this problem is to specify two strings that represent where to begin searching in the response and where to end searching:

```
private static bool IsThere(string strToSearch,
                            string strTarget,
                            string strBegin, string strEnd)
{
  int start = strToSearch.IndexOf(strBegin);
  int end = strToSearch.IndexOf(strEnd);
  int numCharsToSearch = end - (start + strBegin.Length);
  if (strToSearch.IndexOf(strTarget, start, numCharsToSearch) >= 0)
    return true;
  else
    return false;
}
```

(This code assumes that strTarget and strBegin are not the same.) In other words, even though multiple occurrences of some target string may appear in your HTTP response, if you can limit somewhat where a target string must be found, you can search for the nonunique target. With such a method, you can search through an HTTP response:

```
string entireResponse = sr.ReadToEnd();
string target = "red";
if (IsThere(entireResponse, target, "<form", "</form>"))
  Console.WriteLine("Pass");
else
  Console.WriteLine("*FAIL*");
```

This code will return true if "red" is found between "<form" and "</form>" in the HTTP response. Notice the missing ">" to terminate "<form>" because the response looks like

```
<form name="Form1" method="post" action="WebForm.aspx" id="Form1">
...
</form>
```

rather than

```
<form>
...
</form>
```

An alternative approach to the problem of searching for nonunique target strings in an HTTP response stream is to use regular expressions. Regular expressions are more powerful than simple string search methods, but in general, regular expressions are harder to code, modify, and maintain.

5.12 Example Program: RequestResponseTest

This program combines several of the techniques in this chapter to create a lightweight test automation harness to test the ASP.NET Web application shown earlier in Figure 5-1. The program reads test case data from a "!" delimited text file, TestCases.txt:

```
0001!DropDownList1=red&Button1=clicked!You picked red
0002!DropDownList1=red&Button1=clicked!Bad choice!deliberate fail
0003!DropDownList1=green&Button1=clicked!You picked green
```

The first field is a test case ID, the second field is HTTP request POST data, the third field is an expected string in the HTTP response, and the fourth field (e.g., "deliberate fail") is an optional comment. The test harness reads the test case file a line at a time, and then parses the test case ID, input POST data string, and the expected target string. For each test case, the input is sent to the Web AUT using HttpWebRequest, the response is captured with an HttpWebResponse, and the response is examined to determine whether the expected string is in the response. The complete lightweight test harness is listed in Listing 5-1. When run, the output appears as shown in Figure 5-2 at the beginning of this chapter.

Listing 5-1. *Program RequestResponse Test*

```
using System;
using System.Net; // WebClient
using System.Text; // Encoding
using System.IO; // Streams
using System.Web; // request-response classes
using System.Web.Util; // HttpUtility.UrlEncode

namespace RequestResponseTest
{
  class Class1
  {
    [STAThread]
    static void Main(string[] args)
    {
      try
      {
        Console.WriteLine("Start test run\n");
        string uri = "http://localhost/TestAuto/Ch5/WebForm.aspx";
        FileStream fs = new FileStream("..\\..\\TestCases.txt",
                                     FileMode.Open);
        StreamReader sr = new StreamReader(fs);
        string line;

        while ((line = sr.ReadLine()) != null)
        {
          string[] tokens = line.Split('!');
          string data = tokens[1];
          string expected = tokens[2];
          string vs = ViewState(uri);
          vs = HttpUtility.UrlEncode(vs);
          data += "&__VIEWSTATE=" + vs;

          Console.WriteLine("==========");
          Console.WriteLine("TestCase ID = " + tokens[0]);
          Console.WriteLine("Sending: " + data);
          Console.Write("Looking for: '" + expected + "'");
          Console.WriteLine(" in HTTP response stream");

          if (ResponseHasTarget(uri, data, expected))
            Console.WriteLine("Pass");
          else
            Console.WriteLine("*FAIL*");
        }
```

```
      Console.WriteLine("==========");
      Console.WriteLine("\nEnd test run");
    }
  catch(Exception ex)
  {
      Console.WriteLine("Fatal error: " + ex.Message);
  }
} // Main()

private static string ViewState(string uri)
{
  try
  {
    WebClient wc = new WebClient();
    Stream st = wc.OpenRead(uri);
    StreamReader sr = new StreamReader(st);
    string res = sr.ReadToEnd();
    sr.Close();
    st.Close();
    int start = res.IndexOf("__VIEWSTATE", 0) + 20;
    int end = res.IndexOf("\"", start);
    string vs = res.Substring(start, (end-start));
    return vs;
  }
  catch
  {
    throw new Exception("Fatal error finding ViewState");
  }
}

private static bool ResponseHasTarget(string uri,
                                      string postData,
                                      string target)
{
  byte[] buffer = Encoding.ASCII.GetBytes(postData);

  HttpWebRequest req = (HttpWebRequest)WebRequest.Create(uri);
  req.Method = "POST";
  req.ContentType = "application/x-www-form-urlencoded";
  req.ContentLength = buffer.Length;
  req.Timeout = 5000;

  Stream reqst = req.GetRequestStream();
  reqst.Write(buffer, 0, buffer.Length);
```

```
      reqst.Flush();
      reqst.Close();

      HttpWebResponse res = (HttpWebResponse)req.GetResponse();
      Stream resst = res.GetResponseStream();
      StreamReader sr = new StreamReader(resst);

      string result = sr.ReadToEnd();

      sr.Close();
      resst.Close();

      if (result.IndexOf(target) >= 0)
        return true;
      else
        return false;
    }

  } // class
} // ns
```

CHAPTER 6

Script-Based Web UI Testing

6.0 Introduction

The simplest form of Web application testing is manual testing through the UI; however, because manual testing is often slow, inefficient, and tedious, a good strategy is to supplement manual testing with basic Web application UI test automation. You can do this in several ways. The oldest technique uses JavaScript to manipulate a Web application's controls through the Internet Explorer Document Object Model (IE DOM). The best way to demonstrate this type of testing is visually, so Figure 6-1 shows a sample run of a script-based Web UI test harness.

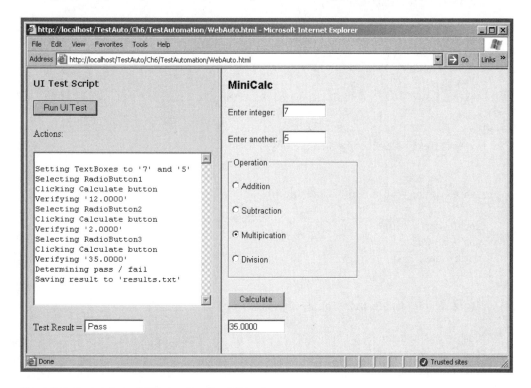

Figure 6-1. *Script-based Web application UI testing*

If you examine Figure 6-1, you'll see that the test harness is a Web page with two frames. The right frame hosts the Web AUT; its display title is MiniCalc. In this example, the application is a simple calculator program. The left frame hosts JavaScript functions that manipulate the Web AUT, examine the resulting state of the application, and log test results to an external file. This chapter presents the various techniques you need to perform script-based Web UI test automation.

Most of the sections in this chapter reference the Web application shown in the right frame in Figure 6-1. The application is named WebApp.aspx. The entire code for the application is

```
<%@ Page Language="C#" Debug="true" %>

<script language="c#" runat="server">
  private void Button1_Click(object sender, System.EventArgs e)
  {
    int alpha = int.Parse(TextBox1.Text.Trim());
    int  beta = int.Parse(TextBox2.Text.Trim());

    if (RadioButton1.Checked)
    {
      TextBox3.Text = Sum(alpha, beta).ToString("F4");
    }
    else if (RadioButton2.Checked)
    {
      TextBox3.Text = Diff(alpha, beta).ToString("F4");
    }
    else if (RadioButton3.Checked)
    {
      TextBox3.Text = Product(alpha, beta).ToString("F4");
    }
    else
     TextBox3.Text = "Select method";
    }

    private static double Sum(int a, int b)
    {
      double ans = 0.0;
      ans = a + b;
      return ans;
    }

    private static double Diff(int a, int b)
    {
      double ans = 0.0;
      ans = a - b;
      return ans;
    }
```

```
    private static double Product(int a, int b)
    {
      double ans = 0.0;
      ans = a * b;
      return ans;
    }
</script>

<html>
  <head><title>WebApp.aspx</title></head>
  <style type="text/css">
   fieldset { width: 16em }
   body { font-size: 10pt; font-family: Arial }
  </style>
  <body bgColor="#ccffff">
    <h3>MiniCalc</h3>
    <form method="post" name="theForm" id="theForm" runat="server">
      <p><asp:Label id="Label1" runat="server">Enter integer:  
        </asp:Label>
      <asp:TextBox id="TextBox1" size="6" runat="server" /></p>
      <p><asp:Label id="Label2" runat="server">Enter another: 
        </asp:Label>
      <asp:TextBox id="TextBox2" size="6" runat="server" /></p>
      <p></p>

      <fieldset>
       <legend>Operation</legend>
       <p><asp:RadioButton id="RadioButton1" GroupName="ops"
         runat="server"/>Addition</p>
       <p><asp:RadioButton id="RadioButton2" GroupName="ops"
         runat="server"/>Subtraction</p>
       <p><asp:RadioButton id="RadioButton3" GroupName="ops"
         runat="server"/>Multipication</p>
       <p><asp:RadioButton id="RadioButton4" GroupName="ops"
         runat="server"/>Division</p>
       <p></p>
      </fieldset>

      <p><asp:Button id="Button1" runat="server" text=" Calculate "
        onclick="Button1_Click" /> </p>

      <p><asp:TextBox id="TextBox3" size="10" runat="server" />
    </form>
  </body>
</html>
```

For simplicity, all the Web application code is contained in a single source file rather than the more usual approach of separating HTML display code and C# (or other .NET-compliant language) code into two separate files. If you examine this code, you'll see that the UI contains two text fields where the user enters two integers, four radio button controls that the user selects to indicate which of four arithmetic operations to perform (addition, subtraction, multiplication, division), a button control to submit the calculation request, and a third text field that displays a result with four decimals.

■**Note** Notice that the label next to the multiplication radio button control is misspelled as "Multipication". Typographical errors in AUTs are common during the testing phase, so be prepared to deal with them when writing automation.

This Web application is simplistic, and your Web AUTs are likely to be much more complex. However, this application has all the key components necessary to demonstrate script-based UI testing. Even if your Web AUT does sophisticated numerical processing or fetches complex data from a SQL data store, each HTTP request-response will result in a new page state that is reflected in the UI.

The code in this chapter assumes that the automation is organized with a root folder containing two subfolders named `TheWebApp` and `TestAutomation`. The `TheWebApp` folder holds the Web AUT (`WebApp.aspx`). The `TestAutomation` folder contains the main test harness structure as a single Web page (`WebAuto.html`) and the page that houses the JavaScript code which runs the test scenario (`TestCode.html`).

Related but lower-level techniques to test a Web application through its UI are presented in Chapter 7. The techniques in this chapter can handle most basic UI testing situations but cannot deal with configurations that have JavaScript disabled. These techniques also cannot manipulate objects that are outside the browser client area (such as alert dialog boxes). The test harness that produced the test run shown in Figure 6-1 is presented in Section 6.8.

6.1 Creating a Script-Based UI Test Harness Structure

Problem

You want to create a structure for a script-based Web application UI test harness that allows you to programmatically manipulate, synchronize, and examine the Web AUT.

Design

Create an HTML page with two frames. One frame hosts the AUT. The second frame hosts the test harness script. The containing HTML page holds synchronization variables and test scenario meta-information.

Solution

```html
<html>
  <head>
    <script language="JavaScript">
      var description = "Description of test scenario";
      var loadCount = 0;
      var pass = true;
    </script>
  </head>

  <frameset cols="40%,*">
    <frame src="TestCode.html" name="leftFrame">
    <frame src="../TheWebApp/WebApp.aspx" name="rightFrame"
      onload="leftFrame.updateState();">
  </frameset>
</html>
```

Comments

Although you can structure a script-based Web application UI test harness in several ways, the organization presented here has proven simple and effective in practice. The `<script>` portion of the HTML harness holds three key variables. Notice we use the `language="JavaScript"` attribute. In a pure Microsoft technology environment, you might want to use `"JScript"` to emphasize the fact that you are using the IE DOM to access Web page controls. The first variable, `description`, is test scenario meta-information. You may want to include other meta-information here such as a test scenario ID or the date and time when the scenario was run. The second variable, `loadCount`, is the key to test harness synchronization. Because HTTP is a stateless protocol, each request-response pair is independent. You need some way to know which state the Web application is in. The easiest way to do this is to use a global variable where a value of 0 indicates an initial state, a value of 1 indicates the next state (after a user clicks a submit button for example), and so on. Observe that when the Web page/document under test finishes loading into the right frame of the test harness, control is transferred to a function `updateState()` located in the page in the left (test code) frame:

```
onload="leftFrame.updateState();"
```

Section 6.2 describes the `updateState()` function. The third variable in the HTML harness page, `pass`, represents the test scenario pass or fail result.

The body of the HTML test harness page just contains two frames, `leftFrame` and `rightFrame`, in this solution. The frames are organized into two columns with the first (left) column receiving 40% of the display area. There's nothing special about the column organization or frame names used here. Using the names `leftFrame` and `rightFrame` implies you have the frames organized in a particular way, but experience has shown that using positionally oriented frame names tends to be easier to read than functionally oriented names such as `frameWithWebApp` and `frameWithHarnessCode`, although this is a matter of personal preference. Frame `rightFrame` holds the AUT. The application does not need to be instrumented in any way, and the techniques in this chapter apply to both classic ASP Web applications and ASP.NET Web applications. Frame `leftFrame` holds the test scenario JavaScript code that manipulates the AUT.

A common mistake when performing script-based UI testing is to attempt to synchronize events by using the setTimeout() method to pause the test automation. Calling setTimeout() stops the thread of execution. Unfortunately, because IE runs under a single thread of execution (with a few rare exceptions), you end up pausing both your test automation and the AUT.

6.2 Determining Web Application State

Problem

You want to determine the state of the Web AUT.

Design

In the TestCode.html page that holds the JavaScript test harness code in the preceding solution, write a function updateState() that increments the global state counter variable and then calls the main test logic.

Solution

```html
<html>
  <head>
    <script language="JavaScript">
      function updateState()
      {
        parent.loadCount++;
          if (parent.loadCount > 1) // > 0 for full-automation
            runTest();
      } // updateState()

      function runTest()
      {
        // runTest() code here
      }

      // other test functions here

    </script>
  </head>
  <body bgColor="#aaff99">
    <h3 style="font-size: 14; font-family: Verdana">UI Test Script
    </h3>
    <p><input type="button" value="Run UI Test" onclick="runTest();">
    </p>
    <p>Actions:</p><p><textarea id="comments" rows="15" cols="34">
    </textarea></p>
    <p>Test Result = <input type="text" name="result" size="12"></p>
  </body>
</html>
```

Comments

If you create a test harness structure as described in Section 6.1, when the Web AUT finishes loading into the test harness right frame, control is transferred to function `updateState()` located in the script part of the page located in the left frame. This state-updating function first increments the global application state counter:

```
parent.loadCount++;
```

Because the state counter is located in the main test harness structure page, you must access it using the `parent` keyword. Next, the `updateState()` function checks if the value of the global state counter is greater than 1. Because the counter is initialized to 0, the counter has a value of 1 when the test harness first launches, which, in turn, loads the Web AUT. If you check for a value greater than 1, the condition is false on the initial page load so the thread of execution stops. This allows you to manually view the test harness and Web AUT, and then launch the test automation manually. If you want full automation, you can edit the condition to

```
if (parent.loadCount > 0)
  runTest();
```

This condition is true on the initial application page load into the test harness structure, and control is immediately transferred to function `runTest()`.

In this solution, the page located in the left frame of the containing test harness page is named `TestCode.html`. In a fully automated situation, such as just described, you do not need any UI for page `WebAuto.html`. However, some minimal UI is required if you want to manually launch the test automation:

```
<body bgColor="#aaff99">
  <h3 style="font-size: 14; font-family: Verdana">UI Test Script</h3>
  <p><input type="button" value="Run UI Test" onclick="runTest();"></p>
  <p>Actions:</p>
  <p><textarea id="comments" rows="15" cols="34"></textarea></p>
  <p>Test Result = <input type="text" name="result" size="12"></p>
</body>
```

You give a title to the page containing the JavaScript automation code so that other testers and developers can clearly distinguish which frame holds the AUT and which frame holds the test automation. You supply a button control so that testers can manually launch the test automation as described previously. An HTML `<textarea>` element is handy to display messages containing information about the progress of the test automation as shown in Figure 6-1. Finally, you add a text field so that the overall test scenario pass/fail result can be displayed in a way that stands out from other messages.

6.3 Logging Comments to the Test Harness UI

Problem

You want to display messages that detail the progress of the test automation.

Design

Write a JavaScript helper function `logRemark()` that uses the IE DOM `value` property to set a value into an HTML `<textarea>` comments field.

Solution

```
function logRemark(comment)
{
  var currComment = document.all["comments"].value;
  var newComment = currComment + "\n" + comment;
  document.all["comments"].value = newComment;
} // logRemark()
```

Comments

Although the goal of any test scenario is to produce a pass or fail result, it's useful to have a way to display the progress of the automation. This helps you diagnose the inevitable problems you'll run into and sometimes reveals bugs in the Web AUT as well. The simple `logRemark()` function accepts a comment to log as the single input argument. Notice that JavaScript is a nontyped language, so you don't specify exactly what data type the comment parameter is. The function first grabs any existing content in the `textarea` named `"comments"` using the `value` property and the `document.all` collection. See Section 6.2 for the definition of the comments HTML `<textarea>` element. The function then appends a newline character to the existing comments contents and then appends the text of the input argument comment using the JavaScript + string concatenation operator. The `logRemark()` function finishes by replacing the value of the old comments contents with the newly updated value.

With this helper function in hand, you can enhance the readability and clarity of your test harness output by displaying various messages as the test scenario runs. For example:

```
logRemark("Starting test automation");
logRemark("About to set TextBoxes to '7' and '5'");
```

6.4 Verifying the Value of an HTML Element on the Web AUT

Problem

You want to verify that an HTML element on the Web AUT has a certain value and set a test scenario pass/fail result to the appropriate value.

Design

Write a function `verify()` that accepts a reference to a control element and an expected value for the element and sets a global pass/fail result variable that has been initialized to true (to false if the actual value of the control does not equal the expected value).

Solution

```
function verify(ctrl, val)
{
  if (parent.rightFrame.document.all[ctrl].value != val)
    parent.pass = false;
}
```

Comments

The verify() function accepts a reference to a control and an expected value for the control. The function assumes the existence of a global variable pass located in the containing harness structure Web page as described in Section 6.1. Notice that to access a control in the Web AUT from the left frame, you must "go up" one page using the parent keyword and then "down" one page into the application using the frame name. If the actual value in the specified control is not equal to the expected value argument, the global pass variable is set to false. This scheme assumes that variable pass has been initialized to true. In other words, the logic used here is that you assume the test scenario will pass. After each state change, you check one or more controls looking for an inconsistent value; if you find such a problem, you set pass to false. An alternative approach is to assume the test scenario will fail. Then after all the state changes, you check for a series of consistency values and set pass to true only if all expected conditions/values are met.

The heart of the techniques in this chapter is the capability to access the HTML elements on a Web page using the IE DOM. This is a large topic because the IE DOM has more than 500 properties and nearly as many methods. From a testing point of view, you'll use the value property most often to verify the state of an HTML element, but you'll find other properties useful too. For example, suppose you need to check whether the background color of the Web AUT is pure red. You can write code like this:

```
if (parent.rightFrame.document.bgColor == "#FF0000")
  backgroundIsRed = true;
```

As another example, suppose you want to check whether some Label element is visible to the user. You can write code like this:

```
if (parent.rightFrame.document.all["Label1"].visibility == "visible")
  logRemark("The Label control is visible");
```

After you understand the test structure presented in the techniques in this chapter, your next step is to get a firm grasp of the IE DOM. The better you understand the DOM, the more powerful automation you'll be able to write.

One common situation that can cause trouble is when you need to access text on a Web page/application that is not part of any HTML element other than the body. One way to do this is to use the document.body.innerText property. Another way is to use the createTextRange() and findText() methods:

```
var trange = parent.rightFrame.document.body.createTextRange();

if (trange.findText("foo") == true)
  logRemark("Found 'foo' on the Web page");
else
  logRemark("No 'foo' found");
```

6.5 Manipulating the Value of an HTML Element on the Web AUT

Problem

You want to manipulate an HTML element on the Web AUT to simulate user actions such as typing data into a text field and clicking on buttons.

Design

Use methods and properties of the IE DOM, such as the checked property and the click() method. You need to take into account the state of the Web AUT.

Solution

For example:

```
function runTest()
{
  try {
    if (parent.loadCount == 1)
    {
      parent.rightFrame.document.theForm.TextBox1.value = "7";
      parent.rightFrame.document.theForm.TextBox2.value = "5";
      parent.rightFrame.document.all["RadioButton1"].checked = true;
      parent.rightFrame.document.theForm.Button1.click();
    }
    else if (parent.loadCount == 2)
    {
      parent.rightFrame.document.all["RadioButton3"].checked = true;
      parent.rightFrame.document.theForm.Button1.click();
    }
    else if (parent.loadCount == 3)
    {
        // determine pass or fail result here
        // save test scenario results here
    }
  }
  catch(e) {
    logRemark("Unexpected fatal error: " + e);
  }
} // runTest ()
```

This code simulates a user typing 7 and 5 into the input fields, checking the RadioButton1 control (for addition), clicking the Button1 control (to calculate), and then after the Web application reloads, checking RadioButton3 for multiplication and clicking the Button1 control again. On the third page load, you verify the state of the application (see Section 6.4) and save the scenario result (see Sections 6.6 and 6.7).

Comments

To simulate user interaction with a Web AUT, you first need to determine what user action you want to simulate. In the case of test automation, this is usually placing text into an HTML element to simulate typing, selecting an option from a drop-down control, clicking on a button control, or checking a radio button control. Each of these actions has an intuitively named method or property such as value, click(), and checked. There are hundreds of other properties and methods too. For example, you can simulate a user scrolling a scrollbar component using the scrollTo() method, you can set the focus of an element using the focus() method, and you can highlight text using the select() method. The IE DOM gives you virtually full control over the client area of an HTML Web page. The real trick is knowing which method or property to use. This is a combination of art and science because it's not practical to learn the details of all the IE DOM methods and properties. Fortunately, the methods and properties have meaningful names and are well documented.

Notice that you are constructing a test scenario here rather than a test case. The terms are often used interchangeably, but in general the term *test scenario* refers to test automation that changes the SUT through several states. For instance, in the techniques in this chapter, each part of the test code triggers a new HTTP request-response, which creates a new state of the application that is reflected in the UI. *Test case* normally refers to a testing situation/item in which the test automation manipulates the SUT through one (or possibly two) state changes. For example, in API test cases, inputs are sent to the method under test, and a return value is produced. Web application UI testing is usually performed as a test scenario because most bugs are found when transitioning through multiple states of the Web application; single state bugs are usually detected during the development process.

When constructing test scenarios like the one in this section, you can organize your test effort in one of two ways. You can hard-code the scenario input values into the test script and maintain a lot of separate scenario scripts. A second approach is to write just a few scripts, which are then parameterized to read input files, and maintain a lot of scenario input files. In practice, most test efforts primarily use the first approach, even though it has the disadvantage of requiring you to manage a large number of test scripts.

6.6 Saving Test Scenario Results to a Text File on the Client

Problem

You want to save your test scenario pass/fail result to an external text file on the test client machine.

Design

Instantiate a Scripting.FileSystemObject ActiveX object and then use the object's CreateTextFile() and WriteLine() methods.

Solution

```
function saveResults()
{
  var fso = new ActiveXObject("Scripting.FileSystemObject");
  var f = fso.CreateTextFile("C:\\results.txt", true, false);
  f.WriteLine("Description = " + parent.description);
  if (parent.pass == true)
    f.WriteLine("Result = Pass");
  else
    f.WriteLine("Result = FAIL");
  f.Close();
}
```

The JavaScript language by itself does not contain any native file IO routines, so if you want to save results to file, you must use a JavaScript add-on. Microsoft created script-friendly libraries called ActiveX technologies that essentially extend JavaScript functionality. To write to a text file, the first step is to instantiate a `Scripting.FileSystemObject` object. Next, you use that object to create a handle to a file object. The `CreateTextFile()` method accepts one required argument and two optional arguments. The required argument is the name of the text file to create. The first of the two optional arguments is a Boolean flag to indicate whether any existing file with the same name should be overwritten. In this example, you specify true. The second optional argument is a Boolean flag indicating whether to use Unicode encoding. In this example, you set that argument to false, which causes the text file to use the default ASCII encoding.

Comments

When running script-based Web application UI test automation, you'll often want to write test scenario results to external storage. The simplest way to save results is to write the results to a text file on the client machine.

The technique given here assumes the existence of a global variable `pass`. As a general rule, the use of global variables is not recommended because it makes your code harder to read and maintain. In this case, the simplicity gained by using a global variable seems to outweigh the readability and maintainability penalty.

To write to a file from a JavaScript function, you may have to modify IE's security settings. By default, these settings typically do not allow JavaScript to write to the client machine's hard drive. Go to IE's Security settings and modify the Trusted Sites and ActiveX object scripting execution properties. (The exact process to do this varies depending upon your client configuration.)

One alternative to saving your test results to a text file on the test client machine using ActiveX technology is to save results as a `Cookie` object on the client machine. This approach is more troublesome in general than saving results as a text file because cookies are stored in a binary format, so you have to write an auxiliary JavaScript helper program to read the cookie from disk and then parse the results. In general, you should use this approach only when other approaches are not feasible. A second alternative to saving scenario results as a text file on the client is to save the results into a lightweight database. This technique is described in Section 6.7.

Several of the techniques in Chapter 1 show how to time-stamp the file name of a results file and how to create a time-stamped folder to hold results files. You can adapt the techniques in Chapter 1 to a JavaScript coding environment by using the Date object and the Date. toDateString() and Date.toTimeString() methods.

6.7 Saving Test Scenario Results to a Database Table on the Server

Problem

You want to save your script-based UI test scenario results into a lightweight database on the Web server.

Design

Create an Access database on the Web server. Then post the test results from the client machine via an HTML Form element back to the server and execute an ASP/VBScript program on the server to save the results into the Access database.

Solution

First you create an Access database on the Web server. For example, you could create an Access database named dbResults.mdb with two columns. The first column is named scenarioID, has type AutoNumber, and is a primary key. The second column is named scenarioResult and is type Text. Of course, you may want to add other columns to hold information, such as the date and time of the test run, and so on.

Next, because you need to post the scenario results back to the Web server, you need to place the results text field in the test harness UI into an HTML Form element:

```
<form name="theForm" method="Post" action="..\\SaveResults.asp">
  <p>Test Result = <input type="text" name="result" size="12"></p>
  <p><input type="submit" name="sender" value="Save Results"></p>
</form>
```

You give the Form element a name and specify which script to run (SaveResults.asp) when the form data is posted to the Web server. You also need to edit any lines of code in the test harness that reference the result field to its new name theForm.result. For example:

```
theForm.result.value = " Pass ";
```

You then write a script called SaveResults.asp and save it on the Web server:

```
<html>
<body>
  <%
    strResult = Request.Form("result")
  %>
  <h4>Save Test Results Page</h4>
  <%
    Response.Write("<p>Scenario result = " & strResult & "<BR>")
    Response.Write("<p>Saving result to Access database dbResults.mdb</p>")
```

```
      Const adOpenStatic = 3
      Const adLockOptimistic = 3
      Set objConnection = CreateObject("ADODB.Connection")
      Set objRecordSet = CreateObject("ADODB.Recordset")
      objConnection.Open _
      "Provider = Microsoft.Jet.OLEDB.4.0; " & _
        "Data Source = C:\Inetpub\wwwroot\TestAuto\Ch6\dbResults.mdb"
      objRecordSet.Open "SELECT * FROM tblResults" , _
      objConnection, adOpenStatic, adLockOptimistic
      objRecordSet.AddNew
      objRecordSet("scenarioResult") = strResult
      objRecordSet.Update

      objRecordSet.Close
      objConnection.Close
      Response.Write("Done")
   %>
   </body>
<html>
```

With this code in place, to manually save results after the test scenario runs, you can click on the Save Results button. This action posts the Form element to the Web server and invokes the SaveResults.asp script that will retrieve the test scenario result from the posted Form object and save it into the dbResults.mdb Access database.

Comments

You may want to save your test scenario results on the Web server machine instead of the client machine as described in Section 6.6. One way to do this is to create a lightweight Access database on the Web server and write a script that saves scenario results into the database.

VBScript is used traditionally for server-side scripts, but you can use JavaScript if you prefer. The SaveResults.asp script grabs the test scenario result from the Form using the Request.Form() method. Next, you open a connection to the dbResults.mdb database using the CreateObject() method, which is part of ADO technology. You can think of ADO (ActiveX Data Objects) as a code library that adds database functionality to JavaScript and VBScript. You can add data to a database using ADO in several ways. The simplest technique, as used in this section, is to create a RecordSet object, fill it with the existing data in the database, add a new row to the RecordSet, add the test scenario result to the new row, and then insert using the RecordSet.Update() method.

If you want to save test results programmatically, you can write a saveResults() function that directly submits the Form element containing the scenario result:

```
function saveResults()
{
  document.all["theForm"].submit();
}
```

You can also indirectly submit the Form element by simulating a user click on the save-results button:

```
function saveResults()
{
  document.all["sender"].click();
}
```

When saving results to the SUT Web server, instead of saving to a database, you can save as a text file. You would use the techniques presented in Section 6.6 by creating a `Scripting.FileSystemObject`. If you use this approach, you must modify the Web server security permissions to allow the virtual user/context under which the saving script executes to have permission to write to the hard drive. Exactly how to do this varies from system to system and can be tricky. Additionally, when creating the results file with the `CreateTextFile()` method, you'll either have to specify the full path to the file or use the `MapPath()` method because the IIS Web Server interprets relative paths incorrectly for use with file operations.

6.8 Example Program: ScriptBasedUITest

This program combines several of the techniques in this chapter to create a lightweight test automation harness to test the ASP.NET Web application shown in the right frame in Figure 6-1. The test automation consists of three files. The first file, `WebForm.aspx`, is presented in the introduction section of this chapter. It is a simple client-server calculator demonstration program. The second file is named `WebAuto.html`. This HTML container houses two frames, one for the Web AUT and one for the test harness code. Following is the code for `WebAuto.html`:

```html
<html>
  <head>
    <script language="JavaScript">
      var description = "Demo Test Scenario";
      var whenRun = new Date();
      var loadCount = 0;
      var pass = true;
    </script>
  </head>

  <frameset cols="40%,*">
    <frame src="TestCode.html" name="leftFrame">
    <frame src="../TheWebApp/WebApp.aspx" name="rightFrame"
      onload="leftFrame.updateState();">
  </frameset>
</html>
```

The third file that makes up the test scenario is named `TestCode.html`. This HTML page houses the JavaScript test harness code. The entire page is provided in Listing 6-1. When run, the output will be as shown in Figure 6-1 in the introduction section of this chapter. The code in this section assumes that the automation is organized with a root folder containing two subfolders named `TheWebApp` and `TestAutomation`. The `TheWebApp` folder holds the Web AUT (`WebApp.aspx`). The `TestAutomation` folder contains the main test harness structure as a single Web page (`WebAuto.html`) and the page that houses the JavaScript code which runs the test scenario (`TestCode.html`).

Listing 6-1. *Test Harness File* TestCode.html

```
<html>
  <head>
    <script language="JavaScript">
      function updateState()
      {
        parent.loadCount++;
          if (parent.loadCount > 1)
            runTest();
      } // updateState()

      function runTest()
      {
      try {
        if (parent.loadCount == 1)
        {
          logRemark("Setting TextBoxes to '7' and '5'");
          logRemark("Selecting RadioButton1");
          logRemark("Clicking Calculate button");
          parent.rightFrame.document.theForm.TextBox1.value = "7";
          parent.rightFrame.document.theForm.TextBox2.value = "5";
          parent.rightFrame.document.all["RadioButton1"].checked = true;
          parent.rightFrame.document.theForm.Button1.click();
        }
        else if (parent.loadCount == 2)
        {
          logRemark("Verifying '12.0000'");
          verify("TextBox3", "12.0000");
          logRemark("Selecting RadioButton2");
          logRemark("Clicking Calculate button");
          parent.rightFrame.document.all["RadioButton2"].checked = true;
          parent.rightFrame.document.theForm.Button1.click();
        }
        else if (parent.loadCount == 3)
        {
          logRemark("Verifying '2.0000'");
          verify("TextBox3", "2.0000");
          logRemark("Selecting RadioButton3");
          logRemark("Clicking Calculate button");
          parent.rightFrame.document.all["RadioButton3"].checked = true;
          parent.rightFrame.document.theForm.Button1.click();
        }
```

```
    else if (parent.loadCount == 4)
    {
      logRemark("Verifying '35.0000'");
      verify("TextBox3", "35.0000");
      logRemark("Determining pass / fail");
      if (parent.pass == true)
        theForm.result.value = " Pass ";
      else
        theForm.result.value = " *FAIL* ";
      logRemark("Saving result to 'results.txt'");
      saveResults();
      logRemark("Run at " + parent.whenRun);
    }
  }
  catch(e) {
    logRemark("Unexpected fatal error: " + e);
  }
} // runTest()

function logRemark(comment)
{
  var currComment = document.all["comments"].value;
  var newComment = currComment + "\n" + comment;
  document.all["comments"].value = newComment;
} // logRemark()

function verify(ctrl, val)
{
  if (parent.rightFrame.document.all[ctrl].value != val)
    parent.pass = false;
}

function saveResults()
{
  var fso = new ActiveXObject("Scripting.FileSystemObject");
  var f = fso.CreateTextFile("C:\\results.txt", true, false);
  f.WriteLine("Description = " + parent.description);
  if (parent.pass == true)
    f.WriteLine("Result = Pass");
  else
    f.WriteLine("Result = FAIL");
  f.Close();
  // document.all["sender"].click();
  //document.all["theForm"].submit();
} // saveResults()
```

```
      </script>
    </head>
    <body bgColor="#aaff99">
      <h3 style="font-size: 14; font-family: Verdana">UI Test Script
      </h3>
      <p><input type="button" value="Run UI Test" onclick="runTest();">
      </p>
      <p>Actions:</p><p><textarea id="comments" rows="15" cols="34">
      </textarea></p>

      <form name="theForm" method="Post" action="..\\SaveResults.asp">
        <p>Test Result = <input type="text" name="result" size="12"></p>
        <p><input type="submit" name="sender" value="Save Results"></p>
      </form>
      <p>
    </body>
</html>
```

■■■

CHAPTER 7

Low-Level Web UI Testing

7.0 Introduction

The techniques in this chapter show you how to perform Web application UI testing by making calls to low-level API functions. These techniques are closely related to those in Chapter 6, which manipulate the client area of a Web application using JavaScript calls to the Internet Explorer Document Object Model (IE DOM). The techniques in this chapter are more powerful, meaning they give you greater control and flexibility over your test automation. This allows you to perform more complex UI testing. The heart of these low-level techniques is calling directly into the `mshtml.dll` and `shdocvw.dll` libraries to access and manipulate HTML objects in the client area of IE. Although these techniques have been available for several years, before .NET your only option was to write fairly complex COM code. The .NET environment greatly simplifies writing test automation code using this low-level technique. Figure 7-1 shows a sample run of a low-level Web UI test scenario.

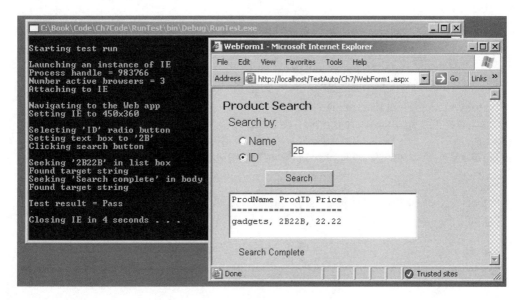

Figure 7-1. *Low-level Web application UI testing*

If you examine Figure 7-1, you'll see that the test harness is a console application. The test harness launches an instance of the IE browser and attaches to it, loads the Web AUT into the browser, manipulates the browser, simulates a user exercising a product-search Web application, and checks the application state to determine a test scenario pass or fail result.

Many of the techniques in this chapter make reference to the Web application shown in the foreground of Figure 7-1. The application was created using Visual Studio .NET 2003 and has the default WebForm1.aspx name. The application has three Label controls, a RadioButtonList control, a TextBox control, a Button control, and a ListBox control. For simplicity, all the names of the controls are the Visual Studio defaults: Label1, Label2, Button1, and so on. Obviously, your Web AUTs will be more complex than this, but the demonstration application has all the key features necessary to illustrate low-level Web application UI testing. The Web application searches through a data store of product information, filtering by product name or product ID. A realistic Web application would likely search through a SQL database of product information. However, the demonstration application searches through a local data store implemented as an ArrayList of Product objects. The local Product class is defined as

```
class Product
{
  public string name;
  public string id;
  public double price;

  public Product(string name, string id, double price)
  {
    this.name = name;
    this.id = id;
    this.price = price;
  }
}
```

and the data store is created when the Web application loads

```
private System.Collections.ArrayList al =
  new System.Collections.ArrayList();

private void Page_Load(object sender, System.EventArgs e)
{
  Product p1 = new Product("widgets", "1A11A", 11.11);
  Product p2 = new Product("gadgets", "2B22B", 22.22);
  Product p3 = new Product("foozles", "3C33C", 33.33);

  al.Add(p1);
  al.Add(p2);
  al.Add(p3);

  Label3.Visible = false; // "Search Complete" message
}
```

The key code for the Web AUT search functionality is

```
private void Button1_Click(object sender, System.EventArgs e)
{
  ListBox1.Items.Clear();
  string filter = TextBox1.Text;
  ListBox1.Items.Add("ProdName ProdID Price");
  ListBox1.Items.Add("=====================");

  if (RadioButtonList1.SelectedValue == "Name")
  {
    foreach (Product p in al)
    {
      if (p.name.IndexOf(filter) >= 0)
        ListBox1.Items.Add(p.name + ", " + p.id + ", " + p.price);
    }
  }
  else if (RadioButtonList1.SelectedValue == "ID")
  {
    foreach (Product p in al)
    {
      if (p.id.IndexOf(filter) >= 0)
        ListBox1.Items.Add(p.name + ", " + p.id + ", " + p.price);
    }
  }

  Label3.Visible = true;

}
```

When testing an application through its UI, it does not particularly matter where or how the new application state is determined. In other words, in UI testing, you don't care if the application is searching through a SQL database, a text file, or a local data store. Each user action on the application (for example, clicking on the Search button) ultimately causes the state of the application to change, which will be reflected in the UI (for example, the text displayed in the ListBox control). Testing situations like this, in which you do not have access to the source code of the AUT/SUT, are often referred to as *black box testing*. If you have full access to the source code, the situation is often called *white box testing*. These two terms, along with variations such as *gray box* and *clear box testing*, are probably the most overused terms in software testing. The terms themselves are not important, but the principles behind them help you identify the limitations on the types of testing you can perform. For example, in a black box testing situation, you must rely on general testing principles when creating test cases; however, in a white box testing situation, you can create test cases specifically designed to exercise a particular code path in the SUT.

Related but higher-level techniques to test a Web application through its UI were presented in Chapter 6. Those techniques access the client area of a Web application using the IE DOM. You can think of the IE DOM as essentially a wrapper around functions in the mshtml.dll and shdocvw.dll libraries. The techniques in this chapter are called low-level because they call directly into `mshtml.dll` and `shdocvw.dll` functions, in effect operating at one level of abstraction lower than the techniques presented in Chapter 6. The techniques in this chapter, combined with those in Chapter 3, allow you to access all areas of a Web application—the client area, the browser shell, and external windows. The test harness that produced the test run shown in Figure 7-1 is presented in Section 7.9.

7.1 Launching and Attaching to IE

Problem

You want to launch an instance of an IE browser and attach to it in a way that will allow you to programmatically manipulate, synchronize, and examine the Web AUT.

Design

Launch an instance of IE using the `Process.Start()` method and retrieve the returned process object. Then instantiate an `InternetExplorer` object and associate the `InternetExplorer` object handle to the process handle.

Solution

```
try
{
  InternetExplorer ie = null;
  Console.WriteLine("\nLaunching an instance of IE");
  Process p = Process.Start("iexplore.exe", "about:blank");
  if (p == null)
    throw new Exception("Could not launch IE");
  Console.WriteLine("Process handle = " + p.MainWindowHandle.ToString());

  SHDocVw.ShellWindows allBrowsers = new SHDocVw.ShellWindows();
  Console.WriteLine("Number active browsers = " + allBrowsers.Count);

  if (allBrowsers.Count == 0)
    throw new Exception("Cannot find IE");

  Console.WriteLine("Attaching to IE");
  int i = 0; // attach to correct browser
  while (i < allBrowsers.Count && ie == null)
  {
    InternetExplorer e = (InternetExplorer)allBrowsers.Item(i);
    if (e.HWND == (int)p.MainWindowHandle)
      ie = e;
    ++i;
  }
```

```
  if (ie == null)
    throw new Exception("Failed to attach to IE");
}
catch(Exception ex)
{
  Console.WriteLine("Fatal error: " + ex.Message);
}
```

You can use the static `Process.Start()` method from the `System.Diagnostics` namespace to launch the IE program. However, you now have two different processes, and the test harness cannot directly communicate with the Web browser. To solve this problem, you instantiate an `InternetExplorer` object from the `shdocvw.dll` library and then assign the process handle of the IE program/process to the `InternetExplorer` object. This allows you to directly access the IE program from your test harness.

Comments

You begin by calling `Process.Start()` with arguments `"iexplore.exe"` and `"about:blank"`. Notice you must fetch the return value from `Start()` into a `Process` object. Instead of loading the virtual page `"about:blank"`, you could load the Web AUT at this time. However, experience has shown that you are less likely to run into problems with your test automation if you load the AUT only after you have attached to the IE program. Additionally, if IE fails to launch at this point in your automation, you know that the AUT was not the source of the error.

After launching an instance of the IE program, you instantiate and fetch a collection of all active browser objects using the `ShellWindows()` method. The `ShellWindows()` method is housed in the `shdocvw.dll` API library. To access `ShellWindows()` you must add a project reference to your test automation harness that points to the Microsoft Internet Controls component in the classic COM list of references. (Notice that unlike using .NET references, determining the name of the COM component that houses a particular DLL or function is sometimes not obvious.) The .NET Framework marshals `shdocvw.dll` to a .NET namespace aliased to `SHDocVw`; this lets you add

```
using SHDocVw;
```

to your test harness if you want to avoid fully qualifying the `InternetExplorer` class and other classes and objects you use from the `shdocvw.dll` library.

The collection of browser objects returned by `ShellWindows()` includes the instance of IE you just launched, any previously launched IE programs, and running instances of Windows Explorer. You must iterate through the collection to find exactly which one is your test instance. To do this, you first instantiate an `InternetExplorer` object. This object is also defined in the `SHDocVw` namespace. The solution here loops through the shell windows collection using an index variable initialized to 0 and a `while` loop:

```
while (i < allBrowsers.Count && ie == null)
```

The loop exits if all available shell window objects have been examined but the test IE program was not found or if the `InternetExplorer` object is not `null`. In the first case, a fatal logic flaw exists in the test harness, and you can throw an exception. In the second case, you have successfully found the test IE program. The actual attaching of the `InternetExplorer` object to the running IE program occurs when a match is found between the `HWND` (handle to window) of the current shell window object being examined and the `MainWindowHandle` property of the test IE process:

```
if (e.HWND == (int)p.MainWindowHandle)
  ie = e;
```

Notice that because `shdocvw.dll` is a pre-.NET unmanaged library, the `HWND` member of an `InternetExplorer` object is a handle that is really just an alias for an integer. But the .NET process object's `MainWindowHandle` is type `IntPtr`, which is a platform-specific .NET type used to represent either a pointer (memory address) or a handle. To make these two values comparable with the `==` operator, you cast the `IntPtr` type to an `int`.

In some testing situations, you may want to set a precondition that no other instances of IE or other browsers may be running. This prevents any possible browser interaction side effects. If this is the case, after launching an IE process, you can check to make sure no other browser instances are active and then attach to the single item in the `ShellWindows` collection:

```
InternetExplorer ie = null;
if (allBrowsers.Count > 1)
  throw new Exception("Other browser instances found");
else
  ie = (InternetExplorer)allBrowsers.Item(0);
```

7.2 Determining When the Web AUT Is Fully Loaded into the Browser

Problem

You want to determine whether the Web AUT is completely loaded into the test IE browser.

Design

Register a `DWebBrowserEvents2` interface event handler and synchronize the handler with a class-scope `AutoResetEvent` object and class-scope method delegate.

Solution

```
class Class1
{
  static AutoResetEvent documentComplete = new AutoResetEvent(false);

  static void Main(string[] args)
  {
    SHDocVw.InternetExplorer ie = null;
    // launch Internet Explorer program - see Section 7.1
    // attach object ie to IE program process - see Section 7.1
```

```
ie.DocumentComplete += new
  DWebBrowserEvents2_DocumentCompleteEventHandler(ie_DocumentComplete);
Console.WriteLine("\nNavigating to the Web app");
object nil = new object();
ie.Navigate("http://server/path/WebApp.aspx", ref nil, ref nil,
           ref nil, ref nil);

documentComplete.WaitOne();
} // Main()

private static void ie_DocumentComplete(object pDisp, ref object URL)
{
  documentComplete.Set();
}
} // class
```

A surprisingly tricky task when writing low-level Web application UI automation is determining exactly when the AUT is completely loaded into the test IE browser. This is essential because otherwise your automation may attempt to manipulate the AUT before it's ready, which almost certainly causes an exception to be thrown. The `InternetExplorer` object in the `shdocvw.dll` library contains a `DocumentComplete` event, which is associated with the `DWebBrowserEvents2` interface. (This interface replaces an older, obsolete `DWebBrowserEvents` interface.) It designates an event sink interface that your automation harness can implement to receive event notifications from the IE program. The second piece of the solution is to use an `AutoResetEvent` object to synchronize your test automation control flow.

Comments

After you've created an `InternetExplorer` object and attached it to a running IE process (as described in Section 7.1), you can register an event handler using the `DWebBrowserEvents2` interface and associate it with the `InternetExplorer.DocumentComplete` event. The constructor accepts a method delegate that is an alias for a real method to transfer control to when the `DocumentComplete` event fires. In this solution, you transfer control to a method that just sets an `AutoResetEvent` synchronizing object to `signaled`. In other words, when the IE process finishes loading its HTTP response page, the `DocumentComplete` event fires and control transfers to the method delegate that sets the `AutoResetEvent` object to `signaled`. So, you can pause your test automation at any point by inserting an `AutoResetEvent.WaitOne()` call. The thread of execution is blocked until `AutoResetEvent.Set()` is called, which only happens when the current document in IE has finished loading completely. Notice that as written, your automation could wait forever if there is a problem, and your Web AUT never finishes loading. To avoid this, you can pass an integer argument and a Boolean flag to the `WaitOne()` method, which will specify a maximum timeout in milliseconds and determine whether or not to exit the synchronization domain for the context before the wait. For example:

```
documentComplete.WaitOne(9000, true);
```

A common, but incorrect way to attempt to pause test automation until a Web AUT is completely loaded into the test IE browser, is to insert `Thread.Sleep()` statements. Because, with few exceptions, IE runs under a single thread of execution, `Thread.Sleep()` will cause both the test automation and IE to halt.

With a mechanism for making sure that a Web page is fully loaded in hand, you can navigate to the AUT using the `InternetExplorer.Navigate()` method. For example:

```
object nil = new object();
ie.Navigate("http://server/path/WebApp.aspx", ref nil, ref nil,
            ref nil, ref nil);
```

The `Navigate()` method accepts five arguments. The first argument is required and is the URL of the application to navigate to. The other four parameters are optional. In most cases, you can pass references to a dummy object for the other four arguments as you've done here. The first optional parameter is a reference to an object holding a constant that specifies whether to add the resource to the history list, whether to read from or write to the cache, and whether to display the resource in a new window. The second optional parameter is a reference to an object holding a string that specifies which frame to display. The third optional parameter is a reference to an object holding a string that is HTTP POST data (typically that data contained in an HTML form element). The fourth optional parameter is a reference to an object holding a string that specifies additional HTTP headers to send to the Web server. Because your automation manipulates IE through its UI, you do not need to pass any of these optional arguments. For example, instead of using the argument that directly sends HTTP POST data, you just simulate a click on the submit button associated with a form element.

7.3 Manipulating and Examining the IE Shell

Problem

You want to programmatically manipulate and examine the test IE browser to simulate user actions such as resizing the browser and reading the status bar.

Design

Use the methods and properties of the `InternetExplorer` object such as `Height`, `Width`, and `StatusText`.

Solution

```
InternetExplorer ie = null;
// attach ie to test Internet Explorer process - see Section 7.1


Console.WriteLine("Setting IE to size 450x360");
ie.Width = 450;
ie.Height = 360;
Thread.Sleep(1000);
```

```
if (ie.StatusText.IndexOf("Done") == -1)
  Console.WriteLine("Could not find 'Done' in status bar");
else
  Console.WriteLine("Found 'Done' in status bar as expected");
Thread.Sleep(1000);

Console.WriteLine("Moving IE to position (50,100)");
ie.Left = 50;
ie.Top = 100;
Thread.Sleep(1000);

Console.WriteLine("Checking address bar value");
if (ie.LocationURL != "http://server/path/WebApp.aspx")
  pass = false;
```

Comments

When writing Web application UI test automation, there are three different areas of IE to take into account—the client area, which holds the Web page under test; the shell area, which holds IE controls such as the Address bar and the Back button; and the windows, such as alert boxes, which are separate from IE altogether. The InternetExplorer object has methods and properties you can use to manipulate the shell (to simulate user actions) and to examine the shell (to determine a test scenario pass/fail result). These properties and methods are fully documented, but here are nine of the most useful ways to manipulate the shell:

- GoBack(): Navigate backward one item in the history list.

- GoForward(): Navigate forward one item in the history list.

- GoHome(): Navigate to the current home page.

- Refresh(): Refresh the page currently loaded in IE.

- Quit(): Close IE.

- Height, Width: Set the height/width of the shell (in pixels).

- Top, Left: Set the top/left location of the shell (in pixels).

In addition to the methods and properties listed here, following are five useful properties you can use to determine a test scenario pass/fail result:

- FullScreen: Returns true if IE is in full-screen mode.

- MenuBar: Returns true if the IE menu bar is visible.

- Resizable: Returns true if IE is resizable.

- LocationURL: Returns the URL of the current page being displayed in IE.

- StatusText: Returns the text in the IE status bar.

7.4 Manipulating the Value of an HTML Element on the Web AUT

Problem

You want to manipulate an HTML input element on the Web AUT to simulate user actions such as typing data into a text field and clicking on buttons.

Design

Create a reference to the Web application document body using the `Document` property of the `InternetExplorer` object. Then use the `getElementById()` method from the `mshtml.dll` library to get a reference to the HTML element you want to manipulate and set the `value` or other appropriate property of the element object to the desired value.

Solution

```
HTMLDocument theDoc = (HTMLDocument)ie.Document;

Console.WriteLine("\nSelecting 'Name' radio button");
HTMLInputElement radioButton =
  (HTMLInputElement)theDoc.getElementById("RadioButtonList1_0");
radioButton.@checked = true;

Console.WriteLine("Setting text box to 'foo'");
HTMLInputElement textBox =
  (HTMLInputElement)theDoc.getElementById("TextBox1");
textBox.value = "foo";

Console.WriteLine("Setting dropdown list to 'blue'");
HTMLSelectElement dropdown =
  (HTMLSelectElement)theDoc.getElementById("DropDownList1");
dropdown.value = "blue";

Console.WriteLine("Clicking search button");
HTMLInputElement butt =
  (HTMLInputElement)theDoc.getElementById("Button1");
butt.click();

documentComplete.WaitOne(); // see Section 7.2
```

This example assumes you have created and attached to an `InternetExplorer` object as described in Sections 7.1 and 7.2. You declare an `HTMLDocument` object and assign it to a reference to the application document body. The `HTMLDocument` type is defined in the `mshtml.dll` library. To access this library, you can add a project reference to the .NET `Microsoft.mshtml` component. This managed code library maps to the `mshtml` namespace, so you can add the statement

```
using mshtml;
```

to your test harness to avoid having to fully qualify the HTMLDocument type and other classes you want to use. After you have an HTMLDocument object, you can obtain a reference to an HTML element that has an ID string by using the getElementByID() method. After you have this object, you can simulate a user manipulating the element by assigning a value using the value property. In the preceding solution, to simulate a user checking the radio button control, you must use @checked because checked is a keyword in the C# language.

Comments

The technique to manipulate controls on your Web AUT is relatively simple in the .NET programming environment, at least compared with doing the same task using unmanaged code. Notice that because the getElementById() method is used to obtain a reference to the element/control you want to manipulate, the control must have an ID attribute that uniquely identifies it. If your Web AUT is created by Visual Studio .NET UI designer, this is not a problem because all controls receive an ID attribute. However, ID attributes are optional, so Web applications created manually, using Notepad for example, may need to be modified to include an ID attribute to use the technique presented here.

A key tool to help you understand and extend this solution is the Object Browser in Visual Studio .NET. If you point the Object Browser to the mshtml reference and expand the tree control, you'll see literally thousands of classes and methods that are available to you. There is far more data here than you can possibly memorize, but fortunately, very few of these classes are needed to write effective test automation. To determine which object interface in the mshtml namespace you need to use, probe an object on your Web application. For example, notice that in the preceding solution, both a button control and a text box control are type HTMLInputElement but a drop-down control is type HTMLSelectElement. Just how can you know this? You can determine the correct class to use with code like this:

```
object o1 = (object)theDoc.getElementById("TextBox1");
Console.WriteLine("The textbox has type "+ o1.GetType().ToString());

object o2 = (object)theDoc.getElementById("DropDownList1");
Console.WriteLine("The dropdown has type " + o2.GetType().ToString());
```

The techniques in this section manipulate only controls in the client area of the IE browser. To manipulate menu bar items or windows that are not part of the client area, you can use the techniques in Chapter 3.

7.5 Verifying the Value of an HTML Element on the Web AUT

Problem

You want to verify that an HTML element on the Web AUT has a certain value so you can set a test scenario pass/fail result to the appropriate value.

Design

Create a reference to the Web application document body using the Document property of the InternetExplorer object. Then use the getElementsByTagName() method from the mshtml.dll library to get a collection of HTML elements, followed by the item() method to get the particular element you want to examine. You can then retrieve the actual value of the HTML element using the InnerText property.

Solution

Suppose, for example, a Web AUT has several `<p>` elements, a `<div>` element with ID "div2", and a single `<select>` element. This code will look for "aloha" in the `<p>` element, "adios" in the `<div>` element, and "ciao" in the `<select>` element:

```
bool pass = true;

// get HTMLDocument object theDoc -- see Section 7.4

Console.WriteLine("Seeking 'aloha' in <p>[2]");
HTMLParaElement paraElement =
  (HTMLParaElement)theDoc.getElementsByTagName("p").item(2, null);
if (paraElement.innerText.ToString().IndexOf("aloha") >= 0)
{
  Console.WriteLine("Found target 'aloha'");
}
else
{
  Console.WriteLine("*Target string not found*");
  pass = false;
}

Console.WriteLine("Seeking 'adios' in <div id='div2'>");
HTMLDivElement divElement =
  (HTMLDivElement)theDoc.getElementsByTagName("div").item("div2", null);
if (divElement.innerText.ToString().IndexOf("adios") >= 0)
{
  Console.WriteLine("Found target 'adios'");
}
else
{
  Console.WriteLine("*Target string not found*");
  pass = false;
}

Console.WriteLine("\nSeeking 'ciao' in list box");
HTMLSelectElement selElement =
  (HTMLSelectElement)theDoc.getElementsByTagName("select").item(0, null);
if (selElement.innerText.ToString().IndexOf("ciao") >= 0)
```

```
{
  Console.WriteLine("Found target 'ciao'");
}
else
{
  Console.WriteLine("*Target string not found*");
  pass = false;
}
```

The parameters to the `item()` method are a bit tricky. The first parameter can be either an integer that is interpreted as a 0-based index value, or the parameter can be a string that is interpreted as the tag name. The second argument to `item()` is also an index value, but it is only used when the `item()` method returns a collection instead of an atomic object. In the preceding solution, the code

```
getElementsByTagName("p").item(2, null);
```

gets a collection of all the <p> elements, and then returns the particular <p> element that has index [2], that is, the third <p> element.

Comments

You'll often need to programmatically examine HTML element values on the document body of the AUT that are not part of any child HTML element. Here's one way to do that:

```
Console.WriteLine("Seeking 'howdy' in body");
HTMLBody body =
  (HTMLBody)theDoc.getElementsByTagName("body").item(0, null);
if (body.createTextRange().findText("howdy", 0, 0) == true)
{
  Console.WriteLine("Found target 'howdy'");
}
else
{
  Console.WriteLine("*Target string not found*");
  pass = false;
}
```

You get a reference to the document body and use the `textRange` object and its `findText()` method to search for a target string. The `findText()` method accepts two optional arguments after a required target string argument. The first optional argument specifies the number of characters to search. A positive value means to search forward from the beginning of the `textRange`. A negative value means to search backwards from the end. A value of 0 means to search the entire `textRange` from the beginning. The second optional argument to `findText()` is a flag that indicates the search type according to Table 7-1.

Table 7-1. *Search-Type Flags for* findText()

Value	Meaning
0	Match partial words (default)
1	Match backwards
2	Match whole words only
4	Case-sensitive matching
131072	Match by comparing byte values
536870912	Match diacritical marks
1073741824	Match Kashida characters
2147483648	Match AlefHamza characters

These flag values may be combined. So the call

```
bool result = body.createTextRange().findText("foo", 0, 6);
```

will perform a case-sensitive, whole-word search of the entire body object. Notice that passing a positive-valued first optional argument (meaning to search forward a certain number of characters) is inconsistent with passing 1 as the second optional argument (meaning to search backwards).

7.6 Creating an Excel Workbook to Save Test Scenario Results

Problem

You want to create an Excel workbook to act as a data store to hold the results of test scenario runs.

Design

Use an OleDbConnection object from the System.Data.OleDb namespace to connect to the target machine where you want to store data. Then use an OleDbCommand object, with an appropriate CommandText property, and the ExecuteNonQuery() method.

Solution

```
Console.WriteLine("\nCreating Excel database");

string connStr = "Provider=Microsoft.Jet.OLEDB.4.0;" +
                 "Data Source=C:\\Results\\results.xls;" +
                 "Extended Properties=\"Excel 8.0;HDR=YES\"";
```

```
OleDbConnection conn = new OleDbConnection();
conn.ConnectionString = connStr;
conn.Open();
OleDbCommand cmd = new OleDbCommand();
cmd.Connection = conn;
cmd.CommandText = "CREATE TABLE tblResults (ScenarioID char(5),
                   Result char(4), WhenRun char(19))";
cmd.ExecuteNonQuery();
conn.Close();
```

This example creates a new Excel file named results.xls with a single worksheet named tblResults. The worksheet has three columns with headers named ScenarioID (in cell A1), Result (in cell B1), and WhenRun (in cell C1).

Comments

You may sometimes want to store your test scenario results in an Excel workbook instead of a text file, SQL database, or other more usual data stores. If so, you must create an Excel workbook in such a way that the workbook can programmatically accept data. The easiest way to programmatically interoperate between .NET and Excel is by using OLE DB technology. You start by creating a connection string. You have to be somewhat careful with the syntax. Notice that in the DataSource attribute, you use the double backslash sequence (to represent a single backslash), and in the Extended Properties attribute, you use a \" sequence to embed a double quote character into the connection string. The HDR=YES part of the connection string means to create a header in the first row of the Excel workbook. The "Excel 8.0" part does not directly refer to the version of the Excel spreadsheet program on your computer; it refers to the Jet database ISAM (Indexed Sequential Access Methods) format installed. You can verify the version on the test client machine by viewing system registry setting HKEY_LOCAL_MACHINE\Software\Microsoft\Jet\4.0\ISAM Formats.

After creating an appropriate connection string, you create an OleDbCommand object that will create a worksheet in the workbook specified in the connection string. The creation of the file is implicit—you don't use a Create() or similar method as you might expect. Notice that OLE DB data types are assigned to each column. In this example, you have five characters for a test scenario ID ("12345", for example), four characters for a scenario result ("pass" or "fail"), and 19 characters for information about when the scenario was run ("2006-10-27T13:42:25", for example). You can specify other OLE DB data types, such as int, date, and so on, but generally you are better off making all your data columns type char. Three different data models are in play—C# data types, OLE DB data types, and Excel data types. Experience has shown that using just char data avoids a lot of potential data type conversion problems when you insert test scenario results. If you intend to perform numerical analysis of your test results directly in the Excel results workbook, however, you may want to consider storing directly as type int and so on. For example

```
cmd.CommandText = "CREATE TABLE tblResults (ScenarioID int,
                   Result char(4), WhenRun date)";
```

will create the scenario ID column as a column of integers, the result column as text, and the time when run column as a date (stripping away the time part of the WhenRun variable).

The solution assumes that file `results.xls` does not already exist. If it does exist, an exception will be thrown. The solution also assumes the existence of folder `C:\Results`. When storing test results into an Excel workbook, you can use several organizational strategies. First, you can create just one Excel results file and insert the results of many different test scenario runs into the file. Alternatively, you can create a new Excel results file for each test run. If you are creating many Excel results files, check whether a file with the same name already exists by using the `File.Exists()` method from the `System.IO` namespace.

Several of the techniques in Chapter 1 show how to time-stamp the file name of a results file and how to create a time-stamped folder to hold results files. You can use those same techniques with Excel data files.

7.7 Saving Test Scenario Results to an Excel Workbook

Problem

You want to save your test scenario result into an existing Excel workbook.

Design

Use the `OleDbConnection` and `OleDbCommand` classes in the `System.Data.OleDb` namespace, combined with a `CommandText` property set to an appropriate insert statement.

Solution

```
// run test scenario here
// determine pass/fail result, save in string variable 'result'

string id = "00001";
string whenRun = DateTime.Now.ToString("s");

string connStr = "Provider=Microsoft.Jet.OLEDB.4.0;" +
                 "Data Source=C:\\Results\\results.xls;" +
                 "Extended Properties=\"Excel 8.0;HDR=YES\"";

conn.ConnectionString = connStr;
conn.Open();
OleDbCommand cmd = new OleDbCommand();
cmd.Connection = conn;

cmd.CommandText = "INSERT INTO tblResults (ScenarioID, Result, WhenRun)
           values ('" + id + "', '" + result + "', '" + whenRun + "')";

cmd.ExecuteNonQuery();
conn.Close();
```

This code assumes you have created an Excel file named `results.xls`, which has a worksheet named `tblResults` and a header row with labels `ScenarioID`, `Result`, and `WhenRun`. (See Section 7.6 for details.) After opening a connection to the Excel existing data store, you create an `INSERT` command where the Excel workbook name acts as a table name, and where the Excel headers act as column names.

Comments

It's very easy to make syntax mistakes when constructing the `INSERT` string for the `OleDbCommand` object. For example, suppose an `INSERT` statement with two literals looks like:

```
INSERT INTO table (col1, col2) values ('abc', 'xyz')
```

If the values for `col1` and `col2` are stored in variables, you need to break the `INSERT` statement into five parts: the part up to the first single quote character, the value for `col1`, the part from the second single quote to the third single quote, the value for `col2`, and finally the part from the fourth single quote to the end of the statement:

```
string part1 = "INSERT INTO table (col1, col2) values ('";
string part2 = col1Value.ToString();
string part3 = "', '";
string part4 = col2Value.ToString();
string part5 = "')";
```

There is no shortcut to crafting `INSERT` statements; you just have to be careful.

7.8 Reading Test Results Stored in an Excel Workbook

Problem

You want to programmatically read test results that have been stored in an Excel workbook.

Design

Create an `OleDbConnection` object that points to the workbook, then create an `OleDbCommand` object that has a `SELECT` statement, and then use an `OleDbDataReader` object to iterate through the workbook one row at a time.

Solution

```
string connStr = "Provider=Microsoft.Jet.OLEDB.4.0;" +
                 "Data Source=C:\\Results\\results.xls;" +
                 "Extended Properties=\"Excel 8.0;HDR=YES;IMEX=0\"";
OleDbConnection conn = new OleDbConnection();
conn.ConnectionString = connStr;
conn.Open();
```

```
OleDbCommand cmd = new OleDbCommand();
cmd.CommandText = "SELECT * FROM tblResults";
cmd.Connection = conn;

OleDbDataReader rdr = cmd.ExecuteReader();
while (rdr.Read() == true)
{
  Console.WriteLine(rdr.GetString(0) + " " + rdr.GetString(1) + " " +
                    rdr.GetString(2));
}
rdr.Close();
conn.Close();
```

Here you select all the data columns from an Excel worksheet/table named tblResults. You can also select just some columns using SQL syntax like this:

```
SELECT ScenarioID, Result FROM tblResults WHERE Result='Pass'
```

This pulls out just the ScenarioID values and the Result values for rows of data where the Result value is "Pass". Notice the IMEX=0 part of the Extended Properties attribute portion of the connection string. Using IMEX is optional and specifies the import/export mode. IMEX can take one of three possible values:

- 0 = Export mode (used when reading from Excel)

- 1 = Import mode (used when inserting into Excel)

- 2 = Linked mode (used for full Excel update capabilities)

If all the data in Excel is type text, then specifying an IMEX has no effect. But if you have mixed data types, you should use an IMEX value. The interaction between data types through the ISAM driver can be very complex, so in a test automation scenario, you are generally better off by simply making all data text for import/output purposes.

Comments

As an alternative to using an OleDbDataReader solution for programmatically reading data from an Excel workbook, you can read all data into an in-memory DataSet object. For example:

```
string connStr = "Provider=Microsoft.Jet.OLEDB.4.0;" +
                 "Data Source=C:\\Results\\results.xls;" +
                 "Extended Properties=\"Excel 8.0;HDR=YES;IMEX=0\"";
OleDbConnection conn = new OleDbConnection(connStr);

string select = "SELECT * FROM tblResults";
OleDbDataAdapter oda = new OleDbDataAdapter(select, conn);

DataSet ds = new DataSet();
oda.Fill(ds);
```

```
foreach (DataRow dr in ds.Tables[0].Rows)
{
  Console.WriteLine(dr["ScenarioID"] + " " + dr["Result"] +
                    " " + dr["WhenRun"]);
}

conn.Close();
```

The `DataSet` class is defined in the `System.Data` namespace. You can essentially read the entire Excel worksheet into memory and then iterate through the result set. This technique has more system overhead than using an `OleDbDataReader` object but is useful if you want to perform some processing of the Excel data. Having your data in a `DataSet` object is also useful if you need to make a backward pass through the data because an `OleDbDataReader` object is a forward-only reader.

In addition to saving test scenario results into an Excel workbook, you may also want to store your test case input data in Excel and programmatically read from the workbook. The basic techniques for reading test case input data are exactly the same as reading test results data. As discussed previously in the context of result data, you should probably store all test case input data as type `char`. Then you can read the `char` test case input data and convert to other types if necessary. The situation is very similar to reading test case data from a text file as described in several of the sections in Chapter 1.

7.9 Example Program: LowLevelUITest

This program combines several of the techniques in this chapter to create a lightweight test automation harness to test an ASP.NET Web application through its UI (see Listing 7-1). When run, the output will be as shown in Figure 7-1 earlier in this chapter.

Listing 7-1. *Program LowLevelUITest*

```
using System;
using SHDocVw; // COM component = Microsoft Internet Controls. IE object
using mshtml;  // .NET component = Microsoft.mshtml. HTML interfaces
using System.Diagnostics; // Process
using System.Threading;   // Sleep()

namespace RunTest
{
  class Class1
  {
    static AutoResetEvent documentComplete = new AutoResetEvent(false);
```

```csharp
[STAThread]
static void Main(string[] args)
{
  try
  {
    Console.WriteLine("\nStarting test run");

    bool pass = true; // assume test run will pass
    SHDocVw.InternetExplorer ie = null;

    Console.WriteLine("\nLaunching an instance of IE");
    Process p = Process.Start("iexplore.exe", "about:blank");
    if (p == null)
      throw new Exception("Could not launch IE");
    Console.WriteLine("Process handle = " + p.MainWindowHandle.ToString());

    SHDocVw.ShellWindows allBrowsers = new SHDocVw.ShellWindows();
    Console.WriteLine("Number active browsers = " + allBrowsers.Count);

    if (allBrowsers.Count == 0)
      throw new Exception("Cannot find IE");

    Console.WriteLine("Attaching to IE");
    int i = 0;
    while (i < allBrowsers.Count && ie == null)
    {
      InternetExplorer e = (InternetExplorer)allBrowsers.Item(i);
      if (e.HWND == (int)p.MainWindowHandle)
        ie = e;
      ++i;
    }

    if (ie == null)
      throw new Exception("Failed to attach to IE");

    ie.DocumentComplete += new
DWebBrowserEvents2_DocumentCompleteEventHandler(ie_DocumentComplete);

    Console.WriteLine("\nNavigating to the Web app");
    object nil = new object();
    ie.Navigate("http://localhost/TestAuto/Ch7/WebForm1.aspx",
                ref nil, ref nil, ref nil, ref nil);

    documentComplete.WaitOne();
```

```
Console.WriteLine("Setting IE to size 450x360");
ie.Width = 450;
ie.Height = 360;
Thread.Sleep(1000);

HTMLDocument theDoc = (HTMLDocument)ie.Document;

Console.WriteLine("\nSelecting 'ID' radio button");
HTMLInputElement radioButton =
(HTMLInputElement)theDoc.getElementById("RadioButtonList1_1");
radioButton.@checked = true;

Console.WriteLine("Setting text box to '2B'");
HTMLInputElement textBox =
(HTMLInputElement)theDoc.getElementById("TextBox1");
textBox.value = "2B";

Console.WriteLine("Clicking search button");
HTMLInputElement butt =
(HTMLInputElement)theDoc.getElementById("Button1");
butt.click();

documentComplete.WaitOne();

// non-HTML element
Console.WriteLine("Seeking 'Search Complete' in body");
HTMLBody body =
(HTMLBody)theDoc.getElementsByTagName("body").item(0, null);
if (body.createTextRange().findText("Search Complete", 0, 4)
    == true)
{
  Console.WriteLine("Found target string");
}
else
{
  Console.WriteLine("*Target string not found*");
  pass = false;
}

if (pass)
  Console.WriteLine("\nTest result = Pass\n");
else
  Console.WriteLine("\nTest result = *FAIL*\n");
```

```
      Console.WriteLine("Closing IE in 4 seconds . . . ");
      Thread.Sleep(4000);
      ie.Quit();

    Finish:

      Console.WriteLine("\nEnd test run");
      Console.ReadLine();
    }
    catch(Exception ex)
    {
      Console.WriteLine("Fatal error: " + ex.Message);
      Console.ReadLine();
    }

  } // Main()

  private static void ie_DocumentComplete(object pDisp, ref object URL)
  {
    documentComplete.Set();
  }

  } // class Class1
} // ns RunTest
```

CHAPTER 8

Web Services Testing

8.0 Introduction

The techniques in this chapter show you how to test ASP.NET Web services. You can think of a Web service as a collection of methods that resides on a server machine, which can be called by a client machine over a network. Web services often expose data from a SQL database. For example, suppose you own a company that sells books. You want your book data available to other companies' Web sites to expand your reach. However, you don't want to allow direct access to your databases. One solution to this problem is for you to create an ASP.NET Web service that exposes your book data in a simple, standardized, and secure way. Figure 8-1 shows a demonstration Web application. Users can query a data store of book information. What is not obvious from the figure is that the data displayed on the Web application comes from an ASP.NET Web service, rather than directly from a SQL database.

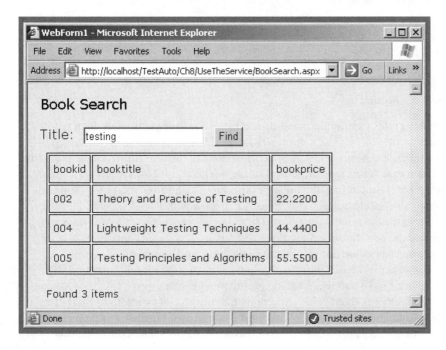

Figure 8-1. *Web application using an ASP.NET Web service*

Behind the scenes, there is an ASP.NET Web service in action. This Web service accepts requests for data from the Web application BookSearch.aspx, pulls the appropriate data from a backend SQL database, and returns the data to the Web application where it is displayed. The Web service has two methods. The first is GetTitles(), which accepts a target string as an input argument and returns a DataSet of book information where the book titles contain the target string. This is the method being called by the Web application in Figure 8-1. The second Web method is CountTitles(), which also accepts a target string but just returns the number of titles that contain the string. The terms Web service and Web method are often used interchangeably.

Testing the methods of a Web service is conceptually similar to the API testing described in Chapter 1—you pass input arguments to the method under test, fetch a return value, and compare the actual return value with an expected value. The main difference is that because Web methods reside on a remote computer and are called over a network, they may be called in several different ways. The fundamental communication protocol for Web services is SOAP (Simple Object Access Protocol). As you'll see, SOAP is nothing more than a particular form of XML. Because of this, Web services are sometimes called XML web services. Although Web services are transport protocol-independent, in practice, Web services are almost always used in conjunction with HTTP. So when a typical Web service request is made, the request is encapsulated in a SOAP/XML packet. That packet is in turn encapsulated in an HTTP packet. The HTTP request packet is then sent via TCP/IP. The TCP/IP packet is finally sent between two network sockets as raw bytes. To hide all this complexity, Visual Studio .NET can call Web methods and receive the return values in a way called a Web service proxy mechanism. Therefore, there are four fundamental ways to call a Web method in an ASP.NET Web service. Listed in order from highest level of abstraction and easiest to code, to lowest level of abstraction, following are the ways to call a Web method:

- Using a Proxy Mechanism (Section 8.1)

- Using HTTP (Section 8.3)

- Using TCP (Section 8.4)

- Using Sockets (Section 8.2)

The techniques in this chapter demonstrate each of these four techniques. Figure 8-2 shows such a run.

Test case #001 in the test run in Figure 8-2 corresponds to the user input and response in Figure 8-1. Each test case is run twice: first by sending test case input and receiving a return value at a high level of abstraction using the proxy mechanism, and second by sending and receiving at a lower level of abstraction using the TCP mechanism. The idea behind testing a system in two different ways is validation. If you test your system in two different ways using the same test case data, you should get the same test results. If you don't get identical results, then the two test approaches are not testing the same thing, and you need to investigate. Notice that test case 002 produces a pass result when calling the GetTitles() method with input *and* via TCP, but a fail result when calling via the proxy mechanism. (Test case 002 contains a deliberately faulty expected value to demonstrate the idea of validation.) Validation is closely related to verification. We often say that verification asks if the SUT works correctly, whereas validation asks if we are testing correctly. However, the two terms are often used interchangeably.

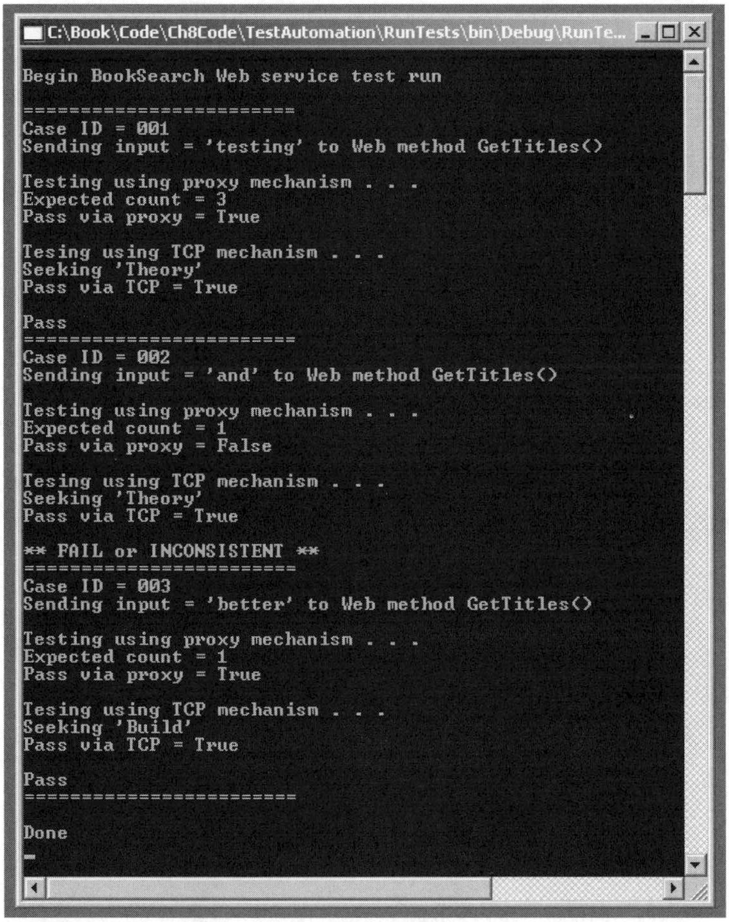

Figure 8-2. *Web service test run with validation*

Many of the techniques in this chapter make reference to the Web service, which supplies the data to the Web application shown previously in Figure 8-1. The Web service is based on a SQL database. The key SQL statements that create and populate the database are

```
create database dbBooks
go

use dbBooks
go

create table tblBooks
(
bookid char(3) primary key,
booktitle varchar(50) not null,
bookprice money not null
)
```

```
go

insert into tblBooks values('001','First Test Automation Principles',11.11)
insert into tblBooks values('002','Theory and Practice of Testing',22.22)
insert into tblBooks values('003','Build Better Software through Automation',33.33)
insert into tblBooks values('004','Lightweight Testing Techniques',44.44)
insert into tblBooks values('005','Testing Principles and Algorithms',55.55)
go

exec sp_addlogin 'webServiceLogin', 'secret'
go

-- grant execute permissions to webServiceLogin here
```

The database dbBooks contains a single table, tblBooks, which has three columns: bookid, booktitle, and bookprice. The table is populated with five dummy records. A SQL login named webServiceLogin is associated with the database. Two stored procedures are contained in the database to access the data:

```
create procedure usp_GetTitles
 @filter varchar(50)
as
 select * from tblBooks where booktitle like '%' + @filter + '%'
go

create procedure usp_CountTitles
 @filter varchar(50)
as
 declare @result int
 select @result = count(*) from tblBooks where booktitle like '%' + @filter + '%'
 return @result
go
```

Stored procedure usp_GetTitles() accepts a string filter and returns a SQL rowset of the rows that have the filter contained in the booktitle column. Stored procedure usp_CountTitles() is similar except that it just returns the number of rows in the rowset rather than the rowset itself.

The Web service under test is named BookSearch. The service has two Web methods. The first method is named GetTitles() and is defined as

```
[WebMethod]
public DataSet GetTitles(string filter)
{
  try
  {
    string connStr =
"Server=(local);Database=dbBooks;UID=webServiceLogin;PWD=secret";
    SqlConnection sc = new SqlConnection(connStr);
    SqlCommand cmd = new SqlCommand("usp_GetTitles", sc);
    cmd.CommandType = CommandType.StoredProcedure;
```

```
    cmd.Parameters.Add("@filter", SqlDbType.VarChar, 50);
    cmd.Parameters["@filter"].Direction = ParameterDirection.Input;
    cmd.Parameters["@filter"].Value = filter;
    SqlDataAdapter sda = new SqlDataAdapter(cmd);
    DataSet ds = new DataSet();
    sda.Fill(ds);
    sc.Close();
    return ds;
  }
  catch
  {
    return null;
  }
} // GetTitles
```

The GetTitles() method calls the usp_GetTitles() stored procedure to populate a DataSet object, which is returned by the method. Similarly, the CountTitles() Web method calls the usp_CountTitles() stored procedure:

```
[WebMethod]
public int CountTitles(string filter)
{
  try
  {
    string connString =
 "Server=(local);Database=dbBooks;UID=webServiceLogin;PWD=secret";
    SqlConnection sc = new SqlConnection(connString);
    SqlCommand cmd = new SqlCommand("usp_CountTitles", sc);
    cmd.CommandType = CommandType.StoredProcedure;
    SqlParameter p1 = cmd.Parameters.Add("ret_val", SqlDbType.Int, 4);
    p1.Direction = ParameterDirection.ReturnValue;
    SqlParameter p2 = cmd.Parameters.Add("@filter", SqlDbType.VarChar, 50);
    p2.Direction = ParameterDirection.Input;
    p2.Value = filter;
    sc.Open();
    cmd.ExecuteNonQuery();
    int result = (int)cmd.Parameters["ret_val"].Value;
    sc.Close();
    return result;
  }
  catch
  {
    return -1;
  }
} // CountTitles()
```

Except for the [WebMethod] attribute, nothing distinguishes these Web methods from ordinary methods; the .NET environment takes care of all the details for you. These are the two methods we want to test. Now, although not absolutely necessary to write test automation code, it helps to see the key code from the Web application that calls the Web service:

```
private void Button1_Click(object sender, System.EventArgs e)
{
  try
  {
    TheWebReference.BookSearch bs = new TheWebReference.BookSearch();
    string filter = TextBox1.Text.Trim();
    DataSet ds = bs.GetTitles(filter);
    DataGrid1.DataSource = ds;
    DataGrid1.DataBind();
    Label3.Text = "Found " + ds.Tables["Table"].Rows.Count + " items";
  }
  catch(Exception ex)
  {
    Label3.Text = ex.Message;
  }
}
```

This code illustrates the proxy mechanism. Calling a Web method of a Web service follows the same pattern as calling an ordinary method. When you test the Web service using a proxy mechanism, the test automation code will look very much like the preceding application code.

When a Web service accesses a database using stored procedures, the stored procedures are parts of the SUT. Techniques to test stored procedure are presented in Chapter 9. The techniques in this chapter demonstrate how to call and test a Web method with a single test case. To construct a complete test harness, you can use one of the harness patterns described in Chapter 4. The complete test harness that produced the test run shown in Figure 8-2 is presented in Section 8.7.

8.1 Testing a Web Method Using the Proxy Mechanism

Problem

You want to test a Web method in a Web service by calling the method using the proxy mechanism.

Design

Using Visual Studio .NET, add a Web Reference to your test automation harness that points to the Web service under test. This creates a proxy for the Web service that gives the Web service the appearance of being a local class. You can then instantiate an object that represents the Web service, and call the Web methods belonging to the service.

Solution

```
try
{
  string input = "the";
  int expectedCount = 1;
  TheWebReference.BookSearch bs = new TheWebReference.BookSearch();
  DataSet ds = new DataSet();

  Console.WriteLine("Calling Web Method GetTitles() with 'the'");
  ds = bs.GetTitles(input);
  if (ds == null)
    Console.WriteLine("Web Method GetTitles() returned null");
  else
  {
    int actualCount = ds.Tables["Table"].Rows.Count;
    Console.WriteLine("Web Method GetTitles() returned " + actualCount + " rows");
    if (actualCount == expectedCount)
      Console.WriteLine("Pass");
    else
      Console.WriteLine("*FAIL*");
  }

  Console.WriteLine("Done");
  Console.ReadLine();
}
catch(Exception ex)
{
  Console.WriteLine("Fatal error: " + ex.Message);
  Console.ReadLine();
}
```

This code assumes there is a Web service named BookSearch that contains a Web method named GetTitles(). The GetTitles() method accepts a target string as an input parameter and returns a DataSet object containing book information (ID, title, price) of the books that have the target string in their titles. When the Web Reference was added to the harness code, the reference name was changed from the default localhost to the slightly more descriptive TheWebReference. This name is then used as a namespace alias. The Web service name, BookSearch, acts as a proxy and is instantiated just as any local class would be, so you can call the GetTitles() method like an ordinary instance method. Notice that the fact that GetTitles() is a Web method rather than a regular method is almost completely transparent to the calling program.

Comments

Of the four main ways to test an ASP.NET Web service (by proxy mechanism, HTTP, TCP, sockets), using the Visual Studio proxy mechanism is by far the simplest. You call the Web method under test just as an application would. This situation is analogous to API testing where your test harness calls the API method under test just like an application would. Using the proxy mechanism is the most basic way to call a Web service and should always be a part of your test automation effort.

In this example, determining the correct return value from the GetTitles() method is more difficult than calling the method. Because GetTitles() returns a DataSet object, a complete expected value would be another DataSet object. In cases where the Web method under test returns a scalar value, such as a single int value for example, determining a pass/fail result is easy. For example, to test the CountTitles() method:

```
Console.WriteLine("Testing CountTitles() via poxy mechanism");
TheWebReference.BookSearch bs = new TheWebReference.BookSearch();
string input = "testing";
int expected = 3;

int actual = bs.CountTitles(input);

if (actual == expected)
  Console.WriteLine("Pass");
else
  Console.WriteLine("*FAIL*");
```

In the preceding solution, after calling GetTitles(), you compare the actual number of rows in the returned DataSet object with an expected number of rows. But this only checks for the correct number of rows and does not check whether the correct row data has been returned. Additional techniques to deal with complex return types, such as DataSet objects, are presented in Chapter 11.

8.2 Testing a Web Method Using Sockets

Problem

You want to test a Web method in a Web service by calling the method using sockets.

Design

First, construct a SOAP message to send to the Web method. Second, instantiate a Socket object and connect to the remote server that hosts the Web service. Third, construct a header that contains HTTP information. Fourth, send the header plus SOAP message using the Socket.Send() method. Fifth, receive the SOAP response using Socket.Receive() in a while loop. Sixth, analyze the SOAP response for an expected value(s).

Solution

Here is an example that sends the string "testing" to Web method GetTitles() and checks the response:

```
Console.WriteLine("Calling Web Method GetTitles() using sockets");
string input = "testing";

string soapMessage = "<?xml version=\"1.0\" encoding=\"utf-8\"?>";
soapMessage += "<soap:Envelope xmlns:xsi=\"http://www.w3.org/2001/XMLSchema-
            instance\"";
soapMessage += " xmlns:xsd=\"http://www.w3.org/2001/XMLSchema\"";
soapMessage += " xmlns:soap=\"http://schemas.xmlsoap.org/soap/envelope/\">";
soapMessage += "<soap:Body>";
soapMessage += "<GetTitles xmlns=\"http://tempuri.org/\">";
soapMessage += "<filter>" + input + "</filter>";
soapMessage += "</GetTitles>";
soapMessage += "</soap:Body>";
soapMessage += "</soap:Envelope>";

Console.WriteLine("SOAP message is: \n");
Console.WriteLine(soapMessage);

string host = "localhost";
string webService = "/TestAuto/Ch8/TheWebService/BookSearch.asmx";
string webMethod = "GetTitles";

IPHostEntry iphe = Dns.Resolve(host);
IPAddress[] addList = iphe.AddressList; // addList[0] == 127.0.0.1
EndPoint ep = new IPEndPoint(addList[0], 80); // ep = 127.0.0.1:80
Socket socket = new Socket(AddressFamily.InterNetwork, SocketType.Stream,
                        ProtocolType.Tcp);
socket.Connect(ep);
if (socket.Connected)
  Console.WriteLine("\nConnected to " + ep.ToString());
else
  Console.WriteLine("\nError: socket not connected");

string header = "POST " + webService + " HTTP/1.1\r\n";
header += "Host: " + host + "\r\n";
header += "Content-Type: text/xml; charset=utf-8\r\n";
header += "Content-Length: " + soapMessage.Length.ToString() + "\r\n";
header += "Connection: close\r\n";
header += "SOAPAction: \"http://tempuri.org/" + webMethod + "\"\r\n\r\n";
Console.Write("Header is: \n" + header);
```

```
string sendAsString = header + soapMessage;
byte[] sendAsBytes = Encoding.ASCII.GetBytes(sendAsString);
int numBytesSent = socket.Send(sendAsBytes, sendAsBytes.Length,
                               SocketFlags.None);
Console.WriteLine("Sending = " + numBytesSent + " bytes\n");

byte[] receiveBufferAsBytes = new byte[512];
string receiveAsString = "";
string entireReceive = "";
int numBytesReceived = 0;

while ((numBytesReceived = socket.Receive(receiveBufferAsBytes, 512,
        SocketFlags.None)) > 0 )
{
  receiveAsString = Encoding.ASCII.GetString(receiveBufferAsBytes, 0,
                                             numBytesReceived);
  entireReceive += receiveAsString;
}

Console.WriteLine("\nThe SOAP response is " + entireReceive);

Console.WriteLine("\nDetermining pass/fail");

if ( entireReceive.IndexOf("002") >= 0 &&
     entireReceive.IndexOf("004") >= 0 &&
     entireReceive.IndexOf("005") >= 0 )
  Console.WriteLine("\nPass");
else
  Console.WriteLine("\nFail");
```

Each of the six steps when using sockets to call a Web method could be considered a separate problem-solution, but because the steps are so completely interrelated, it's easier to understand them when presented together.

Comments

Of the four main ways to test an ASP.NET Web service (by proxy mechanism, HTTP, TCP, sockets), using sockets operates at the lowest level of abstraction. This gives you the most flexibility but requires the most code.

The first step is to construct a SOAP message. You must construct the SOAP message before constructing the HTTP header string because the header string requires the length (in bytes) of the SOAP message. Constructing the appropriate SOAP message is easier than you might expect. You can get a template of the SOAP message from Visual Studio .NET by loading up the Web service as a project. Next you instruct Visual Studio to run the Web service by pressing F5. Because a Web service is a type of library and not an executable, the service cannot run. Instead, Visual Studio launches a utility application that gives you a template for the SOAP message to send. For example, instructing the BookSearch service to run and selecting the GetTitles() method produces a Web page that contains this template information:

The following is a sample SOAP request and response. The placeholders shown need to be replaced with actual values.

```
POST /TestAuto/Ch8/TheWebService/BookSearch.asmx HTTP/1.1
Host: localhost
Content-Type: text/xml; charset=utf-8
Content-Length: length
SOAPAction: "http://tempuri.org/GetTitles"

<?xml version="1.0" encoding="utf-8"?>
<soap:Envelope xmlns:xsi="http://www.w3.org/2001/XMLSchema-instance"
 xmlns:xsd="http://www.w3.org/2001/XMLSchema"
 xmlns:soap="http://schemas.xmlsoap.org/soap/envelope/">
  <soap:Body>
    <GetTitles xmlns="http://tempuri.org/">
      <filter>string</filter>
    </GetTitles>
  </soap:Body>
</soap:Envelope>
```

The lower part of the template is the SOAP message. You can build up the message by appending short strings together as demonstrated in the preceding solution, or you can simply assign the entire SOAP message as one long string. Notice that SOAP is nothing more than a particular type of XML. In XML, you can use either single quotes or double quotes, so replacing the double quote characters in the template with single quote characters often improves readability. If you want to retain the double quote characters, be sure to escape them using the \" sequence as demonstrated in the "Solution" part of this technique. In the preceding template, `<filter>` corresponds to the input parameter for method `GetTitles()`, and the string placeholder represents the value of the parameter. You have to be careful when constructing the SOAP message because the syntax is very brittle, meaning that it usually only takes one wrong character in the message (a missing blank space for example) to generate a general internal server error message.

The second step when calling a Web method using sockets is to instantiate a `Socket` object and connect to the remote server that hosts the Web service. The `Socket` class is housed in the `System.Net.Sockets` namespace. You can instantiate a `Socket` object with a single statement:

```
Socket socket = new Socket(AddressFamily.InterNetwork,
                    SocketType.Stream, ProtocolType.Tcp);
```

Socket objects implement the Berkeley sockets interface, which is an abstraction mechanism for sending and receiving network data. The first argument to the `Socket()` constructor specifies the addressing scheme that the instance of the `Socket` class will use. The `InterNetwork` value specifies ordinary IP version 4. Some of the other schemes include the following:

- `InterNetworkV6`: Address for IP version 6.

- `NetBios`: NetBios address.

- `Unix`: Unix local to host address.

- `Sna`: IBM SNA (Systems Network Architecture) address.

The second argument to the Socket() constructor specifies one of six types of sockets you can create. Using SocketType.Stream means the socket is a TCP socket. The other common socket type is Dgram, which is used for UDP (User Datagram Protocol) sockets. The third argument to the Socket constructor represents the network protocol that the Socket object will use for communication. The type ProtocolType.Tcp is most common but others such as ProtocolType.Udp are available too. The great flexibility you have when instantiating a Socket object points out some of the situations in which you want to call a Web method using sockets instead of the much easier proxy mechanism—for example, using sockets lets you call a UDP-specific Web service. After you have created a Socket object, you can connect to the server that houses the Web service:

```
IPHostEntry iphe = Dns.Resolve(host);
IPAddress[] addList = iphe.AddressList; // addList[0] == 127.0.0.1
EndPoint ep = new IPEndPoint(addList[0], 80); // ep = 127.0.0.1:80

socket.Connect(ep);
if (socket.Connected)
  Console.WriteLine("\nConnected to " + ep.ToString());
else
  Console.WriteLine("\nError: socket not connected");
```

The Socket.Connect() method accepts an EndPoint object. You can think of an EndPoint as an IP address plus a port number. You can specify the IP address directly like this:

```
IPAddress ipa = IPAddress.Parse("127.0.0.1");
```

You can also get the IP address by calling the Dns.Resolve() method that returns a list of IP addresses that map to the host input argument. After you have the IP address, you can create an EndPoint object and then pass that object to the Socket.Connect() method.

The third step when calling a Web method using sockets is to construct a header that contains HTTP information. You can get this information from the Visual Studio-generated template in the first step described earlier in this "Comments" section. You have to be careful with two minor issues, however. The first issue is that HTTP headers are terminated by a \r\n sequence instead of the \n sequence. Additionally the last line of the HTTP header is indicated by a double set of \r\n sequences. The second issue is the SOAPAction header. This header essentially tells the Web server that the HTTP request has SOAP content. This header has been deprecated in the SOAP 1.2 specification in favor of a new "Content-Type:application/soap+xml" header, but for now most servers are expecting a SOAPAction header.

The fourth step when calling a Web method using sockets is to send the header plus SOAP message using the Socket.Send() method:

```
string sendAsString = header + soapMessage;
byte[] sendAsBytes = Encoding.ASCII.GetBytes(sendAsString);
int numBytesSent = socket.Send(sendAsBytes, sendAsBytes.Length,
                        SocketFlags.None);
Console.WriteLine("Sending header + body = " + numBytesSent + " bytes\n");
```

This part of the process is straightforward. You take the data to send as a string, convert to a byte array using the GetBytes() method (located in the System.Text namespace), and then call Socket.Send() passing in the byte array, its length, and a SocketFlags value. The SocketFlags enumeration is rarely needed. For example, `SocketFlags.DontRoute` means to send the bytes without using any routing tables. The `Socket.Send()` method returns the number of bytes sent, which is useful for diagnosing troubles with your test automation. The `Socket.Send()` method and its counterpart `Socket.Receive()` are synchronous methods. You can send and receive asynchronously using `Socket.BeginSend()` and `Socket.BeginReceive()`.

The fifth step when calling a Web method using sockets is to receive the SOAP response using `Socket.Receive()` inside a while loop:

```
byte[] receiveBufferAsBytes = new byte[512];
string receiveAsString = "";
string entireReceive = "";
int numBytesReceived = 0;

while ((numBytesReceived = socket.Receive(receiveBufferAsBytes, 512,
        SocketFlags.None)) > 0 )
{
  receiveAsString = Encoding.ASCII.GetString(receiveBufferAsBytes, 0,
                                             numBytesReceived);
  entireReceive += receiveAsString;
}
```

This code snippet uses a classic stream-reading technique. You declare a byte array buffer to hold chunks of the return data—there is no way to predict how big the return will be. The size of 512 bytes used here is arbitrary. The `Socket.Receive()` method reads bytes from the associated socket, stores those bytes, and returns the actual number of bytes read. If the number of bytes read is 0, then the return bytes have been used up, and you exit the loop. After each block of 512 bytes is received, it is stored as an ASCII string using the `GetString()` method. A second string accumulates the entire received data by appending as each new block arrives.

At this point, you have the entire SOAP response stored into a string variable. If you are just calling a Web method using sockets, then you are done. But if you are testing the Web method, then you must perform the sixth step in the process, which is to examine the received data for an expected value. This is not so easy to do. In the preceding solution, you check the received string for the presence of three substrings, which are the IDs of the three expected books that have "testing" in their titles:

```
if ( entireReceive.IndexOf("002") >= 0 &&
     entireReceive.IndexOf("004") >= 0 &&
     entireReceive.IndexOf("005") >= 0 )
  Console.WriteLine("\nPass");
else
  Console.WriteLine("\nFail");
```

This approach does not absolutely guarantee that the SOAP response is exactly correct. Because the actual return value when calling a Web method using sockets is a SOAP string, which in turn is a kind of XML, a complete expected value would be another SOAP/XML string. Comparing two XML fragments or documents is rather subtle and is discussed in Chapter 12.

This technique reads the entire SOAP response into a string variable. This string could be very long. An alternative approach is to process each 512-byte string as it arrives. However, this approach is tricky because the target string you are searching for could be chopped by the buffering process. For example, if you were searching for the string "002", the response could conceivably break in the middle of the string with "00" coming as the last two characters of one receive block and "2" coming as the first character of the next receive block.

8.3 Testing a Web Method Using HTTP

Problem

You want to test a Web method in a Web service by calling the method using HTTP.

Design

Create an HTTPWebRequest object that points to the Web method, use the GetResponse() method to send name-value pairs that correspond to parameter-argument pairs, and then fetch the response using the GetResponseStream() method.

Solution

This example sends the string "testing" to Web method GetTitles():

```
Console.WriteLine("Calling Web Method GetTitles() using HTTP");

string input = "testing";
string postData = "filter=" + input;
byte[] buffer = Encoding.ASCII.GetBytes(postData);
string uri =
  "http://localhost/TestAuto/Ch8/TheWebService/BookSearch.asmx/GetTitles";

HttpWebRequest req = (HttpWebRequest)WebRequest.Create(uri);
req.Method = "POST";
req.ContentType = "application/x-www-form-urlencoded";
req.ContentLength = buffer.Length;
req.Headers.Add("SOAPAction: \"http://tempuri.org/GetTitles\"");
req.Timeout = 5000;

Stream reqst = req.GetRequestStream(); // add form data to request stream
reqst.Write(buffer, 0, buffer.Length);

reqst.Flush();
reqst.Close();

HttpWebResponse res = (HttpWebResponse)req.GetResponse();
Stream resst = res.GetResponseStream();
StreamReader sr = new StreamReader(resst);

string response = sr.ReadToEnd();

Console.WriteLine("HTTP response is " + response);
```

```
Console.WriteLine("\nDetermining pass/fail");

if ( response.IndexOf("002") >= 0 &&
     response.IndexOf("004") >= 0 &&
     response.IndexOf("005") >= 0 )
  Console.WriteLine("\nPass");
else
  Console.WriteLine("\nFail");

sr.Close();
resst.Close();
```

Because ASP.NET Web services operate over HTTP, you can use the `HttpWebRequest` class to post data directly to Web methods. Web methods expect data in name-value pairs such as

```
filter=testing
```

where the name part is the Web method parameter name, and the value part is the parameter value. The `HttpWebRequest.GetResponse()` method returns an `HttpWebResponse` object, which, in turn, has a `GetResponseStream()` method that can be used to read the response as string data.

Comments

Of the four main ways to test an ASP.NET Web service, using HTTP operates at the middle level of abstraction. The technique provides a nice compromise between simplicity and flexibility. Just as you can generate a SOAP request template as described in Section 8.2, you can also generate an HTTP request template by instructing Visual Studio to run the Web service.

Depending on the particular configuration of the server that hosts the Web service, you may or may not need to add the special `SOAPAction` header:

```
req.Headers.Add("SOAPAction: \"http://tempuri.org/GetTitles\"");
```

In practical terms, it's often easier to first try the request with the header because unrecognized headers are typically ignored by the server. The pattern to post HTTP data is fairly simple: first create a string of name-value pairs that correspond to the Web method's parameter-argument pairs, and then convert the post string to bytes. Next, create an `HttpWebRequest` object using the factory mechanism with the `WebRequest.Create()` method (as opposed to instantiation using the `new` keyword), and then specify values for the `Method`, `ContentType`, and `ContentLength` properties. Send the HTTP request by writing the `POST` data into a `Stream` object (as opposed to using an explicit `Write()` method of some sort), and fetch the response using a `StreamReader` object. The process is best understood by examining concrete examples like the solution in this section, rather than by general principles.

As discussed in Section 8.2, determining a pass/fail result is harder than calling the Web method under test. One good strategy is to structure your underlying database test bed as much as possible so that the data is easily and uniquely identifiable. This is not always feasible, however, and, in such situations, you must sometimes simply rely on manual testing to supplement your test automation. The essence of calling a Web method using HTTP is programmatically posting data to a Web server; see Chapter 5 for additional techniques.

8.4 Testing a Web Method Using TCP

Problem

You want to test a Web method in a Web service by calling the method using TCP.

Design

First, instantiate a `TcpClient` object and connect to the remote server that hosts the Web service. Second, construct a SOAP message to send to the Web method. Third, construct a header that contains HTTP information. Fourth, instantiate a `NetworkStream` object associated with the `TcpClient` object and send the header plus SOAP message using the `NetworkStream.Write()` method. Fifth, receive the SOAP response using a `NetworkStream.Read()` method in a while loop. Sixth, analyze the SOAP response for an expected value(s).

Solution

This example sends the string `"testing"` to Web method `GetTitles()` via TCP:

```
Console.WriteLine("Calling Web Method GetTitles() using TCP");
string input = "testing";

//TcpClient client = new TcpClient("127.0.0.1", 80);
TcpClient client = new TcpClient(AddressFamily.InterNetwork);
client.Connect("127.0.0.1", 80);

string soapMessage = "<?xml version=\"1.0\" encoding=\"utf-8\"?>";
soapMessage += "<soap:Envelope xmlns:xsi=\"http://www.w3.org/2001/XMLSchema-
  instance\"";
soapMessage += " xmlns:xsd=\"http://www.w3.org/2001/XMLSchema\"";
soapMessage += " xmlns:soap=\"http://schemas.xmlsoap.org/soap/envelope/\">";
soapMessage += "<soap:Body>";
soapMessage += "<GetTitles xmlns=\"http://tempuri.org/\">";
soapMessage += "<filter>" + input + "</filter>";
soapMessage += "</GetTitles>";
soapMessage += "</soap:Body>";
soapMessage += "</soap:Envelope>";

string webService = "/TestAuto/Ch8/TheWebService/BookSearch.asmx";
string host = "localhost";
string webMethod = "GetTitles";

string header = "POST " + webService + " HTTP/1.1\r\n";
header += "Host: " + host + "\r\n";
header += "Content-Type: text/xml; charset=utf-8\r\n";
header += "Content-Length: " + soapMessage.Length.ToString() + "\r\n";
header += "Connection: close\r\n";
header += "SOAPAction: \"http://tempuri.org/" + webMethod + "\"\r\n\r\n";
```

```
Console.Write("Header is: \n" + header);

string requestAsString = header + soapMessage;
byte[] requestAsBytes = Encoding.ASCII.GetBytes(requestAsString);

NetworkStream stream = client.GetStream();
stream.Write(requestAsBytes, 0, requestAsBytes.Length);

byte[] responseBufferAsBytes = new byte[512];
string responseAsString = "";
string entireResponse = "";
int numBytesReceived = 0;

while ((numBytesReceived = stream.Read(responseBufferAsBytes, 0, 512)) > 0)
{
  responseAsString = Encoding.ASCII.GetString(responseBufferAsBytes, 0,
                                              numBytesReceived);
  entireResponse += responseAsString;
}

Console.WriteLine(entireResponse);

if ( entireResponse.IndexOf("002") >= 0 &&
     entireResponse.IndexOf("004") >= 0 &&
     entireResponse.IndexOf("005") >= 0 )
  Console.WriteLine("\nPass");
else
  Console.WriteLine("\nFail");
```

Calling a Web method using TCP is very similar to calling a Web method using sockets. This makes sense because the TcpClient class was designed to act as a friendly wrapper around the Socket class. The two techniques are so similar that it's difficult to choose between them. There are two ways to view the question of which technique to use. One argument is that because using TcpClient is slightly cleaner than using the Socket class, you should use TcpClient when calling a Web service over TCP, and you should use Socket only when calling a Web service that is implemented using a non-TCP protocol. In practical terms, because ASP.NET Web services use HTTP, which, in turn, uses TCP, the first argument simplifies to "always use the TcpClient class to call Web methods at a low level." The second argument about which technique to use is that because using TcpClient and Socket are so similar, you might just as well use the Socket class because it's more flexible. So the second argument simplifies to "always use the Socket class to call Web methods at a low level." Ultimately having two different methods in your skill set is better than having just one to choose from. However, because using TcpClient is so similar to using the Socket class, when you are testing a Web method by calling in two different ways as a means to validate your test automation, you should use one or the other technique but not both.

Comments

Of the four main ways to test an ASP.NET Web service, using TCP operates at a low level of abstraction, one just barely above using sockets. There are six discrete steps to perform when testing a Web method using the TcpClient class. These six steps could be considered separate problem/solution pairs but because the steps are so dependent on each other, it's easier to understand them when presented together. The first step is to instantiate a TcpClient object and connect to the server that hosts the Web service under test:

```
TcpClient client = new TcpClient(AddressFamily.InterNetwork);
client.Connect("127.0.0.1", 80);
```

See Section 8.2 for a discussion of the AddressFamily enumeration. After the TcpClient object has been created, you can connect by passing the server IP address and port number. A minor variation you can employ is to pass the sever IP address and port number to an overloaded version of the constructor and omit the AddressFamily specification because InterNetwork is the default value for the Connect() method:

```
TcpClient client = new TcpClient("127.0.0.1", 80);
```

The second step to call a Web method using TCP is to construct a SOAP message to send to the Web method:

```
string soapMessage = "<?xml version=\"1.0\" encoding=\"utf-8\"?>";
soapMessage += "<soap:Envelope xmlns:xsi=\"http://www.w3.org/2001/XMLSchema-
  instance\"";
soapMessage += " xmlns:xsd=\"http://www.w3.org/2001/XMLSchema\"";
soapMessage += " xmlns:soap=\"http://schemas.xmlsoap.org/soap/envelope/\">";
soapMessage += "<soap:Body>";
soapMessage += "<GetTitles xmlns=\"http://tempuri.org/\">";
soapMessage += "<filter>" + input + "</filter>";
soapMessage += "</GetTitles>";
soapMessage += "</soap:Body>";
soapMessage += "</soap:Envelope>";
```

As described in Section 8.2, you can get a SOAP message template from Visual Studio. The third step is to construct a header that contains HTTP information:

```
string webService = "/TestAuto/Ch8/TheWebService/BookSearch.asmx";
string host = "localhost";
string webMethod = "GetTitles";

string header = "POST " + webService + " HTTP/1.1\r\n";
header += "Host: " + host + "\r\n";
header += "Content-Type: text/xml; charset=utf-8\r\n";
header += "Content-Length: " + soapMessage.Length.ToString() + "\r\n";
header += "Connection: close\r\n";
header += "SOAPAction: \"http://tempuri.org/" + webMethod + "\"\r\n\r\n";
Console.Write("Header is: \n" + header);
```

Again, you can get this information from Visual Studio. The fourth step is to instantiate a NetworkStream object associated with the TcpClient object and send the header plus SOAP message using the NetworkStream.Write() method:

```
string requestAsString = header + soapMessage;
byte[] requestAsBytes = Encoding.ASCII.GetBytes(requestAsString);

NetworkStream stream = client.GetStream();
stream.Write(requestAsBytes, 0, requestAsBytes.Length);
```

This step differs most from using the Socket class. After converting the HTTP header and SOAP message into a byte array using the GetBytes() method, you create a NetworkStream object using TcpClient.GetStream() and then send the data over the network using NetworkStream.Write()—very clean and easy. The fifth step to call a Web method using TCP is to receive the SOAP response using a NetworkStream.Read() method inside a while loop:

```
byte[] responseBufferAsBytes = new byte[512];
string responseAsString = "";
string entireResponse = "";
int numBytesReceived = 0;

while ((numBytesReceived = stream.Read(responseBufferAsBytes, 0, 512)) > 0)
{
  responseAsString = Encoding.ASCII.GetString(responseBufferAsBytes, 0,
                                              numBytesReceived);
  entireResponse += responseAsString;
}
```

This step follows almost the same buffered reading pattern as the one described in Section 8.2. You may find it instructive to compare the two code blocks side by side. After you understand the general pattern, you'll find it useful in a wide range of test automation and development scenarios. The sixth and final step to test a Web method using TCP is to examine the SOAP response for some sort of an expected value:

```
Console.WriteLine(entireResponse);

if ( entireResponse.IndexOf("002") >= 0 &&
     entireResponse.IndexOf("004") >= 0 &&
     entireResponse.IndexOf("005") >= 0 )
  Console.WriteLine("\nPass");
else
  Console.WriteLine("\nFail");
```

As discussed in Sections 8.2 and 8.3, determining a pass or fail result is not easy when the return value is as complex as it is here.

8.5 Using an In-Memory Test Case Data Store

Problem

You want to use an in-memory test case data store rather than use external storage such as a text file or SQL table.

Design

Create a class-scope ArrayList object and use the Add() method to insert test case data. Iterate through the ArrayList object using either a foreach or for loop.

Solution

```
class Class1
{
  static ArrayList testcases = new ArrayList();

  static void Main(string[] args)
  {
    try
    {
      Console.WriteLine("\nBegin test run\n");

      testcases.Add("001:GetTitles:testing:3:Theory");
      testcases.Add("002:GetTitles:and:1:Theory");
      testcases.Add("003:GetTitles:better:1:Build");
      testcases.Add("004:GetTitles:Algorithms:1:Algorithms");

      foreach (string testcase in testcases) // main test loop
      {
        string[] tokens = testcase.Split(':');
        string id = tokens[0];
        string method = tokens[1];
        string input = tokens[2];
        int expectedCount = int.Parse(tokens[3]);
        string hint = tokens[4];

        // call method under test here
        // compare actual result to expected result here
        // display or store test result here
      }
    }
    catch(Exception ex)
    {
      Console.WriteLine("Fatal error: " + ex.Message);
    }
  }
}
```

    As a general rule of thumb, in lightweight test automation situations, external test case storage (in the form of text files, XML files, SQL databases, and so on) is preferable to internal storage. External test case data can be shared among different test harnesses and is easier to edit. But using an in-memory test case data store has certain advantages; keeping the test case data embedded within the test harness makes maintenance somewhat easier. The simplest approach to in-memory test case storage is to use an ArrayList object. In-memory test case storage is particularly appropriate when your number of test cases is relatively small (generally, under 100) or if you want to distribute the harness as a single, stand-alone executable to several people for use as DRT (Developer Regression Test) or BVT (Build Verification Test) regression purposes.

Comments

One alternative to using an ArrayList object for in-memory test case storage is to use an array object. Using an array, the preceding solution becomes

```
class Class1
{
  static string[] testcases =
    new string[] { "001:GetTitles:testing:3:Theory",
                   "002:GetTitles:and:1:Theory",
                   "003:GetTitles:better:1:Build"
                 };

  static void Main(string[] args)
  {
    try
    {
      Console.WriteLine("\nBegin test run\n");

      for (int i = 0; i < testcases.Length; ++i) // main test loop
      {
        string[] tokens = testcases[i].Split(':');
        string id = tokens[0];
        string method = tokens[1];
        string input = tokens[2];
        int expectedCount = int.Parse(tokens[3]);
        string hint = tokens[4];

        // call method under test here
        // compare actual result to expected result here
        // display or store test result here
      }
    }
    catch(Exception ex)
    {
      Console.WriteLine("Fatal error: " + ex.Message);
    }
  }
}
```

This approach has an older, pre-.NET feel but otherwise is virtually equivalent to using an ArrayList object. In theory, using an array object provides better performance than using an ArrayList, but this would only be a factor with a very large number of test cases, which means using an in-memory data store is probably not a good idea anyway.

A second minor variation to using an ArrayList object for in-memory test case data storage is to use a Queue object. The solution using a Queue looks like this:

```
class Class1
{
  static Queue testcases = new Queue();

  static void Main(string[] args)
  {
    try
    {
      testcases.Enqueue("001:GetTitles:testing:3:Theory");
      testcases.Enqueue("002:GetTitles:and:1:Theory");
      testcases.Enqueue("003:GetTitles:better:1:Build");

      while (testcases.Count > 0)
      {
        string testcase = (string)testcases.Dequeue();
        string[] tokens = testcase.Split(':');
        string id = tokens[0];
        string method = tokens[1];
        string input = tokens[2];
        int expectedCount = int.Parse(tokens[3]);
        string hint = tokens[4];

        // call method under test here
        // compare actual result to expected result here
        // display or store test result here
      }
    }
    catch(Exception ex)
    {
      Console.WriteLine("Fatal error: " + ex.Message);
    }
  }
}
```

There are few technical reasons to choose one of these data store objects (ArrayList, array, Queue) over another. Using an ArrayList or array object allows random access to any test case because you can fetch a particular test case by index value. Using an ArrayList or Queue object gives you the possibility of adding test case data programmatically via the ArrayList.Add() or Queue.Enqueue() methods. However, your choice will most often be based on personal coding style preference.

8.6 Working with an In-Memory Test Results Data Store

Problem

You want to save your test results to an in-memory data store in such a way that you can easily determine if a particular test case passed or not before running a new test case.

Design

If your test cases have dependencies, where running one case depends on the result of a previous case, then consider storing test results into a Hashtable object. For general processing of test results, using an ArrayList object is usually the best choice.

Solution

To insert a test result into a Hashtable, use

```
TestResult tr = null;
if (actualResult == expectedResult)
{
  tr = new TestResult(id, "Pass");
  testResults.Add(id, tr);
}
else
{
  tr = new TestResult(id, "FAIL");
  testResults.Add(id, tr);
}
```

where

```
static Hashtable testResults = new Hashtable();

class TestResult
{
  public string id;
  public string pf; // "pass" or "fail"
  public TestResult(string id, string pf)
  {
    this.id = id; this.pf = pf;
  }
}
```

The result of each test case is stored into a Hashtable. Now suppose that all test cases are dependent upon test case 002 passing. You can write code like this snippet:

```
string mustPass = "002";

TestResult tr = testResults[mustPass] as TestResult;

if (tr.pf == "Pass")
{
  Console.WriteLine("The dependency passed so I can run case " + id);
  // run test and store result
}
else
{
  Console.WriteLine("The dependency failed so I will skip case " + id);
  continue;
}
```

You will sometimes have test cases that have dependencies on other test cases, meaning whether or not a test case runs is contingent on whether a previous test case passes (or fails). In situations like this, you should store test results to an in-memory data store. This data store must be searched before executing each test case. Even for a moderate number of test cases, you need a data structure that can be searched as quickly as possible. The Hashtable object is designed for just such situations.

Comments

Working with test case data that has dependencies on the results of other test cases is simple in principle but can be tricky in practice. A Hashtable object accepts a key, which you can think of as an ID, and an object to store. For test case results, the test case ID is a natural choice as a key. Because a Hashtable stores objects, a good design approach is to create a lightweight class to hold test result information so you can call the Hashtable.Add() method passing in a TestResult object as the value to be added.

If the number of test case dependencies is very small, you can hard-code the dependency logic into your test automation harness. If the number of dependencies is large, however, you should first rethink your entire test harness design and see if you can simplify. Then, if the dependencies are unavoidable, you'll want to store the dependencies as part of the test case input data. This pushes you to store test case data in a lightweight class such as

```
class TestCase
{
  public string id;
  public string input;
  public string expected;
  public ArrayList dependencies;

  public TestCase(string id, string input, string expected,
                  ArrayList dependencies)
  {
    // constructor code here
  }
}
```

Then you can structure your test harness (in pseudo-code) like this:

```
loop thru test case collection
  fetch a TestCase object
  bool shouldRun = true;
  loop thru each dependency
  {
    pull dependency result from Hashtable
    if (dependency case failed)
      shouldRun = false;
      break;
  }

  if (shouldRun == true)
  {
    run test;
    store test result;
  }
  else
  {
    skip test;
  }
end loop
```

When using a Hashtable object for an in-memory test results data store, at some point you have to either display the results or save them to external storage. There are several ways to do this. One approach is to maintain two different data structures—one Hashtable to determine test case dependencies and one ArrayList to hold test case results for display/external storage. This is simple but inefficient. A second approach is to keep test results in a Hashtable and then after the main test-processing loop has finished, traverse the Hashtable and save to external storage. For example:

```
Hashtable testResults = new Hashtable();

// run harness, store all results into testResults

FileStream fs = new FileStream("TestResults.txt", FileMode.Create);
StreamWriter sw = new StreamWriter(fs);

foreach (DictionaryEntry de in testResults)
{
  TestResult t = de.Value as TestResult;
  sw.WriteLine(t.id + " " + t.pf);
}
sw.Close();
fs.Close();
```

Because each element in a Hashtable object is a DictionaryEntry object, you can iterate through a Hashtable in this nonobvious way.

8.7 Example Program: WebServiceTest

This program combines several of the techniques in this chapter to create a lightweight test automation harness to test a Web service (see Listing 8-1). When run, the output will be as shown in Figure 8-2 in the introduction to this chapter. The test harness uses an in-memory test case data store. Test case 002 has a deliberate error to demonstrate the concept of validation. The expected count for case 002 should be 2, not 1 as coded. Each test case is used to call the Web method under test, GetTitles(), twice. The first call is via the simple proxy mechanism. The second test call is via the low-level TCP technique.

Listing 8-1. *Program WebServiceTest*

```
using System;
using System.Collections;
using System.Data;
using System.Net.Sockets;
using System.Text;

namespace RunTests
{
  class Class1
  {
    static ArrayList testcases = new ArrayList();

    [STAThread]
    static void Main(string[] args)
    {
      try
      {
        Console.WriteLine("\nBegin BookSearch Web service test run\n");

        testcases.Add("001:GetTitles:testing:3:Theory");
        testcases.Add("002:GetTitles:and:1:Theory"); // error
        testcases.Add("003:GetTitles:better:1:Build");
        // other test cases go here

        foreach (string testcase in testcases)
        {
          string[] tokens = testcase.Split(':');
          string id = tokens[0];
          string method = tokens[1];
          string input = tokens[2];
          int expectedCount = int.Parse(tokens[3]);
          string hint = tokens[4];
```

```
        Console.WriteLine("=========================");
        Console.WriteLine("Case ID = " + id);
        Console.WriteLine("Sending input = '" + input + "' to Web
                        method GetTitles()");

        Console.WriteLine("\nTesting using proxy mechanism . . . ");
        BookReference.BookSearch bs = new BookReference.BookSearch();
        DataSet ds = bs.GetTitles(input);
        Console.WriteLine("Expected count = " + expectedCount);

        bool proxyPass;
        if (ds.Tables["Table"].Rows.Count == expectedCount &&
ds.Tables["Table"].Rows[0]["booktitle"].ToString().IndexOf(hint) >= 0)
            proxyPass = true;
        else
            proxyPass = false;
        Console.WriteLine("Pass via proxy = " + proxyPass);

        Console.WriteLine("\nTesing using TCP mechanism . . . ");
        TcpClient client = new TcpClient(AddressFamily.InterNetwork);
        client.Connect("127.0.0.1", 80);

        string soapMessage = "<?xml version=\"1.0\" encoding=\"utf-8\"?>";
        soapMessage +=
"<soap:Envelope xmlns:xsi=\"http://www.w3.org/2001/XMLSchema-instance\"";
        soapMessage += " xmlns:xsd=\"http://www.w3.org/2001/XMLSchema\"";
        soapMessage +=
"xmlns:soap=\"http://schemas.xmlsoap.org/soap/envelope/\">";
        soapMessage += "<soap:Body>";
        soapMessage += "<GetTitles xmlns=\"http://tempuri.org/\">";
        soapMessage += "<filter>" + input + "</filter>";
        soapMessage += "</GetTitles>";
        soapMessage += "</soap:Body>";
        soapMessage += "</soap:Envelope>";
        // Console.WriteLine("SOAP message is " + soapMessage);

        string webService = "/TestAuto/Ch8/TheWebService/BookSearch.asmx";
        string host = "localhost";
        string webMethod = "GetTitles";

        string header = "POST " + webService + " HTTP/1.1\r\n";
        header += "Host: " + host + "\r\n";
        header += "Content-Type: text/xml; charset=utf-8\r\n";
        header += "Content-Length: " + soapMessage.Length.ToString() + "\r\n";
        header += "Connection: close\r\n";
        header += "SOAPAction: \"http://tempuri.org/" + webMethod + "\"\r\n\r\n";
        //Console.Write("Header is: \n" + header);
```

```csharp
            string requestAsString = header + soapMessage;
            byte[] requestAsBytes = Encoding.ASCII.GetBytes(requestAsString);

            NetworkStream ns = client.GetStream();
            ns.Write(requestAsBytes, 0, requestAsBytes.Length);

            byte[] responseBufferAsBytes = new byte[512];
            string responseAsString = "";
            string entireResponse = "";
            int numBytesReceived = 0;

            while ((numBytesReceived = ns.Read(responseBufferAsBytes, 0, 512)) > 0)
            {
              responseAsString = Encoding.ASCII.GetString(responseBufferAsBytes, 0,
                                                  numBytesReceived);
              entireResponse += responseAsString;
            }

            //Console.WriteLine(entireResponse);
            Console.WriteLine("Seeking '" + hint + "'");
            bool tcpPass;
            if (entireResponse.IndexOf(hint) >= 0)
              tcpPass = true;
            else
              tcpPass = false;
            Console.WriteLine("Pass via TCP = " + tcpPass);

            if (proxyPass == true && tcpPass == true)
              Console.WriteLine("\nPass");
            else
              Console.WriteLine("\n** FAIL or INCONSISTENT **");

          } // main test loop

        Console.WriteLine("=========================");
        Console.WriteLine("\nDone");
        Console.ReadLine();
      }
      catch(Exception ex)
      {
        Console.WriteLine("Fatal error: " + ex.Message);
        Console.ReadLine();
      }

    } // Main()
  } // Class1
} // ns
```

PART 3

■■■

Data Testing

CHAPTER 9

▪ ▪ ▪

SQL Stored Procedure Testing

9.0 Introduction

Many Windows-based systems have a SQL Server backend component. The AUT or SUT often accesses the database using stored procedures. In these situations, you can think of the SQL stored procedures as auxiliary functions of the application. There are two fundamental approaches to writing lightweight test automation for SQL stored procedures. The first approach is to write the automation in a native SQL environment, meaning the harness code is written using the T-SQL language, and the harness is executed within a SQL framework such as the Query Analyzer program or the Management Studio program. The second approach is to write the test automation in a .NET environment, meaning the harness code is written using C# or another .NET language, and the harness is executed from a general Windows environment such as a command shell. This chapter presents techniques to test SQL stored procedures using a native SQL environment. The second approach, using C#, is covered by the techniques in Chapter 11. In general, because the underlying models of SQL and .NET are so different, you should test stored procedures using both approaches. The techniques in this chapter are also useful in situations where you inherit an existing T-SQL test harness.

Figure 9-1 illustrates some of the key techniques in this chapter. The figure shows a portion of a T-SQL test harness (in the upper pane) and sample output (lower pane). The automation is testing a SQL stored procedure named usp_HiredAfter(). The stored procedure accepts a date as an input argument and returns a SQL rowset object of employee information (employee ID, last name, date of hire) of those employees in a table named tblEmployees whose date of hire is after the input argument date. Although the actual and expected values in this situation are SQL rowsets, the test automation compares the two using a binary aggregate checksum. Test case 0002 is a deliberate error for demonstration purposes. The complete source code for the test harness and database under test shown in Figure 9-1 is presented in Section 9.9.

The script shown in Figure 9-1 assumes the existence of test case data and test result storage in another database named dbTestCasesAndResults. The script tests stored procedure usp_HiredAfter(), which is contained in a database named dbEmployees and pulls data from table tblEmployees. When testing SQL stored procedures, you do not want to test against the development database for two reasons. First, testing stored procedures sometimes modifies the containing database. Second, development databases usually do not contain data that is rich enough or designed for dedicated testing purposes. Therefore, you'll create a test bed database that is an exact replica of the development database's structure but fill it with rich data. In this example, the dbEmployees database containing the stored procedure under test is an exact replica of the development database.

Figure 9-1. *Sample test run of a SQL stored procedure*

If your background is primarily in procedural programming, you probably tend to think of SQL stored procedures as much like functions in a traditional programming language. But SQL stored procedures are significantly different from regular functions because, in most cases, they have a logical dependency on a table or other database object. In this example, notice that the return value from stored procedure usp_HiredAfter() depends completely on the data in table tblEmployees. This fact makes testing SQL stored procedures somewhat different from testing regular functions, as you will see. The current version of SQL Server, SQL Server 2005, provides greatly enhanced integration with .NET, including the capability to write stored procedures in C# and other .NET languages. This will certainly increase the use and importance of stored procedures and the importance of thoroughly testing them.

9.1 Creating Test Case and Test Result Storage

Problem

You want to create a SQL data store to hold test case input data and test results.

Design

Write a T-SQL script that creates a database and then creates tables to hold test case input data and test result data. Create a dedicated SQL login if you want to connect to the data stores using SQL authentication. Run the T-SQL script from within Query Analyzer or by using the osql.exe program.

Solution

The following script creates a database named dbTestCasesAndResults containing a table for test case data, a table for test results, and a dedicated SQL login so that programs can connect to the database using either Windows Authentication or SQL Authentication.

```
-- makeDbTestCasesAndResults.sql
use master
go

if exists (select * from sysdatabases where name='dbTestCasesAndResults')
 drop database dbTestCasesAndResults
go

if exists (select * from sysxlogins where name = 'testLogin')
 exec sp_droplogin 'testLogin'
go

create database dbTestCasesAndResults
go

use dbTestCasesAndResults
go

create table tblTestCases
(
 caseID char(4) primary key,
 input char(3) not null, -- an empID
 expected int not null
)
go

-- this is the test case data for usp_StatusCode
-- can also read from a text file using BCP, DTS, or a C# program
```

```
insert into tblTestCases values('0001','e11', 77)
insert into tblTestCases values('0002','e22', 77) -- should be 66
insert into tblTestCases values('0003','e33', 99)
insert into tblTestCases values('0004','e44', 88)
go

create table tblResults
(
 caseID char(4) not null,
 result char(4) null,
 whenRun datetime not null
)
go

exec sp_addlogin 'testLogin', 'secret'
go
exec sp_grantdbaccess 'testLogin'
go

grant select, insert, delete on tblTestCases to testLogin
go

grant select, insert on tblResults to testLogin
go
```

The first step is to set the current database context to the SQL Server master database. This is necessary when creating a new user database. To prevent an error if the database you are about to create already exists, you can check by querying the sysdatabases table before you attempt to drop an old version of the new database. You can then create a test case storage database using the create database statement. Many optional parameters are available for the create database statement, but in a lightweight test automation scenario, accepting all the default values will usually meet your needs.

Next you set the current database context to the newly created database with the use statement. This is important because if you omit this step, all subsequent SQL statement will be directed at the SQL master database, which would be very bad. Now you can create a table to hold test case input. The structure of the table depends on exactly what you will be testing, but at a minimum, you should have a test case ID, one or more test case inputs, and one or more test case expected result values. For the test results table, you need a test case ID column and a test result pass/fail column at a minimum. If you intend to store the results of multiple test runs into the table, as is almost always the case, you need some way to distinguish results from different test runs. One way to do this is to include a column that stores the date/time when the test result was generated. This column acts as an implicit test run ID. An alternative is to create an explicit, dedicated test run ID.

Comments

SQL databases support two different security modes: Windows Authentication, where you connect using a Windows user ID and password, and Mixed Mode Authentication, where you connect using a SQL login ID with a SQL password. If you want the option of connecting to your test database using SQL authentication, you should create a SQL login and associated password using the sp_addlogin() system stored procedure. You can drop a SQL login using sp_droplogin(), after first checking whether the login exists by querying the sysxlogins table. After creating a SQL login, you need to grant permission to the login to connect to the database. Then you need to grant-specific SQL statement permissions, such as SELECT, INSERT, DELETE, and UPDATE, on the tables in the database.

A SQL login is easy to confuse with a SQL user. *SQL logins* are server-scope objects used to control connection permissions to the SQL server machine. *SQL users* are database-scope objects used to control permissions to a database and its tables, stored procedures, and other objects. When you assign permissions to a SQL login, a SQL user with the identical name is also created. So you end up with a SQL login and a SQL user, both with the same name and associated with each other. Although it's possible to have associated logins and users with different names, this can get very confusing, so you are better off using the same-name default mechanism.

When creating SQL test case storage for testing stored procedures, you must decide when and how to insert the actual test case data into the table that holds it. The easiest technique is to add test case data when you create the table. You can do this easily with the INSERT statement as demonstrated in this solution. However, you will almost certainly be adding and removing test case data at many points in your testing effort, so a more flexible approach is to insert data later using BCP (Bulk Copy Program), DTS (Data Transformation Services), or an auxiliary C# helper program. If you intend to insert and delete test case data, then you should grant INSERT and DELETE permissions on the test case data table to the SQL login.

Your SQL test case and results storage creation script can be run in several ways. One way is to open the script in the Query Analyzer program and execute the script using the Execute (F5 is the shortcut key) command. A second way to execute a SQL script is by using the osql.exe program.

Executing SQL scripts is discussed in detail in Section 9.2. Section 9.3 shows how to import and export data into a SQL database using BCP. Chapter 11 shows how to import and export data using C# code.

9.2 Executing a T-SQL Script

Problem

You want to run a T-SQL script.

Solution

You have several alternatives, including using the Query Analyzer program, using the osql.exe program, and using a batch (BAT) file. For example, if you have a script named myScript.sql, then you can execute it using the osql.exe program with the command:

```
C:\>osql.exe -S(local) -UsomeLogin -PsomePassword -i myScript.sql -n > nul
```

This command runs the osql.exe program by connecting to the local machine SQL server, logging in using SQL login someLogin with SQL password somePassword, and using T-SQL script myScript.sql as input. The osql.exe line numbering is suppressed (-n), and miscellaneous shell messages is also suppressed (> nul).

Comments

The osql.exe program, which ships with SQL Server, provides you with an automation-friendly way to run T-SQL scripts. The -S argument specifies the name of the database server to use. You can use "(local)" or "." to specify the local machine, or you can use a machine name or IP address to specify a remote machine. If you want to connect and run your script using SQL authentication, you must specify the SQL login and the SQL password. If you want to connect and run using integrated Windows Authentication, you can do so with the -E argument:

```
C:\>osql.exe -S. -E -i myScript.sql -n   > nul
```

Be careful here because the osql.exe arguments are case sensitive: -E means use Windows Authentication, whereas -e means to echo the input. In a pure Windows environment, you are generally better off using Windows Authentication. Mixed Mode Authentication can be troublesome because it's difficult to diagnose problems that arise when there is an authentication or authorization conflict between the two modes.

A variation on using the osql.exe program to run T-SQL scripts is to use a batch file, which calls an osql.exe command. For example, you could write a batch file such as

```
@echo off

rem File name: runMyScript.bat
rem Executes myScript.sql

echo.
echo Start test run
osql.exe -S(local) -E -i myScript.sql -n   > nul

echo Done
```

This approach allows you to consolidate the execution of several scripts, such as a test harness preparation script, a harness execution script, and a results processing script. With a batch file, you can also schedule the test automation to run using the Windows Task Scheduler or the command line at command.

An alternative to using the osql.exe program to run a T-SQL script is to run the script from the Query Analyzer program. You simply open the .sql file and then use the Execute command (F5 is the shortcut key). This is your best approach when developing scripts because Query Analyzer has a very nice development environment. Figure 9-1 (earlier in this chapter) shows the Query Analyzer program in use.

9.3 Importing Test Case Data Using the BCP Utility Program

Problem

You want to import test case data from a text file into a SQL table using BCP.

Design

Construct a BCP format file that maps the information in the text file you want to import from, to the SQL table you want to import into. Then use the command-line bcp.exe utility program with the format file as an argument.

Solution

Suppose, for example, you have a SQL table defined as

```
create table tblTestCases
(
 caseID char(4) primary key, -- like '0001'
 input char(3) not null,     -- an empID like 'e43'
 expected int not null       -- a status code like 77
)
```

and a text file containing test case data named newData.dat:

```
0020,e13,66
0021,e14,77
0022,e15,88
0023,e16,99
0024,e17,66
```

Create a tab-delimited BCP format file named newData.fmt:

```
8.0
3
1   SQLCHAR   0   4    ","    1    caseID    SQL_Latin1_General_CP1_CI_AS
2   SQLCHAR   0   3    ","    2    input     SQL_Latin1_General_CP1_CI_AS
3   SQLCHAR   0   2    "\r\n" 3    expected  SQL_Latin1_General_CP1_CI_AS
```

The command to import the test case data is

```
C:\>bcp.exe dbTestCasesAndResults..tblTestCases in newData.dat
      -fnewData.fmt -S. -UtestLogin -Psecret
```

This command means run the BCP on SQL table tblTestCases located in database dbTestCasesAndResults, importing from file newData.dat using the mappings defined in file newData.fmt. The instruction is to be executed on the local SQL server machine, connecting using the testLogin SQL login and the testLogin user, with SQL password secret.

The key to using this technique is to understand the structure of the format file used by the `bcp.exe` program. The first line contains a single value that represents the version of SQL server. SQL Server 7.0 is version 7.0, SQL Sever 2000 is version 8.0, SQL Server 2005 is version 9.0, and so on. The second line of the format file is an integer, which is the number of actual mapping lines in the format file. The third through remaining lines are the mapping information. Each mapping line has eight columns. The first five columns represent information about the input data (the text file in this example), and the last three columns represent information about the destination (the SQL table in this example). The first column is a simple 1-based sequence number. These values will always be 1, 2, 3, and so on, in that order. (These numbers, and some of the other information in a BCP format file, seem somewhat unnecessary but are needed for use in other situations.) The second column of a mapping line is the import type. When importing from a text file, this value will always be SQLCHAR regardless of what the value represents. The third column is the prefix length. This is a rather complicated value used for BCP optimization when copying from SQL to SQL. Fortunately, when importing text data into SQL, the prefix length value is always 0. The fourth column is the maximum length, in characters, of the input field. Notice that test case IDs (for example, 0001) have four characters in the input file, test case inputs (such as e29) have three characters, and test case expected values (such as 77) have two characters. The fifth column in a mapping line is the field separator, and comma characters separate all fields. If, for example, fields in the input data file were tab-delimited, you would specify \t. The last mapping line should specify \r\n as the separator when importing data from a text file. The sixth through eighth columns refer to the target SQL table, not the input file. Columns six and seven are the order and name of the SQL columns in the destination table. Notice in this example, the new data is inserted into the SQL table in the same order it is stored in the text file. The eighth column of a mapping line is the SQL collation scheme to use. The SQL_Latin1_General_CP1_CI_AS designator is the default collation for SQL Server.

Comments

Using the BCP utility program gives you a high-performance, automation-friendly way to import test case data from a text file into a SQL test case table. You must be careful of two nasty syntax issues. Your test case data file *must not* have a newline character after the very last line of its data. The newline will be interpreted as an empty line of data. However, the format file *must* have a single newline character after the last mapping line. Without that newline, the BCP program won't read the last line of the format file.

The BCP utility allows you to import data from a text file when the file does not exactly match the structure of the SQL table. In other words, even if the text file has data in a different order from the corresponding SQL columns and/or has extra fields, you can still use BCP. For example, suppose a text file looks like this:

```
0020,66,useless,e13
0021,77,no-need,e14
0022,88,go-away,e15
0023,99,drop-it,e16
```

This file has extra information that you don't want to import, and the order of the fields (case ID, expected value, unneeded data, input value) does not match the order of the SQL columns (case ID, input, expected). The BCP format file for this text file is

```
8.0
4
1  SQLCHAR  0  4  ","    1  caseID    SQL_Latin1_General_CP1_CI_AS
2  SQLCHAR  0  2  ","    3  expected  SQL_Latin1_General_CP1_CI_AS
3  SQLCHAR  0  7  ","    0  junk      SQL_Latin1_General_CP1_CI_AS
4  SQLCHAR  0  3  "\r\n" 2  input     SQL_Latin1_General_CP1_CI_AS
```

The sixth column of the mapping file controls removing an input by specifying a 0 and controls the order in which to insert.

Because bcp.exe is a command-line program, you can run it manually or put the command you want to execute into a simple BAT file that can be called programmatically. If you want to use BCP from within a SQL environment, you can do so using the BULK INSERT command:

```
bulk insert dbTestCasesAndResults..tblTestCases
 from 'C:\somewhere\newData.dat'
 with (formatfile = 'C:\somewhere\newData.fmt')
```

A significant alternative to using BCP for importing data into a database is using the DTS (Data Transformation Services) utility, which can be accessed through the Enterprise Manager program. DTS is a powerful, easy-to-use service that can import and export a huge variety of data stores to SQL. A full discussion of DTS is outside the scope of this book but knowing how to use DTS should certainly be a part of your test automation skill set.

Note In SQL Server 2005, DTS has been enhanced and renamed to SSIS (SQL Server Integration Services).

9.4 Creating a T-SQL Test Harness

Problem

You want to create a T-SQL test harness structure to test a SQL stored procedure.

Design

First, prepare the underlying database that contains the stored procedure under test by inserting rich test bed data. Next, use a SQL cursor to iterate through a test case data table. For each test case, call the stored procedure under test and retrieve its return value. Compare the actual return value with the expected return value to determine a pass or fail result, and display or save the test result.

Solution

```
-- testAuto.sql

-- prepare dbEmployees with rich data (see section 9.9)
truncate table dbEmployees.dbo.tblEmployees
```

```
insert into dbEmployees.dbo.tblEmployees
 values('e11','Adams', '06/15/1998')
insert into dbEmployees.dbo.tblEmployees
 values('e22','Baker', '06/15/2001')
insert into dbEmployees.dbo.tblEmployees
 values('e33','Young', '06/15/1998')
insert into dbEmployees.dbo.tblEmployees
 values('e44','Zetta', '06/15/2001')
-- insert much other rich data here

declare tCursor cursor fast_forward
 for select caseID, input, expected
 from dbTestCasesAndResults.dbo.tblTestCases
 order by caseID

declare @caseID char(4), @input char(3), @expected int
declare @actual int, @whenRun datetime
declare @resultLine varchar(50)

set @whenRun = getdate()

open tCursor
fetch next
 from tCursor
 into @caseID, @input, @expected

while @@fetch_status = 0
begin
 exec @actual = dbEmployees.dbo.usp_StatusCode @input

 if (@actual = @expected)
  begin
   set @resultLine = @caseID + ': Pass'
   print @resultLine
  end
 else
  begin
   set @resultLine = @caseID + ': FAIL'
   print @resultLine
  end
 fetch next
  from tCursor
  into @caseID, @input, @expected
end
```

```
close tCursor
deallocate tCursor
```

```
-- end script
```

If the stored procedure under test depends upon data, as is almost always the case, you must populate the underlying database table(s) with rich test bed data. As discussed in the introduction to this chapter, in a SQL testing environment, you typically have two databases: the development database that developers use when writing code and a testing database that testers use when testing. Because the process of testing stored procedures often changes the database containing the stored procedures (because stored procedures often insert, update, or delete data), you certainly do not want to run tests against the development database. So you make a copy of the development database and use the copy for testing purposes. Now the development database will have "developer data" stored in the tables. This is data necessary for doing rudimentary verification testing while developing the SUT. However, this data is generally not rich enough in its variety or designed with testing in mind to provide you with an adequate base for rigorous testing purposes.

Although there are several ways to iterate through a table of test case data, using a SQL cursor is simple and effective. SQL cursor operations are designed to work with a single row of data rather than rowsets like most other SQL operations such as SELECT and INSERT. You begin by declaring a cursor that points to the SQL table holding your test case data:

```
declare tCursor cursor fast_forward
 for select caseID, input, expected
 from dbTestCasesAndResults.dbo.tblTestCases
 order by caseID
```

Notice that unlike most other SQL variables, cursor variable names are not preceded by the @ character. There are several types of cursors you can declare. Using FAST_FORWARD is most appropriate for reading test case data. Other cursor types include FORWARD_ONLY, READ_ONLY, and OPTIMISTIC. The FAST_FORWARD type is actually an alias for FORWARD_ONLY plus READ_ONLY.

Before using a cursor, you must open it. Then, if you intend to iterate through an entire table, you must perform a priming read of the first row of the table using the fetch next statement:

```
open tCursor
fetch next
 from tCursor
 into @caseID, @input, @expected
```

You need to do a priming read because in order to control the reading loop, you use the @@fetch_status variable that holds a code representing the result of the most recent fetch attempt. The @@fetch_status variable holds 0 if data was successfully fetched. Values of -1 and -2 indicate a failed fetch. So, you can loop through an entire table one row at a time like this:

```
while @@fetch_status = 0
begin

 -- run a test case here

 fetch next
  from tCursor
  into @caseID, @input, @expected
end
```

Inside the main processing loop, you need to call the stored procedure under test, feeding it the test case input. You retrieve the return value and then print a pass/fail message:

```
exec @actual = dbEmployees.dbo.usp_StatusCode @input

if (@actual = @expected)
 begin
  set @resultLine = @caseID + ': Pass'
   print @resultLine
 end
else
 begin
  set @resultLine = @caseID + ': FAIL'
   print @resultLine
 end
```

After using a SQL cursor, you must be sure to close it and then release it as a resource by calling the deallocate command:

```
close tCursor
deallocate tCursor
```

If you forget to deallocate the cursor, your script will fail when the cursor is declared the next time you execute the test harness script.

Comments

Instead of, or in addition to, printing a pass/fail message, you'll probably want to insert test results into a SQL table. This is easy:

```
-- declare @actual int, @whenRun datetime
-- set @whenRun = getdate()

while @@fetch_status = 0
begin
 exec @actual = dbEmployees.dbo.usp_StatusCode @input

 if (@actual = @expected)
  insert into dbTestCasesAndResults.dbo.tblResults values(@caseID, 'Pass',
                                                    @whenRun)
```

```
else
  insert into dbTestCasesAndResults.dbo.tblResults values(@caseID, 'FAIL',
                                                @whenRun)

  fetch next
   from tCursor
   into @caseID, @input, @expected
end
```

You can use the GETDATE() function to retrieve the current system date and time. Using an INSERT statement stores the test case result.

Instead of populating the underlying database tables, which the stored procedure under test accesses by using hard-coded INSERT statements, you can use the BULK INSERT statement as demonstrated in Section 9.3:

```
-- prepare dbEmployees with rich data
truncate table dbEmployees.dbo.tblEmployees

bulk insert dbEmployees.dbo.tblEmployees
 from 'C:\somehere\richTestbedData.dat'
 with (formatfile = 'C:\somewhere\richTestbedData.fmt')
```

This approach has the advantages of making your test harness more modular and more flexible, but has the disadvantage of increasing complexity by adding one more file to a test harness system that already has a lot of objects.

9.5 Writing Test Results Directly to a Text File from a T-SQL Test Harness

Problem

You want your T-SQL test harness to write test case results directly to a text file.

Design

Use ActiveX technology to instantiate a FileSystemObject object. Then use the OpenTextFile() and WriteLine() methods.

Solution

```
declare @fsoHandle int, @fileID int

exec sp_OACreate 'Scripting.FileSystemObject', @fsoHandle out
exec sp_OAMethod @fsoHandle, 'OpenTextFile', @fileID out,
  'C:\pathToResults\Results.txt', 8, 1

-- main test loop
```

```
if (@result = @expected)
 exec sp_OAMethod @fileID, 'WriteLine', null, 'Pass'
else
 exec sp_OAMethod @fileID, 'WriteLine', null, 'FAIL'


-- end main test loop

exec sp_OADestroy @fileID
exec sp_OADestroy @fsoHandle
```

You need a file handle and a file ID, both of which are type int. SQL Server has an
sp_OACreate() stored procedure that can instantiate an ActiveX object. The sp_OACreate()
routine accepts a string, which is the name of the ActiveX object to create, and returns a reference to the created object as an int type in the form of an out parameter. In the case of
Scripting.FileSystemObject, the return value is a reference to a file handle. Next you can
open a file by calling the sp_OAMethod() method. In this example, the first argument is the file
handle created by sp_OACreate(), the second argument is the name of the method you want to
use, the third argument is a variable in which to store a returned file handle, and the fourth
argument specifies the physical file name. The fifth argument is an optional IO mode:

- 1: Open file for reading only (default).

- 2: Open a file for writing.

- 8: Open a file for appending to the end of the file.

The sixth argument is an optional create-flag that specifies whether or not to create the
file if the file name does not exist:

- 0: Do not create a new file (default).

- 1: Create a new file.

The eighth argument is an optional format-flag that specifies the character encoding:

- 0: Open file as ASCII (default).

- 1: Open file as Unicode.

- 2: Open file using system default.

Comments

When running a T-SQL test harness, you have several ways to save test results. If you want to
save test results as a text file, the usual technique is to first save all your results into a SQL table
and then later transfer the results to a text file. An alternative is to write test results directly to a
text file from your T-SQL harness.

The preceding solution uses the OpenTextFile() method of the FileSystemObject class.
This approach essentially assumes that the file you'll be writing to already exists. An alternative is to use the CreateTextFile() method:

```
declare @fsoHandle int, @fileID int

exec sp_OACreate 'Scripting.FileSystemObject', @fsoHandle out
exec sp_OAMethod @fsoHandle, 'CreateTextFile', @fileID out,
  'C:\pathToResults\Results.txt', 0, 0

-- main test loop

 if (@result = @expected)
  exec sp_OAMethod @fileID, 'WriteLine', null, 'Pass'
 else
  exec sp_OAMethod @fileID, 'WriteLine', null, 'FAIL'


-- end main test loop

exec sp_OADestroy @fileID
exec sp_OADestroy @fsoHandle
```

The CreateTextFile() method accepts a required file name and two optional Boolean values. Because SQL does not support a native Boolean data type, you must use integers: 0 for false and 1 for true. The first optional Boolean value specifies an overwrite-flag. A value of true/1 means overwrite the file if it already exists. A value of false/0 means do not overwrite if the file exists. The second optional Boolean parameter is an encoding-flag. A value of true/1 means create the file using Unicode encoding. A value of false/0 means create using ASCII encoding. Both parameters have default values of false/0, or in other words, the default is to not overwrite an existing file and to use ASCII encoding.

In addition to writing data directly to a text file from T-SQL, you can also read text data:

```
declare @fsoHandle int, @fileID int
declare @eof int
declare @line varchar(1000)

exec sp_OACreate 'Scripting.FileSystemObject', @fsoHandle out
exec sp_OAMethod @fsoHandle, 'OpenTextFile', @fileID out,
  'C:\path\FileToRead.txt', 1, 1

set @eof = 0
while @eof = 0
begin
 exec sp_OAMethod @fileID, 'ReadLine', @line out
 print @line
 exec sp_OAMethod @fileID, 'AtEndOfStream', @eof out
end

exec sp_OADestroy @fileID
exec sp_OADestroy @fsoHandle
```

9.6 Determining a Pass/Fail Result When the Stored Procedure Under Test Returns a Rowset

Problem

You want to determine a pass/fail result when the stored procedure under test returns a SQL rowset.

Design

First, create a temporary table. Then, call the stored procedure under test and retrieve the returned rowset into the temporary table. Compute the aggregate checksum of the temporary table and compare against an expected checksum value.

Solution

Suppose your stored procedure under test is named `usp_HiredAfter()`, and it accepts a `datetime` input parameter. The stored procedure selects all employee columns (`empID`, `empLast`, `empDOH`) where the date of hire is greater than the input argument:

```
create procedure usp_HiredAfter
 @dt datetime
as
 select * from tblEmployees where empDOH > @dt
```

First, you create a temporary table to hold the SQL rowset returned by the stored procedure:

```
create table #results
(
 empID char(3) primary key,
 empLast varchar(35) not null,
 empDOH datetime not null
)
```

Notice the # character in front of the table name is used to flag it as a temporary table. You then call the stored procedure under test and save the return rowset into the temporary table:

```
insert #results (empID, empLast, empDOH)
 exec dbEmployees.dbo.usp_HiredAfter '01/01/2000'
```

Next, you compute the aggregate checksum of the temporary table and compare that actual value against an expected value:

```
if (@@rowcount = 0)
 set @actual = 0
else
 select @actual = checksum_agg(binary_checksum(*)) from #results
```

```
if (@actual = 25527856)
 print 'Pass'
else
 print 'FAIL'
```

The built-in SQL `binary_checksum()` function returns the checksum of a row of a SQL table. You can think of it as an integer value that is an alternative representation of the character data in the row. The `checksum_agg()` function returns the aggregate checksum of the values in a group. When used together, they compute a single integer that identifies a rowset.

Comments

Many stored procedures return a SQL rowset object. It's not entirely obvious how to compare an actual rowset returned by a stored procedure under test to an expected value of some sort. One approach is to create your test case data store so that it can hold a close replica of a SQL rowset. This is difficult and sometimes not feasible if the rowset you are dealing with is very large. In most testing situations, a better alternative is to store a single integer value that uniquely maps to an expected rowset object. SQL Server has the `binary_checksum()` and `checksum_agg()` functions that can be used to do exactly this. So, instead of having to go through a very elaborate process of directly comparing an actual rowset with an expected rowset, you can simply compare their checksum values. This approach also greatly simplifies your test case storage. Instead of storing a fairly complex representation of a rowset, you can simply store a single integer.

In addition to the `binary_checksum()` function, SQL contains a `checksum()` function. The `checksum()` function computes its return value in a case-insensitive way. For test automation, you'll generally want to use `binary_checksum()` rather than the `checksum()` method.

Although using a checksum expected/actual return value approach when testing stored procedures has many advantages over alternative approaches, there are two disadvantages. First, when expected rowset values are stored as a single integer value, examining your test case data visually is difficult. For example, if an expected rowset returned from the stored procedure under test when called with test case input '01/01/2000' is

```
e22 Baker 06/15/2001
e44 Zetta 06/15/2001
```

then a test case data file storing test case ID, input, and expected value as a checksum would look like this:

```
'0007','01/01/2000', 25527856
```

It's impossible to directly see the relationship between the rowset and its checksum. Therefore, you have to maintain careful documentation of what each checksum value represents. A second disadvantage of using a checksum approach is that it generally requires more time to create test cases. For each test case input for the stored procedure under test, you have to determine what the resulting rowset should be, and then compute the aggregate binary checksum of that hypothetical rowset. A common mistake is to determine the expected checksum value by calling the stored procedure under test and then computing the checksum of the returned rowset. This approach creates a situation in which test case data validates that the stored procedure under test returns the same, possibly incorrect, results.

When using the checksum technique, you need to remember to delete all the data in the temporary table before each call to the stored procedure:

```
truncate table #results
```

You should also drop the temporary table after all test cases have been run:

```
drop table #results
```

A different approach to testing a stored procedure that returns a rowset is to use just the number of rows returned as actual/expected values:

```
-- read test case input into @caseID, @input, @expected

exec dbEmployees.dbo.usp_HiredAfter @input
set @actual = @@ROWCOUNT

if (@actual = @expected)
 begin
  set @resultLine = @caseID + ': Pass'
  print @resultLine
 end
else
 begin
  set @resultLine = @caseID + ': FAIL'
  print @resultLine
end
```

You can use the @@rowcount function to retrieve how many rows were actually returned by the stored procedure under test and then compare that against an expected number of rows. This technique obviously has some severe limitations, most importantly the fact that you are checking only how many rows are returned by the store procedure under test, and you have no indication whether these rows contain the correct SQL data or are in the correct order. That said, however, this simple technique is sometimes useful by itself or when used in conjunction with the checksum technique as a way to validate your test harness.

9.7 Determining a Pass/Fail Result When the Stored Procedure Under Test Returns an out Parameter

Problem

You want to test a SQL stored procedure that returns a value into an out parameter.

Design

Declare a variable of the appropriate type to accept the out parameter and call the stored procedure under test using the out keyword.

Solution

For example, suppose the database containing the stored procedure under test has a table
defined as

```
create table tblEmployees
(
 empID char(3) primary key,
 empLast varchar(35) not null,
 empDOH datetime not null,
)
```

Suppose the stored procedure under test has an out parameter in which to store a result
and is defined as

```
create procedure usp_GetLast
 @empID char(3),
 @empLast varchar(35) out
as
 select @empLast = empLast from tblEmployees where empID = @empID
 return @@rowcount
```

Then T-SQL code to test the stored procedure could be

```
declare @input char(3)
declare @empLast varchar(35)
declare @retval int

declare @expectedLast varchar(35)
declare @expectedRet int

set @input = 'e22'
set @expectedLast = 'Baker'
set @expectedRet = 1

exec @retval = dbEmployees.dbo.usp_GetLast @input, @empLast out
if (@retval = @expectedRet and @empLast = @expectedLast)
 print 'Pass'
else
 print 'FAIL'
```

The usp_GetLast() stored procedure accepts an input parameter of an employee ID. The
procedure retrieves the row that matches the input employee ID and stores the associated
employee last name into an out parameter. The stored procedure returns the number of rows
returned by the SELECT statement. The idea is that the AUT can use the return value as an
error-checking mechanism: if the return is 0, then no matching employee was found, but if the
return is greater than 1, then more than one employee with a particular ID was found (which
is probably an error in most situations).

Comments

A very common design pattern for SQL stored procedures is one in which the stored procedure returns one or more values into out parameters. This pattern is necessary when the stored procedure returns a value that is not type int because the return keyword only accepts int types. The pattern is also necessary when the stored procedure must return more than one value.

You call a stored procedure with an out parameter just as you would a stored procedure that only has input parameters except that you place the SQL keyword out after the argument that accepts the output. The preceding solution calls by parameter-position. You also can call by parameter-name. However, this way of calling can be messy because after the form "@name = value" has been used, all subsequent parameters must be passed in the form "@name = value" form too.

9.8 Determining a Pass/Fail Result When the Stored Procedure Under Test Does Not Return a Value

Problem

You want to test a SQL stored procedure that performs some action but does not return a value.

Design

Call the stored procedure under test and then compute an aggregate checksum on the object affected by the stored procedure. Compare the computed checksum with an expected checksum value.

Solution

For example, suppose the stored procedure under test deletes specified employee record from a tblEmployees table:

```
create procedure usp_DeleteEmployee
 @empID char(3)
as
 delete from tblEmployees where empID = @empID
```

To test this stored procedure, you can call it, compute an aggregate checksum on table tblEmployees, and then compare against an expected value:

```
declare @input char(3)
declare @expected int
declare @actual int

set @input = 'e22'
set @expected = 150847775

exec dbEmployees.dbo.usp_DeleteEmployee 'e22'
```

```
select @actual = checksum_agg(checksum(*)) from dbEmployees.dbo.tblEmployees
if (@actual = @expected)
 print 'Pass'
else
 print 'FAIL'
```

If the stored procedure does not return a value, then it must perform some action, such as deleting data from a table. To test such stored procedures, you need to compare actual and expected values of the object acted upon by the stored procedure. This situation is very similar to testing stored procedures that return a SQL rowset object.

Comments

Many stored procedures affect an underlying data table. Obvious examples include stored procedures that use an INSERT, DELETE, or UPDATE statement. When testing such stored procedures, you must be sure to reset the state of the underlying data tables to some known state before each call in the test harness. For example, suppose you are testing a stored procedure usp_DeleteEmployee() defined as

```
create procedure usp_DeleteEmployee
 @empID char(3)
as
 delete from tblEmployees where @empID = empID
 return @@rowcount
go
```

If the code in your test harness resembled

```
declare @input char(3)
declare @actualRows int

-- main test loop
--   read test case data into @caseID, @input, @expectedRows

    exec @actualRows = dbEmployees.dbo.usp_DeleteEmployee @input
--   determine pass/fail
--   store or display test case result
-- end main loop
```

then each iteration through the main test loop would be testing against a different state of the database, which would make determining an expected value very difficult. You need to reset the database state before each test harness call to the stored procedure under test:

```
declare @input char(3)
declare @actualRows int

-- main test loop
--   read test case data into @caseID, @input, @expectedRows

    truncate table dbEmployees.dbo.tblEmployees
```

```
    insert into dbEmployees.dbo.tblEmployees
     values('001', 'Adams', '06/15/1998')

    insert into dbEmployees.dbo.tblEmployees
     values('e22','Baker', '06/15/2001')

    -- etc.

    exec @actualRows = dbEmployees.dbo.usp_DeleteEmployee @input
--   determine pass/fail
--   store or display test case result
-- end main loop
```

In most situations, resetting the state of the database under test requires many statements that can make your test harness script very long. So, a good approach is to write an auxiliary stored procedure in your test harness script to handle the task of resetting the database state before each call to the stored procedure under test:

```
if exists (select * from sysobjects where name='tap_Reset')
 drop procedure tap_Reset
go

create procedure tap_Reset
as
 truncate table dbEmployees.dbo.tblEmployees

insert into dbEmployees.dbo.tblEmployees
 values('e11','Adams', '06/15/1998')
insert into dbEmployees.dbo.tblEmployees
 values('e22','Baker', '06/15/2001')
insert into dbEmployees.dbo.tblEmployees
 values('e33','Young', '06/15/1998')
insert into dbEmployees.dbo.tblEmployees
 values('e44','Zetta', '06/15/2001')
-- other data would be inserted too
go
```

Here you create a utility test automation procedure that deletes all the rows in table tblEmployees and then repopulates with rich test bed data. Your script can then call the stored procedure inside the main test loop just before each call to the stored procedure under test. An alternative to hard-coding the INSERT statements that populate the target table is to use the BULK INSERT statement in conjunction with an external data store, as described in Section 9.3.

Do not misinterpret this discussion to mean that you should always reset the database under test to some initial state. You must also perform test scenarios that manipulate system state through several changes. For example, a test scenario could insert five data rows, delete one of the new rows and one of the original rows, then insert three new rows, and delete a row. Each state of the database could be examined for correctness to determine an overall scenario pass/fail result.

9.9 Example Program: SQLspTest

The scripts in this section combine several of the techniques in this chapter to create a lightweight T-SQL test harness system. There are three scripts: script makeDbEmployees.sql, which creates the underlying test bed and the stored procedure under test; script makeDbTestCasesAndResults.sql, which creates test case data and result storage; and script SQLspTest.sql, which is the actual test harness. The stored procedure under test is usp_HiredAfter(), which accepts a datetime input argument and returns a SQL rowset of those employees in tblEmployees whose date of hire is after the input argument. When run, the output will be that shown in Figure 9-1 in the introduction section of this chapter. Listing 9-1 shows the script that creates the underlying database and the stored procedure under test.

Listing 9-1. *Script to Create Test Bed Database and Stored Procedure Under Test*

```
-- ================================================================

-- makeDbEmployees.sql
use master
go

if exists (select * from sysdatabases where name='dbEmployees')
 drop database dbEmployees
go

if exists (select * from sysxlogins where name = 'employeesLogin')
 exec sp_droplogin 'employeesLogin'
go

create database dbEmployees
go

use dbEmployees
go

create table tblEmployees
(
 empID char(3) primary key,
 empLast varchar(35) not null,
 empDOH datetime not null,
)
go

-- this is dev data, not test case data
insert into tblEmployees values('e11','Adams', '06/15/1998')
insert into tblEmployees values('e22','Baker', '06/15/2001')
go
```

```
exec sp_addlogin 'employeesLogin', 'secret'
go
exec sp_grantdbaccess 'employeesLogin'
go

create procedure usp_HiredAfter
 @dt datetime
as
 select * from tblEmployees where empDOH > @dt
go

grant execute on usp_HiredAfter to employeesLogin
go

-- end script
```

Listing 9-2 shows the script that creates a test case data and test result store.

Listing 9-2. *Script to Create Test Case Data and Test Results Stores*

```
-- ============================================================

-- makeDbTestCasesAndResults.sql
use master
go

if exists (select * from sysdatabases where name='dbTestCasesAndResults')
 drop database dbTestCasesAndResults
go

if exists (select * from sysxlogins where name = 'testLogin')
 exec sp_droplogin 'testLogin'
go

create database dbTestCasesAndResults
go

use dbTestCasesAndResults
go

create table tblTestCases
(
 caseID char(4) primary key,
 input datetime not null,
 expectedChecksum int not null
)
go
```

```
-- this is the test case data for usp_HiredAfter using a checksum expected
-- value approach
-- can also read from a text file using BCP, DTS, or a C# program
insert into tblTestCases values('0001','01/01/1998', 1042032)
insert into tblTestCases values('0002','01/01/1998', 9999999) -- deliberate error
insert into tblTestCases values('0003','01/01/2000', 25527856)
insert into tblTestCases values('0004','01/01/2006', 0)
go

create table tblResults
(
 caseID char(4) not null,
 result char(4) null,
 whenRun datetime not null
)
go

exec sp_addlogin 'testLogin', 'secret'
go
exec sp_grantdbaccess 'testLogin'
go

grant select, insert, delete, update on tblTestCases to testLogin
go

grant select, insert, delete, update on tblResults to testLogin
go

-- end script
```

Listing 9-3 is the test harness script.

Listing 9-3. *The Test Automation Harness Script*

```
-- ===============================================================

-- SQLspTest.sql
-- test dbEmployees..usp_HiredAfter
-- reads test case data and writes results
--   to dbTestCasesAndResults

set nocount on
```

```
if not exists
 (select * from master.dbo.sysdatabases where name='dbTestCasesAndResults')
 raiserror('Fatal error: dbTestCasesAndResults not found', 16, 1)
go

if exists (select * from sysobjects where name='tap_Reset')
 drop procedure tap_Reset
go

create procedure tap_Reset
as
 truncate table dbEmployees.dbo.tblEmployees

insert into dbEmployees.dbo.tblEmployees
 values('e11','Adams', '06/15/1998')
insert into dbEmployees.dbo.tblEmployees
 values('e22','Baker', '06/15/2001')
insert into dbEmployees.dbo.tblEmployees
 values('e33','Young', '06/15/1998')
insert into dbEmployees.dbo.tblEmployees
 values('e44','Zetta', '06/15/2001')
-- other data would be inserted too
go

-- prepare dbEmployees with rich data
exec tap_Reset
go

declare tCursor cursor fast_forward
 for select caseID, input, expectedChecksum
 from dbTestCasesAndResults.dbo.tblTestCases
 order by caseID

declare @caseID char(4), @input datetime, @expectedChecksum int
declare @whenRun datetime
declare @resultMsg varchar(80)
declare @actualChecksum int

create table #resultRowset -- for checksum technique
(
 empID char(3) primary key,
 empLast varchar(35) not null,
 empDOH datetime not null,
)
```

```
set @whenRun = getdate()

print 'Stored procedure under test = usp_HiredAfter'
print ' '
print 'CaseID  Input              Expected Actual  Result'
print '================================================'

open tCursor
fetch next
 from tCursor
 into @caseID, @input, @expectedChecksum

while @@fetch_status = 0
begin

 exec tap_Reset -- reset test bed data

 truncate table #resultRowset -- empty out the result rowset

 insert #resultRowset (empID, empLast, empDOH) -- call sp under test
  exec dbEmployees.dbo.usp_HiredAfter @input

 if (@@rowcount = 0)
  set @actualChecksum = 0
 else
  select @actualChecksum = checksum_agg(binary_checksum(*)) from #resultRowset

 if (@actualChecksum = @expectedChecksum)
  begin
   set @resultMsg = @caseID + '    ' + cast(@input as varchar(11)) +
     ' ' + cast(@expectedChecksum as varchar(20)) + ' ' +
         cast(@actualChecksum as varchar(20)) + ' Pass'
   print @resultMsg
   insert into dbTestCasesAndResults.dbo.tblResults values(@caseID, 'Pass',
                                                  @whenRun)
  end
 else
  begin
   set @resultMsg = @caseID + '    ' + cast(@input as varchar(11)) +
     ' ' + cast(@expectedChecksum as varchar(20)) + ' ' +
         cast(@actualChecksum as varchar(20)) + ' FAIL'
   print @resultMsg
   insert into dbTestCasesAndResults.dbo.tblResults values(@caseID, 'FAIL',
                                                  @whenRun)
  end
```

```
 fetch next
  from tCursor
  into @caseID, @input, @expectedChecksum

end

close tCursor
deallocate tCursor

drop table #resultRowset

-- end script
```

CHAPTER 10

■ ■ ■

Combinations and Permutations

10.0 Introduction

Combinations and permutations are fundamental concepts in software testing, and the ability to programmatically generate and manipulate them is an essential test automation skill. An arbitrary *combination* is a subset of k items selected from a larger set of n items, where order does not matter. For example, if you have the 5 items

```
{ "ant", "bug", cat", "dog", "elk" }
```

then the 10 possible combinations of size 3 are

```
{ "ant", "bug", "cat" }
{ "ant", "bug", "dog" }
{ "ant", "bug", "elk" }
{ "ant", "cat", "dog" }
{ "ant", "cat", "elk" }
{ "ant", "dog", "elk" }
{ "bug", "cat", "dog" }
{ "bug", "cat", "elk" }
{ "bug", "dog", "elk" }
{ "cat", "dog", "elk" }
```

You can imagine that these could be test case inputs to a method that accepts three string arguments. Notice that { "cat", "bug", "dog" } is not listed because it is considered the same as { "bug", "cat", "dog" }. A mathematical combination is a generalization of this idea of subsets. Instead of being a subset of arbitrary items, a mathematical combination of order (n, k) is a subset of size k of the integers from 0 up to n-1. So the 10 elements of a mathematical combination of 5 items taken 3 at a time are

```
{ 0, 1, 2 }
{ 0, 1, 3 }
{ 0, 1, 4 }
{ 0, 2, 3 }
{ 0, 2, 4 }
{ 0, 3, 4 }
```

```
{ 1, 2, 3 }
{ 1, 2, 4 }
{ 1, 3, 4 }
{ 2, 3, 4 }
```

In this example, the elements of the combination are listed in lexicographical order (also called lexicographic order or dictionary order). For mathematical combinations, this means that the elements, if interpreted as integers, are listed in increasing order. For example, if $n = 5$ and $k = 3$, the first element is { 0, 1, 2 } and the next element is { 0, 1, 3 } because "12" comes before "13". Notice, too, that the atoms (individual integers) of a combination element also appear in increasing order so there is a kind of dual orderedness to a lexicographical combination. With a lexicographical combination of order (n, k), the identity element is defined to be the first element: { 0, 1, 2, . . . n-k }.

The function that calculates the total number of combinations for given n and k values is a very important function when dealing with combinations. For instance, the previous two examples demonstrate that the total number of combinations of 5 items taken 3 at a time is 10. This helper function is often called Choose. So, you can write Choose(5,3) = 10.

Closely related to combinations are *permutations*. An arbitrary permutation is one of the possible arrangements of a set of n items. For example, if you have the three items

```
{ "Adam", "Barb", "Carl" }
```

then, the six permutations of these items are

```
{ "Adam", "Barb", "Carl" }
{ "Adam", "Carl", "Barb" }
{ "Barb", "Adam", "Carl" }
{ "Barb", "Carl", "Adam" }
{ "Carl", "Adam", "Barb" }
{ "Carl", "Barb", "Adam" }
```

Notice that unlike combinations, permutations take order into account by definition. A mathematical permutation is a generalization of this idea of rearrangements. Instead of being a rearrangement of arbitrary items, a mathematical permutation of order n is a rearrangement of the integers from 0 up to $n-1$. So the six elements of a mathematical permutation of order 3 are

```
{ 0, 1, 2 }
{ 0, 2, 1 }
{ 1, 0, 2 }
{ 1, 2, 0 }
{ 2, 0, 1 }
{ 2, 1, 0 }
```

Permutations can be lexicographical as in this example—notice that if the permutation elements were interpreted as integers, you would have { 12, 21, 102, 120, 201, 210 }. The total number of permutations of order n is given by n factorial, often denoted by $n!$ or Factorial(n). So in the preceding two examples, because we are dealing with $n = 3$, the total number of permutations is $3! = 3 * 2 * 1 = 6$.

Combinations and permutations occur in many aspects of software testing. For example, suppose you had a program with a UI that has three drop-down controls. You need to analyze how many different combinations and permutations of user inputs there are so you can design your test cases. Or suppose you are testing a program designed for multiple hardware configurations. You need to analyze the different combinations and permutations of the configurations so you can plan your test effort.

You can write combination and permutation methods that work directly on type string. But a more flexible approach is to write methods that work on integers and then map these mathematical combination and permutation methods to string arrays.

10.1 Creating a Mathematical Combination Object

Problem

You want to create an object to represent a mathematical combination.

Design

Use an object-oriented design to create a Combination class with an array of type long to hold a combination element, and long values n and k to hold the total number of integers and subset size, respectively.

Solution

```
public class Combination
{
  private long n = 0;
  private long k = 0;
  private long[] data = null;

  public Combination(long n, long k)
  {
    if (n < 0 || k < 0)
      throw new Exception("Negative argument in constructor");
    this.n = n;
    this.k = k;
    this.data = new long[k];
    for (long i = 0; i < k; ++i)
      this.data[i] = i;
  }
}
```

Comments

A mathematical combination lends itself nicely to implementation as a class. Because a mathematical combination represents a subset of k items selected from a set of integers from 0 through n-1, you need to store those values as well as an array to hold the combination

element's atoms (individual integer values). The letters "n" and "k" are often used in mathematical literature, so we use them instead of more descriptive variable names such as
totalSize and subsetSize. A long array named data is declared to hold the atoms of a specific
combination. Type long is used rather than type int to get a wider range of values (type ulong
can be used to get an even bigger range, of course). The constructor accepts values for n and k,
and checks to see whether either argument is negative.

The constructor allocates a new long array "data" of size k and populates the array with
values from 0 through k-1. For instance if n = 5 and k = 3 are passed to the constructor,
data[0] has 0, data[1] has 1, and data[2] has 2, representing the initial combination element
{ 0, 1, 2 }. You would call the combination constructor like this:

```
Combination c = new Combination(5, 3);
```

You can place your combination class directly in your test harness program, but a more
flexible alternative is to create a separate code library to house the class. It's very useful to have
a display method so you can see a Combination object:

```
public override string ToString()
{
  string s = "{ ";
  for (long i = 0; i < this.k; ++i)
    s += this.data[i] + " ";
  s += "}";
  return s;
}
```

Here you just return a string with the combination atoms separated by blank spaces and
delimited by curly brace characters. So if you wrote

```
Combination c = new Combination(7, 4);
Console.WriteLine(c.ToString());
```

you would see

```
{ 0 1 2 3 }
```

displayed. You can use the StringBuilder class instead of the += operator if efficiency is a major
concern. As it turns out, it's useful to implement a Combination constructor that accepts an
array as an argument:

```
public Combination(long n, long k, long[] a)
{
  if (k != a.Length)
    throw new Exception("Bad array size in constructor");

  this.n = n;
  this.k = k;
  this.data = new long[k];

  for (long i = 0; i < a.Length; ++i)
    this.data[i] = a[i];
}
```

With this constructor, you can write code to initialize a `Combination` object to a specific element:

```
long[] array = new long[] {0, 2, 3, 6};
Combination c = new Combination(7, 4, array);
Console.WriteLine(c.ToString());
```

This auxiliary constructor is useful in its own right, but you'll use it in Section 10.5 to generate a combination element from an index value. Notice that the caller is responsible for ensuring that the values in the array argument are in proper lexicographical order, and n and k are nonnegative.

10.2 Calculating the Number of Ways to Select k Items from n Items

Problem

You want to calculate the total number of combinations for n items taken k at a time.

Design

Write a `Choose()` method that implements the alternative definition of `Choose()` rather than the canonical definition. Be sure to handle arithmetic overflow.

Solution

```
public static long Choose(long n, long k)
{
  if (n < 0 || k < 0)
    throw new Exception("Negative argument in Choose");
  if (n < k)
    return 0;
  if (n == k)
    return 1;

  long delta, iMax;

  if (k < n - k)
  {
    delta = n - k;
    iMax = k;
  }
  else
  {
    delta = k;
    iMax = n - k;
  }
```

```
long answer = delta + 1;
for (long i = 2; i <= iMax; ++i)
{
  checked { answer = (answer * (delta + i)) / i; }
}

return answer;
}
```

Comments

An important function for combinations is the total number of elements for particular n and k values. This function is most often called Choose(). So if n = 5 and k = 3, you can write Choose(5, 3) and it should return 10, meaning that for 5 items taken 3 at a time there are 10 total combination elements. Note that it's easy to confuse a combination of n and k with a Choose() function of n and k. A mathematical combination with order n = 7 and k = 4 (7 items taken 4 at a time) has elements such as { 0, 3, 4, 6 }, whereas the associated Choose(7,4) function returns 35 and is the total number of elements of 7 items taken 4 at a time.

The canonical definition of Choose() is Choose(n, k) = Factorial(n) / (Factorial (k) * Factorial(n-k)). For example, Choose(7, 3) = Factorial(7) / (Factorial(3) * Factorial(7-3)) = 5040 / (6 * 24) = 35. But implementing Choose() directly from the definition is a weak approach because the numerator and denominator can easily overflow for relatively small values of n and k. A better solution uses an alternative definition for Choose():

Choose(n, k) = (n * (n-1) * (n-2) * ... * (n-k+1)) / (1 * 2 * ... * k)

This equation looks a bit confusing at first glance but is understandable with an example:

Choose(7, 3) = (7 * 6 * 5) / (1 * 2 * 3)

Instead of computing the numerator (a big number), then the denominator (a big number), and then dividing, you can calculate partial products and divide as you go. For Choose(7, 3), you first calculate 7 * 6 and divide by 2, getting 21 (skipping the first 1 term on the bottom of the fraction because dividing by 1 has no effect). Then multiplying that partial product (21) by 5 and dividing by 3, you get an answer of 35.

A second optimization for the Choose(n, k) method is a consequence of the following property:

Choose(n, k) = Choose(n, n-k).

For example, Choose(10, 8) = Choose(10, 2). This is not an obvious relationship, but if you experiment with a few examples you'll see why this is true. Calculating Choose(10, 8) directly involves computing seven partial products and seven divisions, but calculating the equivalent Choose(10, 2) requires only one multiplication and one division operation.

The Choose() implementation starts by checking for the case when n < k. We define a 0 result here—for example, the number of ways to select 6 items from 3 items is 0. Next we check if n = k, in which case we return 1—for example, the number of ways to select 5 items from 5 items is 1. If neither special case holds, we use the two shortcuts to calculate the return value. Using the checked keyword causes arithmetic overflow to raise an exception (in an unchecked context, arithmetic overflow is ignored and the result is truncated).

This Choose() method is relatively lightweight but will meet most of your test automation needs. However, there are many algorithms and implementations available through third-party scientific libraries that are optimized for various purposes. For example, an algorithm optimized for performance at the expense of memory could store results up to certain values of n and k in a table for quick retrieval.

10.3 Calculating the Successor to a Mathematical Combination Element

Problem

You want to determine the successor element to a given mathematical combination element.

Design

Write a Successor() method that finds the rightmost atom that must be incremented, increments it, and then increments all atoms to the right of the incremented atom.

Solution

```
public Combination Successor()
{
  if (this.data[0] == this.n - this.k)
    return null;

  Combination ans = new Combination(this.n, this.k);

  for (long i = 0; i < this.k; ++i)
    ans.data[i] = this.data[i];

  long x;
  for (x = this.k - 1; x > 0 && ans.data[x] == this.n - this.k + x;
       --x);

  ++ans.data[x];

  for (long j = x; j < this.k - 1; ++j)
    ans.data[j+1] = ans.data[j] + 1;

  return ans;
}
```

Comments

To iterate through all mathematical combinations of order (n, k) you need to determine the lexicographic successor element to a given element. For example, if n = 7 and k = 4, combination element [0] is { 0, 1, 2, 3 } and its successor element [1] is { 0, 1, 2, 4 }. Start by determining whether you are at the last Combination element so you can return null. Consider the case with n = 7 and k = 4:

```
[0]  { 0, 1, 2, 3 }
[1]  { 0, 1, 2, 4 }
[2]  { 0, 1, 2, 5 }
. . .
[32] { 2, 3, 5, 6 }
[33] { 2, 4, 5, 6 }
[34] { 3, 4, 5, 6 }
```

Notice that the last element is the only one that has atom value n-k at position 0. This property is true in general, so you can use it to identify when you're at the last element. Alternatives to returning null for the successor to the last element include throwing an exception or returning the first element. Next, the Successor() method creates a Combination object to hold the answer. The key to the algorithm is finding which rightmost atom must be incremented. You use an index x and start at the last position within array data and work to the left (decrementing) until you find a false result to the condition

```
ans.data[x] == this.n - this.k + x
```

or hit the beginning of the data array. The atom at this position is incremented. Then every atom to the right of that atom must be incremented also. With this Successor() method in hand, if you write

```
long[] array = new long[] { 2, 3, 5, 6 };
Combination c = new Combination(7, 4, array);
c = c.Successor();
Console.WriteLine("Successor to 2, 3, 5, 6 is: " + c.ToString());
```

the output would be

```
Successor to 2, 3, 5, 6 is: { 2, 4, 5, 6 }
```

It's often useful to implement a Predecessor() method that returns the lexicographic predecessor element to a given element. Here is one possibility:

```
public Combination Predecessor()
{
  if (this.data[k-1] == this.k - 1)
    return null;

  Combination ans = new Combination(this.n, this.k);

  for (long i = 0; i < this.k; ++i)
    ans.data[i] = this.data[i];
```

```
  long x;
  for (x = this.k - 1; x > 0 && ans.data[x] == ans.data[x-1] + 1;
       --x);

  --ans.data[x];

  for (long j = x + 1; j < this.k; ++j)
    ans.data[j] = this.n - this.k + j;

  return ans;
}
```

You start by identifying the case where you're at the first element so you can return null. This happens when the atom at position k-1 in array data has value k-1. For example, if n = 9 and k = 6, element [0] is { 0, 1, 2, 3, 4, 5 } and the atom at position k-1 = 5 has value 5. After instantiating a Combination object to hold the answer, you use an index variable x and start at the rightmost atom and work to the left until the condition

```
ans.data[x] == ans.data[x-1] + 1
```

is not true. The atom at position x must be decremented, and all atoms to the right of that atom must be incremented.

10.4 Generating All Mathematical Combination Elements for a Given n and k

Problem

You want to generate all mathematical combination elements for given values of n and k.

Design

Instantiate a Combination object, and then use the Combination.Successor() method inside a while loop.

Solution

```
Console.WriteLine("\nStart\n");
Combination c = new Combination(5,3);
int i = 0;

while (c != null)
{
  Console.WriteLine("[" + i + "] " + c.ToString());
  c = c.Successor();
  ++i;
}
Console.WriteLine("\nDone\n");
```

Comments

In situations with sufficiently small values for n and k, you can exhaustively list all mathematical combination elements. When the preceding code is run, the result is

```
Start

[0] { 0 1 2 }
[1] { 0 1 3 }
[2] { 0 1 4 }
[3] { 0 2 3 }
[4] { 0 2 4 }
[5] { 0 3 4 }
[6] { 1 2 3 }
[7] { 1 2 4 }
[8] { 1 3 4 }
[9] { 2 3 4 }

Done
```

The call to `Combination.Successor()` returns the next mathematical combination element in lexicographical order or `null` if you are at the last element. So, you can use a `while` loop with `null` as an exit condition to iterate through all elements. Notice that after the loop terminates, the `Combination` object will be `null`, so you need to reinstantiate it if you want to use it further. If you want to explicitly create all possible elements, you can create an array of `Combination` objects and store each object:

```
long ct = Combination.Choose(5,3);
Combination[] combos = new Combination[ct];
combos[0] = new Combination(5,3);

for (long i = 1; i < ct; ++i)
{
  combos[i] = combos[i-1].Successor();
}

for (long i = 0; i < ct; ++i)
{
  Console.WriteLine("[" + i + "] " + combos[i].ToString());
}
```

When this code is run, the output will be the same as the previous example. You determine how many `Combination` objects you'll be creating using the `Combination.Choose()` method and then initialize an array of `Combination` objects with that size. You seed the first array cell with the initial `Combination` object by calling the default constructor. Then each cell in the array is assigned a `Combination` object that has the successor element to the element of the `Combination` object in the previous cell. Using this technique, you'll have all `Combination` elements available to you. Be careful when employing this technique because the number of combination elements can be very large.

10.5 Determining the mth Lexicographical Element of a Mathematical Combination

Problem

You want to determine a specific element of a mathematical combination.

Design

Write a method `Element()` that calculates the combinadic of the specified element and then transform the combinadic to a combination element.

Solution

```
public Combination Element(long m)
{
  long[] ans = new long[this.k];

  long a = this.n;
  long b = this.k;
  long x = (Choose(this.n, this.k) - 1) - m;

  for (long i = 0; i < this.k; ++i) // store combinadic
  {
    ans[i] = LargestV(a,b,x);
    x = x - Choose(ans[i],b);
    a = ans[i];
    b = b-1;
  }

  for (long i = 0; i < this.k; ++i)
  {
    ans[i] = (n-1) - ans[i];
  }

  return new Combination(this.n, this.k, ans);
}

// return largest value v where v < a and  Choose(v,b) <= x
private static long LargestV(long a, long b, long x)
{
  long v = a - 1;

  while (Choose(v,b) > x)
    --v;

  return v;
}
```

Comments

Computing a specific Combination from a specified lexicographical index is often useful. For example, if you call the code in this solution

```
Combination c = new Combination(7,4);
Console.WriteLine("Element[17] is: " + c.Element(17));
```

you determine combination element [17], and the output is

```
Element[17] is: { 0 3 4 6 }
```

This problem is not as trivial as it may first appear. A brute force solution to generating the mth lexicographical combination element would be to start with the first element and then iterate, calling a successor method or code, m times. This approach works, but the technique is bad when the value of m is large. And, unfortunately, m can be very, very large. For example, if you have a combination of n = 200 items taken k = 10 at a time, there are 22,451,004,309,013,280 possible elements. Using the naive looping technique described on a reasonably fast desktop machine, calculating element [999,999,999,999] for n = 200 and k = 10 takes more than 100 hours. But by using an interesting mathematical idea called the combinadic of a number, the preceding solution calculates the [999,999,999,999] element for n = 200 and k = 10 in approximately 1 second.

The combinadic of an integer is an alternative representation of the number based on combinations. As it turns out, the combinadic of some integer m maps directly to the mth combination element. Consider, for example, the number 27. If you fix n = 7 and k = 4, the combinadic of 27 is (6 5 2 1). This means that

```
27 = Choose(6,4) + Choose(5,3) + Choose(2,2) + Choose(1,1).
```

With n = 7 and k = 4, any number z between 0 and 34 (the total number of combination elements for n and k) can be uniquely represented as

```
z = Choose(c ,4) + Choose(c ,3) + Choose(c ,2) + Choose(c ,1)
           1              2              3              4
```

where $n > c1 > c2 > c3 > c4$. Notice that n is analogous to a base because all combinadic digits are between 0 and n-1 (just like all digits in ordinary base 10 are between 0 and 9). The k value determines the number of terms in the combinadic. The combinadic of a number can be calculated fairly quickly, so the idea to generate the mth combination element is to compute the combinadic of m and then transform the combinadic into a combination element.

The relationship between the combinadic of a number and the mth lexicographical element of a combination uses the concept of the dual of each lexicographic index. Suppose n = 7 and k = 4. There are Choose(7, 4) = 35 combination elements, indexed from 0 to 34. The dual indexes are the ones on opposite ends of the index list—indexes 0 and 34 are duals, indexes 1 and 33 are duals, indexes 2 and 32, and so forth. Notice that each pair of dual indexes sum to 34, so if you know any index, it's easy to compute its dual.

Suppose you are somehow able to find the combinadic of 27 and get (6 5 2 1). Now suppose you subtract each digit in the combinadic from n-1 = 6 to get (0 1 4 5). Interestingly, this gives you the combination element [7], which is the dual index of 27. So, to find the combination element for some index m, first find its dual and call that x. Next, find the combinadic of x. Then subtract each digit of the combinadic of x from n-1 and the result is the mth lexicographic combination element. Table 10-1 shows the relationships among m, the dual of m, Combination.Element(m), the combinadic of m, and (n-1) - ci for n=5 and k=3.

Table 10-1. *Relationships Between an Integer* m *and Its Combinadic*

m	dual(m)	Element(m)	combinadic(m)	(n-1) − ci
0	9	{ 0 1 2 }	(2 1 0)	(2 3 4)
1	8	{ 0 1 3 }	(3 1 0)	(1 3 4)
2	7	{ 0 1 4 }	(3 2 0)	(1 2 4)
3	6	{ 0 2 3 }	(3 2 1)	(1 2 3)
4	5	{ 0 2 4 }	(4 1 0)	(0 3 4)
5	4	{ 0 3 4 }	(4 2 0)	(0 2 4)
6	3	{ 1 2 3 }	(4 2 1)	(0 2 3)
7	2	{ 1 2 4 }	(4 3 0)	(0 1 4)
8	1	{ 1 3 4 }	(4 3 1)	(0 1 3)
9	0	{ 2 3 4 }	(4 3 2)	(0 1 2)

So, the real problem is finding the combinadic of a number. Now you'll see how to find the combinadic of 28. Most of the work of finding the combinadic is done with an unusual little helper method, LargestV(). The basic structure of the combinadic of 28 will be (c1, c2, c3, c4), where

$$28 = Choose(c_1,4) + Choose(c_2,3) + Choose(c_3,2) + Choose(c_4,1)$$

So, you need to find values c1, c2, c3, and c4. Method LargestV(a,b,x) returns the largest value v that is less than a given value a, and so that Choose(v,b) is less than or equal to x. To compute c_1, you call LargestV(7,4,28), the largest value v less than 7, so that Choose(v,4) is less than or equal to 28. In this case, LargestV() returns 6 because Choose(6,4) = 15, which is less than 28. The value 6 is the first number c1 of the combinadic.

Now to compute the c2 value, you subtract 15 from 28, and now you only have 13 left to consume because you used up 15 for the c1 coefficient. Call LargestV(6,3,13), which returns 5 and note that Choose(5,3) is 10, leaving you with 3. The combinadic is now (6 5 ? ?). Next, you call LargestV(4,2,10) and get 3 for c3, noting that Choose(3,2) is 3, leaving you with 0 left. Finally, to compute c4, you call LargestV(3,1,0), which returns 0.

Now that you have the combinadic (6 5 3 0), map it to a combination element by subtracting each of the combinadic values from n-1 = 6, which gives you (0 1 3 6). Finally, pass the answer array to the auxiliary Combination constructor to convert it into a combination object and you get { 0, 1, 3, 6 }—combination element [6] in lexicographical order for n = 7 and k = 4.

Notice that the LargestV(a,b,x) method calls the Choose(n,k) method in such a way that n can be less than k. This is why we allow this possibility in the Choose() method, and also in the Combination constructor.

10.6 Applying a Mathematical Combination to a String Array

Problem

You want one or more combinations of a set of strings.

Design

Write a Combination.ApplyTo() method that accepts an array of strings and returns a subset array corresponding to the Combination element context.

Solution

```
public string[] ApplyTo(string[] sa)
{
  if (sa.Length != this.n)
    throw new Exception("Bad array size in ApplyTo()");

  string[] result = new string[this.k];

  for (long i = 0; i < result.Length; ++i)
    result[i] = sa[this.data[i]];

  return result;
}
```

Comments

In software test automation situations, you usually want to generate combinations of strings. If you called the code in this solution

```
string[] animals = new string[]{"ant", "bat", "cow", "dog", "emu"};
Combination c = new Combination(5,3);
string[] subset = new string[3];
Console.WriteLine("All combinations taken 3 at a time are:\n");
while (c != null)
{
  subset = c.ApplyTo(animals);
  Console.WriteLine(subset[0] + " " + subset[1] + " " + subset[2]);
  c = c.Successor();
}

c = new Combination(5,3);
Console.WriteLine("\nJust element[5] is:\n");
subset = c.Element(5).ApplyTo(animals);
Console.WriteLine(subset[0] + " " + subset[1] + " " + subset[2]);
```

the output would be

```
All combinations taken 3 at a time are:

ant bat cow
ant bat dog
ant bat emu
ant cow dog
ant cow emu
ant dog emu
bat cow dog
bat cow emu
bat dog emu
cow dog emu

Just element[5] is:

ant dog emu
```

Suppose you have a Combination object with n = 5 and k = 3. The object will have a data array with atoms from 0 to n-1, which represent a mathematical combination, for instance, { 0, 3, 4 }. The ApplyTo() method accepts a string array that contains n = 5 strings. That input array is indexed from 0 to n-1. The idea is to create an answer array of size k and store into that answer array the string values that correspond to the atoms of the Combination element. For example, if you pass array "animals" with "ant" at [0], "bat" at [1], "cow" at [2], "dog" at [3], and "emu" at [4] to ApplyTo() where the Combination object context has 0 at data[0], 3 at data[1], and 4 at data[2], the method will place "ant" into result[0], "dog" into result[1], and "emu" into result[2].

Although strings are the most common items to take combinations of in a software-testing situation, you can modify the ApplyTo() method to work with any type. One way to do this is to recast ApplyTo() to accept and return arrays of type object, and then use explicit type casts when calling this new version. Another alternative is to use the generics mechanism; the C# language in Visual Studio .NET 2003 and the .NET Framework 1.1 does not support generics, but generics are supported in Visual Studio 2005 with .NET Framework 2.0.

A lightweight alternative for generating all combinations of a set of strings is to use nested for loops. The technique is best explained by an example. Suppose you have the five animals from the previous example: "ant", "bat", "cow", "dog", "emu".

```
Console.WriteLine("\nAll elements of 5 animals, 3 at a time: ");
string[] animals = new string[]{"ant", "bat", "cow", "dog", "emu"};
for (int i = 0; i < animals.Length; ++i)
{
  for (int j = i+1; j < animals.Length; ++j)
  {
    for (int k = j+1; k < animals.Length; ++k)
    {
      Console.WriteLine( "{ " + animals[i] + ", " + animals[j] +
                       ", " + animals[k] + " }" );
    }
  }
}
```

This technique has the advantage of avoiding the overhead of a Combination object, and is somewhat easier to understand than using a Combination object. However, this simple technique has three disadvantages. First, the technique works well if you want to generate all elements of a combination, but what if you only want some of the elements or a particular element? Second, this technique is very specific to a particular problem and doesn't generalize well. And third, it works nicely when the number of items in each subset element, k, is small, but what if k is very large? If you were interested in n = 100 items taken k = 50 at a time, you would have to code 50 for loops.

10.7 Creating a Mathematical Permutation Object

Problem

You want to create an object to represent a mathematical permutation.

Design

Use an object-oriented approach and write a Permutation class with an array of type int to represent each permutation element, and a single int value named order to represent the subset size.

Solution

```
public class Permutation
{
  private int[] data = null;
  private int order = 0;

  public Permutation(int n)
  {
    this.data = new int[n];

    for (int i = 0; i < n; ++i)
      this.data[i] = i;

    this.order = n;
  }
}
```

Comments

A mathematical permutation lends itself nicely to implementation as a class. Because a mathematical permutation of order n represents an arrangement of the set of integers from 0 through n-1, you need an array to store those values as well as a single integer field to hold the order value. An integer array named data is declared to hold the atoms of a specific permutation. The constructor accepts values for the order but does not check to see whether that value is negative (which will throw an exception).

The constructor allocates a new int array data of size n and populates the array with values from 0 through n-1. For instance, if n = 4 is passed to the Permutation constructor, data[0] gets 0, data[1] gets 1, data[2] gets 2, and data[3] gets 3 to represent the initial identity permutation element { 0, 1, 2, 3 }. You would call the permutation constructor like this:

```
Permutation p = new Permutation(4);
```

You can place your Permutation class directly into your test harness program, but a more flexible approach is to create a separate library to house the Permutation class. It's very useful to have a display method so you can see a Permutation object:

```
public override string ToString()
{
  string s = "% ";
  for (int i = 0; i < this.order; ++i)
    s += this.data[i] + " ";
  s += "%";
  return s;
}
```

Here you just return a string with the permutation atoms separated by blank spaces and delimited by % characters. The % is arbitrary and used instead of the more natural curly brace characters just so that you can distinguish a Permutation representation from a Combination. If you wrote

```
Permutation p = new Permutation(6);
Console.WriteLine(p.ToString());
```

you would see

```
% 0 1 2 3 4 5 %
```

displayed. As you'll see, it's useful to implement an auxiliary Permutation constructor that accepts an array as an argument:

```
public Permutation(int[] a)
{
  this.data = new int[a.Length];
  for (int i = 0; i < a.Length; ++i)
    this.data[i] = a[i];
  this.order = a.Length;
}
```

With this constructor, you can write code to initialize a Permutation object to a specific element

```
int[] a = new int[] { 2, 0, 3, 1 };
Permutation p = new Permutation(a);
Console.WriteLine("\nPermutation from array [ 2, 0, 3, 1 ] is:");
Console.WriteLine(p.ToString());
```

which would display:

```
Permutation from array [ 2, 0, 3, 1 ] is:
% 2 0 3 1 %
```

10.8 Calculating the Number of Permutations of Order n

Problem

You want to calculate the total number of permutations for n items.

Design

The total number of permutations of order n is given by n! (n factorial) so write a `Factorial()` method. Avoid calculating n! directly, if possible, and use some form of lookup instead. But if you absolutely must calculate, code the `Factorial()` method so that it catches arithmetic overflow.

Solution

```
public static int Factorial(int n)
{
  int answer = 1;
  for (int i = 1; i <= n; ++i)
  {
    checked { answer *= i; }
  }
  return answer;
}
```

Comments

Dealing with n factorial is problematic because the result becomes very large, very quickly. For example, although 6! = 6 * 5 * 4 * 3 * 2 * 1 = only 720, the value of 64! is

```
64 * 63 * 62 * . . . * 1 =
126,886,932,100,000,000,000,000,000,000,000,000,000,000,000,000,000,
000,000,000,000,000,000,000
```

approximately. With the C# type int, the largest factorial that can be stored is 12! = 479,001,600. Even with type ulong

```
public static ulong Factorial(int n)
{
  ulong answer = 1;
  for (int i = 1; i <= n; ++i)
  {
    checked { answer *= (ulong)i; }
  }
  return answer;
}
```

you can calculate at most 20! = 2,432,902,008,176,640,000. With such small result sets, you might as well just do a simple lookup:

```
public static int FactorialLookUp(int n)
{
  int[] answers = new int[] { 1, 2, 6, 24, 120, 720, 5040, 40320,
                          362880, 3628800, 39916800, 479001600 };
  if (n > 12)
    throw new Exception("Factorial overflow");

  return answers[n-1];
}
```

If you must calculate a factorial, be sure to use the checked keyword to force arithmetic overflow to throw an exception. Without checked, instead of throwing an exception, results may wrap around int.MaxValue (depending on factors such as compiler options). For example, without checked, this

```
for (int i = 11; i < 20; ++i)
{
  Console.WriteLine(i + "! = " + Permutation.Factorial(i));
}
```

produces this output:

```
11! = 39916800
12! = 479001600
13! = 1932053504
14! = 1278945280
15! = 2004310016
16! = 2004189184
17! = -288522240
18! = -898433024
19! = 109641728
```

Notice that all the results past 12! are incorrect, but no exception was thrown.

10.9 Calculating the Successor to a Mathematical Permutation Element

Problem

You want to determine the successor element to a given mathematical permutation element.

Design

This is a very tricky algorithm. Locate two atoms in the current permutation element to swap, swap them, and then shuffle the tail atoms that are to the right of the swap position.

Solution

```
public Permutation Successor()
{
  Permutation result = new Permutation(this.order);

  int left, right;

  for (int k = 0; k < result.order; ++k)
  {
    result.data[k] = this.data[k];
  }

  left = result.order - 2;
  while ((result.data[left] > result.data[left+1]) && (left >= 1))
  {
    --left;
  }
  if ((left == 0) && (this.data[left] > this.data[left+1]))
    return null;

  right = result.order - 1;
  while (result.data[left] > result.data[right])
  {
    --right;
  }

  int temp = result.data[left];
  result.data[left] = result.data[right];
  result.data[right] = temp;

   int i = left + 1;
  int j = result.order - 1;
```

```
  while (i < j)
  {
    temp = result.data[i];
    result.data[i++] = result.data[j];
    result.data[j--] = temp;
  }

  return result;
}
```

Comments

To iterate through all mathematical permutations of order n, you must be able to determine the lexicographic successor element to a given element. For example, if n = 4, permutation element [0] is { 0, 1, 2, 3 } and its successor element [1] is { 0, 1, 3, 2 }.

The main trick involves finding the two swap positions that are called left and right in the code. Now you'll see how the algorithm finds the successor to the { 2 1 3 5 4 0 } permutation element. To find position left, you start with an index at the second value from the right and move left until the value at index+1 is greater than that at index. In this example, left stops when it points to the 3 in the permutation. To find position right, you start with an index at the rightmost value and move left until you find a value that is greater than that pointed to by left. In this example, right stops when it points to the 4. Now you swap to get an intermediate result of

(2 1 4 5 3 0)

Finally, you perform a shuffle of the values between left and the right end to get the successor permutation:

(2 1 4 0 3 5)

The Successor() method returns null when applied to the last permutation of a particular order. Although we could have checked to see if the permutation is in the form (n-1 n-2 . . . 0), it's easier to observe that this state will occur when index left walks all the way down to the data element at index 0. With this Successor() method, if you write

```
int[] array = new int[] { 2, 0, 3, 1 };
Permutation p = new Permutation(array);
p = p.Successor();
Console.WriteLine("Successor to 2, 0, 3, 1 is: " + p.ToString());
```

the output would be

Successor to 2, 0, 3, 1 is: % 2 1 0 3 %

There are many well-known algorithms that return the lexicographic successor of a permutation. This algorithm is a general-purpose one, but you can find algorithms that optimize for performance or memory use.

10.10 Generating All Mathematical Permutation Elements for a Given n

Problem

You want to generate all mathematical permutation elements for given values of n.

Design

Instantiate an identity Permutation object and then use the Permutation.Successor() method inside a while loop.

Solution

```
Console.WriteLine("\nStart\n");
Permutation p = new Permutation(3);
int i = 0;

while (p != null)
{
  Console.WriteLine("p[" + i + "] = " + p.ToString());
  p = p.Successor();
  ++i;
}

Console.WriteLine("\nDone\n");
```

Comments

In situations with sufficiently small values for n, you can exhaustively list all mathematical permutation elements. When the preceding code is run, the result is

```
Start

p[0] = % 0 1 2 %
p[1] = % 0 2 1 %
p[2] = % 1 0 2 %
p[3] = % 1 2 0 %
p[4] = % 2 0 1 %
p[5] = % 2 1 0 %

Done
```

The call to `Permutation.Successor()` returns the next mathematical permutation element in lexicographical order, or `null` if you are at the last element. You can use a `while` loop with `null` as an exit condition to iterate through all elements. Notice that after the loop terminates, the `Permutation` object will be `null`, so you'll need to reinstantiate it if you want to use it further. If you want to explicitly create all possible permutation elements, you can create an array of `Permutation` objects and store each object:

```
long ct = Permutation.Factorial(3);
Permutation[] perms = new Permutation[ct];
perms[0] = new Permutation(3);

for (int i = 1; i < ct; ++i)
{
  perms[i] = perms[i-1].Successor();
}

for (int i = 0; i < ct; ++i)
{
  Console.WriteLine("p[" + i + "] = " + perms[i].ToString());
}
```

When this code is run, the output will be the same as the previous example. You determine how many `Permutation` objects you'll be creating using the `Permutation.Factorial()` method and then initialize an array of `Permutation` objects with that size. You seed the first array cell with the initial identity `Permutation` object by calling the default constructor. Then each cell in the array is assigned a `Permutation` object, which has the successor element to the element of the `Permutation` object in the previous cell. Using this technique, you'll have all `Permutation` elements available to you. Be careful when employing this technique because the number of permutation elements can be very large.

10.11 Determining the kth Lexicographical Element of a Mathematical Permutation

Problem

You want to determine a specific element of a mathematical permutation.

Design

Write an auxiliary `Permutation` constructor that calculates the factoradic of the specified element and then transforms the factoradic into a permutation element.

Solution

```
public Permutation(int n, int k)
{
  this.data = new int[n];
  this.order = this.data.Length;

  int[] factoradic = new int[n];

  for (int j = 1; j <= n; ++j)
  {
    factoradic[n-j] = k % j;
    k /= j;
  }

  int[] temp = new int[n];

  for (int i = 0; i < n; ++i)
  {
    temp[i] = ++factoradic[i];
  }

  this.data[n-1] = 1;

  for (int i = n-2; i >= 0; --i)
  {
    this.data[i] = temp[i];
    for (int j = i+1; j < n; ++j)
    {
      if (this.data[j] >= this.data[i])
        ++this.data[j];
    }
  }

  for (int i = 0; i < n; ++i)
  {
    --this.data[i];
  }

}
```

Comments

It's often useful to be able to create a specific Permutation from a specified lexicographical index. For example, if you call the code in this solution such as

```
Permutation p = new Permutation(4,0);
Console.WriteLine(p.ToString());
p = new Permutation(4,23);
Console.WriteLine(p.ToString());
```

you would create permutation element [0] and element [23] (i.e., the first and last elements of order 4), and the output is

```
% 0 1 2 3 %
% 3 2 1 0 %
```

This problem is not as simple as you might first think. A brute force solution to generating the kth lexicographical permutation element would be to start with the first element and then iterate, calling a successor method or code, k times. This approach works, but the technique is bad when the value of k is large. And, unfortunately, k can be very large because it can be up to n! where n is the order of the permutation. For example, if you are interested in permutations of order 20, there are 2,432,902,008,176,640,000 different permutations. Using the naive looping technique even on a fast desktop machine is often just not feasible. But by using a mathematical concept called the factoradic of a number, the preceding solution calculates permutation element [999,999,999,999] in well under 1 second.

You can think of a factoradic as an alternate representation of an integer. Consider the integer 859, which can be represented as

```
(8 * 100) + (5 * 10) + (9 * 1)
```

Or another way of looking at it is as based on a fixed radix (base) of powers of 10:

$$(8 * 10^2) + (5 * 10^1) + (9 * 10^0)$$

The factoradic of an integer is its representation based on a variable base corresponding to the values of n factorial. It turns out that any integer i can be uniquely represented in the form

```
  (a0 * 1!) + (a1 * 2!) + (a2 * 3!) + . . .
= (a0 * 1) + (a1 * 2) + (a2 * 6) + . . .
```

For example, the integer 859 can be represented as

```
  (1 * 1!) + (0 * 2!) + (3 * 3!) + (0 * 4!) + (1 * 5!) + (1 * 6!)
= (1 * 1) + (3 * 6) + (1 * 120) + (1 * 720)
= 1 + 18 + 120 + 720
= 859
```

So you can represent 859 in factoradic form as { 1 1 0 3 0 1 } where the rightmost digit is the value of the 1!'s. It will be easier to convert a factoradic to a permutation if you append a trailing 0 onto the right end of all factoradics, so you get { 1 1 0 3 0 1 0 } as the final form. Furthermore, there is a one-to-one mapping between the factoradic of an integer k and the kth permutation of order n, meaning that each factoradic uniquely determines a permutation. To illustrate this, Table 10-2 shows the values of k, the factoradic of k, and the kth permutation for order 4.

Table 10-2. *Relationship Between* k, *Factoradic(*k*), and* kth *Permutation*

k	factoradic(k)	permutation(k)
0	{ 0 0 0 0 }	(0 1 2 3)
1	{ 0 0 1 0 }	(0 1 3 2)
2	{ 0 1 0 0 }	(0 2 1 3)
3	{ 0 1 1 0 }	(0 2 3 1)
4	{ 0 2 0 0 }	(0 3 1 2)
5	{ 0 2 1 0 }	(0 3 2 1)
6	{ 1 0 0 0 }	(1 0 2 3)
7	{ 1 0 1 0 }	(1 0 3 2)
8	{ 1 1 0 0 }	(1 2 0 3)
9	{ 1 1 1 0 }	(1 2 3 0)
10	{ 1 2 0 0 }	(1 3 0 2)
11	{ 1 2 1 0 }	(1 3 2 0)
12	{ 2 0 0 0 }	(2 0 1 3)
13	{ 2 0 1 0 }	(2 0 3 1)
14	{ 2 1 0 0 }	(2 1 0 3)
15	{ 2 1 1 0 }	(2 1 3 0)
16	{ 2 2 0 0 }	(2 3 0 1)
17	{ 2 2 1 0 }	(2 3 1 0)
18	{ 3 0 0 0 }	(3 0 1 2)
19	{ 3 0 1 0 }	(3 0 2 1)
20	{ 3 1 0 0 }	(3 1 0 2)
21	{ 3 1 1 0 }	(3 1 2 0)
22	{ 3 2 0 0 }	(3 2 0 1)
23	{ 3 2 1 0 }	(3 2 1 0)

So, an efficient way to derive the kth permutation of order n is to first find the factoradic of k and then transform the factoradic into the corresponding permutation. The factoradic is computed with

```
for (int j = 1; j <= n; ++j)
{
  factoradic[n-j] = k % j;
  k /= j;
}
```

On each pass through the loop, the remainder is calculated using the modulus (%) operator and stored in the rightmost available cell (n-j) of the working array. Then k is reduced by division (k /= j), which, in effect, changes the base for the next pass by doing a reverse factorial calculation. The trickiest part of the algorithm is the computation of the permutation that corresponds to the factoradic. Take, for example, how the algorithm converts the factoradic

{ 1 2 3 2 1 1 0 }

into its corresponding permutation. You first create a temp[ ] array and copy into it the factoradic values incremented by 1:

[2 3 4 3 2 2 1]

You seed the rightmost cell of the result data[ ] array with 1:

[? ? ? ? ? ? 1]

Now starting with the second value from the rightmost value (skip over the rightmost value, which is always 1 because it came from the padded 0 value), you add it to the data[ ] array:

[? ? ? ? ? 2 1]

Now you scan through all the values to the right of the new value and increment by 1 all values that are greater than or equal to the new value. Continuing this process generates:

[? ? ? ? 2 3 1]
[? ? ? 3 2 4 1]
[? ? 4 3 2 5 1]
[? 3 5 4 2 6 1]
[2 4 6 5 3 7 1]

Finally, you traverse the data[ ] array and decrement all values by 1 to put the resulting permutation in 0-based form:

(1 3 5 4 2 6 0)

To summarize, if you want to generate the kth permutation of order n, first you compute the factoradic of k, and then use that result to compute the corresponding permutation. In the preceding example, you started with k = 1,047, computed its factoradic = { 1 2 3 2 1 1 0 }, and then computed the permutation (1 3 5 4 2 6 0). So permutation element [1047] of order 7 is (1 3 5 4 2 6 0).

10.12 Applying a Mathematical Permutation to a String Array

Problem

You want one or more permutations of a set of strings.

Design

Write a Permutation.ApplyTo() method that accepts an array of strings and returns a rearranged array corresponding to the Permutation element context.

Solution

```
public string[] ApplyTo(string[] sa)
{
  if (sa.Length != this.order)
    throw new Exception("Bad array size in Permutation.ApplyTo()");

  string[] result = new string[this.order];

  for (long i = 0; i < result.Length; ++i)
    result[i] = sa[this.data[i]];

  return result;
}
```

Comments

In software test automation situations, you usually want to generate permutations of strings. If you called the code in this solution such as

```
string[] names = new string[]{"Adam", "Barb", "Carl"};
Permutation p = new Permutation(3);
string[] rearrange = new string[3];
Console.WriteLine("All perms of the 3 are:\n");
while (p != null)
{
  rearrange = p.ApplyTo(names);
  Console.WriteLine(rearrange[0] + " " + rearrange[1] +
                                  " " + rearrange[2]);
  p = p.Successor();
}

p = new Permutation(3,4);
Console.WriteLine("\nJust element[4] is:\n");
rearrange = p.ApplyTo(names);
Console.WriteLine(rearrange[0] + " " + rearrange[1] +
                                " " + rearrange[2]);
```

the output would be

All perms of the 3 are:

Adam Barb Carl
Adam Carl Barb
Barb Adam Carl
Barb Carl Adam
Carl Adam Barb
Carl Barb Adam

Just element[4] is:

Carl Adam Barb

Suppose you have a Permutation object of order 5. The object will have a data array with atoms from 0 to n-1 = 4 that represent a mathematical permutation, for instance { 0, 3, 4, 2, 1 }. The ApplyTo() method accepts a string array that contains n = 5 strings. That input array will be indexed from 0 to n-1. The idea is to create an answer array of size n = 5 and store into that answer array the string values that correspond to the atoms of the Permutation element. For example, if you pass an array "animals" with "ant" at [0], "bat" at [1], "cow" at [2], "dog" at [3], and "emu" at [4] to ApplyTo() where the Permutation object context has values { 0, 3, 4, 2, 1 } in its data array, then the ApplyTo() method will place "ant" into result[0], "dog" into result[1], "emu" into result[2], "cow" into result[3], and "bat" into result[4].

10.13 Example Program: ComboPerm

Listing 10-1 combines several of the techniques in this chapter to create a demonstration program that shows how to manipulate combinations and permutations. The program creates a string array with 13 values such as As and 8s to represent a shortened deck of playing cards consisting only of spades (As = ace of spade, 8s = eight of spades, and so forth). The program generates all five-card combinations of the shortened deck and generates all permutations of one specific combination. When run, the program produces this output:

Combination & Permutation demonstration

There are 1287 combinations of 13 cards taken 5 at a time.

They are:
[0] As Ks Qs Js Ts
[1] As Ks Qs Js 9s
[2] As Ks Qs Js 8s

(much output deleted)

```
[1284] 7s 6s 4s 3s 2s
[1285] 7s 5s 4s 3s 2s
[1286] 6s 5s 4s 3s 2s

Just hand[1286] is:
6s 5s 4s 3s 2s

There are 120 permutations of this 5-card hand.

They are:
[0] 6s 5s 4s 3s 2s
[1] 6s 5s 4s 2s 3s
[2] 6s 5s 3s 4s 2s

(much output deleted)

[117] 2s 3s 5s 4s 6s
[118] 2s 3s 4s 6s 5s
[119] 2s 3s 4s 5s 6s

Done
```

Listing 10-1. *Program ComboPerm*

```
namespace ComboPerm
{
  class Class1
  {
    [STAThread]
    static void Main(string[] args)
    {
      try
      {
        Console.WriteLine("Combination & Permutation demonstration");
        string[] shortDeck = new string[] { "As", "Ks", "Qs", "Js",
              "Ts", "9s", "8s", "7s", "6s", "5s", "4s", "3s", "2s" };

        long ct = Combination.Choose(13,5);
        Console.WriteLine("\nThere are " + ct + " combinations of 13
                          cards taken 5 at a time.");
        Console.WriteLine("\nThey are: ");
```

```
    Combination c = new Combination(13,5);
    string[] hand = new string[5];
    int i = 0;
    while (c != null)
    {
      hand = c.ApplyTo(shortDeck);
      Console.WriteLine("[" + i + "] " + hand[0] + " " + hand[1]
              + " " + hand[2] + " " + hand[3] + " " + hand[4]);
      c = c.Successor();
      ++i;
    }

    Console.WriteLine("\nJust hand[1286] is: ");
    c = new Combination(13,5).Element(1286);
    hand = c.ApplyTo(shortDeck);
    Console.WriteLine(hand[0] + " " + hand[1] + " " + hand[2] +
                        " " + hand[3] + " " + hand[4]);

    Console.WriteLine("\nThere are " + Permutation.Factorial(5) +
                      " permutations of this 5-card hand.");
    Console.WriteLine("\nThey are:");
    Permutation p = new Permutation(5);
    string[] rearrangement = new string[5];
    i = 0;
    while (p != null)
    {
      rearrangement = p.ApplyTo(hand);
      Console.WriteLine("[" + i + "] " + rearrangement[0] + " " +
              rearrangement[1] + " " + rearrangement[2] + " " +
                  rearrangement[3] + " " + rearrangement[4]);
      p = p.Successor();
      ++i;
    }

    Console.WriteLine("\nDone\n");
    Console.ReadLine();
  }
  catch(Exception ex)
  {
    Console.WriteLine("Fatal error: " + ex.Message);
    Console.ReadLine();
  }

  } // Main()
} // Class1
```

```
public class Combination
{
  private long n = 0;
  private long k = 0;
  private long[] data = null;

  public Combination(long n, long k)
  {
    if (n < 0 || k < 0)
      throw new Exception("Negative argument in constructor");
    this.n = n;
    this.k = k;
    this.data = new long[k];
    for (long i = 0; i < k; ++i)
      this.data[i] = i;
  }

  public Combination(long n, long k, long[] a)
  {
    if (k != a.Length)
      throw new Exception("Bad array size in constructor");
    this.n = n;
    this.k = k;
    this.data = new long[k];
    for (long i = 0; i < a.Length; ++i)
      this.data[i] = a[i];
  }

  public static long Choose(long n, long k)
  {
    if (n < 0 || k < 0)
      throw new Exception("Negative argument in Choose");
    if (n < k)
      return 0;
    if (n == k)
      return 1;
    long delta, iMax;

    if (k < n - k)
    {
      delta = n - k;
      iMax = k;
    }
    else
    {
      delta = k;
      iMax = n - k;
    }
```

```
  long answer = delta + 1;
  for (long i = 2; i <= iMax; ++i)
  {
    checked { answer = (answer * (delta + i)) / i; }
  }

  return answer;
}

public Combination Successor()
{
  if (this.data[0] == this.n - this.k)
    return null;

  Combination ans = new Combination(this.n, this.k);

  for (long i = 0; i < this.k; ++i)
    ans.data[i] = this.data[i];

  long x;
  for (x = this.k - 1; x > 0 &&
          ans.data[x] == this.n - this.k + x; --x);

  ++ans.data[x];

  for (long j = x; j < this.k - 1; ++j)
    ans.data[j+1] = ans.data[j] + 1;

  return ans;
}

public Combination Element(long m)
{
  long[] ans = new long[this.k];

  long a = this.n;
  long b = this.k;
  long x = (Choose(this.n, this.k) - 1) - m;

  for (long i = 0; i < this.k; ++i)
  {
    ans[i] = LargestV(a,b,x);
    x = x - Choose(ans[i],b);
    a = ans[i];
    b = b-1;
  }
```

```
      for (long i = 0; i < this.k; ++i)
      {
        ans[i] = (n-1) - ans[i];
      }

      return new Combination(this.n, this.k, ans);
    }

    private static long LargestV(long a, long b, long x)
    {
      long v = a - 1;

      while (Choose(v,b) > x)
        --v;

      return v;
    }

    public string[] ApplyTo(string[] sa)
    {
      if (sa.Length != this.n)
        throw new Exception("Bad array size in ApplyTo()");

      string[] result = new string[this.k];

      for (long i = 0; i < result.Length; ++i)
        result[i] = sa[this.data[i]];

      return result;
    }


} // class Combination

public class Permutation
{
  private int[] data = null;
  private int order = 0;

  public Permutation(int n)
  {
    this.data = new int[n];
    for (int i = 0; i < n; ++i)
    {
      this.data[i] = i;
    }
```

```
    this.order = n;
}

public Permutation Successor()
{
  Permutation result = new Permutation(this.order);

  int left, right;

  for (int k = 0; k < result.order; ++k)
  {
    result.data[k] = this.data[k];
  }

  left = result.order - 2;
  while ((result.data[left] > result.data[left+1]) &&
                                  (left >= 1))
  {
    --left;
  }
  if ((left == 0) && (this.data[left] > this.data[left+1]))
    return null;

  right = result.order - 1;
  while (result.data[left] > result.data[right])
  {
    --right;
  }

  int temp = result.data[left];
  result.data[left] = result.data[right];
  result.data[right] = temp;


  int i = left + 1;
  int j = result.order - 1;

  while (i < j)
  {
    temp = result.data[i];
    result.data[i++] = result.data[j];
    result.data[j--] = temp;
  }

  return result;
}
```

```
    public static ulong Factorial(int n)
    {
      ulong answer = 1;
      for (int i = 1; i <= n; ++i)
      {
        checked { answer *= (ulong)i; }
      }
      return answer;
    }

    public string[] ApplyTo(string[] sa)
    {
      if (sa.Length != this.order)
        throw new Exception("Bad array size in ApplyTo()");

      string[] result = new string[this.order];

      for (long i = 0; i < result.Length; ++i)
        result[i] = sa[this.data[i]];

      return result;
    }

  } // class Permutation
} // ns
```

CHAPTER 11

■ ■ ■

ADO.NET Testing

11.0 Introduction

This chapter presents a variety of test automation techniques that involve ADO.NET technology. ADO.NET is an enormous topic, but the most common development/testing situation is simple: an application (either Windows form-based or Web-based) acts as a front-end interface to select, insert, update, and delete data in a backend SQL database. In addition, test automation often uses ADO.NET to read and write test data to a data store. So the title of this chapter means testing Windows programs that use ADO.NET technology, and/or writing test automation that uses ADO.NET, but does not mean testing ADO.NET technology itself.

Consider the demonstration Windows application shown in Figure 11-1. It is a simple but representative program that accesses a SQL database of employee information using ADO.NET technology. In particular, the application calls local method GetEmployees(), which accepts a string, uses a SqlDataAdapter object to connect to and retrieve employee data where the employee last name contains the input string, and returns a DataSet object containing the employee data. The DataSet then acts as a data source for a DataGrid control.

Figure 11-1. *Application under test that uses ADO.NET*

Here is the key code for the application:

```
private void button1_Click(object sender, System.EventArgs e)
{
  string filter = textBox1.Text.Trim();
  DataSet ds = GetEmployees(filter);
  if (ds != null)
    dataGrid1.DataSource = ds;
}
```

where:

```
private DataSet GetEmployees(string s)
{
  try
  {
    string connString = "Server=(local);Database=dbEmployees;
                         Trusted_Connection=Yes";

    SqlConnection sc = new SqlConnection(connString);
    string select = "SELECT empID, empLast, empDOB FROM tblEmployees
                    WHERE empLast LIKE '%" + s + "%'";
    SqlCommand cmd = new SqlCommand(select, sc);
    sc.Open();

    DataSet ds = new DataSet();
    SqlDataAdapter sda = new SqlDataAdapter(select, sc);
    sda.Fill(ds);
    sc.Close();
    return ds;
  }
  catch
  {
    return null;
  }
}
```

One important aspect of testing the application shown in Figure 11-1 is testing the application's ADO.NET plumbing. The screenshot shown in Figure 11-2 shows a sample run of a test harness that tests the GetEmployee() method used by the application. The complete source code for the test harness shown in Figure 11-2 is presented in Section 11.10.

The techniques in this chapter are closely related to those in Chapter 9 and Chapter 12. Several of the sections in this chapter describe testing SQL stored procedures from within a .NET environment (as opposed to the SQL environment techniques discussed in Chapter 9). And there is a strong connection between XML and ADO.NET DataSet objects.

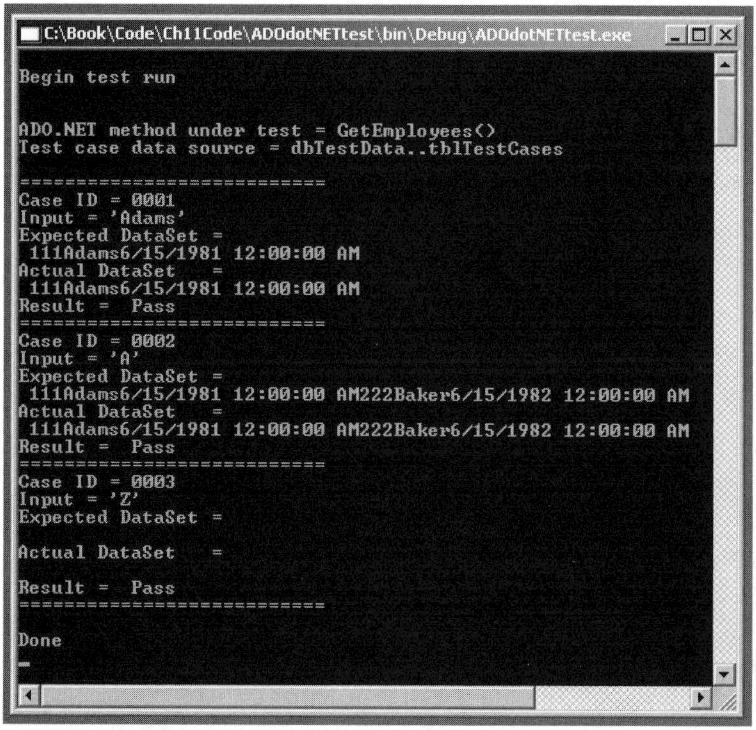

Figure 11-2. *Sample test run*

11.1 Determining a Pass/Fail Result When the Expected Value Is a DataSet

Problem

You want to determine if a test case or a scenario passes or fails in a situation where the actual and expected values are DataSet objects.

Design

Iterate through each row in the DataTable object in the actual DataSet object and build up a string that represents the aggregate row data. Compare that string with an expected string. Alternatively you can compute a hash of the aggregate string and compare with an expected hash.

Solution

For example, suppose a SQL table of product information has a product ID like "001" and a product description like "Widget." The system under test uses a SqlDataAdapter object to read data from the table into a DataSet object. Suppose that for a particular test case input, the expected DataSet should contain three rows of data:

```
001 Widget
002 Wadget
003 Wodget
```

Then an expected aggregate string is:

```
001Widget002Wadget003Wodget
```

and you can check whether the actual DataSet object contains expected row data with code like this:

```
DataSet ds = new DataSet();
// run test, store actual result into DataSet ds


string expectedData = "001Widget002Wadget005Wodget";
string actualData = null;

DataTable dt = ds.Tables[0];
foreach (DataRow dr in dt.Rows)
{
  foreach (DataColumn dc in dt.Columns)
  {
    actualData += dr[dc];
  }
}

if (actualData == expectedData)
  Console.WriteLine("Pass");
else
  Console.WriteLine("FAIL");
```

You first retrieve the DataTable object in the actual DataSet, then iterate through the DataRow collection, grabbing each column value, and appending onto a string variable.

Comments

This approach to determining a pass/fail result when the expected value is a DataSet object is simple and effective. However, the technique does have three drawbacks. First, this solution assumes the actual and expected DataSet objects contain only a single table. Second, this solution only checks table data and does not check other DataSet components such as Constraint objects and Relation objects. Third, this solution is not feasible if the actual and expected table data is very large. If you need to compare the data in multiple DataTable objects, you can refactor this solution into a helper method that compares the aggregate row data with an expected string:

```
static bool IsEqual(DataTable dt, string s)
{
  string aggregate = null;
  foreach (DataRow dr in dt.Rows)
```

```
  {
    foreach (DataColumn dc in dt.Columns)
    {
      aggregate += dr[dc];
    }
  }
  return (s == aggregate);
}
```

and instead of using a single aggregate string as an expected value, maintain an array of expected strings. Then iterate over the DataTable collection. For example, suppose the system under test should return a DataSet with two tables where the first table should hold:

```
001 Widget
004 Wudget
009 Wizmo
```

and the second table should hold:

```
005 Gizmo
007 Gazmo
```

then you can determine a pass/fail result like this:

```
string[] expecteds = new string[] { "001Widget004Wudget009Wizmo",
                                     "005Gizmo007Gazmo" };
bool pass = true;

for (int i = 0; i < expecteds.Length; ++i)
{
  if (!IsEqual(ds.Tables[i], expecteds[i]))
    pass = false;
}
```

Now if the expected data is very large, instead of comparing an aggregate string variable consisting of row data appended together, you can compute and compare hashes of the data. Using this approach, the original solution becomes:

```
DataSet ds = new DataSet();

// run test, store actual result into ds

//string expectedData = "001Widget002Wadget005Wodget";
string expectedHash = "EC-5C-E5-E5-6D-1D-8C-DD-6E-2A-2B-6B-D3-CB-C1-28";
string actualData = null;
string actualHash = null;
```

```
DataTable dt = ds.Tables[0];
foreach (DataRow dr in dt.Rows)
{
  foreach (DataColumn dc in dt.Columns)
  {
    actualData += dr[dc];
  }
}

MD5CryptoServiceProvider md5 = new MD5CryptoServiceProvider();
byte[] ba = md5.ComputeHash(Encoding.ASCII.GetBytes(actualData));
actualHash = BitConverter.ToString(ba);

if (actualHash == expectedHash)
  Console.WriteLine("Pass");
else
  Console.WriteLine("FAIL");
```

By comparing an MD5 (Message Digest version 5) hash of the expected table data, you can avoid storing huge expected string data because all MD5 hashes are size 16 bytes. You can loosely think of an MD5 hash as "one-way encryption": a sequence of input bytes of any size is mapped to a sequence of 16 bytes in such a way that even if you have the hashing algorithm, you cannot determine the original input from the result hash. Furthermore, a slight change in the input to a hash algorithm produces a huge change in the resulting output byte array. These are very tricky concepts if you are new to hashing. The whole purpose of crypto-hashes (as opposed to hash table–related hashes) is to produce a fingerprint, or a digest, of a sequence of bytes. Because the hashing process is not reversible, hashes are used only for identification, not encryption/decryption. Here we use the hashes to identify aggregate row data in a table in a DataSet.

Because the ComputeHash() method returns a byte array, in a testing situation it is usually convenient to convert the 16-byte array to a more friendly string form using the BitConverter class. The BitConverter.ToString() method returns a string of hexadecimal digits separated by hyphens.

The MD5 routines are part of the System.Security.Cryptography namespace. In addition to the MD5 hashing class, the .NET Framework has an SHA1 (Secure Hash Algorithm version 1) class. The only real difference between the two from a testing point of view is that SHA1 returns a 20-byte array instead of a 16-byte array. SHA1 uses a different algorithm and is considered more secure than MD5; but for testing purposes either hashing algorithm is fine.

11.2 Testing a Stored Procedure That Returns a Value

Problem

You want to test a SQL stored procedure that explicitly returns an int value.

Design

Create a `SqlCommand` object and set its `CommandType` property to `StoredProcedure`. Add input parameters and a return value using the `Parameters.Add()` method, and specify `ReturnValue` for the `ParameterDirection` property. Call the stored procedure under test using the `SqlCommand.ExecuteScaler()` method. Compare the actual return value with an expected return value.

Solution

Suppose, for example, you want to test a stored procedure `usp_PricierThan()` that returns the number of movies in a SQL table that have a price greater than an input argument:

```
create procedure usp_PricierThan
 @price money
as
 declare @ans int
 select @ans = count(*) from tblPrices where movPrice > @price
 return @ans
go
```

Notice that the stored procedure accepts an input parameter named @price and returns an int value. You can test the stored procedure like this:

```
int expected = 2;
int actual;
string input = "30.00";

string connString = "Server=(local);Database=dbMovies;UID=moviesLogin;
                     PWD=secret";
SqlConnection sc = new SqlConnection(connString);
SqlCommand cmd = new SqlCommand("usp_PricierThan", sc);
cmd.CommandType = CommandType.StoredProcedure;

SqlParameter p1 = cmd.Parameters.Add("ret_val", SqlDbType.Int);
p1.Direction = ParameterDirection.ReturnValue;
SqlParameter p2 = cmd.Parameters.Add("@price", SqlDbType.Money);
p2.Direction = ParameterDirection.Input;
p2.Value = input;
sc.Open();

cmd.ExecuteScalar();
actual = (int)cmd.Parameters["ret_val"].Value;
sc.Close();

if (actual == expected)
  Console.WriteLine("Pass");
else
  Console.WriteLine("FAIL");
```

Comments

This solution begins by connecting to the SQL server that houses the stored procedure under test, using SQL authentication mode. This assumes that the database contains a SQL login named moviesLogin, with password "secret," and that the login has execute permissions on the stored procedure under test. If you want to connect using Windows authentication mode, you can do so like this:

```
string connString = "Server=(local);Database=dbMovies;
                      Trusted_Connection=Yes";
```

The SqlCommand() constructor is overloaded and one of the constructors accepts the name of a stored procedure as its argument. However, you must also specify CommandType.StoredProcedure so that the SqlCommand object knows it will be using a stored procedure rather than a text command. The key to calling a stored procedure that returns an explicit int value is to use the ParameterDirection.ReturnValue property. Before you write this statement you must call the SqlCommand.Parameters.Add() method:

```
SqlParameter p1 = cmd.Parameters.Add("ret_val", SqlDbType.Int);
```

The Add() method returns a reference to a SqlParameter object to which you can specify the ParameterDirection.ReturnValue property. The Add() method accepts a parameter name as a string and a SqlDbType type. You can name the parameter anything you like but specifying a string such as "ret_val" or "returnVal," or something similar, is the most readable approach. The SqlDbType enumeration will always be SqlDbType.Int because SQL stored procedures can only return an int. (Here we mean an explicit return value using the return keyword rather than an implicit return value via an out parameter, or a return of a SQL rowset, or as an effect of the procedure code.) Unlike return value parameters, with input parameters, the name you specify in Add() must exactly match that used in the stored procedure definition:

```
SqlParameter p2 = cmd.Parameters.Add("@price", SqlDbType.Money);
```

Using anything other than @price would throw an exception. The Add() method accepts an optional third argument, which is the size, in SQL terms, of the parameter. When using fixed size data types such as SqlDbType.Int and SqlDbType.Money, you do not need to pass in the size, but if you want to do so, the code will look like this:

```
SqlParameter p1 = cmd.Parameters.Add("ret_val", SqlDbType.Int, 4);
p1.Direction = ParameterDirection.ReturnValue;
SqlParameter p2 = cmd.Parameters.Add("@price", SqlDbType.Money, 8);
```

because the SQL int type is size 4 and the SQL money type is size 8. The only time you should definitely specify the size argument is when using variable size SQL types such as char and varchar.

Notice that when you assign a value to an input parameter, you can pass a string variable if you wish, rather than using some sort of cast:

```
string input = "30.00";

// other code
SqlParameter p2 = cmd.Parameters.Add("@price", SqlDbType.Money, 8);

// other code

p2.Value = input;
```

Although we specify that input parameter p2 is type SqlDbType.Money, we can assign its value using a string. This works because the SqlParameter.Value property accepts an object type which is then implicitly cast to the appropriate SqlDbType type. In other words, we can write:

```
double input = 30.00;

// other code
SqlParameter p2 = cmd.Parameters.Add("@price", SqlDbType.Money, 8);

// other code

p2.Value = input;
```

and the test automation will work exactly as before. Actually calling the stored procedure under test uses a somewhat indirect mechanism:

```
cmd.ExecuteScalar();
actual = (int)cmd.Parameters["ret_val"].Value;
```

You call the SqlCommand.ExecuteScalar() method. This calls the stored procedure and stores the return value into the SqlCommand.Parameters collection. Because of this mechanism, you can call SqlCommand.ExecuteNonQuery(), or even SqlCommand.ExecuteReader(), and still get the return value from the Parameters collection.

11.3 Testing a Stored Procedure That Returns a Rowset

Problem

You want to test a stored procedure that returns a SQL rowset.

Design

Capture the rowset into a DataSet object, then compare this actual DataSet with an expected DataSet. First, create a SqlCommand object and set its CommandType property to StoredProcedure. Add input parameters using the Parameters.Add() method. Instead of calling the stored procedure directly, instantiate a DataSet object and a SqlDataAdapter object. Pass the SqlCommand object to the SqlDataAdapter object, then fill the DataSet with the rowset returned from the stored procedure.

Solution

For example, suppose you want to test a stored procedure usp_PricierThan() that returns a SQL rowset containing information about movies that have a price greater than an input argument:

```
create procedure usp_PricierThan
 @price money
as
 select movID, movPrice from tblPrices
 where movPrice > @price
go
```

Notice that the stored procedure returns a rowset via the SELECT statement. You can populate a DataSet object with the returned rowset and test like this:

```
string input = "30.00";
string expectedHash = "EC-5C-E5-E5-6D-1D-8C-DD-6E-2A-2B-6B-D3-CB-C1-28";
string actualHash = null;

string connString = "Server=(local);Database=dbMovies;
                     Trusted_Connection=Yes";
SqlConnection sc = new SqlConnection(connString);
SqlCommand cmd = new SqlCommand("usp_PricierThan", sc);
cmd.CommandType = CommandType.StoredProcedure;
SqlParameter p = cmd.Parameters.Add("@price", SqlDbType.Money, 8);
p.Direction = ParameterDirection.Input;
p.Value = input;
sc.Open();

DataSet ds = new DataSet();
SqlDataAdapter sda = new SqlDataAdapter(cmd);
sda.Fill(ds);

// compute actualHash of DataSet ds - see Section 11.1

if (actualHash == expectedHash)
  Console.WriteLine("Pass");
else
  Console.WriteLine("FAIL");
```

This code fills a DataSet with the rowset returned by the usp_PricierThan() stored procedure. To test the stored procedure you will have to compare the actual rowset data with expected rowset data. Techniques for doing this are explained in Section 11.1.

Comments

Many stored procedures call the SQL SELECT statement and return a rowset. To test such stored procedures you can capture the rowset into a DataSet object. The easiest way to do this is to use a SqlDataAdapter object as shown in the previous solution. Once the rowset data is in a DataSet, you can examine it against an expected value using one of the techniques described in Section 11.1. An alternative approach is to capture the rowset into a different in-memory data structure, such as an `ArrayList` or an array of type `string`. Using this approach, the easiest way to capture the rowset data is to use a `SqlDataReader` object. For example, this code will capture the rowset data returned by the `usp_PricierThan()` stored procedure into an `ArrayList`:

```
string connString = "Server=(local);Database=dbMovies;
                     UID=moviesLogin;PWD=secret";
SqlConnection sc = new SqlConnection(connString);
SqlCommand cmd = new SqlCommand("usp_PricierThan", sc);
cmd.CommandType = CommandType.StoredProcedure;
SqlParameter p = cmd.Parameters.Add("@price", SqlDbType.Money, 8);
p.Direction = ParameterDirection.Input;
p.Value = input;
sc.Open();

ArrayList list = new ArrayList();
string line;
SqlDataReader sdr = cmd.ExecuteReader();
while (sdr.Read() == true)
{
  line = "";
  line += sdr.GetString(0) + " " + sdr.GetDecimal(1);
  list.Add(line);
}
```

Storing rowset return data into an `ArrayList` object instead of a `DataSet` object is sometimes useful in situations where you want to do processing of the return data before placing it into memory, as, for example, when normalizing the rowset data into a standard form so you can more easily compare the data with an expected value. After reading a row of data with `SqlDataReader()` you can manipulate it and then store into an `ArrayList` object. Although data in `DataSet` objects is in general easy to manipulate, sometimes an `ArrayList` is easier to use.

11.4 Testing a Stored Procedure That Returns a Value into an out Parameter

Problem

You want to test a SQL stored procedure that returns a value into an `out` parameter.

Design

Create a `SqlParameter` object for the `out` parameter and specify `ParameterDirect.Output` for it. Call the stored procedure using the `SqlCommand.ExecuteScaler()` method, and then fetch the value of the `out` parameter from the `SqlCommand.Parameters` collection.

Solution

Suppose a stored procedure under test, usp_GetPrice(), accepts a movie ID as an input parameter and stores the price of the corresponding movie into an out parameter:

```
create procedure usp_GetPrice
 @movID char(3),
 @price money out
as
 select @price = movPrice from tblPrices where movID = @movID
go
```

You can test the stored procedure like this:

```
decimal expected = 33.3300M;
decimal actual;
string input = "m03";

string connString = "Server=(local);Database=dbMovies;
                     Trusted_Connection=Yes";
SqlConnection sc = new SqlConnection(connString);
SqlCommand cmd = new SqlCommand("usp_GetPrice", sc);
cmd.CommandType = CommandType.StoredProcedure;

SqlParameter p1 = cmd.Parameters.Add("@movID", SqlDbType.Char, 3);
p1.Direction = ParameterDirection.Input;
p1.Value = input;

SqlParameter p2 = cmd.Parameters.Add("@price", SqlDbType.Money);
p2.Direction = ParameterDirection.Output;

sc.Open();
cmd.ExecuteScalar();

actual = (decimal)cmd.Parameters["@price"].Value;
sc.Close();

if (actual == expected)
  Console.WriteLine("Pass");
else
  Console.WriteLine("FAIL");
```

You set up the call to the stored procedure by preparing an input parameter using the Parameters.Add() method, setting the ParameterDirection property to Input, and supplying a value for the input parameter. You prepare the out parameter similarly except you specify ParameterDirection.Output. Calling the ExecuteScalar() method will invoke the stored procedure and place the value of the out parameter in the SqlCommand.Parameters collection where you can retrieve it and compare it against an expected value.

Comments

Testing a stored procedure that returns a value into an out parameter is a very common task. This is a consequence of the fact that SQL stored procedures can only return an int type using the return keyword. So when a stored procedure must return a non-int type, or must return more than one result, using an out parameter is the usual approach taken. In the solution above, the stored procedure places a SqlDbType.Money value into the out parameter. This data type maps to the C# decimal type. Type decimal literals are specified using a trailing "M" character.

The input argument is a SqlDbType.Char type. Because this type can have variable size, we must be sure to pass the optional size argument to the Parameter.Add() method. In this case we pass 3 because the input is a movie ID that is defined as char(3) in the movies table.

Stored procedures often place a return value in an out parameter and also explicitly return a value using the return keyword. The explicit return value is typically used as an error-check of some sort. For example, suppose you wish to test this stored procedure:

```
create procedure usp_GetPrice2
 @movID char(3),
 @price money out
as
 declare @count int
 select @price = movPrice from tblPrices where movID = @movID
 select @count = count(*) from tblPrices where movID = @movID
 return @count
go
```

The procedure works as before except that in addition to storing the price of a specified movie into an out parameter, it also returns the number of rows with the specified movie ID. (Note: This stored procedure code is particularly inefficient but makes the idea of a hybrid-return approach clear.) The explicit return value can be used as an error-check; it should always be 1 because a value of 0 means no movie was found and a value of 2 or more means there are multiple movies with the same ID. In such situations you can either ignore the explicit return value, which is not such a good idea, or you can test like this:

```
decimal expected = 33.3300M;
decimal actual;
int retval;
string input = "m03";

string connString = "Server=(local);Database=dbMovies;Trusted_Connection=Yes";
SqlConnection sc = new SqlConnection(connString);

SqlCommand cmd = new SqlCommand("usp_GetPrice2", sc);
cmd.CommandType = CommandType.StoredProcedure;

SqlParameter p1 = cmd.Parameters.Add("@movID", SqlDbType.Char, 3);
p1.Direction = ParameterDirection.Input;
p1.Value = input;
```

```
SqlParameter p2 = cmd.Parameters.Add("@price", SqlDbType.Money);
p2.Direction = ParameterDirection.Output;

SqlParameter p3 = cmd.Parameters.Add("@ret_val", SqlDbType.Int);
p3.Direction = ParameterDirection.ReturnValue;

sc.Open();
cmd.ExecuteScalar();
actual = (decimal)cmd.Parameters["@price"].Value;
retval = (int)cmd.Parameters["@ret_val"].Value;
sc.Close();

if (actual == expected && retval == 1)
  Console.WriteLine("Pass");
else
  Console.WriteLine("FAIL");
```

As mentioned above, the SQL data type SqlDbType.Money maps to the C# type decimal. When writing lightweight test automation in C# that involves ADO.NET, you will often have to convert between a SQL data type and the corresponding C# data type. Table 11-1 lists most of the common SQL data types and their corresponding C# data types that you are likely to encounter.

Table 11-1. *SQL Data Types and Corresponding C# Types*

SQL Data Type	Equivalent C# Data Type
Bit	bool
Decimal, Money, SmallMoney	decimal
DateTime, SmallDateTime	DateTime()
Int	int
SmallInt	short
Real	float
Float	double
Char, NChar, NText, NVarchar, Text, VarChar	string
TinyInt	byte
Binary, Image, TimeStamp, VarBinary	byte[]
Variant	object

11.5 Testing a Stored Procedure That Does Not Return a Value

Problem

You want to test a SQL stored procedure that performs an action but does not explicitly return a value.

Design

Call the stored procedure under test and then check the database object affected by the call.

Solution

For example, suppose you wish to test this stored procedure that adds movie data into the main table and the prices table:

```
create procedure usp_AddMovie
 @movID char(3),
 @movTitle varchar(35),
 @movRunTime int,
 @movPrice money
as
 insert into tblMain values(@movID, @movTitle, @movRunTime)
 insert into tblPrices values(@movID, @movPrice)
go
```

Notice that there is no explicit return value; the stored procedure affects database tables tblMain and tblPrices by inserting data. To test such a stored procedure you must examine the state of the affected objects (in this case the two tables) and compare with some expected values. The simplest way to do so is to compute a hash of the affected objects. We start by setting up the input arguments and expected values:

```
string inMovieID = "m06";
string inMovieTitle = "F is for Function";
int inMovieRunTime = 96;
decimal inMoviePrice = 66.6600M;

string expectedMainHash = "2F-63-51-A8-C6-E2-CC-C2-1C-1C-A0-A2-A5-41-D9-79";
string expectedPriceHash = "21-E5-23-85-C3-F7-02-9C-0D-F5-85-72-78-A0-52-91";

string actualMainHash = null;
string actualPriceHash = null;
```

Here we are going to add data for a movie with ID "m06," title "F is for Function," and so forth. Of course, in a full test harness you would probably read these values in from external test case storage. The expected hash values are MD5 hashes of all of the data in the main movie table and the prices table after the usp_AddMovie() stored procedure has been called. See Section 11.1 for a discussion of this process. Next we set up the SqlConnection to the target database:

```
string connString = "Server=(local);Database=dbMovies;
                     Trusted_Connection=Yes";
SqlConnection sc = new SqlConnection(connString)
SqlCommand cmd = new SqlCommand("usp_AddMovie", sc);
cmd.CommandType = CommandType.StoredProcedure;
```

This process is explained in Section 11.2. The next step is to prepare the four input arguments:

```
SqlParameter p1 = cmd.Parameters.Add("@movID", SqlDbType.Char, 3);
p1.Direction = ParameterDirection.Input;
p1.Value = inMovieID;

SqlParameter p2 = cmd.Parameters.Add("@movTitle", SqlDbType.VarChar, 35);
p2.Direction = ParameterDirection.Input;
p2.Value = inMovieTitle;

SqlParameter p3 = cmd.Parameters.Add("@movRunTime", SqlDbType.Int);
p3.Direction = ParameterDirection.Input;
p3.Value = inMovieRunTime;

SqlParameter p4 = cmd.Parameters.Add("@movPrice", SqlDbType.Money);
p4.Direction = ParameterDirection.Input;
p4.Value = inMoviePrice;
```

This process is discussed in detail in Sections 11.2 and 11.3. Next we call the stored procedure under test:

```
sc.Open();
cmd.ExecuteScalar();
```

At this point, the stored procedure under test has been executed, so now we need to determine a pass/fail result. We must examine the two affected tables, tblMain and tblPrices, to verify that the new data was actually inserted. We do this by capturing all the data in the tables into a DataSet object, iterating through each row and building up an aggregate result string. We then compute an MD5 hash of the aggregate string and compare against an expected value:

```
// get both tables into a DataSet
DataSet ds = new DataSet();
SqlDataAdapter sda = new SqlDataAdapter("select * from tblMain", sc);
sda.Fill(ds, "tblMain");

sda = new SqlDataAdapter("select * from tblPrices", sc);
sda.Fill(ds, "tblPrices");

// get agregate row data for tblMain
string aggregateMain = null;
foreach (DataRow dr in ds.Tables["tblMain"].Rows)
{
  foreach (DataColumn dc in ds.Tables["tblMain"].Columns)
  {
    aggregateMain += dr[dc];
  }
}
```

```
// compute hash for tblMain
MD5CryptoServiceProvider md5 = new MD5CryptoServiceProvider();
byte[] ba = md5.ComputeHash(Encoding.ASCII.GetBytes(aggregateMain));
actualMainHash = BitConverter.ToString(ba);

// get agregate row data for tblPrices
string aggregatePrices = null;
foreach (DataRow dr in ds.Tables["tblPrices"].Rows)
{
  foreach (DataColumn dc in ds.Tables["tblPrices"].Columns)
  {
    aggregatePrices += dr[dc];
  }
}

// compute hash for tblPrices
ba = md5.ComputeHash(Encoding.ASCII.GetBytes(aggregatePrices));
actualPriceHash = BitConverter.ToString(ba);

// determine pass/fail
if (actualMainHash == expectedMainHash &&
    actualPriceHash == expectedPriceHash)
  Console.WriteLine("Pass");
else
  Console.WriteLine("FAIL");
```

Comments

Using MD5 or SHA1 hashes is an effective way to determine a pass/fail result for stored procedures that do not return a value. An alternative approach is to store an in-memory facsimile of the expected result and compare with an in-memory facsimile of the actual result. This will most often be facsimiles of a SQL data table. A particularly easy way to do this in a .NET environment is to store the expected facsimile as an XML file. Then you can read the XML facsimile into a DataSet object in memory. Next you can call the stored procedure under test. Then you read the affected table into a second DataSet object. You determine a pass/fail result by comparing the values in the two DataSet objects. The techniques in Chapter 12 will show several ways to read XML into a DataSet object, and Section 11.7 demonstrates how to compare two DataSet objects. In pseudo-code, the technique looks like this:

```
DataSet ds1 = new DataSet();
// read XML facsimile of an expected table result into ds1

DataSet ds2 = new DataSet();
// call stored procedure under test
// read affected table (actual table result) into ds2

// compare ds1 and ds2 to determine pass/fail
```

11.6 Testing Systems That Access Data Without Using a Stored Procedure

Problem

You want to test an application that accesses a SQL database directly rather than through a stored procedure.

Design

Use the same techniques as those used when testing an application that accesses a SQL database through a stored procedure, except access the backend database in the same way used by the application under test.

Solution

Suppose an application under test contains this code:

```
string connString = "Server=(local);Database=dbMovies;
                      Trusted_Connection=Yes";
SqlConnection sc = new SqlConnection(connString);
string command = "INSERT INTO tblMain VALUES('m07', 'G is for GUI', 97)";
SqlCommand cmd = new SqlCommand(command, sc);
cmd.CommandType = CommandType.Text;
sc.Open();
int rowsAffected = cmd.ExecuteNonQuery();
Console.WriteLine("Affected = " + rowsAffected + " rows");
sc.Close();
```

Notice that instead of using a stored procedure to insert data into the application backend database, the application calls a SQL INSERT command directly. There is no explicit return value to test against; the application affects a database table. This situation corresponds to Section 11.5, which explains how to test a stored procedure that does not return a value. Your test code will resemble this:

```
string inMovieID = "m07";
string inMovieTitle = "G is for GUI";
int inMovieRunTime = 97;

string expectedHash = "4A-65-6E-6E-69-66-65-72-20-4A-69-6E-68-6F-6E-67";
string actualHash;
```

```
string connString = "Server=(local);Database=dbMovies;Trusted_Connection=Yes";
SqlConnection sc = new SqlConnection(connString);
string command = "INSERT INTO tblMain VALUES('" + inMovieID +
                 "', '" + inMovieTitle + "'," + inMovieRunTime + ")";
SqlCommand cmd = new SqlCommand(command, sc);
cmd.CommandType = CommandType.Text;
sc.Open();
cmd.ExecuteNonQuery();
sc.Close();

// compute actualHash of tblMain here - see Section 11.5

if (actualHash == expectedHash)
  Console.WriteLine("Pass");
else
  Console.WriteLine("FAIL");
```

Comments

Many systems under test that access an underlying SQL database do so without using stored procedures. Although access through a stored procedure provides more flexibility, better performance, and better security, it is common for very simple data access needs to just call a SQL command directly. Or you may be testing a new application that accesses a legacy back-end database system where there are no stored procedures. The techniques used to test stored procedures can be used when the application under test issues SQL commands directly. Here is a second example. Suppose an application under test fills a DataSet object:

```
string connString = "Server=(local);Database=dbMovies;
                     Trusted_Connection=Yes";
SqlConnection sc = new SqlConnection(connString);
string command = "SELECT * FROM tblMain WHERE movTitle > 'M'";
sc.Open();

DataSet ds = new DataSet();
SqlDataAdapter sda = new SqlDataAdapter(command, sc);
sda.Fill(ds);
sc.Close();
```

The application calls an explicit SELECT statement rather than calling a stored procedure. The result is a SQL rowset. This situation corresponds to Section 11.3 where we examined testing a stored procedure that returns a SQL rowset. Your test code will look like this:

```
string input = "M";
string expectedHash = "4A-65-6E-6E-69-66-65-72-20-4A-69-6E-68-6F-6E-67";
string actualHash;
```

```
string connString = "Server=(local);Database=dbMovies;
                     Trusted_Connection=Yes";
SqlConnection sc = new SqlConnection(connString);
string command = "SELECT * FROM tblMain WHERE movTitle > '" +
                 input + "'";
sc.Open();

DataSet ds = new DataSet();
SqlDataAdapter sda = new SqlDataAdapter(command, sc);
sda.Fill(ds);
sc.Close();

// compute actualHash of ds here - see Section 11.1

if (actualHash == expectedHash)
  Console.WriteLine("Pass");
else
  Console.WriteLine("FAIL");
```

One final example should make the idea of this technique clear. Suppose an application under test inserts data into an ArrayList object using a SqlDataReader object like this:

```
string connString = "Server=(local);Database=dbMovies;
                     Trusted_Connection=Yes";
SqlConnection sc = new SqlConnection(connString);
string command = "SELECT * FROM tblPrices WHERE movPrice < 40.00";
SqlCommand cmd = new SqlCommand(command, sc);
cmd.CommandType = CommandType.Text;
sc.Open();

SqlDataReader sdr = cmd.ExecuteReader();

ArrayList list = new ArrayList();

while (sdr.Read() == true)
{
  string s = sdr.GetString(0);
  s += sdr.GetDecimal(1).ToString();
  list.Add(s);
}

sc.Close();
```

Then, using the key idea of this section, your test automation code will look something like this:

```
string input = "40.00";
string[] expecteds = new string[] { "m01 11.1100", "m03 33.3300" };
```

```
string connString = "Server=(local);Database=dbMovies;
                     Trusted_Connection=Yes";
SqlConnection sc = new SqlConnection(connString);
string command = "SELECT * FROM tblPrices WHERE movPrice < " + input;
SqlCommand cmd = new SqlCommand(command, sc);
cmd.CommandType = CommandType.Text;
sc.Open();

SqlDataReader sdr = cmd.ExecuteReader();
ArrayList list = new ArrayList();

while (sdr.Read() == true)
{
  string s = sdr.GetString(0);
  s += " " + sdr.GetDecimal(1).ToString();
  list.Add(s);
}
sc.Close();

// determine pass/fail
bool pass = true;
for (int i = 0; i < expecteds.Length; ++i)
{
  string s = (string)list[i];
  if (s != expecteds[i])
    pass = false;
}

if (pass == true)
  Console.WriteLine("Pass");
else
  Console.WriteLine("FAIL");
```

Here we write code that manipulates the state of the system under test just like the application does. In the previous example, the application uses a SqlDataReader object to store rowset data into an ArrayList object, so our test code does the same. Exactly how you check an expected value in order to determine a pass/fail result will depend on the system under test. Here the expected result is an ArrayList that contains the string "m01 11.1100" at index position 0, and the string "m03 33.3300" at index position 1. The test code declares a string array, expecteds, with these two values, and compares each string in the expecteds array with the corresponding string in the DataSet result.

11.7 Comparing Two DataSet Objects for Equality

Problem

You want to compare the data in two DataSet objects for equality.

Design

Write an IsEqual() helper method that does a string comparison of each row of each table in the two DataSet objects.

Solution

```
static bool IsEqual(DataTable dt1, DataTable dt2)
{
  if (dt1.Rows.Count != dt2.Rows.Count)
    return false;

  if (dt1.Columns.Count != dt2.Columns.Count)
    return false;

  for (int r = 0; r < dt1.Rows.Count; ++r)
  {
    for (int c = 0; c < dt1.Columns.Count; ++c)
    {
      if (dt1.Rows[r][c].ToString() != dt2.Rows[r][c].ToString())
        return false;
    }
  }
  return true;
}

static bool IsEqual(DataSet ds1, DataSet ds2)
{
  if (ds1.Tables.Count != ds2.Tables.Count)
    return false;

  for (int t = 0; t < ds1.Tables.Count; ++t)
  {
    if ( !IsEqual(ds1.Tables[t], ds2.Tables[t]) )
      return false;
  }
  return true;
}
```

The first IsEqual() method compares two DataTable objects and returns true if each of the tables has the same string data in each corresponding row and column location. The first two checks in IsEqual() determine whether the two tables being compared have the same number of rows and columns. Once past those criteria, we can imagine the two tables as being matrices with rows and columns, and then do a cell-by-cell comparison of the string representation in each corresponding cell. This approach assumes that the column values can be meaningfully mapped to type string.

The second IsEqual() method compares two DataSet objects by calling the first helper method. Notice that this approach does not do a full comparison of the DataSet objects; it checks the data in the tables but does not check things like Constraint objects, column names, and so on. You may need to customize this code to suit your particular definition of DataSet equality.

Comments

When testing applications that use ADO.NET technology, it is very common to have to compare two DataSet objects for equality in order to determine a pass/fail result. The important design decision you must make when comparing two DataSet objects is what exactly constitutes equality in your particular testing situation. DataSet objects are fairly complex. Doing a full comparison of two DataSet objects is not simple but it can be done. The real problem with a full comparison of all the attributes in two DataSet objects is storing meaningful test case expected value data. If you are going to do a complete comparison of an actual DataSet returned by a call to the system under test with an expected DataSet, your test case expected value data could be huge. Comparing just the string representations of the data in two DataSet objects is usually a reasonable approach in lightweight test automation scenarios.

An alternative approach for comparing two DataSet objects is to just compare their respective sizes and a small subset of the data in each table. For example:

```
static bool IsEqual2(DataTable dt1, DataTable dt2)
{
  if (dt1.Rows.Count != dt2.Rows.Count)
    return false;

  if (dt1.Columns.Count != dt2.Columns.Count)
    return false;

  int col = 0;
  for (int r = 0; r < dt1.Rows.Count; ++r)
    if ( dt1.Rows[r][col].ToString() != dt2.Rows[r][col].ToString() )
      return false;

  return true;
}
```

This helper method examines only the values in the first column of each row of the two DataSet objects being compared. You might want to consider such an approach when the DataSet objects you are comparing are very large and you have many thousands of test cases. Obviously using an approach like this makes the determination of a pass/fail result somewhat probabilistic. However, all software testing is probabilistic to some extent, and in a lightweight testing environment, practicality often trumps theory.

11.8 Reading Test Case Data from a Text File into a SQL Table

Problem

You want to read test case data from a text file and store into a SQL table using ADO.NET technology.

Design

Use a `StreamReader` object to iterate through the text file you wish to store into the SQL table. Parse the text file and load the parsed tokens into the SQL table using a `SqlCommand` object with command text containing a SQL `INSERT` statement.

Solution

For example, suppose you have a SQL table of test case data defined as:

```
create table tblTestCases
(
 caseID char(5) primary key,
 input varchar(35) not null,
 expected int not null
)
go
```

and you have a tab-delimited text file containing this data:

```
00001    foobar    1
00002    bizbaz    2
00003    wixtel    3
```

The data fields are a test case ID, a test case input, and an expected result. You want to store the text data into the SQL table. This code will do that:

```
FileStream fs = new FileStream("..\\..\\TestCases.txt", FileMode.Open);
StreamReader sr = new StreamReader(fs);

string line;
string[] tokens;
string command;

string connString = "Server=(local);Database=dbTestData;
                     UID=testDataLogin;PWD=thepwd";
SqlConnection sc = new SqlConnection(connString);
sc.Open();
SqlCommand cmd = null;
```

```
while ((line = sr.ReadLine()) != null)
{
  tokens = line.Split('\t');
  command = "INSERT INTO tblTestCases VALUES('" + tokens[0] + "', '" +
              tokens[1] + "', " + tokens[2] + ")";
  cmd = new SqlCommand(command, sc);
  cmd.CommandType = CommandType.Text;

  cmd.ExecuteNonQuery();
}

sc.Close();
sr.Close();
fs.Close();
```

The only tricky issue here is creating a new INSERT statement during each pass through the loop that iterates through the text file.

Comments

As with most ADO.NET techniques, there are a huge number of alternatives available to you. The solution above is particularly suitable when the structure of the text file you are importing from matches the structure of the SQL table you are storing to. Notice that in the previous example, the number and order of the data fields (test case ID, test case input, expected result) in the text file match the SQL table. This solution can be easily modified for situations where the number and order of fields do not match. For example, suppose the text file you are reading from looks like this:

00001	extradata	1	foobar	extradata
00002	junkydata	2	bizbaz	junkydata
00003	donotneed	3	wixtel	donotneed

The text file has two extra fields, and the order of the fields does not match the SQL table. You just create a second string array to hold the fields you want, copy the needed fields into that array in the correct order, and pass the second array values to the INSERT statement:

```
FileStream fs = new FileStream("..\\..\\TestCases2.txt", FileMode.Open);
StreamReader sr = new StreamReader(fs);

string line;
string[] tokens;
string[] info;
string command;
```

```
string connString = "Server=(local);Database=dbTestData;
                      UID=testDataLogin;PWD=thepwd";
SqlConnection sc = new SqlConnection(connString);
sc.Open();
SqlCommand cmd = null;

while ((line = sr.ReadLine()) != null)
{
  tokens = line.Split('\t'); // parse text file
  info = new string[3];
  info[0] = tokens[0]; // test case ID
  info[1] = tokens[3]; // input
  info[2] = tokens[2]; // expected

  command = "INSERT INTO tblTestCases VALUES('" + info[0] +
          "', '" + info[1] + "', " + info[2] + ")";
  cmd = new SqlCommand(command, sc);
  cmd.CommandType = CommandType.Text;

  cmd.ExecuteNonQuery();
}

sc.Close();
sr.Close();
fs.Close();
```

A significantly different approach to reading a text file into a SQL table is to read the text file data into a DataSet object and then emit the DataSet to the destination SQL table using a SqlDataAdapter.Update() method. For example:

```
FileStream fs = new FileStream("..\\..\\TestCases.txt", FileMode.Open);
StreamReader sr = new StreamReader(fs);

DataSet ds = new DataSet();
ds.Tables.Add("tblTestCases");
ds.Tables["tblTestCases"].Columns.Add("caseID");
ds.Tables["tblTestCases"].Columns.Add("input");
ds.Tables["tblTestCases"].Columns.Add("expected");

string line;
string[] tokens;

while (( line = sr.ReadLine()) != null )
{
  tokens = line.Split('\t');
  ds.Tables["tblTestCases"].Rows.Add(tokens);
}
```

```
sr.Close();
fs.Close();

string connString = "Server=(local);Database=dbTestData;
                     UID=testDataLogin;PWD=thepwd";
SqlConnection sc = new SqlConnection(connString);
SqlDataAdapter sda = new SqlDataAdapter();

SqlCommand cmd = null;
cmd = new SqlCommand("insert into tblTestCases (caseID, input, expected)
                     values(@caseID, @input, @expected)", sc);
cmd.Parameters.Add("@caseID", SqlDbType.Char, 5, "caseID");
cmd.Parameters.Add("@input", SqlDbType.VarChar, 35, "input");
cmd.Parameters.Add("@expected", SqlDbType.Int, 4, "expected");
sda.InsertCommand = cmd;

sda.Update(ds, "tblTestCases");
sc.Close();
```

This approach is useful when you need to do some in-memory processing of the text file data before you send it to the SQL store. With the text data in a DataSet object you can easily process it. We start by creating a DataSet object and then make a DataTable object to hold data from the text file. Here we give the DataTable and its columns the same names as the corresponding objects in the destination SQL table. This is not required but makes our automation code much more readable. After the DataTable is ready, we prepare a SqlDataAdapter object and a SqlCommand object. When we call the SqlDataAdapter.Update() method, it will invoke the prepared InsertCommand.

11.9 Reading Test Case Data from a SQL Table into a Text File

Problem

You want to read test case data from a SQL table and store into a text file using ADO.NET technology.

Design

Use a SqlDataReader object to iterate through each row of the SQL table. For each row, parse the SQL column using the GetString() method if the SQL data is char or varchar, or use another appropriate GetX() method for different types. Write the data using the WriteLine() method of a StreamWriter object.

Solution

Suppose, for example, you have a SQL table that contains test results defined as:

```
create table tblTestResults
(
 caseID char(5) null,
 result char(4) null,
 whenRun datetime null
)
go
```

and you want to read all the data in the table and write it to a tab-delimited text file. Here is one solution:

```
string connString = "Server=(local);Database=dbTestData;
                        UID=testDataLogin;PWD=thepwd";
SqlConnection sc = new SqlConnection(connString);
string select = "SELECT caseID, result, whenRun FROM tblTestResults";
SqlCommand cmd = new SqlCommand(select, sc);
sc.Open();
SqlDataReader sdr = cmd.ExecuteReader();

FileStream fs = new FileStream("..\\..\\TestResults.txt", FileMode.Create);
StreamWriter sw = new StreamWriter(fs);

while (sdr.Read() == true)
{
  sw.WriteLine(sdr.GetString(0) + "\t" +
               sdr.GetString(1) + "\t" +
               sdr.GetSqlDateTime(2).ToString() );
}

sw.Close();
fs.Close();
sdr.Close();
sc.Close();
```

This approach is simple and effective. The SqlCommand.ExecuteReader() method returns a SqlDataReader object that can be used to read through the source SQL table one row at a time. For each column you must use the appropriate GetX() method: Use GetString() for char, varchar, and similar type columns. Use GetSqlDateTime() for datetime columns, and so on.

Comments

This solution can be easily modified if the structure of the source SQL table does not match the structure of the destination text file. You simply read each data column value in the SQL table, then build up an output string using string concatenation, or the StringBuilder class if performance is a major issue.

A significant alternative approach to reading a SQL table and storing into a text file is to read the entire SQL table into memory using a SqlDataAdapter, and then iterate through the DataTable object one row at a time, writing to the destination text file. Here is an example of this approach:

```
string connString = "Server=(local);Database=dbTestData;
                      UID=testDataLogin;PWD=thepwd";
SqlConnection sc = new SqlConnection(connString);
string select = "SELECT caseID, result, whenRun FROM tblTestResults";
SqlCommand cmd = new SqlCommand(select, sc);
sc.Open();

DataSet ds = new DataSet();
SqlDataAdapter sda = new SqlDataAdapter(select, sc);
sda.Fill(ds);

FileStream fs = new FileStream("..\\..\\TestResults.txt", FileMode.Create);
StreamWriter sw = new StreamWriter(fs);

for (int i = 0; i < ds.Tables["Table"].Rows.Count; ++i)
{
  string line = "";
  for (int j = 0; j < ds.Tables["Table"].Columns.Count-1; ++j)
  {
    line += ds.Tables["Table"].Rows[i][j] + "\t";
  }
  line += ds.Tables["Table"].Rows[i][ds.Tables["Table"].Columns.Count-1];
  sw.WriteLine(line);
}

sw.Close();
fs.Close();
sc.Close();
```

This technique is useful if you want to perform some processing of the SQL data before you send it to the destination text file. With the SQL data in a DataSet object, you can easily manipulate it.

You build up a string representing a line of the text file by fetching each column value and appending to a string, then add a tab character as a delimiter. Notice one mildly annoying detail: to avoid having a tab character at the end of each line of the text file, for each row, you have to process all but the last column of SQL data, and then append the last column without adding a tab character.

11.10 Example Program: ADOdotNETtest

The program in Listing 11-1 combines several of the techniques in this chapter to create a test harness that verifies an application method that uses ADO.NET technology. The application under test is the demonstration program shown in Figure 11-1 in the introduction section of this chapter. The method under test, GetEmployees(), accepts a string, then accesses a back-end database, dbEmployees, using ADO.NET, and fills and returns a DataSet object that is then displayed by the application via a DataGrid control.

Listing 11-1. *Program ADOdotNETtest*

```
using System;
using System.Data;
using System.Data.SqlClient;

namespace ADOdotNETtest
{
  class Class1
  {
    [STAThread]
    static void Main(string[] args)
    {
      try
      {
        Console.WriteLine("\nBegin test run\n");
        Console.WriteLine("\nADO.NET method under test = GetEmployees()");
        Console.WriteLine("Test case data source = dbTestData..tblTestCases\n");

        string connString = "Server=(local);Database=dbTestData;
                             Trusted_Connection=Yes";
        SqlConnection sc = new SqlConnection(connString);
        string select = "SELECT caseID, input, expected FROM tblTestCases";
        SqlCommand cmd = new SqlCommand(select, sc);
        sc.Open();
        SqlDataReader sdr = cmd.ExecuteReader();

        string caseID, input, expected, actual;
        DataSet ds;

        while (sdr.Read() == true) // main test loop
        {
          Console.WriteLine("===========================");
          caseID = sdr.GetString(0);
          input = sdr.GetString(1);
          expected = sdr.GetString(2); // aggregate string
          if (expected == "")
            expected = null;

          actual = null;

          ds = GetEmployees(input); // call method under test

          // build aggregate string of actual DataSet
          foreach (DataRow dr in ds.Tables[0].Rows)
```

```
      {
        foreach (DataColumn dc in ds.Tables[0].Columns)
        {
          actual += dr[dc];
        }
      }

      Console.WriteLine("Case ID = " + caseID);
      Console.WriteLine("Input = '" + input + "'");
      Console.WriteLine("Expected DataSet = ");
      Console.WriteLine(" " + expected);
      Console.WriteLine("Actual DataSet   = ");
      Console.WriteLine(" " + actual);

      if (actual == expected)
        Console.WriteLine("Result =  Pass");
      else
        Console.WriteLine("Result =  FAIL");
    }
    Console.WriteLine("============================");

    sdr.Close();
    sc.Close();

    Console.WriteLine("\nDone");
    Console.ReadLine();
  }
  catch(Exception ex)
  {
    Console.WriteLine("Fatal error: " + ex.Message);
    Console.ReadLine();
  }
} // Main()

private static DataSet GetEmployees(string s) // copy from App under test
{
  try
  {
    string connString = "Server=(local);Database=dbEmployees;
                          Trusted_Connection=Yes";
    SqlConnection sc = new SqlConnection(connString);
    string select = "SELECT empID, empLast, empDOB
                     FROM tblEmployees
                     WHERE empLast LIKE '%" + s + "%'";
    SqlCommand cmd = new SqlCommand(select, sc);
    sc.Open();
```

```
        DataSet ds = new DataSet();
        SqlDataAdapter sda = new SqlDataAdapter(select, sc);
        sda.Fill(ds);
        sc.Close();
        return ds;
      }
      catch
      {
        return null;
      }
    }
  } // class
} // ns
```

In situations like this, where significant functionality is embedded directly into the application code (as opposed to a modular approach where the functionality is placed in a code library), you have no choice but to make an exact replica of the application functionality for use by your test harness.

The test harness uses ADO.NET technology to read test case data from a SQL table in database dbTestData. The harness displays results to the command shell, but can be easily modified to save results to a SQL table. When run, the output will be as shown in Figure 11-2 in the introduction section of this chapter. The script that creates the underlying database under test, dbEmployees, is presented in Listing 11-2. The script that creates the test case data, dbTestData, is presented in Listing 11-3.

Listing 11-2. *Script to Create Underlying Database Under Test*

```
-- makeDbEmployees.sql
use master
go

if exists (select * from sysdatabases where name='dbEmployees')
 drop database dbEmployees
go

create database dbEmployees
go

use dbEmployees
go

create table tblEmployees
(
 empID char(3) primary key,
 empLast varchar(35) not null,
 empDOB datetime not null
)
go
```

```
insert into tblEmployees
 values('111', 'Adams', '6/15/1981')
insert into tblEmployees
 values('222', 'Baker', '6/15/1982')
insert into tblEmployees
 values('333', 'Chung', '6/15/1983')
insert into tblEmployees
 values('444', 'Donne', '6/15/1984')
go

-- end script
```

Listing 11-3. *Script to Create TestCase Data*

```
-- makeDbTestData.sql
use master
go

if exists (select * from sysdatabases where name='dbTestData')
 drop database dbTestData
go

create database dbTestData
go

use dbTestData
go

create table tblTestCases
(
 caseID char(4) primary key,
 input varchar(35) not null,
 expected varchar(250) not null
)
go

insert into tblTestCases
 values('0001', 'Adams', '111Adams6/15/1981 12:00:00 AM')
insert into tblTestCases
 values('0002', 'A', '111Adams6/15/1981 12:00:00 AM222Baker6/15/1982 12:00:00 AM')
insert into tblTestCases
 values('0003', 'Z', '')

-- end script
```

CHAPTER 12

XML Testing

12.0 Introduction

This chapter presents a variety of test automation techniques that involve XML data. The most common XML-related tasks in test automation situations are reading/parsing test case data that has been stored as XML, writing test results to external storage as XML, programmatically modifying XML files to match a new test harness or output format, validating XML files, and comparing two XML files for equality to determine a test case pass/fail result. The screenshot in Figure 12-1 demonstrates XML validation and parsing. The program that generated the output shown in Figure 12-1 is presented in Section 12.12.

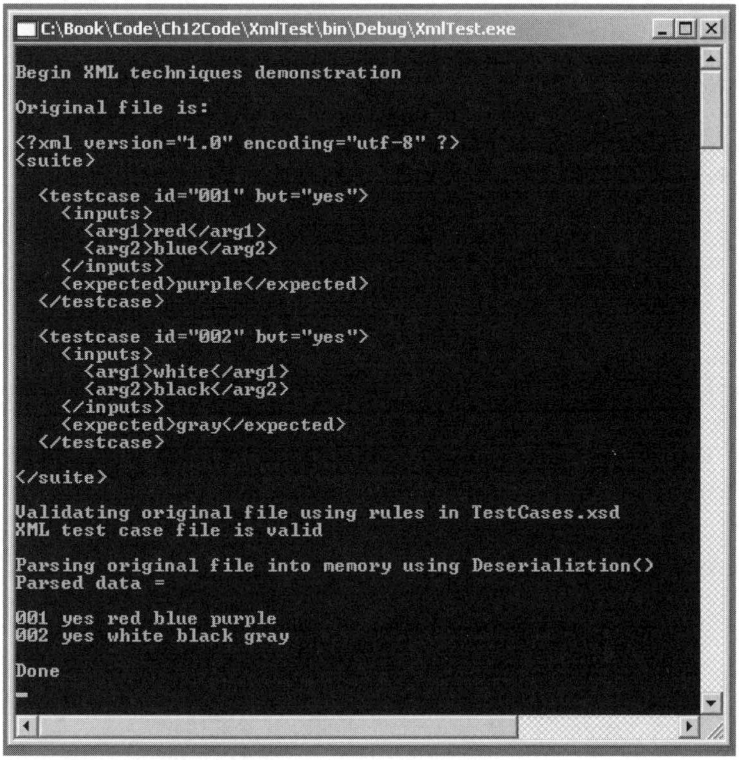

Figure 12-1. *Validating and parsing an XML file*

Most of the example code in this chapter will use a slightly expanded version of the file shown in Figure 12-1:

```xml
<?xml version="1.0" encoding="utf-8" ?>
<suite>

  <testcase id="001" bvt="yes">
    <inputs>
      <arg1>red</arg1>
      <arg2>blue</arg2>
    </inputs>
    <expected>purple</expected>
  </testcase>

  <testcase id="002" bvt="no">
    <inputs>
      <arg1>blue</arg1>
      <arg2>yellow</arg2>
    </inputs>
    <expected>green</expected>
  </testcase>

  <testcase id="003" bvt="yes">
    <inputs>
      <arg1>white</arg1>
      <arg2>black</arg2>
    </inputs>
    <expected>gray</expected>
  </testcase>

</suite>
```

The preceding example is a dummy XML file of hypothetical test case data. Notice that XML data is stored as either an element (such as <arg1>red</arg1>) or as an attribute in an element (such as <testcase id="001" bvt="yes">). Dealing with elements and attributes, and with a nested/hierarchical structure, are key tasks when working with XML. The five parsing techniques in this chapter (Sections 12.1 through 12.5) all parse file testCases.xml into a test case Suite object defined as:

```csharp
namespace Utility
{
  public class TestCase
  {
    public string id;
    public string bvt;
    public string arg1;
    public string arg2;
    public string expected;
  }
```

```
  public class Suite
  {
    public ArrayList cases = new ArrayList();
    public void Display()
    {
      foreach (TestCase tc in cases)
      {
        Console.Write(tc.id + " " + tc.bvt + " " + tc.arg1 + " ");
        Console.WriteLine(tc.arg2 + " " + tc.expected);
      }
    }
  } // class Suite
} // ns Utility
```

The TestCase class represents a single test case and the Suite class represents a collection of TestCase objects. Encapsulating test case data in this way instead of using individual variables usually makes your test harnesses easier to maintain.

12.1 Parsing XML Using XmlTextReader

Problem

You want to parse an XML file using the XmlTextReader class.

Design

Iterate through each node of the XML file using the Read() and ReadElementString() methods of the XmlTextReader class. Use the GetAttribute() method to fetch attribute data, and use the return value from ReadElementString() to fetch element data.

Solution

This code parses file testCases.xml (shown in the introduction to this chapter) into a Suite collection of TestCase objects (also shown in the introduction):

```
Console.WriteLine("Start\n");

Utility.Suite suite = new Utility.Suite();

XmlTextReader xtr = new XmlTextReader("..\\..\\testCases.xml");
xtr.WhitespaceHandling = WhitespaceHandling.None;
xtr.Read(); // read the XML declaration node, advance to <suite> tag

while (!xtr.EOF) //load loop
{
  if (xtr.Name == "suite" && !xtr.IsStartElement()) break;
```

```
  while (xtr.Name != "testcase" || !xtr.IsStartElement() )
  xtr.Read(); // advance to <testcase> tag

  Utility.TestCase tc = new Utility.TestCase();
  tc.id = xtr.GetAttribute("id");
  tc.bvt = xtr.GetAttribute("bvt");
  xtr.Read(); // advance to <inputs> tag
  xtr.Read(); // advance to <arg1> tag
  tc.arg1 = xtr.ReadElementString("arg1"); // consumes the </arg1> tag
  tc.arg2 = xtr.ReadElementString("arg2"); // consumes the </arg2> tag
  xtr.Read(); // advance to <expected> tag
  tc.expected = xtr.ReadElementString("expected"); // consumes </expected> tag
  // we are now at an </testcase> tag
  suite.cases.Add(tc);
  xtr.Read(); // and now either at <testcase> tag or </suite> tag
} // load loop

xtr.Close();
suite.Display(); // show the suite of TestCases

Console.WriteLine("\nDone");
```

When run, this solution will produce this output:

```
Start

001 yes red    blue    purple
002 no   blue  yellow  green
003 yes  white black   gray

Done
```

The XML file has been parsed into its individual data pieces which can then be used as needed, typically as input to a method under test.

The key to understanding this solution is to understand the Read() and ReadElementString() methods of XmlTextReader. To an XmlTextReader object, an XML file is a sequence of nodes. For example:

```
<?xml version="1.0" ?>
<alpha id="001">
  <beta>123</beta>
</alpha>
```

There are six nodes, without counting whitespace: the XML declaration, <alpha id="001">, <beta>, 123, </beta>, and </alpha>. Notice that attributes (id="001") are not considered XML nodes by an XmlTextReader object.

The Read() method advances one node at a time. Unlike many Read() methods in other classes, the System.XmlTextReader.Read() method does not return significant data. The ReadElementString() method on the other hand returns the data between begin and end tags of its argument and advances to the next node after the end tag. Because XML attributes are not nodes, we have to extract attribute data using the GetAttribute() method. The statement:

```
xtr.WhitespaceHandling = WhitespaceHandling.None;
```

is important. It instructs the XmlTextReader object to ignore whitespace characters such as blanks, tabs, and newlines. Without this statement you would have to Read() over all white-space, which is very troublesome and error-prone.

Comments

The main loop in this solution:

```
while (!xtr.EOF) //load loop
{
  if (xtr.Name == "suite" && !xtr.IsStartElement()) break;
  // etc.
}
```

is not particularly elegant but is more readable than alternatives. The loop exits when at EOF or a </suite> tag.

When marching through an XML file, you can either Read() your way one node at a time, or get a bit more sophisticated with code such as this:

```
while (xtr.Name != "testcase" || !xtr.IsStartElement() )
  xtr.Read(); // advance to <testcase> tag
```

The choice of technique you use is mostly a matter of style. Parsing an XML file with XmlTextReader has a traditional, pre-.NET feel to it. You walk sequentially through the file using Read(), and extract data with ReadElementString() and GetAttribute(). Using XmlTextReader is straightforward and effective and is appropriate when the structure of the XML file being parsed is relatively simple and consistent, and when you only need to process the XML in a forward-only manner. In general, using XmlTextReader is the fastest technique when compared with the other parsing techniques in this chapter. Notice that because the logic in this solution depends quite a bit on the XML file having a consistent structure, using XmlTextReader is usually not a good idea if your XML file has an inconsistent structure. Compared to other parsing techniques in this chapter, XmlTextReader operates at a lower level of abstraction, meaning it is up to you as a programmer to keep track of where you are in the XML file and Read() correctly.

12.2 Parsing XML Using XmlDocument

Problem

You want to parse an XML file using the XmlDocument class.

Design

Read the entire XML file into memory using the XmlDocument.Load() method. Fetch node collections using the SelectNodes() method then use the Attributes.GetNamedItem() and SelectSingleNode() methods combined with the InnerText property to get the values of attributes and elements.

Solution

This code parses file testCases.xml (shown in the introduction to this chapter) into a Suite collection of TestCase objects (also shown in the introduction):

```
Utility.Suite suite = new Utility.Suite();

XmlDocument xd = new XmlDocument();
xd.Load("..\\..\\testCases.xml");

// get all <testcase> nodes
XmlNodeList nodelist = xd.SelectNodes("/suite/testcase");
foreach (XmlNode node in nodelist) // for each <testcase> node
{
  Utility.TestCase tc = new Utility.TestCase();

  tc.id = node.Attributes.GetNamedItem("id").Value;
  tc.bvt = node.Attributes.GetNamedItem("bvt").Value;

  XmlNode n = node.SelectSingleNode("inputs"); // get <inputs> node
  tc.arg1 = n.ChildNodes.Item(0).InnerText;
  tc.arg2 = n.ChildNodes.Item(1).InnerText;

  tc.expected = node.ChildNodes.Item(1).InnerText;

  suite.cases.Add(tc);
} // foreach <testcase> node

suite.Display();
```

When run, this solution will produce the exact same output as Section 12.1 (parsing with XmlTextReader):

```
Start

001 yes red    blue    purple
002 no  blue   yellow  green
003 yes white  black   gray

Done
```

XmlDocument objects are based on the notion of XML nodes and child nodes. Instead of sequentially navigating through a file, we select sets of nodes with the SelectNodes() method, or individual nodes with the SelectSingleNode() method. Notice that because XML distinguishes between attributes and elements, we must get the id and bvt attribute values with an Attributes.GetNamedItem() method applied to an element node.

Comments

After loading the XmlDocument, we fetch all the testcase nodes at once with:

```
XmlNodeList nodelist = xd.SelectNodes("/suite/testcase");
```

Then we iterate through this list of nodes and fetch each <input> node with:

```
XmlNode n = node.SelectSingleNode("inputs");
```

and then extract the arg1 (and similarly arg2) value using:

```
tc.arg1 = n.ChildNodes.Item(0).InnerText;
```

In this statement, n is the <inputs> node, ChildNodes.Item(0) is the first element of <inputs>, i.e., <arg1>, and the InnerText property gets the value between <arg1> and </arg1>.

The XmlDocument class is modeled on the W3C XML Document Object Model and may have a somewhat different feel to it than many .NET Framework classes that you are familiar with. Using the XmlDocument class is appropriate if you need to extract data in a nonsequential manner, or if you are already using XmlDocument objects and want to maintain a consistent approach to your test harness code. Because using XmlDocument reads an entire XML document into memory at the same time, using it may not be suitable in situations where the XML file being parsed is very, very large.

In addition to the XmlDocument class, the System.Xml namespace contains a closely related XmlDataDocument class. It is derived from the XmlDocument class and is primarily intended for use in conjunction with DataSet objects. So, in this solution, we could have used the XmlDataDocument class but we would not have gained any advantage by doing so.

12.3 Parsing XML with XPathDocument

Problem

You want to parse an XML file using the XPathDocument class.

Design

Read the entire XML file into memory using the XPathDocument() constructor. Create an XPathNodeIterator object and use it to move through the XPathDocument object with the MoveNext() method. Fetch attribute values using the GetAttribute() method. Fetch element values using the SelectChildren() method and the Current.Value property.

Solution

This code parses file testCases.xml (shown in the introduction to this chapter) into a Suite collection of TestCase objects (also shown in the introduction):

```
Utility.Suite suite = new Utility.Suite();

XPathDocument xpd = new XPathDocument("..\\..\\testCases.xml");
XPathNavigator xpn = xpd.CreateNavigator();
XPathNodeIterator xpi = xpn.Select("/suite/testcase");

while (xpi.MoveNext()) // each testcase node
{
  Utility.TestCase tc = new Utility.TestCase();
  tc.id = xpi.Current.GetAttribute("id", xpn.NamespaceURI);
  tc.bvt = xpi.Current.GetAttribute("bvt", xpn.NamespaceURI);

  XPathNodeIterator tcChild =
    xpi.Current.SelectChildren(XPathNodeType.Element);
  while (tcChild.MoveNext()) // each part of <testcase>
  {
    if (tcChild.Current.Name == "inputs")
    {
      XPathNodeIterator tcSubChild =
 tcChild.Current.SelectChildren(XPathNodeType.Element);
      while (tcSubChild.MoveNext()) // each part of <inputs>
      {
        if (tcSubChild.Current.Name == "arg1")
          tc.arg1 = tcSubChild.Current.Value;
        else if (tcSubChild.Current.Name  == "arg2")
          tc.arg2 = tcSubChild.Current.Value;
      }
    }
    else if (tcChild.Current.Name == "expected")
      tc.expected = tcChild.Current.Value;
  }
  suite.cases.Add(tc);

} // each testcase node

suite.Display();
```

When run, this solution will produce the same output as Section 12.1 (parsing with XmlTextReader) and Section 12.2 (parsing with XmlDocument):

```
Start

001 yes red    blue    purple
002 no  blue   yellow  green
003 yes white  black   gray

Done
```

After loading the XPathDocument object, we get what is, in essence, a reference to the first `<testcase>` node into an XPathNodeIterator object with:

```
XPathNavigator xpn = xpd.CreateNavigator();
XPathNodeIterator xpi = xpn.Select("/suite/testcase");
```

Because XPathDocument does not maintain "node identity," we must iterate through each `<testcase>` node with this loop:

```
while (xpi.MoveNext())
```

Similarly, we have to iterate through the children nodes with:

```
while (tcChild.MoveNext())
```

Comments

Using an XPathDocument object to parse XML has a hybrid feel that is part procedural and lower-level (as in XmlTextReader), and part object oriented and higher-level (as in XmlDocument). You can select parts of the document using the Select() method of an XPathNavigator object and also move through the document using the MoveNext() method of an XPathNodeIterator object.

The XPathDocument class is optimized for XPath data model queries. So using it is particularly appropriate when the XML file to parse is deeply nested, has a complex structure, or requires extensive searching. You might also consider using XPathDocument if other parts of your test harness code use that class, so that you maintain a consistent coding look and feel. An XPathDocument object is read-only, so using XPathDocument is not appropriate if you want to do any direct, in-memory processing of the XML file you are parsing.

12.4 Parsing XML with XmlSerializer

Problem

You want to parse an XML file using the XmlSerializer class.

Design

Prepare a class that is defined so it will accept the result of calling the Deserialize() method of the XmlSerializer class. Then create an instance of the receptacle class and use Deserialize() with a StreamReader object.

Solution

This code parses file testCases.xml (shown in the introduction to this chapter) into a Suite collection of TestCase objects (also shown in the introduction):

```
XmlSerializer xs = new XmlSerializer(typeof(SerializerLib.Suite));
StreamReader sr = new StreamReader("..\\..\\testCases.xml");
SerializerLib.Suite suite = (SerializerLib.Suite)xs.Deserialize(sr);
sr.Close();
suite.Display();
```

where:

```
namespace SerializerLib
{
  [XmlRootAttribute("suite")]
  public class Suite
  {
    [XmlElementAttribute("testcase")]
    public TestCase[] items; // changed name from xsd-generated code
    public void Display() // added to xsd-generated code
    {
      foreach (TestCase tc in items)
      {
        Console.Write(tc.id + " " + tc.bvt + " "  + tc.inputs.arg1 + " ");
        Console.WriteLine(tc.inputs.arg2 + " " + tc.expected);
      }
    }
  }

  public class TestCase  // changed name from xsd-generated code
  {
    [XmlAttributeAttribute()]
    public string id;
    [XmlAttributeAttribute()]
    public string bvt;
    [XmlElementAttribute("inputs")]
    public Inputs inputs; // change from xsd-generated code: no array
    public string expected;
  }

  public class Inputs // changed name from xsd-generated code
  {
    public string arg1;
    public string arg2;
  }
} // ns SerializerLib
```

When run, this solution will produce the same output as in Section 12.1 (parsing with XmlTextReader), Section 12.2 (parsing with XmlDocument), and Section 12.3 (parsing with XPathDocument):

```
Start

001 yes red    blue    purple
002 no  blue   yellow  green
003 yes white  black   gray

Done
```

Using the XmlSerializer class is significantly different from using any of the other five fundamental classes that parse XML, because the in-memory data store must be carefully prepared beforehand. Observe that pulling the XML data into memory is accomplished in a single statement:

```
SerializerLib.Suite suite = (SerializerLib.Suite)xs.Deserialize(sr);
```

This example uses a SerializerLib namespace to hold the definition for a Suite class that corresponds to the testCases.xml file so that the XmlSerializer object can store the XML data into it. The trick of course is to set up this Suite class.

Comments

There are two ways to create a class that is defined so it will accept the result of calling the Deserialize() method of the XmlSerializer class. The first way is to carefully examine the structure of the source XML file and then code the destination/receptacle class by hand. A much easier approach is to use the xsd.exe command line tool that ships with Visual Studio .NET. First, (assuming file testCases.xml is in the C: folder) issue the command:

```
C:\>xsd.exe testCases.xml /o:.
```

This means create an XSD schema definition of file testCases.xml and save the result with default name testCases.xsd in the current directory. The intermediate .xsd file will contain a complete structure definition of the XML file. Next, issue the command:

```
C:\>xsd.exe testCases.xsd /c /o:.
```

This means use the testCases.xsd definition file to generate a set of class definitions that are compatible with the Deserialize() method, using the default C# language, and save with default name testCases.cs in the current directory. Here is the original testCases.cs before some editing:

```
[System.Xml.Serialization.XmlRootAttribute(Namespace="",
  IsNullable=false)]
public class suite
```

```
{
  [System.Xml.Serialization.XmlElementAttribute("testcase",
    Form=System.Xml.Schema.XmlSchemaForm.Unqualified)]
  public suiteTestcase[] Items;
}

public class suiteTestcase
{
  [System.Xml.Serialization.XmlElementAttribute(Form=
    System.Xml.Schema.XmlSchemaForm.Unqualified)]
  public string expected;

  [System.Xml.Serialization.XmlElementAttribute("inputs",
    Form=System.Xml.Schema.XmlSchemaForm.Unqualified)]
  public suiteTestcaseInputs[] inputs;

  [System.Xml.Serialization.XmlAttributeAttribute()]
  public string id;

  [System.Xml.Serialization.XmlAttributeAttribute()]
  public string bvt;
}
public class suiteTestcaseInputs
{
  [System.Xml.Serialization.XmlElementAttribute(Form=
    System.Xml.Schema.XmlSchemaForm.Unqualified)]
   public string arg1;

  [System.Xml.Serialization.XmlElementAttribute(Form=
    System.Xml.Schema.XmlSchemaForm.Unqualified)]
  public string arg2;
}
```

If you examine the resulting class definition code carefully, you will eventually be able to see the relationship between the code and the original XML file:

```
<suite>

  <testcase id="001" bvt="yes">
    <inputs>
      <arg1>red</arg1>
      <arg2>blue</arg2>
    </inputs>
    <expected>purple</expected>
  </testcase>

  (other <testcase> data here)

</suite>
```

At this point you can copy and paste the newly created class definitions directly into your test harness and use them as is to instantiate an object to receive the result of the Deserialize() method. Alternatively, you can edit the auto-generated file by removing unneeded code, changing names to those that better match your original XML file, and adding additional methods (such as a display method or get and set properties). The class definition in the solution to this section was created using this approach.

Using the XmlSerializer class provides a very elegant solution to the problem of parsing an XML file. Compared with the other four techniques in this chapter, XmlSerializer operates at the highest level of abstraction, meaning that the algorithmic details are largely hidden from you. But this gives you somewhat less control over the XML parsing process.

Using XmlSerializer for parsing is most appropriate for situations when fine-grained control is not required, the test harness program does not make extensive use of XmlDocument objects, the XML file is relatively shallow rather than deeply nested, and the application is not primarily an ADO.NET application.

12.5 Parsing XML with a DataSet Object

Problem

You want to parse an XML file using a DataSet object.

Design

Read the entire XML file into a DataSet object using the ReadXml() method. Then iterate through each DataTable in the DataSet, and extract related data by using the GetChildRows() method in conjunction with table relation names.

Solution

This code parses file testCases.xml (shown in the introduction to this chapter) into a Suite collection of TestCase objects (also shown in the introduction):

```
DataSet ds = new DataSet();
ds.ReadXml("..\\..\\testCases.xml");

Utility.Suite suite = new Utility.Suite();
foreach (DataRow row in ds.Tables["testcase"].Rows)
{
  Utility.TestCase tc = new Utility.TestCase();
  tc.id = row["id"].ToString();
  tc.bvt = row["bvt"].ToString();
  tc.expected = row["expected"].ToString();

  DataRow[] children = row.GetChildRows("testcase_inputs"); // relation name
```

```
    tc.arg1 = (children[0]["arg1"]).ToString(); // there is only 1 row in children
    tc.arg2 = (children[0]["arg2"]).ToString();

    suite.cases.Add(tc);
}

suite.Display();
```

When run, this solution will produce the same output as in Section 12.1 (parsing with XmlTextReader), Section 12.2 (parsing with XmlDocument), Section 12.3 (parsing with XPathDocument), and Section 12.4 (parsing using XmlSerializer):

Start

001 yes red   blue   purple
002 no blue   yellow green
003 yes white black   gray

Done

We start by reading the XML file directly into a System.Data.DataSet object using the ReadXml() method. A DataSet object can be thought of as an in-memory relational database. The key to parsing XML using a DataSet object is to understand how XML, which is inherently hierarchical, is mapped to a set of DataTable objects, which are inherently flat. Each level of the source XML file will generate a table in the DataSet. Recall the structure of the source XML file:

```
<suite>

  <testcase id="001" bvt="yes">
    <inputs>
      <arg1>red</arg1>
      <arg2>blue</arg2>
    </inputs>
    <expected>purple</expected>
  </testcase>

  (other <testcase> nodes

</suite>
```

The top-level, <testcase>, produces a DataTable named testcase. The next level, <inputs>, produces a DataTable named inputs. A relation named testcase_inputs is created which links the DataTable objects. Notice that the XML root level does not generate a table and that the lowest level (in his case the <arg> data) does not generate a table either.

Comments

In practice, when parsing XML using a DataSet object, a good approach is to do some preliminary investigation. Although you could create a custom DataSet object with completely known characteristics, it is much quicker to let the ReadXml() method do the work and then examine the result. Read the source XML file into a DataSet and then programmatically examine it to determine the number and names of the DataTable objects that are created. This utility method will usually reveal all the information you need:

```
// names of tables, columns, relations in ds
public static void DisplayInfo(DataSet ds)
{
  foreach (DataTable dt in ds.Tables)
  {
    Console.WriteLine("\n=========================================");
    Console.WriteLine("Table = " + dt.TableName + "\n");
    foreach (DataColumn dc in dt.Columns)
    {
      Console.Write("{0,-14}", dc.ColumnName);
    }
    Console.WriteLine("\n-----------------------------------------");

    foreach (DataRow dr in dt.Rows)
    {
      foreach (object data in dr.ItemArray)
      {
        Console.Write("{0,-14}", data.ToString());
      }
      Console.WriteLine();
    }
    Console.WriteLine("=========================================");
  } // foreach DataTable

  foreach (DataRelation dr in ds.Relations)
  {
    Console.WriteLine("\n\nRelations:");
    Console.WriteLine(dr.RelationName + "\n\n");
  }

} // DisplayInfo()
```

The first table, testcase, holds the data that is one level deep from the XML root: id, bvt, and expected. The second table, inputs, holds data that is two levels deep: arg1 and arg2. In general if your XML file is n levels deep, ReadXml() will generate n-1 tables (or n-2 tables, depending on your exact definition of levels).

Extracting the data from the parent testcase table is easy. Just iterate through each row of the table and access by column name. To get the data from the child table inputs, get an array of rows using the GetChildRows() method:

```
DataRow[] children = row.GetChildRows("testcase_inputs"); // relation name
```

Because each <testcase> node has only one <inputs> child node, the children array will only have one row. The trickiest aspect of this technique is to extract the child data:

```
tc.arg1 = (children[0]["arg1"]).ToString(); // there is only 1 row in children
```

Using the DataSet class to parse an XML file has a very relational database feel. Compared with the other parsing techniques in this chapter, it operates at a middle level of abstraction. The ReadXml() method hides a lot of details, but you must traverse through relational tables.

Using a DataSet object to parse XML files is particularly appropriate when your test harness program is using ADO.NET classes so that you maintain a consistent look and feel. Using a DataSet object has relatively high overhead and would not be a good choice if performance is an issue. Because each level of an XML file generates a table, if your XML file is deeply nested, then using DataSet would not be a good choice. If you need to perform extensive in-memory processing of the XML file being parsed and the XML is not deeply nested, using a DataSet approach is generally a good choice because you can easily manipulate the data stored in DataTable objects.

12.6 Validating XML with XSD Schema

Problem

You want to validate an XML file using an XSD schema definition.

Design

Read through the XML file you wish to validate using an XmlValidatingReader object. If the XML file is invalid, control is transferred to a delegate method where you can print an error message. If the XML file is valid, control does not transfer to the delegate.

Solution

This code will validate file testCases.xml (shown in the introduction to this chapter) using a schema file named testCases.xsd:

```
try
{
  Console.WriteLine("\nStarting XML validation");
  XmlSchemaCollection xsc = new XmlSchemaCollection();
  xsc.ValidationEventHandler += new ValidationEventHandler(ValidationCallBack);
  xsc.Add(null, "..\\..\\testCases.xsd");
  XmlTextReader xtr = new XmlTextReader("..\\..\\testCases.xml");
  XmlValidatingReader xvr = new XmlValidatingReader(xtr);
  xvr.ValidationType = ValidationType.Schema;
  xvr.Schemas.Add(xsc);
  xvr.ValidationEventHandler += new ValidationEventHandler(ValidationCallBack);
  while (xvr.Read()); // note empty loop
```

```
  Console.WriteLine("If no error message then XML is valid");
  Console.WriteLine("Done");
  Console.ReadLine();
}
catch(Exception ex)
{
  Console.WriteLine("Generic exception: " + ex.Message);
  Console.ReadLine();
}

Console.WriteLine("\nDone");
Console.ReadLine();
```

where:

```
private static void ValidationCallBack(object sender, ValidationEventArgs ea)
{
  Console.WriteLine("Validation error: " + ea.Message);
  Console.ReadLine();
}
```

and file testCases.xsd is:

```
<?xml version="1.0" encoding="utf-8"?>
<xs:schema id="suite" xmlns="" xmlns:xs="http://www.w3.org/2001/XMLSchema"
xmlns:msdata="urn:schemas-microsoft-com:xml-msdata">
  <xs:element name="suite" msdata:IsDataSet="true">
    <xs:complexType>
      <xs:choice maxOccurs="unbounded">
        <xs:element name="testcase">
          <xs:complexType>
            <xs:sequence>
              <xs:element name="inputs" minOccurs="1"
              maxOccurs="unbounded">
                <xs:complexType>
                  <xs:sequence>
                    <xs:element name="arg1" type="xs:string"
                    minOccurs="1" />
                    <xs:element name="arg2" type="xs:string"
                    minOccurs="1" />
                  </xs:sequence>
                </xs:complexType>
              </xs:element>
              <xs:element name="expected"
                type="xs:string" minOccurs="0"
                msdata:Ordinal="1" />
            </xs:sequence>
            <xs:attribute name="id" type="xs:string" />
            <xs:attribute name="bvt" type="xs:string" />
```

```
            </xs:complexType>
          </xs:element>
        </xs:choice>
      </xs:complexType>
    </xs:element>
</xs:schema>
```

You can generate an XSD schema definition by hand, or you can use the xsd.exe tool as described in Section 12.4 to generate one for you to use as a starting point.

Comments

When using XML in lightweight software test automation situations, you will often need or want to check that various XML files are valid. For example, if your test case data is stored as XML you will likely want to validate it before launching a test run. Or if you store test results as XML, you may want to validate the results file before distributing the results. Validating XML with XSD schema is relatively easy. You create an `XmlValidatingReader` object and set the `ValidationType` property to `ValidationType.Schema`. You add the validating schema definition file through an `XmlSchemaCollection`; this approach allows multiple schema definitions to be used against a single XML file. The only unusual aspect of the validation process is that when you read through the XML file being validated, instead of getting a return result indicating success or failure, a delegate method will be called if the XML is invalid, and nothing will happen if the XML is valid. So you have to create a callback method to handle the validation error. In this example, we would simply print the validation message.

Generating XSD schema definition files from scratch is not so much fun. A better approach is to use the xsd.exe tool to generate an initial XSD file to be used as a starting point, and then manually edit the generated file as needed. For example, when xsd.exe was applied to the testCases.xml file (presented in the introduction to this chapter), the resulting XSD file contained this:

```
<xs:element name="testcase">
 <xs:complexType>
  <xs:sequence>
   <xs:element name="expected" type="xs:string" minOccurs="0"
     msdata:Ordinal="1" />
   <xs:element name="inputs" minOccurs="0" maxOccurs="unbounded">
     <xs:complexType>
       <xs:sequence>
         <xs:element name="arg1" type="xs:string" minOccurs="0" />
         <xs:element name="arg2" type="xs:string" minOccurs="0" />
       </xs:sequence>
     </xs:complexType>
   </xs:element>
  </xs:sequence>
  <xs:attribute name="id" type="xs:string" />
  <xs:attribute name="bvt" type="xs:string" />
 </xs:complexType>
</xs:element>
```

This is close to, but not exactly, what is needed for this solution. Notice that the expected result is mistakenly defined to come before the inputs, and that `arg1` and `arg2` were defined to allow 0 occurrences. You can easily make changes because the XML format of XSD files is very readable (for example, `minOccurs=0`) and is self-explanatory.

An alternative approach to validating XML files using XSD schema is to validate using DTD (Document Type Definition) files. DTD is an older technology that is somewhat easier to use than XSD, but not as powerful as XSD schema validation.

12.7 Modifying XML with XSLT

Problem

You want to generate a modified version of an XML file using XSLT (Extensible Stylesheet Language Transformations).

Design

Create an XSLT template file, then create an `XslTranform` object. Use the `Load()` and `Transform()` methods to generate the modified version of the original XML file.

Solution

Suppose you wish to modify the testCases.xml file from its original form:

```
<?xml version="1.0" encoding="utf-8" ?>
<suite>

  <testcase id="001" bvt="yes">
    <inputs>
      <arg1>red</arg1>
      <arg2>blue</arg2>
    </inputs>
    <expected>purple</expected>
  </testcase>

  (other <testcase> nodes here)

</suite>
```

to a modified version that looks like this:

```
<?xml version="1.0" encoding="utf-8"?>
<allOfTheCases>
  <aCase caseID="001">
    <bvt>yes</bvt>
    <expRes>purple</expRes>
```

```
    <inputs>
      <input1>red</input1>
      <input2>blue</input2>
    </inputs>
  </aCase>

  (other <aCase> nodes here)

</allOfTheCases>
```

The names of all nodes are different in the modified XML file; the bvt attribute in the original file is replaced by an element in the modified file; and the expected result comes before the inputs in the modified file. First, create an XSLT file like this:

```
<?xml version="1.0" encoding="UTF-8" ?>
<xsl:transform version="1.0" xmlns:xsl="http://www.w3.org/1999/XSL/Transform">
<xsl:output method="xml" indent="yes"/>

<xsl:template match="/">
<allOfTheCases>
  <xsl:for-each select="//testcase">
    <aCase>
      <xsl:attribute name="caseID"><xsl:value-of select="@id"/></xsl:attribute>
      <bvt><xsl:value-of select="@bvt"/></bvt>
        <expRes><xsl:value-of select="expected"/></expRes>
        <inputs>
          <xsl:for-each select="inputs">
            <input1><xsl:value-of select="arg1"/></input1>
            <input2><xsl:value-of select="arg2"/></input2>
          </xsl:for-each>
        </inputs>
    </aCase>
  </xsl:for-each>
</allOfTheCases>

</xsl:template>
</xsl:transform>
```

and then programmatically apply the transform using C# code like this:

```
Console.WriteLine("\nStarting XSLT Transformation");
XslTransform xst = new XslTransform();
xst.Load("..\\..\\testCasesModifier.xslt");
xst.Transform("..\\..\\testCases.xml", "..\\..\\testCasesModified.xml");
Console.WriteLine("Done. New XML file is testCasesModified.xml");
```

Comments

You may want to generate an XML file that is a modified version of some other XML file. For example, in a testing situation you may want to use an existing test case data file created by some other group as input to one of your test harnesses, but you need to modify the XML to conform to the structure expected by your harness. One way to do this is to use XSLT technology. The problem boils down to creating the appropriate .xslt transform template. If you examine the example in this section, you'll see that XSLT is fairly intuitive. The xsl:for-each tag is used for iteration; the xsl:value-of tag is used for assignment; and XPath syntax is used for specifying particular attributes and elements. Once you have created the XSLT modification file, applying it with the XslTranform class is also very obvious.

The potential problem with XSLT is not so much technical as it is psychological; using XSLT has a very different feel than normal procedural-style programming. Because of this, many testers prefer a completely different approach to generating a modified version of an XML file, which does not use XSLT—they parse the original XML file into memory using one of the techniques presented in this chapter, modify the in-memory image of the original file to match the target structure, then write the modified image to file. This alternate technique is common. However, there may be situations in which you inherit a system that makes heavy use of XSLT.

12.8 Writing XML Using XmlTextWriter

Problem

You want to write to an XML file using the XmlTextWriter class.

Design

Use the WriteStartElement() method to write XML element tags. Use the WriteAttributeString() method to write attribute values. Use the WriteString() method to write element values.

Solution

For example, this code:

```
string caseID = "0001";
string result = "Pass";
string whenRun = "01/23/2006";

XmlTextWriter xtw = new XmlTextWriter("..\\..\\Results1.xml",
  System.Text.Encoding.UTF8);
xtw.Formatting = Formatting.Indented;
xtw.WriteStartDocument();
xtw.WriteStartElement("Results");
xtw.WriteStartElement("result");
xtw.WriteAttributeString("id", caseID);
xtw.WriteStartElement("passfail");
xtw.WriteString(result);
```

```
xtw.WriteEndElement();
xtw.WriteStartElement("whenRun");
xtw.WriteString(whenRun);
xtw.WriteEndElement();
xtw.WriteEndElement();
xtw.WriteEndElement();
xtw.Close();
```

will produce as output:

```
<?xml version="1.0" encoding="utf-8"?>
<Results>
  <result id="0001">
    <passfail>Pass</passfail>
    <whenRun>01/23/2006</whenRun>
  </result>
</Results>
```

Comments

Writing XML results using an XmlTextWriter object is simple and straightforward. In theory, all you need is the XmlTextWriter.WriteString() method, which simply writes its argument to output. But if you only use WriteString() you will not get the benefit of the XmlTextWriter class and you could just as well have used a series of StreamWriter.WriteLine() statements to write the XML file. The preceding solution uses explicit WriteStartElement() and WriteEndElement() calls like this:

```
xtw.WriteStartElement("whenRun");
xtw.WriteString(whenRun);
xtw.WriteEndElement();
```

Alternatively, you can use WriteElementString() like this:

```
xtw.WriteElementString("whenRun" , whenRun);
```

The XmlTextWriter class has many useful methods such as WriteComment() and WriteCData().

12.9 Comparing Two XML Files for Exact Equality

Problem

You want to compare two XML files for exact equality.

Design

Write a helper method that iterates through each file using two FileStream objects. Read each file byte-by-byte, and return false if you hit a byte mismatch.

Solution

This method will compare two XML files for exact equality:

```
private static bool XMLExactlySame(string file1, string file2)
{
  FileStream fs1 = new FileStream(file1, FileMode.Open);
  FileStream fs2 = new FileStream(file2, FileMode.Open);

  if (fs1.Length != fs2.Length) // number bytes
    return false;
  else
  {
    int b1 = 0;
    int b2 = 0;

    while ((b1 = fs1.ReadByte()) != -1)
    {
      b2 = fs2.ReadByte();
      //Console.WriteLine("b1 = " + b1 + " b2 = " + b2);
      if (b1 != b2)
      {
        fs1.Close();
        fs2.Close();
        return false;
      }
    }
    fs1.Close();
    fs2.Close();
    return true;
  }
} // XMLExactlySame()
```

This code assumes the two files passed in as input arguments exist. First we check the size of the two files; if the sizes are different, the two files cannot possibly be identical. Next, we iterate through both files, and read one byte from each, and compare the two byte values. If the byte values differ, we know the files are different, so we can close the FileStream objects and return false. If we make it all the way through both files, they must be identical.

Comments

In software test automation, if the system under test produces an XML file as output, you will have to compare an actual XML file with an expected XML file. One of several ways to do this is to store an expected XML file and then compare byte-by-byte. Because XML files are just a particular type of text file, the technique in this section will work for any text file.

12.10 Comparing Two XML Files for Exact Equality, Except for Encoding

Problem

You want to compare two XML files for exact equality except for their encoding.

Design

Read each of the two files being compared into a string variable. Then compare the two strings using the ordinary == Boolean comparison operator.

Solution

```
private static bool XMLExactlySameExceptEncoding(string file1, string file2)
{
  FileStream fs1 = new FileStream(file1, FileMode.Open);
  FileStream fs2 = new FileStream(file2, FileMode.Open);
  StreamReader sr1 = new StreamReader(fs1);
  StreamReader sr2 = new StreamReader(fs2);

  string s1 = sr1.ReadToEnd();
  string s2 = sr2.ReadToEnd();
  //Console.WriteLine(s1);
  //Console.WriteLine(s2);
  sr1.Close();
  sr2.Close();
  fs1.Close();
  fs2.Close();

  return (s1 == s2);
}
```

Comments

In testing situations, you may want to compare an actual XML file with an expected XML file but you do not care if the encoding schemes are different. In other words, if the actual and expected XML files both have the same character data but one file is encoded using UTF-8 and the other is encoded using ANSI, the files are equivalent from your perspective. One way to perform such a comparison is to simply read both files into string variables and compare using the overloaded == operator. The Boolean == operator is overloaded to take into account character encoding. This approach may not be feasible if the two XML files being compared are very, very large. In this situation, you can adapt Section 12.9 by reading through each file a character at a time and doing a character-by-character comparison.

12.11 Comparing Two XML Files for Canonical Equivalence

Problem

You want to compare two XML files for canonical equivalence. You can think of canonical equivalence as meaning "the same for most practical purposes."

Design

Perform a C14N canonicalization on the two XML files being compared using the XmlDsigC14NTransform class and then compare the two files in memory using two MemoryStream objects.

Solution

```
// using System.Security.Cryptography.Xml;

string f1 = "..\\..\\Books1.xml";
XmlDocument xd1 = new XmlDocument();
xd1.Load(f1);

XmlDsigC14NTransform t1 = new XmlDsigC14NTransform(true);
// true = include comments

t1.LoadInput(xd1);
Stream s1 = t1.GetOutput() as Stream;
XmlTextReader xtr1 = new XmlTextReader(s1);
MemoryStream ms1 = new MemoryStream();
XmlTextWriter xtw1 = new XmlTextWriter(ms1, System.Text.Encoding.UTF8);
xtw1.WriteNode(xtr1, false);
// false = do not copy default attributes

xtw1.Flush();
ms1.Position = 0;
StreamReader sr1 = new StreamReader(ms1);
string str1 = sr1.ReadToEnd();
//Console.WriteLine(str1);

//Console.WriteLine("\n======\n");

string f2 = "..\\..\\Books2.xml";
XmlDocument xd2 = new XmlDocument();
xd2.Load(f2);
XmlDsigC14NTransform t2 = new XmlDsigC14NTransform(true);
t2.LoadInput(xd2);
```

```
Stream s2 = t2.GetOutput() as Stream;
XmlTextReader xtr2 = new XmlTextReader(s2);
MemoryStream ms2 = new MemoryStream();
XmlTextWriter xtw2 = new XmlTextWriter(ms2, System.Text.Encoding.UTF8);
xtw2.WriteNode(xtr2, false);
xtw2.Flush();
ms2.Position = 0;
StreamReader sr2 = new StreamReader(ms2);
string str2 = sr2.ReadToEnd();
Console.WriteLine(str2);

if (str1 == str2)
  Console.WriteLine("Files canonically equivalent");
else
  Console.WriteLine("Files NOT canonically equivalent ");
```

Comments

Suppose an XML file Books1.xml looks like this:

```
<?xml version="1.0" encoding="utf-8" ?>
<books>

  <book>
    <title isbn='1111'    storeid="A1A1">
All About Apples</title>
    <author>
      <last>Anderson</last>
      <first>Adam</first>
    </author>
  </book>
</books>
```

and suppose that a second XML file, Books2.xml, looks like this:

```
<books>
  <book>
    <title storeid="A1A1" isbn="1111">
      All About Apples
    </title>
    <author>
      <last>Anderson</last>
      <first>Adam</first>
    </author>
  </book>

</books>
```

If the code in this solution is run against these two files, the message "Files canonically equivalent" would be displayed—these two files are canonically equivalent. The whitespace differences do not matter; the use of single-quote and double-quote characters does not matter; XML declarations do not matter; and the order of attributes does not matter. C14N canonical equivalence is fairly complex. It is defined by the W3C and is primarily used in security contexts. In order to determine if an XML file has been accidentally or maliciously changed during transmission over a network, you can compare crypto-hashes of the transmitted file and the received file. However, because networks may modify the files, we need a way to determine canonical equivalence. This explains why the XmlDsigC14NTransform class is in the System.Security.dll assembly.

12.12 Example Program: XmlTest

The program in Listing 12-1 demonstrates XML validation using an XSD schema definition, and XML parsing using the XmlSerializer class. When run, the output will be that shown in Figure 12-1 in the introduction to this chapter.

Listing 12-1. *Program XmlTest*

```
using System;
using System.IO;
using System.Xml;
using System.Xml.Schema; // validation
using System.Xml.Serialization; // deserialization

namespace XmlTest
{
  class Class1
  {
    [STAThread]
    static void Main(string[] args)
    {
      try
      {
        Console.WriteLine("\nBegin XML techniques demonstration\n");

        Console.WriteLine("Original file is: \n");
        FileStream fs = new FileStream("..\\..\\TestCases.xml",
                                      FileMode.Open);
        StreamReader sr = new StreamReader(fs);
        string line;
        while((line = sr.ReadLine()) != null)
        {
          Console.WriteLine(line);
        }
        sr.Close(); fs.Close();
```

```csharp
        Console.WriteLine("\nValidating original file using
                        rules in TestCases.xsd");
        XmlSchemaCollection xsc = new XmlSchemaCollection();
        xsc.ValidationEventHandler +=
         new ValidationEventHandler(ValidationCallBack);
        xsc.Add(null, "..\\..\\testCases.xsd");
        XmlTextReader xtr = new XmlTextReader("..\\..\\testCases.xml");
        XmlValidatingReader xvr = new XmlValidatingReader(xtr);
        xvr.ValidationType = ValidationType.Schema;
        xvr.Schemas.Add(xsc);
        xvr.ValidationEventHandler +=
         new ValidationEventHandler(ValidationCallBack);
        while (xvr.Read()); // note empty loop

        Console.WriteLine("XML test case file is valid");

        Console.WriteLine("\nParsing original file into memory
                        using Deserialization()");
        XmlSerializer xs =
          new XmlSerializer(typeof(SerializerLib.Suite));
        sr = new StreamReader("..\\..\\TestCases.xml");
        SerializerLib.Suite suite =
         (SerializerLib.Suite)xs.Deserialize(sr);
        sr.Close();
        Console.WriteLine("Parsed data = \n");
        suite.Display();

        Console.WriteLine("\nDone");
        Console.ReadLine();
      }
      catch(Exception ex)
      {
        Console.WriteLine("Fatal error: " + ex.Message);
        Console.ReadLine();
      }

      } // Main()

    private static void ValidationCallBack(object sender, ValidationEventArgs ea)
    {
      Console.WriteLine("Validation error: " + ea.Message);
      Console.ReadLine();
    }
    } // class

  namespace SerializerLib
  {
```

```
[XmlRootAttribute("suite")]
public class Suite
{
  [XmlElementAttribute("testcase")]
  public TestCase[] items; // changed name from xsd-generated code
  public void Display() // added to xsd-generated code
  {
    foreach (TestCase tc in items)
    {
      Console.Write(tc.id + " " + tc.bvt + " "  + tc.inputs.arg1 + " ");
      Console.WriteLine(tc.inputs.arg2 + " " + tc.expected);
    }
  }
}

public class TestCase  // changed name from xsd-generated code
{
  [XmlAttributeAttribute()]
  public string id;
  [XmlAttributeAttribute()]
  public string bvt;
  [XmlElementAttribute("inputs")]
  public Inputs inputs; // change from xsd-generated code: no array
  public string expected;
}

public class Inputs // changed name from xsd-generated code
{
  public string arg1;
  public string arg2;
}
} // ns SerializerLib

} // ns
```

Index

Symbols

== (Boolean comparison operator), 358
@@rowcount function, 254

A

accessing
   backend databases for testing, 318–321
   control properties, 50–53
   form properties, 44–47
   text on Web page/application, 175
Add() method, 226–228
ADO.NET testing
   comparing two DataSet objects for
      equality, 321–323
   determining pass/fail result when
      expected value is DataSet
      object, 303–306
   example program, 329–333
   overview of, 301–302
   reading test case data
      from SQL table into text file, 327–329
      from text file into SQL table, 324–327
   stored procedure
      that does not return value, 314–317
      that returns rowset, 309–311
      that returns value, 306–309
      that returns value into out
         parameter, 311–314
   of systems that access data without using
      stored procedure, 318–321
aggregate checksum, computing, 256–258
AllowAutoRedirect property
      (HttpWebRequest class), 141
API (Application Programming Interface)
      testing
   calculating summary results, 17–18
   converting test case data, 9–11
   description of, 3–4
   determining test case result, 11–13
   empty string input arguments, dealing
      with, 24–26
   launching test harness
      automatically, 28–29
   logging test case result, 13–15
   methods that throw exceptions, dealing
      with, 22–23
   null input/null expected results, dealing
      with, 20–22

   parsing test case, 8–9
   program example, 29–32
   reading test case data, 7–8
   sending e-mail alerts on test case
      failures, 26–28
   storing test case data, 6–7
   test automation run, 5
   test run total elapsed time,
      determining, 19–20
   time-stamping test case result, 16
API functions. *See* low-level Web UI testing
application state
   checking with Windows-based UI
      testing, 89–91
   description of, 187
application under test (AUT)
   checking contents of control on, 89–91
   color-mixer example, 66
   description of, 4
   determining when fully loaded into
      browser, 190–192
   launching
      reflection-based UI testing, 35–38
      Windows-based UI testing, 66–67
   manipulating value of HTML element
      on, 194–195
   obtaining handle to main window of,
      Windows-based UI testing, 68–73
   typographical errors in, 170
   verifying value of HTML element
      on, 195–198
applications under development, unrefined
      nature of, 34
applying
   mathematical combination to string
      array, 278–280
   mathematical permutation to string
      array, 291–293
ArrayList collection
   SQL file data, 123–125
   text file data, 104–108
   XML file data, 113–117
ArrayList object, 226–231, 311
ASP Web page, sending simple HTTP POST
      request to, 143–145
ASP.NET Web application, sending simple
      HTTP POST request to, 145–150
ASP.NET Web services, 207–208

You Need the Companion eBook

Your purchase of this book entitles you to its companion eBook for only $10.

We believe this Apress title will prove so indispensable that you'll want to carry it with you everywhere, which is why we are offering the companion eBook for $10 to customers who purchase this book now. Convenient and fully searchable, the eBook version of any content-rich, page-heavy Apress book makes a valuable addition to your programming library. You can easily find, copy, and apply code—and then perform examples by quickly toggling between instructions and the application. Even simultaneously tackling a donut, diet soda, and complex code becomes simplified with hands-free eBooks!

Once you purchase this book, getting the $10 companion eBook is simple:

❶ Visit **www.apress.com/promo/tendollars/**.

❷ Complete a basic registration form to receive a randomly generated question about this title.

❸ Answer the question correctly in 60 seconds and you will receive a promotional code to redeem for the $10 eBook.

2560 Ninth Street • Suite 219 • Berkeley, CA 94710

eBookshop

THE EXPERT'S VOICE™

Offer valid through 11/06.